INSIDE
the President's Helicopter

INSIDE
the President's Helicopter

LTC Gene T. Boyer with Jackie Boor

CABLE PUBLISHING

Brule, Wisconsin

INSIDE THE PRESIDENT'S HELICOPTER
Reflections of a White House Senior Pilot

First Edition

Published by:
    Cable Publishing
    14090 E Keinenen Rd
    Brule, WI 54820

    Website: www.cablepublishing.com
    E-mail: nan@cablepublishing.com

© 2011 by Gene T. Boyer and Jackie Boor
All rights reserved. Published in 2011

Hardcover: ISBN 13: 978-1-934980-90-3
              ISBN 10: 1-934980-90-0

Soft cover: ISBN 13: 978-1-934980-91-0
              ISBN 10: 1-934980-91-9

Library of Congress Control Number: 2010933995

Printed in the United States of America

Dedication

This book is dedicated to the spirit and achievements of the courageous helicopter aviators and flight crews who have flown in battle. Thank you for the lives you saved, the sacrifices you made and the incomparable legacy you leave to a grateful nation.

Praise for LTC Gene T. Boyer and Inside the President's Helicopter

INSIDE THE PRESIDENT'S HELICOPTER *is a story of high adventure, courage and history-making moments. Whether piloting the President and First Lady into an active combat zone in Vietnam in 1969 or landing at 11,000 feet in a devastated mountain village in the Andes, author Gene Boyer takes the reader along. What makes* INSIDE THE PRESIDENT'S HELICOPTER *such compelling reading is that on one level, it is the saga of an Army veteran of Korea and Vietnam; on another, the book is the history of the evolution of the Presidential helicopter; and, finally, it is a very human, up-close look at the Presidency. It is must reading for anyone interested in the White House.*

— Julie Nixon Eisenhower

Gene Boyer provides ten years of closely held information on the comings and goings of three sitting, one future, and two former U.S. presidents as well as national leaders worldwide. This kind of information was available only to one who had close contact and an insider's access in a most critical job requiring exceptional aviation skills, strong and informed leadership, and dedication to the nation. Having traveled extensively with the President in Gene's care during the Watergate years, I am proud to have served with him at the White House.

— Colonel Bill Golden, Army aide to President Nixon

I was the guy who closed up shop after the U.S. Army's Executive Flight Detachment was disbanded in 1976. If not for Gene Boyer's headstrong determination, the history of that unit and the prominent role it played in providing 20 years of helicopter service to the White House might have been lost forever. For ten of those years, I was one of Boyer's pilots and I can promise anyone reading this book they will experience a lot of what I did flying with him. Get ready for some unforgettable rides!

— CW4 Carl Burhanan, first black aviator to fly for the White House

Sit down, buckle up, and get ready for an exciting ride with a White House helicopter pilot for Presidents Johnson, Nixon, and Ford at the controls. Filled with candid observations about presidential personalities and private lives, LTC Boyer's INSIDE THE PRESIDENT'S HELICOPTER *reveals scores of historic happenings that were never mentioned by the media. It's a fascinating inside look at the most important piloting job in the world.*

— Flint Whitlock, co-author of *Capt. Jepp and the Little Black Book: How Barnstormer & Aviation Pioneer Elrey B Jeppesen Made the Skies Safer for Everyone*

As a retired Marine Colonel and the proud son of a former Executive Flight Detachment Pilot, I am extremely grateful that LTC Gene Boyer has captured this very important and interesting part of American history in his book, INSIDE THE PRESIDENT'S HELICOPTER. *These brave young men were the very best our country had to offer. Most had previous combat experience flying in the jungles of Vietnam, but their new assignment found them landing on the manicured lawns of the White House, safely returning the President of the United States. They were a fine "band of brothers" whose bravery, professionalism, and devotion to duty are amply documented in Gene's book. With a unique perspective on such a pivotal time in our past, this is more than a gripping story, it is an important part of history. Gene's book is not only an interesting and wonderful story of days past; it is also an excellent tribute to some of our finest American heroes.*

— Colonel Greg Woodward, USMC

The minute Lt. Col. Gene Boyer told me, when I interviewed him for American Veteran *magazine, that he had flown President Richard Nixon off the White House lawn on that fateful day after Nixon chose to resign rather than face possible impeachment over the Watergate scandal, I knew he had to write a book about his experiences flying, not only Nixon, but several of America's presidents in Army One. And now he's done it. Co-written with Jackie Boor, it is a stirring, informative work that will put you square in the right seat of many of the chopper flights Gene commanded. From the jungles of Vietnam to the pyramids of Egypt, we gain insight into the driven character of the always mission-oriented Boyer and the men who were at the helm of our country. From LBJ and Nixon to Ford, each of these Presidents placed their countenance in Gene Boyer.* INSIDE THE PRESIDENT'S HELICOPTER *will show you why and is well worth the read.*

— Marc Phillip Yablonka, author,
Distant War: Recollections of Vietnam, Laos and Cambodia

Gene Boyer is as interesting a person as the celebrities and distinguished politicians he transported over the years. I worked with Gene on the restoration of the #617 Presidential Helicopter and loved it when he would digress and reminisce with stories like the Brezhnev and Nixon bad weather account. I often thought that he was privy to more inside observations than the media could ever imagine. As I read through the pages of his book I once again found myself in the midst of the persons that shaped our history in the 1970s and privy to firsthand observations that only a person who was there could share. This is truly a case where a third party has something more interesting to share than the scripted evening news accounts. The book is fascinating in the way pilot Gene Boyer becomes a player in one of the biggest games there is, politics. As you turn each page, those days come alive again on each page — but this time from the eyes of a different observer.

— Patricia Korzec, Executive Director
March Field Air Museum

PHOTO INDEX

Table of Contents

Prologue

The cockpit of Army One was more familiar to me than any room in my home and the start-up and shut-down checklist had long ago become second nature to me.

Strapped into the right seat where the flight commander always sat, I methodically moved through the series of routine tasks we performed for lift-off from the South Lawn of the White House. I scanned instrument indicators, made sure people on the ground were at a safe distance, and checked clearance over the radio with Washington National air traffic control, the White House switchboard, the Secret Service, and Andrews Air Force Base. To my left, co-pilot Chief Warrant Officer-4 (CW-4) Carl Burhanan pushed the auxiliary power unit button and reached for the overhead throttle, poised to engage the transmission to release the rotor blades to spin.

I glanced over my left shoulder. The President's silhouette paused in the open helicopter doorway, turned to a transfixed crowd outside and, with cameras rolling, gave a robust, sweeping salute. He raised both arms for the signature dual-fisted "V" for victory gesture before promptly stepping into Army One's cocooned shadows and out of the searing spotlight of public examination.

"Cut!" someone yelled from the movie production crew clustered outside the helicopter.

Burhanan and I relaxed for a moment and then repositioned ourselves for what would be at least a dozen takes that clear fall day in 2007 for director Ron Howard's latest film, Frost/Nixon. The scene was a re-creation of the iconic moment the world had viewed thousands of times since August 9, 1974 – an ignominious President Richard Nixon boarding Army One and waving farewell to a wounded and disheartened nation.

I was 78 and Burhanan, the first black pilot to fly for the White House, was 74. We had no speaking parts, but we did hold the distinction of being the only cast members playing ourselves. Amazingly, I could still fit into the very flight suit I had worn the day of Nixon's "last flight," but Burhanan needed a few seam adjustments. Still, not bad for two old Army guys.

Burhanan and I had first met in 1953 during helicopter flight school at Fort Sill, Oklahoma, and we both served in Korea and Vietnam. When I took command of the White House Executive Flight Detachment in 1969, he was one of my first crew selections. It had not been his first attempt to join the unit. Several years earlier, President John Kennedy's pilot had interviewed Burhanan for the position and at one point, gestured to a nearby Sikorsky VH-3A helicopter like the one we used to fly Nixon.

"You think you could fly that big helicopter?" he asked very condescendingly.

"Colonel," Burhanan replied with his quiet brand of arrogance, "I could fly the box it came in."

Burhanan didn't get the job that day, but it was precisely that determination and self-assurance that convinced me to bring him on board when I had the chance. In fact, he was so exceptionally thorough and capable that I assigned him to fly President Nixon in my absence when I had back surgery in 1974. And, if Burhanan had held a higher rank at the time of my retirement in 1976, I would have recommended him to take my place as the Exec Flight's senior pilot and commanding officer at the White House.

Now, decades later, here we were in a film directed by "Opie from Mayberry," pretending to fly the very helicopter we had piloted so long ago, mingling with movie stars, grinning like school boys, thinking "we still got it."

"Can you believe we're doing this?" I asked Burhanan.

"Amazing, isn't it?" he answered.

"Sure brings it all back," I said, imagining the piercing ring of the hotline telephone that interrupted dinner with my wife CeCe and our two young children the night of August 8, 1974, in our Fort Belvoir home near Washington, D.C.

Introduction

While gathering information for this book, I asked Lieutenant Colonel Bob Shain, the man who replaced me as the Exec Flight commanding officer in 1975, to forward any records he may have retained upon his departure in 1976 when the unit was disbanded. He sent a small packet with a cover letter explaining that they had been instructed by President Ford's Military Office Director, Marine Master Sergeant Bill Gulley, to destroy all records.

"Consequently," wrote Shain, "this is basically what was in my desk. Most of the items pertaining to the disestablishment were never given to me. They were 'gleaned' from files I 'found' when I went to work in the Pentagon. To the best of my knowledge, some of them are no longer in any archives, particularly the personal notes...."

I was disappointed, although not surprised – given the Exec Flight's struggle for acknowledgement through the years – that the history of the Army's White House helicopter unit had been all but "lost." I knew then, more than ever, that telling our story was going to be a very steep hill to climb, but if I didn't do it, a valuable part of Army and White House history would continue to be misrepresented or even worse, disappear.

Now, as much as I and many of those who flew with me between 1964 and 1975 are able to recall has landed between the covers of this book. To characterize the quality of those pilots and crewmembers, I am reminded that the U.S. Army did not officially activate its 1st Special Operations Command (Airborne) until 1983. However, many years earlier, the Army's Exec Flight had the flight time, the combat experience, the technical know-how and the core survival instincts to have converted to a "special operations" unit in a red-hot minute.

This book is a tribute to them as well as my fellow soldiers in all branches of the military who serve selflessly and without hesitation to protect the freedom and safety of the United States of America. I am eternally proud to be one of some 46,681 helicopter pilots who flew in Southeast Asia – 2,202 of those men

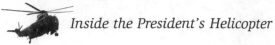

lost their lives. Of those killed in action 1,869 were in the Army and include Captain Dale Dwyer and Chief Warrant Officer Dusty Rhodes who flew with me at the White House during the Johnson years. Few men have ever been more dedicated and courageous.

Finally, it is my heartfelt hope that the reflections of a "no-name helicopter pilot" will help my two terrific adult children, Robin and Curtis, better comprehend what Dad was doing all that time he was away during their childhoods. Nothing means more to me than their understanding, respect and love.

The First White House Flight

Every helicopter pilot entering the White House Executive Flight Detachment in the early 1960s heard the same story from his commanding officer:

The day before John F. Kennedy's inauguration as the 35th President of the United States in 1961, he met with outgoing President Dwight D. Eisenhower in the Oval Office. In the process of briefing the former Massachusetts senator, Eisenhower invited Kennedy to stand with him behind the massive wooden desk.

"See that button?" Eisenhower said, pointing to a small disk affixed to the edge of the desk. "If you punch it, a helicopter will be here in five minutes."

Eisenhower promptly pushed the button and, sure enough, not more than five minutes later they heard the muffled flutter of approaching helicopter blades.

Only four years earlier, on July 12, 1957, Eisenhower became the first Chief Executive to travel by helicopter in an Air Force Bell UH-13-J from the White House to a Camp David bomb shelter in an emergency evacuation drill for "Operation Alert," one of several national civil defense exercises conducted between 1954 and 1961. As the Cold War stewed in the "atomic age," the estimated time for an intercontinental ballistic missile launched by Russia to reach Washington, D.C. was 35 minutes – a few minutes more than the time it took to fly a helicopter from the South Lawn to Camp David.

Operation Alert: First official White House helicopter flight
Bell UH 13-J, U.S. Air Force
President Dwight D. Eisenhower, July 12, 1957
(Boyer Family Archives)

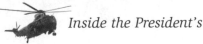

Deeply devoted to his own family, Eisenhower had another comment for Kennedy.

"If I were a pilot," he said, "with missiles coming and a family in Virginia, I'd consider saving them instead of flying to the White House. After all, we at least have a bomb shelter."

The reason for telling us this story was clear, especially for new pilots: "You can think it but don't do it. The president is more important than your life or anyone else's."

The mission established late in 1957 has remained virtually unchanged to this day. The president's helicopter must be capable of operating day and night, in adverse weather and all climates worldwide, and be prepared for a variety of threats ranging from mechanical malfunctions to nuclear war.

The task of locating the first presidential helicopter and pilot was assigned to Eisenhower's chief pilot and Air Force aide, Colonel William G. Draper. According to a June 19, 1957, *Time* magazine article, "The Air Force culled its files for helicopter pilots who had 2,000 to 4,000 hours of flight time without accident... Chosen for the job: steady, blue-eyed Major Joseph E. Barrett, 33, a tough but affable World War II veteran from Rule, Texas."

Only the best flew for the White House and Barrett, as the first presidential helicopter pilot, set a high bar.

While tremendous technological strides in the design and function of helicopters have been made since 1957, additional contributors to the security, safety, convenience and comfort of the president are *when, where and how* he is flown. The pilot, the flight crew, the Secret Service, the MP guards, the advance team, maintenance, operations and the support network on the ground must function as a well-oiled machine. A trip, whether five minutes long or an hour, has a strict, intentional protocol with numerous contingency plans in the event of unforeseen developments. As a result, each take-off and landing is aptly called "a mission."

Emergency landing sites are always pre-designated and protective systems always on standby. If the worst happens, and the president's helicopter is attacked, the best defense is evasion and relocation to the nearest secure facility, such as Air Force One or a Top Secret bunker.

Once the Secret Service was convinced helicopters were a safe, more efficient and cost-effective way to travel than a traditional ground motorcade, the White House contacted Sikorsky to upgrade its single-engine H-34 Choctaw model for VIP use by the President of the United States. Also during this time, the mission was transferred from the Air Force to the Army which established the H-34 Detachment in the fall of 1957 at Davison Army Airfield, Fort Belvoir, Virginia. Not long after, the Marines came on board with the Sikorsky HUS-1 Seahorse from their helicopter squadron (HMX-1), based at the U.S. Marine Corps Air Station in Quantico, Virginia. That joint mission would be shared for nearly 19 years.

WWII veteran Lieutenant Colonel William Howell was the first commander and number one pilot for the Army helicopter unit. Besides emergency evacuation, responsibilities included transporting Eisenhower and other dignitaries to destinations such as Camp David, National Airport and his Gettysburg farm where a strobe light mounted on a barn guided incoming helicopters. Flying by helicopter also made it convenient for Eisenhower to get to any number of area golf courses – a favorite pastime of more presidents to come.

President Dwight D. Eisenhower and French President Charles de Gaulle
Sikorsky H-34, Gettysburg Farm helipad, April 24, 1960
(National Park Service, U.S. Department of the Interior)

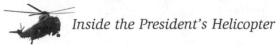

In the summer of 1958, the Army's H-34 Detachment was renamed the Executive Flight Detachment. By January of 1961, the Exec Flight had flown Eisenhower on more than 100 presidential missions and included two international goodwill trips.

Presidential pilots were required to wear helmets, given the propensity for helicopters to crash. However, the helmet rule was lifted after Kennedy was elected for three main reasons: improved pilot skill, better built aircraft, and to instill passenger confidence, which was known to quickly erode upon boarding a helicopter where only the pilots and not the passengers had helmets.

Originally designed for the Navy as a carrier-based helicopter, the H-34 aircraft was replaced by eight "customized" Sikorsky CH-3A fleet models early in the Kennedy administration. Once upgraded, the six-ton CH-3A became a VH-3A – the "V" signifying use by "very important people." Four were assigned to the Army and four to the Marines.

Also known as the "Sea King," the CH-3A was nicknamed the "Jolly Green Giant" in Vietnam where it was used for rescue missions and troop resupply. The state-of-the-art helicopter was powered by two 1,500 horsepower T58-GE-83 turbines and could carry a crew of three with up to 16 passengers at a cruising speed of 140 mph over a range of 600 miles.

Perfect for VIP transport and able to land in tight surroundings, the normal bare-bones interior had a folding door that separated the cabin from the flight deck. Decorated in the style of the era, the wall-to-cockpit carpeting was a dark variegated aqua, the bench sofas upholstered in harvest gold tweed fabric and the president and first lady's individual plush seats were burnt orange. A red cradle telephone was mounted by the window adjacent to the president's seat. With no less than 15 built-in ashtrays, there was also air conditioning, a closet toilet, sound-proof wall paneling and a fully-stocked wet bar – a creature comfort highly favored by President Lyndon B. Johnson.

The VH-3A had a flotation hull and its fuel tanks were self-sealing and crash-resistant. Two airstair doors were also installed to eliminate the need for a mobile staircase normally used by passengers to board and exit from either the forward or aft end of the cabin. Each president had his own gold-embossed, personalized glassware which frequently disappeared as souvenirs discreetly tucked into the pockets and purses of guest passengers.

The classified portion of the Exec Flight established under Eisenhower was supported by five 24-hour helicopters on duty at the Anacostia Naval Station where the Defense Information Systems Agency is located. By the time Johnson became president in 1963, the Exec Flight had grown to about 220 people and had close to 18 helicopters ready to immediately evacuate him and other national security officials to a secure site.

When flown by an Army pilot with a president on board, the helicopter call-sign was Army One. If the pilot was a Marine, the helicopter was called Marine One, even it happened to be same aircraft. Three removable plexiglass plaques – the first reading "Welcome," the second "Aboard" and the third, either "Army One" or "Marine One," could be inserted beneath the stairway steps leading up to the door to further signify which military branch was flying the president. Many historians, journalists, and even some First Family members often miss this distinguishing nuance.

As to what goes on *inside* the president's helicopter, I have a few stories to share....

Jacoby Road 1

Life is like a landscape. You live in the midst of it, but can describe it only from the vantage point of distance.
– Charles Lindberg

"Back in the old days," I told my two children, Robin and Curtis, about growing up during the Great Depression in Ohio, "before television, computers, video games, cell phones, credit cards and $100 shoes that grow out of style faster than any kid could ever wear them out, we had it pretty tough."

Now sharing those memories with my grandchildren, Aryn and Ryan, I begin with "Back in *ancient* times, if we couldn't afford it, we didn't buy it. If we had extra, we shared. If we went without, no one judged us."

In those ancient times during the 1930s, when I was a skinny, barefoot youngster, gratitude prevailed. Complaints floated into thin air. Family was everything. That way of thinking kept us moving forward in the hardest of times and we definitely had our share.

My very non-identical twin brother Jack and I were born in Akron, Ohio, on July 24, 1929, to working-class parents George and Edna Boyer. Our collective weight was about 16 pounds, not much more than our older brother Dick who had tipped the scales at 13 pounds as a solo arrival two years earlier. Once my parents had counted all our fingers and toes, their attention turned to Jack's black eye. It raised questions about how well we had gotten along in tight quarters.

"Looks like we have a couple of boxers," Dad told Mom.

As a result, I was named Gene Tunney Boyer and my brother Jack Dempsey Boyer after two of the 20th century's greatest prizefighters. For all the things my father did right, I think he might have gotten this one wrong. Tunney was extremely intellectual. Dempsey was a barroom brawler. My brother had the high IQ and I – well, I was innovative. I also had ahead of me

more than a few random frays and explained Jack's black eye by saying he had thrown the first punch.

Amusing as it tended to be, being named after such distinguished fighters, we always felt a keen obligation to perform "all out," no matter the job. Jack was smaller and smarter, I was taller and, as I said, innovative. To no one's surprise, we beat out several hundred other sets of fraternal twins to place second as the "Least Alike" at the 1984 Twins Day Festival in Twinsburg, Ohio. The first place finishers had a height differential of six inches, plus they were born in different years having straddled the strike of midnight on New Year's Eve. As twins go, Jack and I were uncharacteristically detached and did not grow close until well into adulthood.

Older brother Dick's full name was Wallace Richard Boyer, so named by my creative father in honor of Henry Wallace, the Iowa-based editor of *Wallaces Farmer,* a farming magazine founded in 1998. A controversial advocate of government intervention in agricultural production, Wallace later became Secretary of Agriculture under Franklin Delano Roosevelt and eventually, in 1940, his vice president. However, four years later in 1944, after Wallace's increasing left-wing views began to raise Democratic eyebrows, Roosevelt replaced him as vice president with Harry Truman.

I'm not sure what my father saw in Henry Wallace the spring of 1927 that moved him to name his first son after the man, but clearly Wallace was not afraid to "stir it up" and that tendency had been a celebrated forte in our family for hundreds of years.

My father was born in a small town outside of Athens, Ohio, in 1906. His parents had left the family stronghold of Boyerstown, Pennsylvania, to chase industrial jobs in Ohio. Before my father's first birthday, his father, a railroad engineer, was killed in a train wreck in Columbus. Not long after, my grandmother married local farmer John Davis. She bore five more sons, two of whom were identical twins and both served in the Army during WWII – one in the Pacific and one in Europe. They came back home to work on the farm and live out their lives, never to be separated again.

My mother was born in Athens, Tennessee, in 1909 on a

My parents, George and Edna (Monroe) Boyer
Akron, Ohio, about 1930
(Boyer Family Archives)

1,600-acre farm. The Monroe family had received its property in a land grant as a result of military service under General George Washington before he became our first president. Like Dad, Mom was also one of six children (she the youngest) and had also lost a parent early in life. Her mother had been one of the some 30 million victims of the worldwide influenza pandemic of 1918-1919, which is still considered to be one of the most devastating epidemics in recorded history.

A distant relative of President James Monroe, my mother's "Munro" ancestors first arrived in the "colonies" from Scotland in 1620 as indentured servants. They were under contract with a variety of "employers" who financed their transportation, lodging and other living expenses. They were gradually released from bonded obligations through the years by fighting in the French and Indian War (1754-1763), the Revolutionary War (1775-1783) and the War of 1812.

When I trace the branches of my family tree, I am always struck by how many relatives served in the military fighting and, in some cases, dying for freedom and independence. I

know that experience instilled in their offspring, me included, a visceral sense of patriotism and duty.

Dad was born too late to serve in WWI and too early for WWII. He was a dyed-in-the-wool Democrat and fancied himself a civic soldier of sorts – pro working man, pro labor, pro union. A skilled tire builder in the heart of Akron, the Rubber Capital of the World, he was already an active union organizer in 1926, the year he met my mother at a community dance. Battling for better wages, keeping jobs from going overseas and preventing small business takeovers by the Big Four – Goodyear, Goodrich, Firestone and U.S. Rubber – kept my father fired up and sometimes even fired. But day by day, month by month, year by year, the jobs dried up.

The greatest struggle for the young Boyer family and millions of others came between 1930 and 1940. During that time, one third of the nation's work force plunged into unemployment in the wake of the October 1929 stock market crash and the widespread drought to follow in 1930 that ravaged the heart of American agriculture.

Our lives became a daily ordeal of keeping food on the table, clothes on our backs and a roof over our heads. Sometimes our dinner menu had only two items: macaroni and cheese or leftover macaroni and cheese. No turkey has ever tasted as good as the one anonymously donated to our family one Thanksgiving.

We lived in at least ten different places in and around Akron, from drafty shacks to tiny cramped houses, often without electricity or plumbing. As the auto industry steadily declined, tire builders were no longer in demand and Dad scrambled to take any hard labor job he could find.

There wasn't much time for lofty daydreams about what I wanted to be when I grew up when each day dawned with urgencies a child could sense but not fully understand. The notion of ever being a pilot, even when living so close to Dayton, the birthplace of the Wright brothers, never entered my head. Occasionally, we crafted a crude kite out of newspaper and twigs, but even if we managed to get it airborne I thought it was a boring way to pass time.

In and out of school, my brothers and I took odd jobs like

Gene Tunney Boyer (right) and Jack Dempsey Boyer, born July 24, 1929
(Boyer Family Archives)

picking crops and mowing lawns. One of our best customers was the owner of the Mason Canning Jar Company. Mom worked as a cook when she could. When no one had work, we retreated to the Davis farm on a rolling hillside outside Athens, 175 miles south of Akron, where Dad's mother and stepfather housed up to 20 floundering relatives at a time.

Dick, Jack and I slept in the hayloft in the barn and took on chores as directed, which included milking cows, feeding the livestock, and working in the garden. I especially liked taking laundry off the clothesline. Stiff as it was, nothing smelled better. With our few precious moments of idle time, we scooted into the spacious crawl space under the house and plowed race tracks for our toy cars in the cool, powdery dirt. If we had a craving for apples we knew whose neighboring orchard wouldn't notice a few pint-sized thieves. If a car broke down or clothing got torn, there was always someone at the farm who could fix it with their bare hands. Often short on tableware at mealtime, Grandpa Davis made each of us a personal soup cup out of a buffed tin can to which he soldered a handle. Iced tea was served in glass Mason canning jars.

One of my fondest memories was watching my grandmother strike a wooden match and light one by one the natural gas lanterns anchored on the walls throughout the small, two-story house. The golden warmth of those entrancing lamps somehow softened the hardship of a long, hot day as it faded into the quiet, slightly cooler night.

I loved the farm for its stability and the always welcoming arms of my grandparents. Naturally, of the several times I tried to run away from home in my pre-high school years, the farm was my destination. Hard as I try, I can't recall what types of disagreement with my parents caused me to hop a bike, provision free, and earnestly peddle south. More than likely it was something standard like wanting to play with friends instead of doing chores.

My Boy Scout days, age 11
(Boyer Family Archives)

Usually, I turned around after about ten miles and was home by dark. My parents counted on it and rarely said anything. I like to imagine they understood the need for a juvenile hothead to cool off. However, I do recall my father confessing he gave up punishing me for misbehaving because it didn't seem to do any good. Horseplay was horseplay and whether my pals and I were sneaking a smoke or hurling rotten eggs at a passing car, no one ever went to jail.

I was still in junior high the last time I tried to run away from home. It was a hot, summer day and I was determined to not turn around this time and make it all the way to Grandma's farm. I had peddled about 25 of the 175 miles south to Massillon, the birthplace of pro football, when hunger pangs compelled me to scout for something to eat. Oblivious to a state police car driving by, I wandered into a roadside grocery store planning to steal a candy bar, but before "Lightfingers" Boyer could strike, I heard a deep male voice behind me.

"Are you Gene Boyer?"

I turned to look up into the stern face of a towering policeman and swallowed hard. "Yes, Sir."

"Your parents are looking for you."

I lowered my head and planted my hands into the empty pockets of my blue jeans, hoping he didn't detect the unexpected surge of relief coursing through my entire body.

"Come on, I'll give you and your bike a lift home."

I never ran away again. Reflecting on that incident, I am struck by the contrast of today's world and can't help but yearn for a way of life that made it possible for a kid to act out, get rescued and still be loved unconditionally by the parents to whom he had caused so many headaches.

"You're heading in the wrong direction," Dad cautioned me on more than one occasion. "What do you plan to make of your life?"

Not much, I thought, since all I had ever known was "not much" beyond the boundaries of my upbringing. I couldn't imagine a world that didn't reek of raw rubber and overcooked cabbage. I hated cabbage. Stewed cabbage and carrots. Steamed cabbage and potatoes. Creamed cabbage sometimes with ham.

Easy to grow and versatile, the indestructible, odorous vegetable was a Depression staple and I would rather go hungry than eat it; although once an uncle offered me a staggering 50 cents to wolf down a helping of the slimy limp-leaf vegetable. Upon completing the challenge, I collected the payment and promptly ran behind the house to vomit. Yes, it was worth it. I was going to the movies.

In a cruel twist of fate, the tire-building business picked up in 1939 when world conflicts increased the demand for United States military products. Hitler was on the march in Europe and Dad was working double shifts at Goodyear in Akron, often napping in his car. My brothers and I were back in school. However, we had been away so long we had to take a test to determine in which grade we belonged. Jack passed his exam, but Dick and I weren't as lucky and were placed one grade lower than we would normally qualify based on age. Even though being "put back" was not unusual for the time given all the family instabilities, I was nonetheless ashamed and resentful of my twin's accomplishment – another good reason to act out and not take school seriously. I will say I was a good listener in class, but otherwise could not sit still long enough to study, read or write.

The gut-wrenching fierceness of the Depression years definitely helped implant in me a gritty brand of willpower. As a Gene Tunney namesake, I was always running into someone who wanted to pick a fight with "a boxer." Being small for my age, I wish I could say I learned to avoid confrontation or at least be smart about it like Tunney, but no such luck. I never backed down, sometimes threw the first punch and as a result, I won some and lost some. I even tried out for Golden Gloves but didn't make the cut and quickly abandoned any hope of defending my prestigious name in the ring. I would have to make my mark someplace else.

By 1941, things were looking up. We were renting a four-room brick house with an outhouse on about 12 acres west of Akron, growing most of our own food, and earning enough money to open a savings account in the local bank. My first awareness of the turmoil churning on the other side of the world in Europe came one afternoon when, midway through a bag of popcorn at an afternoon matinee with Jack in the small town of Barberton, the movie screen went black. We thought the projector had malfunctioned until an older man in a white shirt and dark slacks stepped out of the shadows onto the narrow stage.

"We're interrupting the movie," he announced with a tremor in his voice, "to let you know the Japanese have attacked Pearl Harbor and we are headed to war."

I remember looking at Jack who was as dumbfounded as I was. If we had been old enough, the two of us would have walked out of that theater and enlisted. I honestly can't recall what movie we were watching or if we even finished it, but I'll never forget how upset my father was when we climbed into the car for him to drive us home. Listening to the latest news bulletins on the radio, Dad had a grip on the steering wheel so tight I wasn't sure he would ever let go. On December 7, 1941, I realized the world was bigger than Akron, Ohio. Life stood still until the next day when our family huddled around the living room radio to hear President Franklin Roosevelt issue a declaration of war.

"Japan has therefore undertaken a surprise offensive extending throughout the Pacific area," the third-term president conveyed to a spellbound nation. "The facts of yesterday and today speak for themselves... No matter how long it may take us to overcome this premeditated invasion, the American people, in their righteous might, will win through to absolute victory...."

Everyone from the milk man to rubber industry barons felt the swell of patriotism and a hammering desire to contribute, to do our part to protect the country we loved. The country pulled together with clear purpose and a willingness to sacrifice. In an odd way, it felt good to go to war. Years later, after Korea and Vietnam, I saw firsthand the immense and grim absurdity of how warfare is "good for the economy" and yet so otherwise completely devastating and costly to individuals, their families and their homelands, no matter which side.

As more and more able-bodied men joined the military to fight in WWII, the workforce made room for women as well as teenage boys willing to lie about their age. At 14, I was posing as a 16-year-old doing heavy lifting in a Quaker Oats warehouse and chasing girls who weren't interested in me, oblivious to the ones who were. Thank goodness for football.

For the three Boyer boys as well as the entire community, sports of any kind were both an outlet and entertainment. Sledding and ice skating in the winter, swimming in Barberton Reservoir during the summer, and baseball, basketball or football as the season dictated – usually with the reigning family mutt dog trailing along. When I entered Copley High School as a freshman in 1944, my brother Jack was a sophomore and Dick

Brother Jack and I (left) peddled 20 miles roundtrip to play for the
Bantam Weight Barberton Barons, Akron, Ohio, 1943
(Boyer Family Archives)

Gene Tunney Boyer, left, and Jack Dempsey Boyer, twins on the Barberton Barons squad, don't mind a bit of a workout on their bikes before the workout on the gridiron. They live in Copley, ride their bikes to Barberton high school for practice.

was a junior. With a student body numbering less than 150, the school was too small to field a junior varsity team. Consequently, all three of us were on the varsity team which had about 24 guys, most of whom played both defense and offense.

Mostly, I played end. Jack was a guard and Dick a tackle. We wore leather helmets without face guards and our pads were a fraction of the size of today's protective equipment. Our home football field was the least favorite in the league because the north end was substantially higher than the south, not to mention the lumpy and often muddy playing surface. As much as we liked playing offense downhill and grumbled about running defense uphill, we adapted and played our hearts out.

From 1944 to 1948, Dick, Jack and I all had a turn as captain of the Copley High Indians football team. Our normally reserved parents were faithful supporters. Whether they were pacing the sidelines or perched in the bleachers, they were not shy about cheering often and loud – especially at football games. There were always at least two Boyer boys on the field and sometimes, best of all, three! We played rain or shine, blizzard or thunderstorm, sprained ankle or broken nose. No one ever wanted to sit on the bench, but since we had so few players that rarely happened anyway.

My greatest lessons learned at Copley High came as a result of the intelligence and influence Coach Eli Floison brought to a ragtag bunch of adolescent football players. A tall, husky man not more than 25 years old and a graduate of Ohio University in Athens where he had played football and earned a doctorate in Education, Floison was ahead of his time. Like all superior football coaches, he was hard-driving, but perhaps not so common, he was tactful and evenhanded. Not inclined to tirades or personal grillings, he was especially gifted at motivating his players to make adjustments on their own.

"Boyer?" he would say when, for instance, I ran off the field after a demoralizing turnover. "You know what you did wrong?"

"Yeah," I answered, knowing I missed a block or had run the wrong pattern.

"Good." That's all he said. Good. And with a single nod, convince me I had what it took to make a change for the better.

"Work to win," Coach Floison drummed into us. "If you're a passive participant, then don't be surprised if you don't amount to anything." His imprint on my youth remains to this day – perform with fairness and be aggressive. Even though I didn't know where I was headed, I was unknowingly developing the fortitude necessary to get there.

Amazingly, between my sophomore and junior year of high school, our team averaged 52 points a game and pounded our way up and down the gridiron to win 17 games in a row. I was among an unprecedented eleven first string players to land college football scholarships and four of us were headed to Ohio University.

Off the football field, I took a theater class to get closer to the girls, but never had a steady girlfriend. I knew myself well enough to know I was not the commitment type. History was my favorite class and was, in addition to news reels and the radio, my number one source of learning about world affairs and the war. I was easily mesmerized with news related to any number of battles and remember paying close attention to the graphic horrors of the Normandy Invasion and the Battle of the

Me (far left) and brothers Dick and Jack
Copley High Varsity Football, 1947
(Boyer Family Archives)

Bulge. Never did I imagine two decades later that I would pilot President Dwight Eisenhower and famed CBS anchorman Walter Cronkite over Omaha Beach, once so littered with blood-soaked bodies, to document the 20th anniversary of D-Day.

When the Germans surrendered in May of 1945, the Boyers piled into the family car to join thousands of others in downtown Akron for a jubilant rally, thrilled we had whipped the bad guys. Three months later, the United States brought WWII to a cataclysmic end by dropping two atomic bombs on Hiroshima and Nagasaki, Japan. More than 220,000 people were killed. Japan soon surrendered, but the relief that washed across America was short-lived in our family. Dick was drafted into the Army out of high school and sent to Korea as part of the forces assigned to prevent further Russian expansion into Asia.

"Don't worry," he told my concerned but proud parents, "I'll be back soon."

I envied his determination and wished I was older so I could go with him. His confidence was so convincing, I never doubted he would return. If there was one thing the Boyers knew how to do, it was survive, and Dick did just that.

About that same time, Dad and Mom had managed to save enough to buy a 1.5-acre plot of land on Jacoby Road in the rural outskirts west of Akron. Only recently subdivided, there were a few other small houses in the area, but no trees yet along the freshly black-topped road. Dad and Mom had dreamed for years about building their own home, periodically revising crude sketches of the two-story, three-bedroom wood-frame house that would have a basement, indoor plumbing and enough land for both a vegetable and flower garden. Finally, that vision was about to take shape, one board at a time.

Ever thrifty and resourceful, Dad got the rights to disassemble bunk houses and storage sheds at an abandoned Civil Conservation Corps camp. About five miles from the site of our new house, the facility once housed government-employed workers who had helped build many of the local schools, bridges and roads. Day after day, Jack and I worked with Dad to pull nails and load the free lumber into a truck borrowed from a neighbor.

To repay our neighbor for use of his truck, we put in hours helping him with his cement finishing business. As a result, we learned how to construct our own basement which is where we lived while we built the rest of the house over us. Some of the people who passed by made a point of looking down their noses at us using old lumber and scavenged plumbing fixtures to build a new house. Dad just smiled and waved.

For me, the best find at the CCC Camp was a large claw-foot bathtub. Soaking in a full tub of warm water in the days after we finished the house generated a rare feeling of privilege and indulgence. We had built a dream with our own hands! Little has ever felt more satisfying.

Although, there was that ingenious scheme Jack and I cooked up when he started working at the first drive-in theater in Summit County. To promote the new business, the company held a raffle drawing for a new Philco table-top television set. When the big day came for the drawing, Jack's girlfriend "somehow" managed to draw a ticket with my name out of the bin.

"And the winner is," she declared, "Gene Boyer!"

I'm not quite sure how we rationalized the impropriety at the time, but sitting with my brother watching grainy Westerns on a six-inch screen was the height of brotherly bonding if ever there was one. I'm sure our parents never knew the real story. Otherwise they would not have kept reminding friends and relatives through the years that the Boyers had the first television set in Summit County, Ohio.

A house with electricity, a huge bathtub, a record-breaking football season, plenty of girls willing to be kissed, *and* a television set – life was the best it had ever been.

When I graduated from high school in 1948, a gallon of gas was 14 cents, the average annual income was $3,000, Harry Truman was president and the Cleveland Browns became the first unbeaten team in professional football history.

Thanks to Coach Floison, I was accepted by Ohio University on a football scholarship, and in the fall of 1948 began plodding through one course after another to preserve my eligibility, uncertain as to whether to major in Business Administration or Physical Education. Either way, I expected to return to the

Akron area where I knew my way around and people knew me.

Jack was already at Kent State and would earn his degree in Business Administration by the age of 19 before spending two years in Germany with the Army. After his discharge, Jack embarked on a successful banking career with the Federal Deposit Insurance Corporation. He never married.

Dick married his high school sweetheart, a cheerleader from a rival school, and upon returning from Korea earned a Civil Engineering degree from Ohio University. After accepting an Air Force commission in 1951, he went back to Korea as a B-26 bomber pilot. He retired from military service in 1970, got a teaching credential and taught math at a high school near Vandenberg AFB in California, where he also coached the girls' softball team to a state championship. He and his wife, Elizabeth, had five children.

High school graduation, 1948
(Boyer Family Archives)

My twin brother, Jack Dempsey Boyer
(Boyer Family Archives)

My older brother, Wallace (Dick) Richard Boyer
(Boyer Family Archives)

The house on Jacoby Road is still standing inside a lush canopy of mature trees. Who knows how many people have lived there unaware of the family that built it and what it took to accomplish a dream one used piece of lumber at a time. I will always admire and envy the simplicity of how my parents thought and lived. They were honest, tireless, never drank, always had a garden, treated all people with respect, loved their three boys completely and were so devoted to each other that only three months after my father passed away in 1988, my mother followed.

I credit my parents most of all for helping me to keep my feet on the ground when my head was in the clouds or someplace much worse.

"If you're not happy with what you have," Dad drilled into me, "work harder."

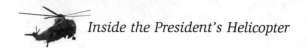

Higher Education 2

Professor Focke and his technicians standing below grew even smaller as I continued to rise straight up, 50 metres, 75 metres, 100 metres. This was intoxicating! I thought of the lark, so light and small of wing, hovering over the summer fields. Now man had wrested from him his lovely secret.
– Hanna Reitsch, German pilot describes first helicopter flight

A football scholarship was my ticket to college.

Located in Athens, Ohio, and founded in 1804, Ohio University was a nationally ranked business school. Approximately ten percent of my fellow students came from New York and countless alumni advanced on to prominent, distinguished careers. Among the most well-known are: George Voinovich, Sammy Kaye, Clarence Page, Matt Lauer, Erma Bombeck, Arsenio Hall, Joe Eszterhas, and Nancy Cartwright – the voice of cartoon character Bart Simpson. Paul Newman attended one year, was expelled for undisclosed reasons, but went on to graduate from Kent State. My own teammate, Vince Costello, became a Cleveland Browns defensive linebacker great (1957-67) who went on to coach with the Browns, the Cincinnati Bengals, and the Kansas City Chiefs.

Costello was one year younger than me and he had about 20 pounds more muscle. He was also Ohio-born and bred, and we were on the same athletic scholarship that paid for books and tuition. Ohio U Bobcat football players were mostly housed in small dorms and obligated to work in the off-season as servers and busboys in the girls' cafeteria. None of us objected to that job. Costello and I were both as adept at dishing out flirtatious one-liners as we were bacon, eggs and hotcakes.

"Want some sugar with that?" was one of my favorite lines. Although relentless in our self-promotion, Costello and I were rarely successful in captivating the object of our affection and football remained our single highest priority.

In 1949, famed Ohio State Buckeye head coach Carroll Widdoes joined forces with rising star line coach Howard Brinker at Ohio U. Like my high school coach, they were patient, stalwart, methodical thinkers able to corral hotheads like me. Couple their influence with the crushing, face-to-face scrimmages I had against the likes of Costello, and I had to reach deeper than ever to compete.

As probably the smallest offensive guard in the conference at 175 pounds tops, I knew fighting hard for something meant getting nicked up. The blows were slightly softened when we retired our leather headgear in exchange for the first plastic helmets. (My son still points to the "leatherhead" era as a contributor to some of my dingy thinking.) Unfortunately, face masks were still about five years away and I lost count of the number of times my nose was broken. Such injuries were part of the game, viewed as a badge of honor and, for reasons I still don't understand, fascinated the girls.

Offensive Guard, First String
Ohio University Bobcats, 1948-52
(Boyer Family Archives)

1951 OHIO UNIVERSITY FOOTBALL SQUAD

Front row (left to right) John Halak, Mgr., Bill Haffner, Tom Anderson, Frank Underwood, Vic Pikus, Ron Foliano, John Ohrman, John Turk, Vince Costello, Tom Lee, Bill Ellis, Bill Bevan, Frank Richey.

Second row (left to right) Coach Jim Snyder, Coach Carroll Widdoes, Paul Winemiller, Bill Castc, Nick Fogoros, Al Dunn, Gene Boyer, Charlie Wilson, Captain Al Scheider, Duke Anderson, Don Miller, Gene Nuxhall, Ed Roberts, Coach Howard Brinker.

Third row (left to right) Coach Kermit Blosser, Sam Carpenter, Dick Fleitz, Larry Lawrence, Bill Scheider, Elmer Apel, Leon Wilson, Bob Haug, John Bedosky, Wally Platzenburg, Demus Jones, Wally Duemer, Don Essey, Merle Hurmell, Coach Bob Wren.

Back row (left to right) Fred Schleicher, Trainer, Tom Ascani, Dick Phillips, Jerry Hannah Lou Sawchik, Sam Greiner, Art Aspengren, Bob Marchi, Stan maschino, Bill Mason, Bob Penrod, Dick Evans, Dick Sump, Jim Umstead, Roger Crabtree, Matyas Belle, team doctor

(Boyer Family Archives)

Our playing schedule matched us against several worthy
adversaries such as Illinois, West Virginia, Bowling Green,
Temple, Cincinnati, and Kent State. About half the team was ex-
military and going to school on the GI Bill. In their late 20s and
fresh from combat, they had a bigger interest in getting an education and moving on with their lives than those of us just out
of high school. Most of that group, including me, were also
enrolled in ROTC (Reserved Officers' Training Corps) courses
and pocketed a hard-earned $21 per month.

In 1950, the Big Ten Football Conference had an open slot for
membership. I remember cruising along in the team bus on the
375-mile trip from Athens to Champaign, Illinois, watching the
blur of farmland out the window, our hopes riding high that we
could earn a Big Ten spot. Then, just seeing the immense size
of the Illini Stadium compared to ours instantly convinced us
we were out of our league, but we still played like we owned the
place. We lost to Illinois 28-2 and were summarily removed
from Big Ten contention.

As disappointing as that game was, we endured an even
worse assault later that season when we traveled across the
Mason-Dixon Line to still-segregated Huntington, West Virginia,
to play Marshall University. Blind-sided by a wrenching act of
racism, I remember stopping in my tracks the instant I found
out Frank Underwood and Charlie Wilson, the only black players on the team, would not be allowed to stay with us at our
hotel. The first two black athletes to receive a full-ride scholarship to Ohio U, they were forced to sleep at a "colored-only"
hotel on the other side of town and dutifully complied without
protest. Shocked as I was, I didn't know how to speak up or to
whom, but I felt to my core it was all wrong. How could this be
happening?

President Truman had integrated the military, plus half our
football squad were ex-GIs. Wasn't that the same thing? We
were a unit, too. If we're fighting wars together, why couldn't
we eat, sleep and play ball together? It didn't make sense and
it damn sure wasn't fair.

The next day I watched Underwood and Wilson warm up
like nothing had happened and figured this was not the first

time they had weathered such discrimination. But it was my first hard encounter with Jim Crow America and stirred in me a private and lasting outrage.

Our Ohio U football team always played hard, but that day in West Virginia, we were definitely more steamed up than usual. Every play was a full-out clash of bodies and personal dispositions. I'm only guessing, but that may be why I took a brutal kick to my face. Four top teeth were broken off at the gum line. I was in surgery the next day, but relief from the injury and pain of racism was a long way off for Underwood and Wilson.

Wilson later joined the Army and rose to the rank of Lieutenant Colonel. Underwood went on to build a distinguished military career with the Army, served in Vietnam where he was severely wounded, and retired as a full colonel. His son Frank, Jr. became an accomplished artist and son Blair is an award-winning television and film actor.

While I lettered three times and only missed two games in four years due to illness, there was no denying the blunt reality that I was too small for pro football. I graduated in 1952 with a Bachelor's Degree in Business Administration.

I grudgingly bid farewell to my gridiron days and braced myself for a dull and tedious march toward what my mother called "something sensible and stable." To me, that translated into a boring, entry-level, dead-end management position at an Akron rubber company. While I didn't know for certain what I wanted to do with my life, I definitely knew what I didn't want and was filled with gnawing regret for having taken my family's advice to abandon an interest in Physical Education and becoming a coach.

Thankfully, Uncle Sam stepped in and drafted me just in the nick of time. Contrary to what I might think if I were a young man today facing the prospect of being sent to an ill-conceived war in Iraq or Afghanistan, I welcomed my country's call to serve and relished the adventure that surely must lie ahead. After all, my brother Dick had come back from Korea in one piece. Plus, what better reason could there be than to fight the spread of communism and protect world peace?

I reported to Camp Pickett in rural southeast Virginia for

Me (upper left) with brothers Jack (right) and Dick
(Boyer Family Archives)

basic training the fall of 1952. While I was traversing obstacle courses and target shooting, Ohio University was marching toward their first and only Mid-American Conference title, and on the other side of the world in Korea, our country's first Vietnam raged. Eventually tagged The Forgotten War, the plight of North and South Korea remains to this day a tragic, unre-solved byproduct of WWII.

Koreans had jubilantly celebrated Japan's surrender and withdrawal from their country in 1945 but were unprepared for how the United States and our then-ally, the Soviet Union, would forever compromise that short-lived independence. In 1948, the opposing ideologies of communism and democracy etched a jagged boundary line near the 38th parallel and the Republic of Korea (ROK) was formed in the South and a com-munist regime was established in the North.

The once unified country less than 600 miles long and 175 miles wide erupted in war in 1950 when the Soviet-backed North Korean army invaded South Korea. First under the command of General Douglas McArthur and then LT General Matthew Ridgway, United States forces rushed to the aid of South Korea. While the newly formed United Nations and President Harry Truman's efforts to negotiate a peace agreement ran hot and cold, the Chinese sent in 180,000 men to back up North Korea. The fighting was ferocious, bloody and costly. Approximately 4 million lives would be lost, which included civilians and more than 25,000 American troops.

Fragments of gruesome stories from the battlefields wound their way to Camp Pickett where I spent eight weeks. But as young soldiers are prone to do, we simply stoked the fires of invincibility and charged forward – except for one kid from New York who reminded us we were not all eager recruits.

I can still see the lean, dark-haired private from my barracks, half-conscious, curled up on a stretcher being loaded into an Army ambulance. While on latrine duty he had caved into the pressures and swallowed a dose of Drano. The acid-based cleaning granules had eaten through his gums and throat even before he reached the hospital. Little could be done but keep him sedated until he died.

For many, basic training was sheer torture, but I never imagined the stress could get so bad that anyone would be driven to take his own life and in such a terrible way. It was the first time most of us had had someone close to us die. Regardless, we instinctively knew not to dwell on what had happened – that kind of loss and the waste of human life was part of the terrain upon which we were now traveling. We were headed into combat and, in one of warfare's greater ironies, we were expected to place our lives in each other's hands, but not get too close. If we felt too deeply, we risked becoming our own worst enemy – just like the kid who committed suicide. That day, contrary to everything I had learned playing football and the value of building team camaraderie, I concluded that being in the Army was no time to make a lot of friends.

Survival. It is a sobering and supreme leveling force.

On July 29, 1953, a Korean armistice was signed by delegates from the United Nations, North Korea and China.

"We have won an armistice on a single battleground," said newly elected President Dwight D. Eisenhower, "but not peace in the world."

His sentiments reflected what most anticipated – sporadic fighting would continue, the United States would remain in a peacekeeping role in the region, and our military would continue to train and deploy troops.

I was fortunate to be one of a few in my platoon of 40 to qualify for Infantry Officer's Candidate School (OCS). Instead of going straight to Korea like most of my fellow trainees, I was assigned to Fort Benning, Georgia. Located near the Alabama border, Benning covers more than 180,000 acres of rolling red clay hills and pine forests thick with tangled underbrush. Mountain training was held in Dahlonega, Georgia, and river, swamp and coastal training to the south at Fort Eglin Air Force Base. When I traveled through Fort Benning's main gates in a bus crowded with other enlisted personnel, my attention riveted on a wooden "control descent" tower used to train paratroopers.

"That looks like fun," I said to the guy next to me that chilly spring day in 1953.

But I wasn't there to learn to jump, I was there to get a commission.

Of the some 220 of us in the 19th Officer Candidate Company, Class No. 69, more than half would wash out. The rest would emerge at the end of 16 weeks as Second Lieutenants, otherwise known as the 45th man – able to lead a 44-man platoon and according to my OCS class book read, "a man developed through rigorous training, intensive mental application, exacting military discipline, group cooperation, social good will and firm moral courage... The 45th man is the United States' most valued weapon. He is the combat infantry platoon leader."

For all the robust build-up and endless, punishing demands on our mental and physical stamina, a deeper motivation to excel was rooted in simply sensing we were part of something bigger than ourselves that had come before. We were now responsible for perpetuating that legacy of endurance, service and duty.

Our daily routine began at 4:00 a.m. with a five-mile run and calisthenics before breakfast, then another five-mile run with weapon training that included everything from grenades to rocket launchers, flame throwers to land mines, M-1s to the recoilless rifles we called "cosmic peashooters." Classroom courses concentrated on subjects like communications, chemical warfare and leadership proficiency. We broke for a 30-minute lunch, then back to work until dinner at 6:00 p.m., after which we studied until it was impossible to keep our eyes open or lights out – whatever came first.

Letters from home were always a boost. Just reading in my mother's own handwriting that she wished I was there to have a slice of the apple pie she had in the oven warmed me inside. Dad would usually scribble the same short note at the bottom of her letter reminding me to work hard and stay out of trouble. What he said wasn't near as important as him taking the time to connect.

Opportunities to cut loose were few and far between, but when we had the chance we made the most of it. Jamming shoulder to shoulder into local bars, we consumed gallons of beer, tried to dazzle the ladies, swapped off-color jokes and foraged for any reason to make fun of each other. Everybody seemed to have a nickname: Handy Andy, Ripple, Johnny Reb, Little Caesar, Blue Suede, Mighty Mouse and Blitz.

Not surprisingly, I was called a lot of things, but nothing stuck unless you count what a self-appointed commentator wrote in my class book: "Gene labored hard and long, but he was never allowed to forget the time he spent in ROTC. The original 'Thug,' he forced us to admit that even a "Rotcee" could soldier. Gene showed us many amazing things and we just can't believe he learned them all in college."

Only a few of my classmates were college graduates. Several had volunteered or were drafted straight out of high school, while others had been in the Army for up to six or seven years. I was an easy target for good-natured ribbing because I had a college degree and four "easy" years of ROTC. Fortunately, I was in the best physical shape of my life and was able to dispel most doubts about not having the guts to get the job done by drawing

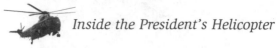
on the teachings of my father and football coaches: work harder, don't be afraid of getting banged up and always be a team player.

Unlike my college days, class studies and athletics were integrated disciplines at Fort Benning. Consequently, I hit the books as I never had before and to my parents' delight and my own amazement – or maybe it was the other way around – I finished near the top of my class. Three of us performed and tested at a high

My next assignment was a six-week course during the fall of 1953 in emergency medical treatment and battlefield support at Fort Sam Houston northeast of San Antonio, Texas. Different than Fort Benning with its rows of wood-framed structures, Fort Houston was built using classic southwestern mission architecture with stucco walls and red tile roofs. Known as the home of the combat medic, the fort remains one of the most progressive medical training facilities in the world. Besides learning advanced first aid, wound treatment and minor surgery techniques, I was also preparing to take command of about 100 medics assigned to infantry units, companies and battalions on the ground in Korea. MSC training concentrated on developing techniques for keeping the injured alive while in transport to a Mobile Army Surgical Hospital (MASH) located to the rear of the front lines. In Korea, that translated to all-terrain travel by land rig or by a recently introduced new mode of transportation – the helicopter.

Sometimes described as "an assembly of forty thousand loose pieces, flying more or less in formation," credit for the modern helicopter belongs to Russian immigrant Igor Sikorsky. (One of my most prized possessions is a personally inscribed photograph given to me by Sikorsky.) Known as the father of the helicopter, he did not invent the first vertical flight aircraft, but did design and build the first helicopter able to fly with consistent reliability.

In May of 1942, Sikorsky's XR-4 was delivered to the U.S. Army Air Corps as a prototype that would be reproduced in quantity for military service. Midway through WWII, a small fleet of fabric-covered helicopters flew the first combat rescue missions. Able to travel into areas unreachable by any other vehicles and also greatly reduce transport time, their versatility appealed to both military and civilian operations. By the mid-

1950s, advancements in power and design had produced helicopters sophisticated enough for routine use in medical evacuation, search and rescue, utility missions and VIP shuttles in Korea.

Near the end of training at Fort Sam Houston in late 1953, I noticed a crisp, freshly printed announcement tacked to a hallway bulletin board. One of the Army's first classes for commissioned officers to become helicopter pilots was scheduled to start at Fort Sill, Oklahoma. Prior to then, most air ambulance helicopter pilots were required to train first in a fixed-wing aircraft. With that pre-requisite eliminated, I saw nothing but a rack of green lights and the chance for another great adventure. I applied that day.

Looking back, that class may have attracted more than a few of us who were just nuts enough to ignore the hazards of flying such an untested and unpredictable contraption. No matter – we were invincible, right?

For anyone reviewing those of us standing in formation the day we reported to Helicopter Flight School, I was the one with two shiny black eyes – the result of a "sub-mucus resection" to remove damaged bones and scar tissue in my nose. The nasal surgery was one prerequisite I had not anticipated. Apparently, the Army felt it was important to have pilots who could breathe normally, so they undertook the task of correcting the side effects of multiple broken noses.

Swollen snout aside, I felt better than I looked. With the promise of rain gathering in the Oklahoma sky, I listened intently with about two dozen others to a captain foretelling what to expect in the weeks to come.

"This is going to be hard work," he said, sizing us up. "The helicopter is difficult to fly and about half of you won't finish."

The rumble of an approaching low-boy truck distracted us. On the trailer was a crumpled three-seat Hiller – often referred to as Hiller the Killer because it was so dangerous to fly. The captain didn't miss a beat.

"If you don't pay attention," he warned, "that's how you'll end up."

My first thought: "I don't need to worry, because I won't let that happen." The line between courage and stupidity has always been a blur for me.

We later learned that both pilots had died in the crash, the result of a phenomenon called mast bumping – a condition that occurs when winds come from one direction as an updraft and hits against one side of the mast (the drive shaft to which the blades are attached) causing it to bounce back and forth. The only way to regain stability is to flatten the rotor blades by lowering the collective pitch allowing the helicopter's nose to come up. The cyclic stick stays in neutral. If not corrected, the nose continues to drop, and the helicopter pitches to the right and crashes. Like driving a car that starts sliding on ice and knowing to turn the wheels into the slide, a skilled helicopter pilot learns to perform contrary to instinct.

After a week in the classroom pouring over aerodynamics, helicopter mechanics, principles of navigation, and radio communications protocol, I finally climbed aboard my first helicopter – a two-seat Bell H13-D. Hiller the Killer would come later. As we buckled our lap belts, I glanced at my instructor pilot – a trim, slightly older first lieutenant with a buzz haircut. Close to breaking a sweat sitting still, even in winter, I hoped I had mixed the right internal fortitude cocktail of enthusiasm, knowledge and caution. Helicopter pilots don't use parachutes and show-offs get killed.

"I'll tell you right now," the lieutenant said before we took off. "You won't be able to keep it over this field when you hover. It's that sensitive. What you have to do with a helicopter is just *think* about moving and it will move just enough for you to control it."

"And always take off into the wind," I said, offering a meager scrap of what I had already learned.

Each trainee was given 15 hours of flight time in which to qualify. During the next several days, we practiced how to take off and hold, fly in a straight line, make a turn, land, and hardest of all – hover. As the lieutenant predicted, I was all over the place and he saved me countless times from certain disaster by taking over the controls.

I didn't get airsick and, more importantly, wasn't scared. I was far too occupied trying to understand why one maneuver yielded a totally different result than I had intended. Hour by hour, one failed movement after another, I fought to ignore an insistent inner voice declaring over and over: "You'll never learn to fly this #*!%&! thing."

In the most basic sense, flying a helicopter is a synchronized balancing act. The brain, each hand and foot, both eyes and ears are all fully engaged in the process of managing direction, navigating and coordinating radio communications. It didn't take long for me realize the helicopter made the rules and my job was to learn how to become an extension of that mechanism – a mechanism that functions like no other.

Rotary flight relies on two rotor blades and controlling the angle at which they spin. The large, main rotor enables the aircraft to rise vertically, to hover and when tilted, to move in the direction of that pitch. The tail rotor, controlled by foot pedals, functions much like the rudder of a boat and makes it possible to turn right or left. Unlike an airplane, the engine only turns the blades and does not provide thrust like an airplane. Helicopters are pulled through the air or, as one of my favorite coffee mugs reads: "Helicopters don't fly. They beat the air into submission."

Steering is done with two control levers. On the left side is the collective stick, which raises or lowers the helicopter by setting both rotors at the same collective pitch. Movement to the right or left, forward or, particularly difficult, backward, is done by the cyclic control stick held by the right hand. Hovering requires that stick to be in neutral.

When I talk with children about flying a helicopter, I sometimes describe the task this way: "Sit down and pretend you are gripping an extra-large wet noodle in your right hand, the cyclic stick. Your job is to next rotate your left hand over your head counter-clockwise and alternate your feet in pumping motions on two imaginary pedals. Every once in a while, you grab a throttle, the collective stick, near your left hip and give it the gas. If you can do all of this without moving the tail of the noodle, you can fly a helicopter."

At Fort Sill, I struggled in the bottom third of my class for several weeks. Most had only a high school education, including Sergeant Ray Bowers from Washington State. A towering, thin guy with a can-do attitude, Bowers was a diligent student.

Through the years, every time our paths crossed, he asked me the same thing: "How the hell could you sleep so much in class and still learn all that stuff?"

"Just lucky," I said, and never told him about all the nights, after lights out, I hunkered in the corner of the latrine beneath a dim light bulb cramming for the next day's lessons. I had never studied so hard in my life and I knew the only way I would leave that program was if someone ordered me out. I was too bull-headed to ever give up.

During my last pre-solo flight, in the intimidating Hiller the Killer, all the pieces inexplicably came together. It was a classic, irreversible, breakthrough moment. Golfers know the feeling when a fairway iron finally hits the sweet spot and sends that little white ball on a poetic trajectory to an intended target. The next trick is figuring out how to normalize an intentional action into an instinctive motion. That comes only with practice.

My final check ride lasted about an hour and by the end of that flight, my instructor was smiling almost as much as I was. I was doing it all – bank turns, vertical ascents and descents, maximum performance take-offs, running landings and even emergency put-downs on sloping hillsides. That skeptical inner voice vaporized and I soloed the next day, executing a pre-scribed flight pattern with precision and whooping and cheering at the top of my lungs.

I was hooked!

As predicted by the captain the first day of flight school, only half of the 54-G class earned their wings in March of 1954. Most were ordered to Europe – also known as "the fast lane to the good life" – where the booze flowed in torrents and the girls were…friendly. In my case, luck took a hard-earned day off and I was among the three new pilots sent to Korea.

Before shipping out, I took the train back to Ohio on a week's leave to show off my wings to my thrilled parents and to all the skeptics from high school who, if given the chance, would have voted me "most likely to end up in jail," which, so far, hadn't happened. And, of course, I wanted to impress any passing girl who dared to take notice of the shiny pair of wings neatly pinned above my heart on my uniform pocket.

At a neighborhood watering hole, owned by a boisterous Greek-Italian-American named Jerry Columbus, I settled in at the bar anxious to "talk shop" and expound upon my latest escapades. Jerry had been an instructor pilot during WWII. The next thing I knew I had made the mistake of getting into a small plane with him at the controls, but I had never flown in one and I couldn't turn down the chance. Mae West said it best: "I try to avoid temptation unless it's something I can't resist!"

I climbed into the open cockpit behind Jerry and strapped into the surplus fixed-wing trainer he had purchased for a song from the Army Air Corps. Parked in a parched, hard dirt field on

Helicopter Flight School, Fort Sill, Oklahoma, 1954
(Boyer Family Archives)

a cloudless day, Jerry started the single propeller and we were off, rolling over the bumpy field, increasing speed and so jarring my brain I thought I would have a concussion before we left the ground. That worry shifted to a suffocating fear that we were going to die when we hit on one wheel, dipped to the opposite side, then bounced back to the other wheel, lurched into the air, hit the ground again and then finally, mercifully lifted up the instant I thought we were about to cartwheel into the great beyond.

Once airborne, terror transformed to exhilaration. We flew for about 30 minutes, cruising low over the gently sloping countryside, skimming the treetops, pointing out familiar landmarks like the newly built high school football stadium, friends' houses and in the distance, the Cuyahoga River – once so polluted with rubber plant debris and chemicals the surface caught fire and burned.

Circling to land, I hollered "This is great!" for the umpteenth time. The landing was a white-knuckle repeat of the take-off and all I could think of as we rolled to a stop was how we had cheated the local newspaper out of a spectacular headline about two popular local men dying in an airplane crash. Well, at least Jerry was popular.

The night before I left for Korea, I borrowed my father's Ford sedan to do what most 25-year-olds would do – meet up with some buddies at a bar, find some girls and "drink up." Shortly before dawn, after I had slept off most of my drunkenness on a friend's davenport, I carefully drove back to my parents' place on Jacoby Road. Concentrating so hard on staying in my lane and observing the 35-mile-per-hour speed limit, I didn't notice a police car parked on a side street until I passed by. As soon as it slowly pulled in behind me, I became so fixated on the headlights in the rearview mirror that I missed an upcoming turn at the bottom of the hill and drove straight into a bridge abutment. Had I been going any faster, I would have probably broken my nose yet again on the steering wheel.

Uninjured, adrenaline pumping through my veins like hot oil, I knew the car was too crunched to be drivable. I turned off the ignition and rolled down the window to greet the approaching officer.

"You all right?" he asked.

"Yes, Sir." I felt like a moron. I could fly a helicopter practically with my eyes closed, but couldn't drive a tank-size car along a road I knew like the back of my hand.

"Okay," he said, moving away from the car. "Get out."

This was it. I was finally going to jail. I staggered out and tried in vain to walk a straight line toward the officer.

"You drunk?"

"Yes, Sir." I stopped in front of the broad man who had both hands planted on his hips. "I've been celebrating. Headed to Korea…"

"That so?" he questioned, eyeballing me from head to toe.

I stole a look at my father's car in the light of dawn. Regret clogged my throat. I knew in the next few hours, the man who had bragged about me all over town was about to get a call from both the jail and the towing yard. The officer grumbled beneath his breath. I held mine. And then he said, "Well, son, I was in the Army and I know how you're feeling."

Instead of writing me a ticket and hauling my sorry ass off to the pokey, he drove me the remaining 15 miles to my parents' house, where my father met us in the driveway.

Dad was so boiling mad, I thought he was going to explode. I quickly eased by him to go inside the house where Mom dished out her own special brand of tight-lipped glares as she handed me a cup of coffee and then helped get my gear together. After the officer explained everything was fine and that he had called a tow truck, Dad cooled down enough to borrow a neighbor's car.

Surprisingly, that brush with the law would be as close as I ever got to jail. It was an important wake-up call for a young man who sometimes flirted too much with the odds. I look back and know if I had screwed up like that today, I probably would have been serving time instead of my country.

On the way to the Cleveland-Hopkins Airport about 40 miles north, the tension between Dad and me ebbed. Soon we were laughing about what had happened, the look on his face, the look on mine, and the throbbing headache I had and deserved.

The last five miles, before he dropped me off to catch a plane to San Francisco, I was confident in his unwavering support and he was confident I had found the new love of my life – helicopters.

By Example 3

If your actions inspire others to dream more, learn more, do more, and become more, you are a leader.
– John Quincy Adams

Like most GIs who returned from WWII and Korea, my brother Dick had little to say about the experience other than it was "pretty tough." His best advice for me on my way to Korea was to prepare for extreme weather.

"Worse than Ohio?" I asked, thinking our snowy winters and steamy summers were a fair measure.

"Worse than Ohio," he confirmed.

My commanding officers at Fort Sill added slightly more insight. Speaking in generalities, they briefed us about the strained political situation between North and South Korea and the dangerous conditions along the DMZ. Approximately two-and-a-half miles wide and 150 miles long, the demilitarized buffer zone angled roughly east to west across the 38th parallel. The mostly mountainous region included the vibrant Han River Delta that fed the extensive grasslands and hundreds of acres of abandoned rice paddies.

There were many outposts along the south line of the DMZ occupied by a combination of South Korean and American troops. Heavily barricaded with barbed wire and riddled with land mines, the DMZ was treated with Agent Orange in the late 1960s. The public would not know about the use of the cancer-causing defoliant in Korea until the latter stages of the Vietnam War, when the herbicide's lethal side effects could no longer be concealed. Two years earlier, in 1952, when I was first drafted by the Army, the fighting had been intense and widespread. Post-armistice, North Korea and China were still constantly testing the frail peace agreement and provoking sporadic skirmishes, but nothing, so far, had escalated.

I slept most of the way from Cleveland to San Francisco,

where I caught a bus to Travis Air Force Base about 50 miles inland. From there, I flew to Tokyo and then took a 600-mile-plus train ride to the southernmost portion of Honshu, Japan's main island. Crossing over the Kanmon Straits to the nondescript port of Kokura, situated on the northern tip of Kyusha, I gazed at the Sea of Japan's choppy, gray waters. About 90 miles to the west, Korea waited just beneath the horizon. I was on the other side of the world.

Japan was surprisingly neat and tidy. I saw not one enclave that came close to resembling the shanty towns or big city slums I had seen in the States. Well-insulated by the U.S. military transportation system, I had no opportunity to interact with the culture I later came to know as polite, artistic and industrious.

After nearly a week's worth of travel, my first assignment was to escort about a dozen doctors and surgeons from Kokura, Japan, to Pusan, Korea, for dispatch to MASH hospital units. We were put on board an LST or "landing ship tank," a huge, box-like, amphibious craft first used to move Allied men and equipment onto the beaches of Normandy in WWII and, in September of 1950, for the American landing at Inchon, Korea.

Congregating in the mess hall, the doctors held ranks from major up to a full colonel. Suffice it to say, as a second lieutenant, I was along for the ride – and what a ride it was with churning seas beneath us and an endless stream of resentment pouring from the men who were already counting the hours until they would be headed back home.

"What the hell are we doing here?" one doctor grumbled.

"Damn sure isn't what I signed up for," chimed in another.

Both men reflected a shared viewpoint that when WWII ended, their battlefield expertise would no longer be needed. Some were new draftees, but others were returning veterans pulled from growing families and established practices, and strongly believed they had already served their time.

Shortly, the to-and-fro pitch of the vessel got the best of a couple and they darted to the head to heave their guts out. "This whole thing," one shouted from down the hall, "is making me sick!" His colleagues all laughed and he vomited again.

From behind my weak smile, I quickly realized MASH doctors

had their own culture. As would later be depicted on the popular *M*A*S*H* television show that premiered in 1972, they were highly skilled and very adept at relieving the enormous pressures under which they had to perform. If they got into any trouble with military officials regarding protocol or regulations, they knew they were as close to being indispensable as most anyone could be. Most were stand-up guys who worked miracles in rudimentary, tent hospitals patching up gaping chest wounds and shattered skulls. For all of us, humor was a quick escape, a ready coping mechanism in the midst of unimaginable circumstances.

"So what are you going to do to me?" a reprimanded MASH doctor might reply. "Send me home? Well then, please do!"

Upon arrival in Pusan, Korea, I got my first whiff of kimchi, a pungent pickled vegetable dish that usually includes my nemesis – cabbage. I rarely saw one of the oft-buried crocks with its fermenting contents, but the gag-worthy smell, especially during the warmer months, was everywhere. The city – one of only two the North Koreans failed to strike – was a moving portrait of poverty and despair. I was appalled by the squalor, rampant starvation and the number of orphaned children begging in the streets. An even worse smell than rotting cabbage was that of human feces.

On virtually every corner, the locals would dump their solid waste in large metal pots. Every evening after the sun set, dutiful workers emptied the containers into huge "honey bucket" carts pulled by donkeys and then form a "night train" to the rice paddies where the contents were strewn about as fertilizer. I couldn't believe my eyes. Back in Ohio, anyone who drilled a well or planted a garden always made sure there was no seepage or cross contamination from an outhouse or septic tank. Yet the "night train" ritual was so obviously entrenched in this ancient culture, I could do nothing but accept it and watch where I stepped.

From Pusan, it was a 30-hour train ride north to Seoul through fallow, muddy farmland before climbing into mountain crevices. Early European visitors to Korea thought the landscape resembled "a sea in a heavy gale" because of the large number of successive mountain ranges that rippled across the peninsula.

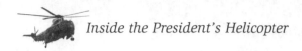

Bouncing along the last 35 miles of my journey in an open-air jeep toward the 24th Infantry's Division Headquarters located about four miles south of the DMZ, I concluded I had actually traveled beyond the other side of the world and was now closer to what poets and preachers called the "ends of the earth."

My initial duty was flying "ash and trash" for a MASH hospital staffed by about 100 people two miles from the DMZ. In other words, I was transporting supplies in and garbage out. We had four choppers and five pilots, ten mechanics and ten other support people. I was the executive officer and together we spent hour upon hour learning the lay of the land and how to fly against the wild, thrashing winds that circulated through the deep, narrow valleys.

Days and sometimes weeks would pass without a single combat casualty. Caseloads for MASH doctors were similar to that of a country doctor with a steady stream of cuts, scrapes, sprains and an occasional broken bone. The number one affliction for which I was not prepared was boredom – abject, eye-crossing boredom. If it was raining, we were in our tents reading,

Bell H-13, Mobile Army Surgical Hospital (MASH) helicopter, Korea, 1955
(Boyer Family Archives)

playing cards, writing letters, sketching or just shooting the bull. If it wasn't raining, we were cleaning equipment, watching movies on the side of a tent or playing some pick-up version of basketball, baseball or, my favorite, football. Mail call always perked us up and after we would read our own letters, we would read each others'. A single newspaper from someone's hometown made the rounds no matter how old it was.

Helicopters during the Korean conflict evacuated more than 22,000 causalities from front-line locations and were directly responsible for reducing to a then all-time low the percentage of those who died from wounds. Long before the helicopter became an eye in the sky for traffic reports, a troop and equipment transport in Vietnam, or a luxury shuttle flying important people to and from important business, it was a life-saver.

One clear, bone-chilling night, a call came in from headquarters requesting me to transport a South Korean soldier from the east coast 45 miles away back to our MASH facility. The patient had a severe gunshot wound to his chest. Climbing into the Bell H-13, even though I was heavily dressed, was like crawling inside a refrigerator. When I lifted off, I had two concerns: what kind of battle was ahead with the wicked, erratic air currents and would I freeze to death?

Guided by a single landing light and fighting unceasing gusts of wind, I followed the line of a familiar road to the ROK company headquarters close to where the DMZ dipped into the Sea of Japan. After I put down, blades still running, I helped several ROK personnel secure the cocoon-like stretcher holding the unconscious young man to the helicopter's right litter, which was equipped with a heating tube.

Within seconds, after anchoring a clear, hard plastic canopy over him, we were airborne and running at full power against pounding headwinds. Once oriented, I glanced at my patient in the ambient light. Tiny droplets of blood were collecting on the hood of the canopy each time he exhaled. "Hang on," I told us both.

The temperature had dropped below zero and my hands were now so numb I couldn't feel the stick. I had no choice but to steal a few precious minutes and land on the road to thaw my fingers. Standing with my gloved hands pressed against the

chopper's hot exhaust pipe, I looked at the lifeless solder through the frozen bubbles of blood clinging to the inside of the canopy. He was still breathing. I had transported trauma cases before, but nothing like this. Here we were, both of us some-one's son and brother, sent to war by people who would never know us, trapped in a freezing nightmare. What a god-awful flight I was giving him.

Twenty minutes later, I landed back at the MASH hospital. Medics rushed from the shadows to meet us, but it was too late. "Damn," I thought to myself, hoping the memory of his blood-smeared face would somehow die, too. So far, that hasn't happened.

With U.S. troops continuing to downsize in 1955, many of us were moved around in the process. Not long after being promot-ed to first lieutenant, I was transferred to the junior aide posi-tion for Major General Stanhope Brassfield Mason, commanding general of the 24th Division. That division was in charge of enforcing compliance with the terms of the Armistice. I was elated to bid farewell to the MASH doldrums.

A medium-sized man, the general had a professorial demeanor and loved classical music. A West Point graduate, he had commanded a regiment in the 1st Infantry Division in WWII and distinguished himself in battles across Europe including the Normandy Invasion and The Battle of the Bulge. A talented pianist, he eventually retired as a three-star general.

Mason led by example and was uniquely forward thinking. Before he introduced me to his senior aide, a captain, he called me into his office for a chat. Mason listed the captain's many service awards for bravery earned during some of the most bru-tal confrontations of the Korean War.

"He's on his second tour and," the general said, settling onto the edge of his desk, "there's also something else I want you to know since you'll probably figure it out on your own."

"Yes, sir."

"He's homosexual."

Admittedly, with my limited worldly awareness, the full impli-cations of homosexuality in a military setting were over my head.

"And that's just between you and me," Mason firmly added. "Most important thing is he's damn good at his job and that's what matters."

For me, it was a profound display of discretion and acceptance, and helped shape a personal perspective anchored in tol-
erance and common sense. Many years later, after I had
received my White House assignment, I met the captain for
lunch in New York where he worked as a stockbroker and was
managing my modest portfolio. After a few comments in the
vein of my being a "man or a mouse," he convinced me – a
meat and potato connoisseur – to try lobster for the first time.
Absolutely delicious.

General Mason was among the first military leaders to recognize the helicopter's exceptional utility and worth beyond that
of performing medical evacuations. Until the Korean War, helicopters were little more than an aeronautical curiosity for the
military. Mason helped change that.

Intent on personally connecting with the nearly 18,000
troops under his command, he decided to use a helicopter
instead of traversing bumpy, rutted roads in a jeep. I became his
personal pilot and for nearly three weeks we traveled throughout the division, landing at compounds for him to inspect troops
and interact with their officers.

During more than one flight, Mason expounded on his belief
that I was a "rough-cut gem" and he would sooner or later
knock off some of the sharp edges. Consequently, I got mini-
tutorials on leadership skills, social graces and, yes, even classical music, which he frequently played on his nicked-up, old
phonograph. The lilting melodies of Bach, Beethoven, and
Mozart pouring out of Mason's tent reminded us that somewhere, beyond this hell-hole, civilization awaited our return.

On the other hand, while the General worked to guide and
reassure me, I managed to rattle him with a few unnerving incidents. Once, on a routine approach to a company landing site,
with the General in the seat beside me, I caught sight of a hor-
izontal communications wire about ten feet ahead stretched
between two trees. Moving at about 12 knots and only 50 feet
above ground, I instantly pulled back on the cyclic stick,
increased power, and worked the pedals back and forth like
crazy to stall the helicopter to keep from hitting the wire. Mason
froze like a statue.

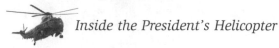

Wire strikes are one of the greatest hazards to helicopter pilots because the lines are generally not seen until it's too late. A heavy wire, if struck at 120 to 130 knots, can either sheer off a mast or flip a helicopter upside down.

The thick wire lodged against the rounded face of the cockpit and, as we hovered in place, it began to gradually slip upward. Downward would have been a lot better. To back up or fly in reverse, absent a monster headwind, is an unnatural behavior for helicopters, but that was our only option to prevent the worst from happening.

The wire inched higher.

Ever so delicately, I raised the helicopter in place just enough to let the wire slip to the skids below. With seconds passing like hours, the helicopter finally surrendered to my gyrations and we backed away enough to lift above the lines.

"That was a close one," Mason said after we had landed.

"Yes, sir," I answered, wondering if he was going to chew my ass.

"Good job," he said, and within a few days distributed a division-wide memorandum with guidelines for running communication wires in areas frequented by helicopters. Those regulations were widely adapted throughout the military.

Back in the United States, similar policies were being instituted. For instance, after building a series of dams, the Tennessee Valley Authority, responsible for controlling hydroelectricity, was the first to use large plastic balls on high tension wires and cables to alert low-flying pilots. Without question, these balls, now used prolifically throughout the world, have saved countless lives and General Mason's memo most assuredly accomplished the same in Korea.

I logged close to 500 hours with Mason, puddle jumping and crisscrossing South Korea with the life of our Division Commander in my hands. The wire incident had clarified for me that I was far less afraid of killing myself than I was of causing injury or death to someone who trusted me to keep them safe. My mother had a name for this kind of thinking. She called it responsibility.

Just when I was about to grant Mason sainthood, he announced the day before Thanksgiving, 1955, that he wanted me to fly him into the DMZ. "We're going to go kill our Thanks-giving dinner," he said, and grabbed a shotgun and shells.

Holy crap.

Since the creation of the DMZ two years earlier, the land was swiftly reverting back to its natural state and had become a wildlife refuge for, among other animals, panthers, bear, egrets and – our game of choice – pheasants. Former farmland was now overgrown with wild rice. It was a hunter's paradise.

Flying north, Mason spoke exuberantly about what a big morale booster it was going to be to put pheasant on the table for his 20 staff members. "Don't worry," he said, grinning, "the North Koreans don't have the weapon power to reach us. But just in case we better stay under a hundred feet."

So this is it. I'm going to die hunting birds.

I had to admit it was a decent plan and by the time we sailed over the barbed wire barricade, I was all-in and thinking, "Damn, I like this guy."

With Mason literally riding "shotgun" and no doors on the helicopter, I buzzed a brush thicket and flushed out a flock of pheasants. The General took aim and fired and we circled back for me to hover as low as I could for him to snag the dead birds with a crude gaff hook and pull them into the cockpit.

We repeated the drill several times, being extra careful not to touch down on the ground that concealed any number of live land mines. One after the other, pheasants piled up around our feet. I wasn't keeping count, but about 30 minutes later, when our bounty reached about twenty, I knew there were too many on board. The helicopter lost its center of gravity and suddenly pitched forward.

"We're in trouble!" I shouted. "I've got to put down. Hang on."

We braced for a running landing and prayed with every nerve the ground ahead was mine-free. Clumsy as it was, we landed safely and nothing blew up.

"I think," I advised Mason, who was as bathed in relief as me, "we better throw one back."

He promptly heaved a bird out the door and we called it a day.

Thanksgiving dinner was fantastic – give or take a few resid-ual buckshot pellets. The staff applauded our account of such a

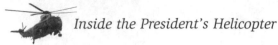

bold venture and the general ordered everyone to enjoy the pheasant. "You will take pleasure in every bite, gentlemen," he told us, "because we almost killed ourselves getting them here."

About 25 years later, I couldn't help but watch the antics of television *M*A*S*H* doctors Hawkeye and Trapper John and imagine what a comical scene it would have been for the two of them to go pheasant hunting in the DMZ.

Before I ended my tour in Korea, General Mason invited me to accompany him to Seoul for a dinner with Syngman Rhee, President of the South Korean Republic. Rhee ruled from 1948 until he was forced to resign at the age of 85 in 1960 during the so-called Student Revolution. Never imagining I would meet a president from any country, I was honored by the opportunity. General Mason and I were the only guests to arrive by helicopter at the palace 90 miles south of our headquarters. Naturally, Rhee wanted a closer look and Mason graciously offered the President the use of the helicopter if needed.

Among General Mason's last efforts to smooth a few of my "rough edges," he encouraged me to put in for regular commission in the Army. "Keep all your doors open," advised the wise man who so instilled the value of leading by example.

After 18 months in Korea, I returned to Fort Benning in early 1956 as a reserve officer and was put in charge of about a half dozen first-aid stations. The work was routine, predictable and land-based. I missed flying, but managed to finagle an hour or two every weekend to keep logging flight hours. It was never enough.

Being at the controls of a helicopter was like writing myself into a chapter of some dime-store novel. There was a mission at my fingertips and no matter how certain I was about how the plot might unfold, there was always a twist. I loved the element of surprise, like catching sight of a tractor below turning up peanut plants in a field or a fisherman casting a line on the Chattahoochee River.

As usual, when the workload slackened, I found my way to a card game or a bull session in the mess hall where, amidst the bravado and poetic license of fellow soldiers, there was also the promise of an yet untold yarn. One afternoon, my boss, an easy-going major with a penchant for good story-telling, reached

Commendation Award from mentor
Major General Stanhope Brassfield Mason, U.S. Army, Korea, 1955
(Boyer Family Archives)

back into his past some 15 years to talk about being drafted into WWII. He had been a student at the University of Tennessee in Knoxville and living in a boarding house with about 30 other young men when they were called to active duty.

"Our landlady was a tough, battle axe of a broad," the major said to the five other officers seated at the table and went on to tell us she had had two or three husbands. With everyone heading out at once she knew it would be impossible to re-rent the

rooms and keep up her mortgage, so she set the place on fire to collect the insurance money.

I started squirming in my chair. The major was talking about my mother's oldest sister, crazy Aunt Ora.

"All my shit burned up and I had to report with nothing but the clothes on my back," he said.

I quickly changed the subject to something less inflammatory. How was I going to tell my boss this "resourceful" nut-ball of a woman was my aunt? It took a few days to get the right words together, but I finally let the major know she was a relative and did do a fair amount of jail time for her crime. We had a good laugh and I assured him I was nothing like Aunt Ora, who out of sheer will and gumption, died shortly before her 100th birthday. I lost count of the husbands.

With the diminishing need for military support in Korea, the Army was rapidly reducing forces and, while I had hoped for a regular commission, I was told it could take more than a year to come through. The last thing I wanted to do was hang around watching people give injections and hand out aspirin, Band-Aids and condoms, and still end up getting *riffed* (reduction in force). As a result, when my tour ended the spring of 1957, I left the service and went home to scout for a civilian flying job or better yet, maybe start my own business.

The unknown was waiting.

Going Mainstream 4

The available helicopters resemble a pretty girl – they are small, nice to look at and to be seen with, exciting, pleasant to take out, apt to be noisy; and the more you have to do with them the more expensive they get and the more problems they bring around your neck.
    – Peter Masefield, CEO British European Airways, 1954

Coming home to my parents home in Akron after nearly five years in the Army was like trying to put on a pair of old shoes I had outgrown. Nothing seemed to fit. The house was smaller, the neighborhood disappointingly predictable, and the weather just as hot and humid with far too many thunderstorms rumbling through.

No one was flying helicopters in the Akron area except for an occasional crop duster. Even though fledgling helicopter airway services had begun in New York, Los Angeles and Chicago, there were likely fewer than 200 rotary aircraft flying American skies and slightly less for the rest of the world. However, I did have one option close to home.

Within President Franklin Roosevelt's New Deal package was the Tennessee Valley Authority Act. In 1933, Congress had created the innovative government agency charged with incorporating integrative solutions related to flood control, reforestation, navigation on the Tennessee River, electric power production, farmland irrigation, and even malaria prevention. Roosevelt described TVA as "a corporation clothed with the power of government but possessed of the flexibility and initiative of a private enterprise."

The Authority was extremely successful and thrives to this day. During the mid-1950s, TVA began using helicopters to monitor the rapidly growing network of power and communication transmission lines running throughout the greater Tennessee region and neighboring states. Crews of two, a pilot and a "spotter"

with binoculars, followed lines through all kinds of terrain looking for fallen wires, damaged poles or cracked porcelain insulators. One helicopter could do in a fraction of the time what took 30 or 40 men in a fleet of trucks months to accomplish.

My maiden entrepreneurial venture involved first working out a deal with Bell to lease an H-13 and then convince the local power utility company to hire me to do line survey work. They could save a ton of money and I would have a job for life flying helicopters. Perfect, except for one thing. I, the son of a union leader, had neglected to consider the power of organized labor. The threat of a full-scale strike if the company brought in a helicopter was enough to ground my plan and send me packing. I had spent almost all of my savings working the angles and I hated feeling like a failure. Today, I can massage the story enough to call myself a progressive thinker ahead of his time, no matter what my father thought about the impact on workers.

Dad was still building tires at Goodyear in 1957 and Mom was tending house and garden. Jack lived in Akron and worked for the FDIC as a senior bank examiner. His area stretched from Wisconsin to Florida. My older brother Dick, now a father of five, was an Air Force major stationed at El Segundo AFB in southern California where he was in charge of construction for Atlas missile sites across the United States.

Fresh out of ideas for starting my own business, I thought, "If I can't bring helicopters to Akron, I'll take myself to where they are." I loaded clothing and a small stereo system in my

Artist vision of the coming helicopter commuter service
that never materialized
(*Look* magazine, May 18, 1954)

new, red and white Ford Fairlane and drove to New York. I'm sure more than one member of my family asked if I knew what I was doing and I'm just as sure I had a smart-aleck remark like, "I always know what I'm doing."

Five years earlier, New York Airways, with the help of generous government subsidies, became the first scheduled helicopter service in the world. The commercial market potential was thought to be enormous, as described by Civil Aeronautics Administrator Frederick B. Lee in a May 15, 1955, *TIME* magazine business article. Lee predicted that in ten years there would be 286 daily helicopter movements between New York and Washington alone and the helicopter passenger market could total 133 million a year, almost four times the number then carried by all airlines.

Using a 12-passenger Sikorsky S-58, they operated between three main airports – La Guardia, Newark and Idlewild (now John F. Kennedy Airport). On average, in the summer of 1957, NYA carried about 9,000 passengers a month along with 60,000 pounds of freight and over 250,000 pounds of mail. Although a convenient and increasingly reliable form of transportation, rotary-wing aircraft, according to a 1958 *Flight* Magazine article, "are still fifteen to twenty-five times as expensive to operate as their fixed-wing brethren." Cost aside, passenger use was growing at more than 100 percent per year and to me that translated into the need for more pilots. Mainstream use of helicopters, as Lee had forecasted, was just around the corner, and I was ready.

I arrived at La Guardia Airport at about 9:00 a.m. and parked in a large paved lot. I locked my car, took a breath and made my way to the New York Airways headquarters housed in a large hangar. I was interviewed, flew a 30-minute check flight, passed my physical and was hired on the spot. A clockwork day until I got back to my car. Someone had broken the front passenger window and stolen my stereo and most of my clothes. Infuriated, I marched back to the office of friendly faces to call the police.

"We should have warned you," said an operations specialist. "That stuff happens all the time."

I was speechless. Now what? Helplessly, I looked around and

into the hallway. I couldn't believe who I saw standing there smiling back at me. I hadn't seen James Flynn since Korea where we had been tent-mates for a brief time. A First Lieutenant Marine, he was ruggedly handsome, a little taller than I, good natured and a very capable pilot.

"Boyer, right?"

"Right," I answered and reached out a hand to shake his. "What are you doing here?"

"Flying for these guys."

"Me, too."

Before the end of the day, Flynn and I were again roommates sharing a two-bedroom walk-up in Jackson Heights about two miles southwest of La Guardia. The biggest difference between flying a MASH helicopter and a NYA Skybus was that I did not have to worry about getting shot at. We had a regular schedule, wore polished dress shoes instead of combat boots, and our uniforms were neatly pressed.

Being the new guys in the lineup, Flynn and I were assigned mostly night flights. As a co-pilot intent on doing whatever I had to do to earn senior pilot status and a day job, I eagerly accepted those responsibilities as we beelined from La Guardia to Newark to Idlewild with frequent stops at the 30th Street helipad. After about two weeks and not having once touched the controls, my enthusiasm faded. Flynn and I both came to the same conclusion: Flying for NYA was not what we thought it would be.

"How can we be bored living in New York City?" I asked Flynn and suggested we take in some sights like Times Square. He passed on the invitation so I drove into the heart of New York late one afternoon and parked on a side street in front of a dive bar. Just as I was walking away from my car toward Times Square, a troll of a man hollered, "You can't park here!"

"Why not?"

"We save it for our customers," he barked, fully prepared for me to spot him a bill or two.

"All I see is a public street," I said, "so my car stays and when I come back it better look just like it does now."

"Don't count on it, punk."

We volleyed a few more insults before I walked on, confident he had gotten a clear message from a guy named after Gene Tunney who had been taught to never back down.

Time Square was a colossal disappointment. As I stood there, trying to figure out why this dark and filthy honky-tonk slum was held in such high regard, I saw passing only a few yards away Joan Riggs, one of the most beautiful girls in my high school class. She was with her father, a vice president at Goodyear. Even though I knew I was out of her league, I had asked her out once when I was at Copley. Not surprising, she had turned me down. After all, I was still getting used to indoor plumbing. But now, I was a distinguished New York Airways pilot (at least I was riding in the cockpit) and didn't hesitate to call out her name.

"Joan!"

She recognized me instantly and introduced me to her father. He had come to New York on business and she had tagged along to do some sightseeing and shopping. We hadn't seen each other for almost ten years and enjoyed catching up. Time had deflated both my teenage crush and her judgment of a kid from the other side of the tracks. We parted with a quick hug and as I walked back to my car, I wondered if I would ever tell her about how all the boys had once taken turns peeking through a crack in the wall of the girls' changing shed at the local swimming hole back home.

My reverie abruptly ended the instant I saw my car. All four tires had been slashed. The crude man with the jowls was nowhere in sight, but a lone beat cop was eyeing the damage. I ran up to him.

"I know who did this and I want to file charges."

"This your car?" asked the policeman.

"Yes, sir."

"Okay," he said and motioned to the bar. "You run inside and get the manager."

Upon seeing the damage, the portly manager was furious, but I couldn't tell if it was because of what had happened to me or having to pay for the four new tires the cop suggested as an alternative to me filing charges. My guess is it was the latter. As

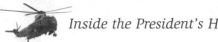

missions go, this one definitely had its own twist. My plan to eyeball one of the over-billed wonders of the world had been thankfully interrupted by Joan and her father, plus I was leaving Times Square with a new set of Goodyear tires – compliments of a beat cop who had connections with the neighborhood tire store. Overall, it had been a great day and gave me new story to tell Dad.

New York Airways, the first commercial passenger service, 1955
(Courtsey of Westchester County Archives)

During the next month, two NYA helicopter incidents made the local news. The first was a fully loaded S-58 that dropped a crankshaft over the Hudson River and was forced to make an emergency landing in a field layered with coffee bean shells in New Jersey. The ground was less firm than it looked. Once it sat down, the helicopter promptly tipped to one side and the rotor blades dug into the earth. Fortunately, no one was injured. The second event was a fatal check-ride crash at La Guardia. All three people aboard were killed.

As a result of such incidents and the skyrocketing cost of maintaining their fleet, Lee's forecast two years earlier of helicopter commercial service outperforming that of fixed-wing airlines never materialized. NYA laid off four pilots, including me and Flynn. He chose to go to Sikorsky in Bridgeport, Connecticut, where he was immediately hired as a test pilot. I decided to go home first before determining my next move.

Helicopter pilots were a small, tight circle in those days, so no sooner was I out of job, than I got a call from Hiller Helicopters in Palo Alto, California. They were recruiting commercial pilots to qualify in the Hiller and had just sold their first group of helicopters to a foreign market – an aviation company doing geological oil line survey work in the jungles of Venezuela. I briefly flashed on the balled up Hiller I had seen the day I reported to helicopter school and hoped appropriate modifications had made the Hiller less a killer.

As usual, at the forefront of my mind was the opportunity to fly and I was ready to go, even to South America. The pay and accommodations were also attractive: $650 base monthly salary; $9 per flight hour with a guaranteed 60 hours per month; room and board and, of course, transportation. Minimally, I would fly for three out of four weeks, and then have a break in Caracas or another nearby city.

South America. Mom and Dad had stopped asking if I knew what I was doing and just wished me good luck. But this time, I needed it more than ever.

I quickly realized the flying challenges of shuttle work in New York paled compared to what awaited me in some faraway jungle. During my check flight in a three-seater H-23 at Hiller, the pilot – who didn't hold back on demonstrating his gung-ho approach to flying – showed no interest in my ability to execute the basics. All business, Hiller's chief pilot went straight to the tough stuff as if to say, "Let's not waste my time or yours."

Most people think a helicopter will drop like a stone if the engine fails, which is completely false. A helicopter can continue to fly without any power by the action of air moving up

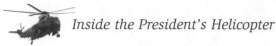
through the rotor rather than the engine driving the blades. "Autorotation" is the term used for "gliding" a helicopter down without power. A pilot has no margin for error and must take immediate action the instant power is lost to flatten the blade pitch to keep them spinning at the same speed. Otherwise, if you're at 500 feet and the blades stop, you'll be mashed potatoes with blood for gravy. It's a one-time shot.

After I performed a power-off landing, the check pilot told me to do a 180-degree low-level autorotation, which meant changing direction in a split second, ideally into the wind. The maneuver is so dangerous most organizations don't want pilots practicing it because the risk for an accident is too high. But apparently, knowing what to do in the event of engine failure was a top priority at Hiller and I was glad to have been so tested. I passed the course, along with an Army major and two Argentine pilots.

By the spring of 1958, the four of us were making history as civilian bush pilots flying the first helicopters in South America. Stationed at a huge houseboat on the Orinoco River in Venezuela about 200 miles southeast of Caracas, we were averaging 100 hours a month flying for a local flight service that had

Oil survey operations, Orinoco Delta, Venezuela, 1958
(Boyer Family Archives)

a contract with the Royal Dutch Shell oil company to do aerial surveys in the Orinoco Delta. Getting that amount of flight time was unheard of in those days given the physical demands on pilots and the mechanics responsible for maintaining the helicopters, but the money was good, so no one complained.

The four H-23s were equipped with cargo racks and floats, and kept parked in an open clearing along the river. Our job was to transport people and equipment to various sites along a pre-designated course that ran up to 30 miles into the steaming rain forest and creature-infested swamps. The survey process involved drilling deep holes, dropping in explosives, then detonating the charges to generate seismic activity recorded and interpreted by geologists. The type and level of sound waves determined whether or not the drill site was above an oil field, of which there were many.

On April 14, 1958, I had just landed on our crude helipad above the river when I saw several men near the houseboat pointing over the dense jungle canopy. What the hell? A huge blinding white fire ball not more than fifty miles away was streaking across the bright blue western sky.

"It's a meteor!" someone shouted.

I had to agree. What else could it be?

A week later, we read in a newspaper that Russia's Sputnik 2, launched some five months earlier, had fallen out of orbit and disappeared into the northern jungles of South America. It had been an amazing sight made only more remarkable by me discovering the origin of the glowing stream of light. The space race was on and I had had a front row seat in, of all places, the tangled depths of Venezuela.

Our closest contact with civilization was 30 miles northwest in Las Barrancas, a bustling little town where we bought groceries, picked up our mail and shuttled arriving and departing geologists, engineers and oil company officials. I rarely deviated from these duties, but two incidents stand out.

The first involved several local hunters who sought me out to lend a hand. They had just stabbed to death a 15-foot anaconda and wanted me to fly it back to their village a few miles away. In the interest of goodwill, I agreed and we soon had the

massive olive-green and black serpent lashed to the helicopter float. As soon as I lifted up, the men hurried off into the trees to meet me back at their village. I climbed to about 100 feet, casually glanced down at the snake and about lost control of my bowels.

The damn thing was moving. Must be the wind. No. It was definitely writhing beneath the rope ties and I had no place to set down. My heart thudded against my chest as I imagined the 140-pound creature slithering free and crawling into the open cockpit for a visit I was unprepared to have. Somebody should have hacked off its head, wherever the hell that was, and we wouldn't be having this problem.

I flew as fast as I could and it was still too slow. A five-minute flight had never taken so long. I practically dropped out of the sky into an open space next to the village and was out of my seat well before the blades stopped turning. Whether it was still alive or misfiring nerve impulses causing involuntary movement, I didn't care and stood back for the experts to retrieve their dinner.

Another seemingly harmless excursion occurred one afternoon when a Canadian geologist about my age asked me to fly him to Las Barrancas "just to see what was going on." When he climbed into the cockpit with a bottle of wine, I knew he had plans to be *part* of whatever was going on. He had finished the entire bottle just as we arrived on the edge of town.

"Fly over there," he directed.

"Where?" I asked.

"That little house with the thatched roof," he said, pointing ahead.

"You know someone there?"

"Yeah."

I fully expected a person to come out of the house to wave at us.

"Closer," pushed my Canadian passenger.

I eased the helicopter forward, but when I saw the edges of the fragile roof start to flutter, I knew I was too close. Before I could pull away, the entire roof lifted like a man tipping his hat and blew off revealing about a half dozen rooms with two scantily clad women scurrying around for protection. I had just blown the top off a whore house.

The local police levied a fine of about $20 which I passed along to my Canadian passenger. Other than that unfortunate incident, day after day, my fellow pilots and I performed without further calamity, knowing what every helicopter pilot knows: if everything is working, something is about to break.

I had just dropped off some workers at a drill site and was following a small tributary leading back to the Orinoco River when I heard a metallic "clunk." Alone, at about 500 feet in the air, I realized I had lost a tail rotor blade. The helicopter started yawing and turning counter-clockwise, the opposite direction of the blades. I hadn't practiced this stunt, but knew the only option was to cut off the engine, go into autorotation and hope I had enough control to skirt the two trees between me and the murky water below teaming with piranha, snakes and crocodiles. Thankfully, I cheated Hiller the Killer and landed upright with no injuries to me or damage to the helicopter.

A ravenous swarm of mosquitoes circled as I scrambled to paddle the helicopter out of the slowly drifting current to lodge against a nearby sand bar beneath a canopy of trees and then radio for help. No answer. Wearing a t-shirt, shorts and tennis shoes, I dug inside the cockpit for my survival kit. No kit. I had left it in another helicopter. Dumb. My next thought was to build a fire for two reasons: smoke out the mosquitoes and signal my whereabouts. I used a lighter to set a chamois used to filter gasoline on fire and fueled the blaze with twigs and brush.

I wasn't missed until later in the day when my co-workers realized I hadn't returned to refuel. They quickly located and retrieved the passengers I had earlier delivered, but by dark, I hadn't been found. I turned on my running lights and swatted mosquitoes until I fell asleep in the cockpit from exhaustion. Waking about an hour later, covered with insect bites, I was about to set the entire helicopter on fire to draw attention when I heard the purring rattle of approaching rotor blades.

Luckily, I suffered only a mild case of malaria and amoebic dysentery, and was allowed to leave two days early for my monthly break and recuperation in Caracas – a colorful city with a pulsating nightlife. On a previous trip I had met and dined with Louis Armstrong. "Ambassador Satch" loved interacting with the local street urchins and always had a pocketful of American silver dollars to toss their way. I will always remember the flash of his trumpet and, from "Up a Lazy River" to finding his thrill on Blueberry Hill, how wonderfully his raspy, bourbon voice could belt a tune.

On May 13, 1958, while I was still in Caracas, then Vice President Nixon and his wife, Pat, led a goodwill delegation to South America. With plans to visit several countries and attend the inauguration of Argentina's first democratically elected president in twenty years, the trip was expanded to include stops to several other countries to counteract anti-American sentiment bolstered by the infiltration of various Communist factions. While in Colombia, Nixon received a message from the Secret Service that the Central Intelligence Agency had heard rumors of a plot to assassinate him in Venezuela.

Nixon's pending visit soon became the talk of the city. I knew little regarding the state of world affairs, only that Americans were generally not well thought of unless involved in a mutually beneficial business such as the oil industry. I had not yet even been in a convenient State-side locale to vote in a presidential election. My shallow-at-best political awareness was modeled after my father's strident, pro-union viewpoints. Republicans were the enemy and Vice President Nixon was a snake in the grass.

From the moment the Vice President and Mrs. Nixon landed at Maiquetia Airport twelve miles outside of Caracas, they encountered hostile crowds angry about U.S. support for their recently overthrown dictator, Marcos Pérez Jiménez. Both were showered with spit at the terminal and Pat Nixon stunned onlookers by reaching over a guard's bayonet to shake the hand of a screeching young woman, hoping to convey the sincere intent of their visit. The disarming moment was short-lived and the Nixons sought refuge in separate cars, which were quickly surrounded by angry protestors and so pelted by rocks that tiny slivers of glass sprayed Nixon and the Venezuelan Foreign Minister. A Secret Service agent threw himself across the back window of car to protect them from attack.

Nixon later wrote that he actually believed they might be

killed and probably would have had they continued on to their
hotel where a mob of several thousand were waiting along with
a cache of Molotov cocktails. Instead, Nixon abandoned the itinerary and went directly to the U.S. Embassy.

Word of the turbulence reached the White House and
Eisenhower ordered a military rescue operation. As troops were
being marshaled at nearby U.S. Caribbean bases in preparation
to rescue the Nixons, U.S. Embassy officials were scrambling for
local options. About the time I thought of locating a helicopter
and finding a way to offer my services, the Nixon party had
managed to motor back to the airport and safely depart by
plane. No other political event up to that time had made a better case for providing White House helicopter support. At the
time, I didn't have the slightest glimmer of a notion that someday he would be President and I would be his senior helicopter
pilot. Being a single, adventurous man, my prevailing thought
was to instead get well and back to flying as soon as possible.

Nixon returned to a hero's welcome in Washington, D.C.
Not long after, a reporter asked then Texas Democratic
Congressman Lyndon Johnson why he had embraced Nixon
upon his return, especially since he had previously called the
Vice President *chicken shit*. Johnson responded in vintage form,
"Son, in politics you've got to learn that, overnight, chicken shit
can turn to chicken salad."

Not long after Nixon's trip, the U.S. Army notified me that
they were expanding and looking for experienced and proven
officers to return to active duty. If I wanted it, I had a regular
Army commission waiting for me back in the States. The timing was perfect. I had had enough of the endless equatorial
summers, the mosquitoes, dysentery, the mosquitoes, the isola-
tion of jungle living, and did I mention the mosquitoes?

By August 1958, I was back in the Army as a first lieutenant
stationed at Fort Eustis, Virginia, home of the Army
Transportation Corps, going to school, teaching and flying.
Regular Army officers were required to be proficient in several
areas such as infantry, transportation, supply, ordnance, personnel or artillery. So six months later, I was transferred to Fort
Benning to complete the Infantry Advanced Course.

When I chose to go through paratrooper training, I was bombarded with a lot of questions about my sanity. I was not the typical candidate. Nearly 30 years old, I out-ranked the other guys in the course (even my trainer), was already an "oldtimer" pilot and if I got hurt, I could lose my flight pay.

But from the moment I had seen Benning's wooden 34-foot-tall "controlled descent" towers when I reported for basic training six years earlier, I thought jumping out of a plane looked like fun. Contrary to what a lot of people think, helicopter pilots don't carry parachutes. Generally, we're flying too low to the ground or if we happen to be higher, the likelihood of a deployed chute getting swept into the rotor blades was all but assured. Above all, when and if I was ever in combat, I wanted to be as prepared as possible for myself and for those I commanded. I had my chance now, and I wasn't going to pass it up.

The first day of paratrooper training was made even more memorable by discovering a former football teammate on the tower platform with me. I was a senior when Chuck Bell arrived as a freshman half-back for Ohio University. A compact, happy-go-lucky guy, he went straight to the starting lineup and always played all out. Bell still holds the Bobcat record for longest kick-off return, an 87-yarder.

"You know we won the conference title the year after you left," he ribbed.

I thought about making a smart-ass comment about me having set a good example, but instead I said what I really felt. "I wish I'd been there."

"Me, too," he said. "I really looked up to you."

Paratrooper school was easier and even more exciting than I had anticipated – until our first night jump. Bell and I were queued up with about two dozen other soldiers in a C-47 flying at no more than 400 feet. We leapt into the darkness with precision speed. The faster out, the closer together we landed on the ground – a critical factor for being able to rapidly organize in a combat zone. I had no idea we were off course until I caught sight of trees streaking by in the shadows. There wasn't time to correct or even recognize the danger. Two seconds later my feet touched the ground and I held my breath, listening as the others landed, one by one. Nobody hit a tree. All safe, we emptied our lungs in a wave of relief among billowing clouds of nylon. Now I knew the true meaning of what it meant to take a "leap of faith," to be both vulnerable and resilient at the same time. We briefly speculated the pilot had overshot the drop zone. It was an important lesson to have learned. Rarely, especially in combat, do missions ever go as planned and it is a waste of time to bitch about anything when you're trying to stay alive.

I grabbed flight time any chance I could and often brought Bell along for the ride. Sometimes, that ride took us about 20 miles north of Benning to the newly built Calloway Gardens Golf Resort and the beach at Mountain Creek Lake. Nestled in the southernmost foothills of the Appalachians, the resort was only a few miles west of Franklin Roosevelt's Little White House in Warm Springs. The lake was an unauthorized landing site if ever there was one, but the summer weekend crowd had too tempting a flock of bathing beauties eager to cluster around the helicopter, daring us to take them for a spin. I venture to say there wasn't an automobile on earth, no matter what color and how much chrome, that drew more attention from the fairer sex than a three-seater Hiller H-23D with two self-described handsome men in uniform on board.

"You could really get nailed for this," said Bell, my self-appointed conscience, one afternoon as we flew along the lake shore.

"You think this is scary?" I shouted over the din of whirling blades. "I've hunted pheasant in the DMZ and bathed with piranhas. This is nothing."

Our "bad boy" attitude served us well when we moved on to nine weeks of Ranger School in July of 1959. A second lieutenant, Bell never let me forget he was a fit three years younger and my "master pilot" rank wasn't going to help me survive the arduous days ahead.

"So why do you want to be my partner?" I had to ask as we strapped on about 100 pounds of gear for a 50-mile mountain survival exercise.

"Because I know you love to fight."

Bell and I managed to battle our way into the pages of the new comprehensive *Department of the Army Field Manual for*

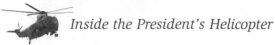
Rangers published in 1962. Below a photo of Bell defending himself against my knife-wielding attack, the caption on page 189 read: "Hand-to-hand combat provides the Soldier with another means to fight or defend himself when unarmed."

Second Lieutenant Chuck Bell (left) getting the best of me at Ranger School
Fort Benning, Georgia, 1959
(Chuck Bell)

Figure 38. Hand-to-hand combat provides the Soldier with another means to fight or defend himself when he is unarmed.

With a snarling look on his face, Bell was clearly the better actor. However, neither one of us could ever agree if my tight-jawed expression was a genuine strain against his attempt to disarm me or if I was just trying not to laugh.

Ranger units using clandestine infiltration tactics pre-date the French and Indian War when Rangers of Captain Benjamin Church brought "King Phillip's War" to a successful end in 1675. Rangers were the first to go ashore in Normandy, but during the late 1950s, instead of being organized into self-contained battalions, they were organized into companies attached to larger units to serve as an elite light infantry special operations force. Ours was one of the first classes of Rangers to be trained since WWII.

Ranger School is divided into three parts: the Fort Benning Phase, the Mountain Phase and the Florida Phase. In addition to rigorous physical fitness requirements, the first phase tests include long-distance running and obstacle courses, a 12-mile foot march, graded field exercises that include day and night land navigation, ambush and reconnaissance patrols, close quarters combat, and air assault operations. The second phase teaches survival techniques, mountain climbing, and how to manage the emotional stress of hunger and sleep deprivation in adverse conditions. The final phase covers ship to shore operations, stream crossings and a host of skills needed to survive in a jungle or swamp environment, where I had a slight edge having done battle with the mosquitoes in Venezuela.

Of the some 45 candidates who started the Airborne Rangers Program, about half washed out. I remember teetering on the verge of complete delirium the final week, but both Bell and I gutted it out and earned our Ranger tab, and, as is so often the case, went our separate ways. Although a trite perspective, the experience reinforced in no uncertain terms – when the going gets tough, the tough get going. Fight on. No matter what, fight on.

I spent the next year as an infantry officer training troops at Fort Riley, Kansas. The summer of 1960, I took my platoon to Fort Niagara, New York, where I was in charge of one of the rifle ranges for the National Rifle Matches. Unlike Times Square, Niagara Falls more than lived up to its majestic reputation and reminded me of a story I had heard in Venezuela about Angel Falls. The world's highest waterfall, at 3,212 feet, it was located in the Gran Sabana region. The height is so great that the water vaporizes before it hits the ground. The falls were unknown to the world until James Crawford Angel, an American aviator, flew over them in 1933 while searching for an ore bed.

I wished I had found a way to fly over the falls when I was in Venezuela, but that opportunity had passed and I couldn't imagine ever again flying in South America. I had my sights set on Hawaii with its warm, sandy beaches, tropical drinks with tiny umbrellas, and sweet-smelling hula girls.

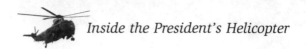

Touch and Go 5

I told them I'm not going to let Vietnam go the way of China. I told them to go back and tell those generals in Saigon that Lyndon Johnson intends to stand by our word, but by God, I want something for my money. I want 'em to get off their butts and get out in those jungles and whip hell out of some Communists.

– President Lyndon B. Johnson

My father was ecstatic when Massachusetts Senator John F. Kennedy narrowly defeated Vice President Richard M. Nixon for president in November of 1960. Dad had watched all four of their debates, the first ever televised, and thought Kennedy and his vice presidential running mate Lyndon B. Johnson embodied the promise of a new day in America.

"Good riddance to that S.O.B.," Dad said of the former vice president with the shifty eyes and anti-labor policies. The notion never entered his head that one day he would shake hands with Nixon at the White House and reluctantly admit, "Okay, he's not such a bad guy."

Military duties had moved me about the country so much that I had yet to be in the right place at the right time to vote for a president. However, I was paying more attention to the increasing threat of nuclear war with Russia and the spread of communism. Tens of thousands of people across America were building fallout shelters and stocking them with enough provisions to sustain a family until a bomb's radiation dissipated and it was safe to emerge. Fear of Soviet expansion escalated as one-time anti-communist alliances began to unravel, the most notable defector being that of Cuba, America's neighbor to the south.

As an Army captain flying helicopters in northeast Kansas, I believed improvement in the current state of world affairs should not depend solely on military strength. Yet, in 1961, Kennedy sent the first American advisors and forces to Vietnam to cope with the surging peasant upheaval; U.S. diplomatic relations broke down with Cuba leading to the failed Bay of Pigs invasion; in Germany, construction began on the Berlin Wall, fortifying the Iron Curtain between Eastern and Western Europe; and the Army's 1st Infantry Division stationed at Fort Riley was put on heightened alert. The Vietnam War was imminent, China could not have been more anti-American, and the Cold War would not end for 30 years.

Diplomacy had a rough road ahead.

A highlight for me at Fort Riley was getting qualified in a Piasecki H-21. Nicknamed the "flying banana" because of the upward angle of the aft fuselage, it carried 14 passengers. It was invented by Polish immigrant Frank Nicholas Piasecki, a fellow pioneer with Sikorsky. The unique tandem rotor aircraft was the predecessor to the Chinook workhorse about to rise to prominence in Vietnam.

A normally reliable machine, the Piasecki was, after all, still a helicopter. During a training flight at the fort, one of our crews lost the front rotor at about 500 feet. The helicopter pitched forward in a nose dive, when suddenly the rear rotor kicked in and tipped the nose skyward. This seesaw motion repeated several times as it descended. The pilots were unable to do anything but pray the nose would be up when they hit the ground. Amazingly, that is exactly what happened. The tail struck first, the helicopter was demolished, and the pilots walked away with only a few scratches.

We could never have too many miracles.

As the officer in charge of maintenance for the helicopters in the 81st Transportation Company, I knew action was intensifying in Southeast Asia when I was ordered to move 24 helicopters to an aircraft carrier bound for Hawaii that was docked at the Alameda Naval Air Station near San Francisco, California. Besides the build-up in Hawaii, we were also shipping military units to Europe as a precaution against a possible war between NATO member nations and Russia.

When I received orders for Hawaii, a senior captain in my unit intervened. He had orders to go to Europe, but being a family man, he convinced our commander to swap our assignments.

Even though I understood, I was still peeved, especially when I landed in Verdun, France, at the onset of winter the end of 1961 and there was not a hula girl to be found.

My bellyaching ended when I heard four months later that the 81st, with that captain, was the first helicopter unit sent to Vietnam. I, on the other hand, was transporting military VIPs in and around Paris from one meeting to another. Most of my passengers were staff from the Supreme Headquarters Allied Powers Europe (SHAPE) and dignitaries from the North Atlantic Treaty Organization (NATO). Fortunately, for the captain and his family, he survived his Vietnam tour. Years later, as a full colonel at the Pentagon, he was among several military personnel listening to me give an informational presentation on the White House Executive Unit. When I spotted him at the back of the room grinning at me, I couldn't resist sharing the story.

"I've had a lot of good things happen to me," I told the group, "and there's someone here today I want to personally thank for helping me get to France." After I talked about the great tan he surely got in Hawaii, I asked him to stand, which he did, red-faced and laughing with the rest of us as we applauded his service.

In Verdun, I was based at a small U.S. installation as the operations officer for the Army's 46th Transportation Company, which flew Sikorsky CH-34 helicopters. Located in northeastern France near the German border, Verdun is 150 miles east of Paris and the sight of the longest and bloodiest battle of WWI. In 1916, within only a six-square-mile area, German and French forces fought for ten months and neither gained any ground. France lost 550,000 men. Germany had 434,000 casualties. At the nearby Ossuaire de Douaumont cemetery there are 25,000 graves. Inside the Ossuary's basement I saw neatly stacked piles of bones and skulls belonging to 130,000 unidentified French and German soldiers. I had two thoughts: What a waste of life and what an irony that the remains of men who had likely killed each other were resting together, bone upon bone, forever.

In the spring of 1962, now with nearly 2,000 flight hours, I was reassigned to the 1st Aviation Detachment, United States European Command (EUCOM) at Orly Airport southeast of

Paris. As the OIC (officer in charge) and senior helicopter pilot, I commanded a detachment of three very plush UH-1B Hueys for VIP use.

Different from flying around New York's orderly grid system, Paris had an intricate and confusing network of narrow streets and boulevards with traffic going every which way. There were four main airports on the outskirts with dozens of planes coming and going at each one. As far as I know, the only helicopters in the area were those under my command. Ever vigilant to other air traffic, we were in constant contact with the control towers. Thankfully, in France and throughout the world, all international air traffic controllers were required to be fluent in English.

Even though the German Army had once marched troops into the heart of Paris, the "City of Lights" appeared unscathed by the events of WWII. A cultural Mecca of architecture, fashion, art and food, the capital of France felt like the center of the universe to me. History lived on every corner. From my 4th floor apartment I had a full view of the Eiffel Tower, a mere quarter mile to the north. With the exception of the occasional "ugly American" or "snotty Frenchman," the city was full of ambitious, vibrant personalities. There was also no shortage of beautiful single women, which included a fling with a James Bond girl fresh from filming _Dr. No_. I loved France – its rich past, the cozy bistros, the red wine, the racy nightclub acts, and all the food, except "steak tartare." It was an uncooked delicacy I associated more with a survival tactic than fine dining.

The spring of 1963, I was killing time at a quarter slot machine at the Camp des Loges Officer's Club, headquarters for SHAPE located west of Paris, when I noticed an attractive tall, blonde woman at a nearby machine. We would later disclose the only jack-pot we hit that day was meeting each other.

Cynthia (CeCe) Wells Campbell was born in 1936 into a prominent family from Pittsburg, Pennsylvania. The younger of two sisters, she attended Lake Erie College in Painesville, Ohio, where she majored in theater and foreign languages. (I liked to call the school Lake College for Eerie Women when I wanted to get under CeCe's skin.) During her junior year, CeCe was a foreign exchange student at the University of Grenoble located on the border of France and Switzerland. After graduation, she worked as an administrative assistant for William (Bill) Porter, the U.S. Ambassador to Algeria. The month we met, CeCe held a similar position for an executive at SHAPE Headquarters.

An intelligent, light-hearted woman, CeCe had an outgoing, adventurous personality. We were a great fit and soon found ourselves touring romantic Italy and dancing at the elaborate NATO Ball hosted by French President Charles de Gaulle at the Palace of Versailles. Within a year, CeCe and I were married in the magnificent American Cathedral in the heart of Paris and I was looking forward to finally starting my own family. I had sown enough wild oats.

Second to my marriage, the highlight of my European tour was being called upon to provide helicopter support for former President Dwight D. Eisenhower and a CBS news crew led by famed broadcaster Walter Cronkite. They had come to France to film a documentary on the twentieth anniversary of D-Day. I

With my wife, Cynthia (CeCe) Wells Campbell
(Boyer Family Archives)

On my honeymoon, Florence, Italy, 1963
(Boyer Family Archives)

had yet to tour Normandy and now I not only had the chance to do that, but did so in the company of the Allied Forces Supreme Commander and the 34th President of the United States.

My first memory of D-Day was sitting by the radio with my parents and brothers in the living room of our Jacoby Road home, waiting for news breaks about the Allied invasion on June 6, 1944. I was almost 15 years old and through the years never tired of hearing accounts related to one of the most complex and massive military actions in world history.

What became known in literature and film as "the longest day" took nearly two years to plan and involved mostly American, British, Canadian and French Resistance troops. General Eisenhower outlined the Allied objective in a speech to the troops just prior to the invasion.

"Soldiers, sailors and airmen of the Allied Expeditionary Force," he said, "you are about to embark upon the great crusade toward which we have striven these many months. The eyes of the world are upon you. The hopes and prayers of liberty-loving people everywhere march with you. In company with our brave Allies and brothers-in-arms on other Fronts, you will bring about the destruction of the German war machine, the elimination of Nazi tyranny over the oppressed peoples of Europe, and security for ourselves in a free world."

Initially stalled by a rain storm, "Operation Overlord" got underway on the morning of June 5, 1944, after a meteorologist assured Eisenhower they had a good break in the weather.

"Okay," Eisenhower said from his position in southeastern England, "We'll go."

Within hours, an armada of some 5,000 ships began leaving English ports. That night, more than 800 aircraft, carrying paratroopers and towing gliders, did their best to "soften" entrenched German forces. In addition to heavy naval and aerial bombardment, close to 12,000 paratroopers were dropped behind German lines. In total, some 13,000 aircraft and 24,000 airborne troops participated. Along a 50-mile stretch of the Normandy coastline, the first wave of about 156,000 Allied troops landed on five different beachheads occupied by five well-armed and heavily barricaded German divisions.

Some described that morning as a "shrieking inferno." Allied casualties the first day were estimated at 10,000, which included about 2,500 dead. Many were paratroopers who drifted off course and were shot out of the sky. The number of dead doubled in the next ten days. By July 2, nearly one million men and 177,000 vehicles had been put ashore. The Germans officially surrendered on May 7, 1945, in General Eisenhower's headquarters in Reims, France.

Now, on this cloudless summer day nearly 20 years later, along the tranquil Normandy shore, families were picnicking and children romped in the surf. In the distance, I could see Eisenhower driving Cronkite in a jeep along the water's edge where the General had come ashore the day after the initial invasion. In his mind's eye, he likely saw much more than any of us who had not been there could even begin to picture. The most visible relics from that blood-soaked ordeal were the remnants of a few German bunkers and sections of the partially submerged Mulberry harbor – a temporary structure – assembled by Allied troops for offloading vehicles and cargo.

I wondered what might have happened had helicopters been part of the invasion. They would have likely replaced the landing crafts and greatly reduced paratrooper exposure to enemy assault. More land might have been conquered in less time. Supplies, ammunition and medical support would have been more accessible. Spent troops could have been more frequently rotated with fresh forces. The trapped and wounded would have been rescued faster. It's fair to conclude, with helicopters, as we learned in Korea and Vietnam, fewer people would have died.

As valuable as I knew helicopters could be in a war zone, I hoped to heaven there was never a need even close to the scale of D-Day. There was no way of predicting that in exactly three years I would be in Vietnam flying helicopters for all the reasons just mentioned, plus dousing the jungles with Agent Orange.

In the *D-Day Plus 20* documentary that was broadcast around the world a year later, Cronkite and Eisenhower discussed planning the attack as they retraced naval routes across the English Channel, visited Omaha Beach, and reminisced with the wife of a local mayor who had lived through the invasion.

President Eisenhower with famed CBS anchor Walter Cronkite
filming a 20th Anniversary of D-Day documentary, Normandy, France, 1963
(Courtesy of the Dwight D. Eisenhower Library)

"One of the most famous pictures of D-Day," Cronkite said to Eisenhower, "was of you talking to the paratroopers in their camouflage. And one of the versions of that visit, I think, said that as you turned away, this reporter saw a tear in your eye."

"Well, I don't know about that," Eisenhower responded. "It could have been possible. Because look, here's the kind of an operation you start. You know there are going to be losses along the line. They're going to be bad. Because we knew this – there were mobile troops, German troops in that area, with all sorts of flak, you know, the anti-aircraft stuff. And there could easily have been fighters coming into these helpless troop carriers. It's...I would think, if a man didn't show a bit of emotion, it would show that he probably was a little bit inhuman."

Considered the invasion that broke the Nazi grip on Western Europe, the Battle of Normandy is forever memorialized in the numerous cemeteries along the French coast that hold the remains of more than 110,000 dead from both sides. The sprawling American Cemetery near Saint Laurent overlooks one of the five landing beaches, code-named Omaha, and covers 172 acres. A serene place of beauty, the graves face westward, toward the United States.

I picked up Eisenhower and Cronkite with a cameraman from the beach in a UH-1B Huey and flew them over the American Cemetery where nearly 10,000 stark white crosses studded the velvet green lawns. We all gazed downward in solemn silence. I circled closer for a better look. I knew the history. I had seen photographs. I had heard stories of sacrifice and survival. But nothing prepared me for the consuming emotion that rocked me to the core.

Below me were the graves of soldiers who had waded through ocean breakers, bodies and bullets, with no place to hide, knowing they were going to die. Where does that kind of courage come from? What kept them moving forward until they were dropped in their tracks? How were the next men able to step over the dead and wounded and press onward?

If there was any more selfless act than dying for the lives and freedom of others, I couldn't think of it; and I was sure neither could the two bigger-than-life men sitting behind me scanning the French countryside spread beneath us like a patchwork quilt. It was a tremendous honor to be their pilot.

Also on that day, I scooped up a handful of sand from Omaha Beach and now, some fifty years later, still have it safely contained in a small apothecary jar. The powder-fine grains churned through the years reveal nothing to the naked eye from that brutal day in 1944.

The first president to fully grasp the value of helicopters for the White House, Eisenhower had once invited visiting Soviet Union Premier Nikita Khrushchev in the fall of 1959 to join him for an aerial tour of Washington, D.C. At first, the often hardheaded Soviet leader declined, but then agreed to the helicopter ride as long as Eisenhower was on board, too. Eisenhower proudly showed off the city's diverse neighborhoods, busy business districts and stately government buildings – all irrefutable symbols of a thriving, democratic system. Khrushchev was amazed at the number of cars traveling the streets below. As the story goes, Eisenhower gave Khrushchev a Lincoln automobile, but he had to order his own helicopter.

Before Eisenhower left office in 1961, his personal helicopter pilot, United States Air Force Major Joseph E. Barrett, had helped convince him to upgrade the White House helicopter fleet by replacing the Sikorsky VH-34 piston-driven models with eight new jet-engine VH-3As. The list of benefits attached to the six-ton Sikorsky Sea King was a long one: it had two engines instead of one, was more reliable, more powerful, faster, held more passengers, and had a travel range of 600 miles. Nearly 73 feet long with a 62-foot rotor diameter, the VH-3A had a cruising speed of 140 miles per hour, a ceiling limit of 14,500 feet and it could fly on its side if evasive action was needed.

Of the eight helicopters, four were assigned to the Army at Fort Belvoir, Virginia, (about 11 to12 minutes south of the White House) and four to the Marines at their Quantico, Virginia, base (23 to 25 minutes from the White House). Rotating standby positions at Anacostia Naval Station less than five minutes from the White House, the VH-3A tail numbers ranged from 150610 to 150618. Odd numbers were assigned to the Army and even numbers to the Marines, although both units flew all eight helicopters at one time or another. Every Sikorsky employee who worked on the state-of-the-art helicopters and those who performed future maintenance underwent extensive security clearance.

Two of the original eight VII-3As would gain historical status – 615, still in use today, was a goodwill gift from Nixon to Egypt's President Anwar Sadat in 1974 and two months later I used 617 to fly Nixon off the White House lawn the day of his resignation. Through the years, there have been many different helicopters used to transport the president. In addition to the Sikorsky CH-3A Sea King, they include the Bell UH-1 Huey, the Sikorsky CH-34C Choctaw, the Boeing CH-46 Sea Knight, the Bell 47-J Sioux, and the Sikorsky UH-60 Black Hawk.

In 1962, the new fleet of helicopters that went into service at the White House was used to fly Kennedy to Air Force One at Andrews AFB, to Camp David, to the Kennedy family compound in Hyannis Port, Massachusetts, and other favorite getaways in Virginia and Florida. Overseas helicopter support had not yet been developed when, in June of 1963, he began a ten-day tour of Europe in West Germany.

I liked Kennedy for all the reasons other people did. He was bold, principled, articulate, and a Democrat. So when I got a letter from the Pentagon in October 1963, informing me I was being considered for assignment as a maintenance officer for the U.S. Army Executive Flight Detachment at the White House, I was thrilled and read the letter several times to make sure it said what I thought it did before I grabbed the nearest phone to call CeCe at her office.

After CeCe quit squealing with delight, I told her we both needed to pass an extensive background check. Her security

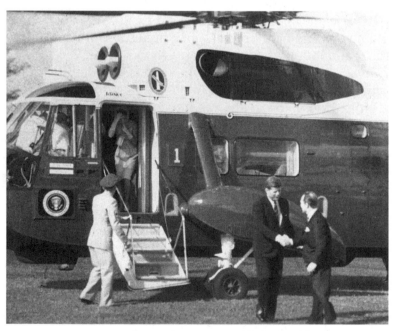

President and Mrs. John F. Kennedy disembarking a Sikorsky VH-3A
Orange Bowl Stadium, Florida
December 29, 1962
(Cecil Stoughton/White House, John F. Kennedy Presidential Library and
Museum, Boston)

clearance came through within only a few weeks. Mine took several months. Understandably, the United States government needed to be absolutely convinced I had no suspicious "affiliations" from my work in South America.

I wrote my parents and brothers about leaving Paris and going to Washington, D.C., to fly for the White House. Not surprisingly, they were shocked by yet another unimagined achievement. My brother Dick made a point of questioning the sanity of the assignment officer at the Pentagon. Ribbing aside, I knew I was up to the task, even if my family was defaulting to doubts rooted in their memories of a kid with a wild streak.

Only a month into the transfer process, on November 22, 1963, CeCe and I were walking along Avenue George V just off the Champs-Elysées on our way to the Officers Club in downtown Paris when we overheard people around us blurting out words of shock and disbelief: Kennedy had been assassinated in Dallas, Texas.

We hurried into the building, caught the elevator up to the club dining room and joined the other grim faces crowded around a single radio. All the euphoria of the last few weeks drained out of me in an instant. It was almost every military pilot's highest aspiration to fly for the White House, but I wanted more than the assignment. I had wanted to someday welcome President John. F. Kennedy aboard Army One.

Countless dreams and expectations, enormously more significant than mine, died with Kennedy that day in Dallas. As our nation mourned the loss of a promising and visionary leader, I kept asking myself, "How could such a thing happen in *this day and age?*"

What the hell was going on?

Were we moving forward or backward?

The answer to that question would land squarely in the lap of our new president – Lyndon Baines Johnson, the tough-talking, former powerhouse senator from Texas who had lost to Kennedy in the Democratic primaries, but was selected as his vice-presidential running mate. Sworn into office aboard Air Force One the day of the assassination, Johnson was a shrewd and seasoned "good old boy," career politician. In 1948, during his bid for the U.S. Senate in a supposedly "rigged" election, Johnson was the first candidate to use a helicopter to fly from stump speech to stump speech in what was dubbed, "The Flying Windmill."

Johnson loved helicopters, but, as I soon discovered, that appreciation translated into more than convenience and security. Flying for President Johnson frequently involved deception, self-serving indulgences, and pilots adept at looking the other way.

By the spring of 1964, CeCe and I were back in the States. After a quick visit to see our parents, I went to Fort Eustis, Virginia, near Williamsburg for several brush-up transportation courses. One of my classmates was West Point graduate Major George Dudley Iverson, the fifth. He was a tall, balding man with a razor-sharp mind, was already working at the Pentagon and generously suggested we stay at his home while we looked for a house to buy. We were both majors and got along great.

"Are you sure?" I asked, more than tempted by the offer, especially since, in four months CeCe and I were expecting our first child.

"Absolutely," he reassured, "We've got lots of room and it's only a 30-minute drive to Belvoir."

I gratefully accepted. Driving to his home in the northern suburbs of Washington, D.C., I thought maybe Iverson had made a wrong turn when he entered the driveway of a large mansion.

I managed to close my mouth long enough to ask, "This is where we're staying?"

"Yeah," said Iverson. "My wife's grandmother gave it to her. You've probably heard of her. Marjorie Merriweather Post."

"You're kidding?" I replied, knowing full well she was one of America's wealthiest women and the founder of General Foods, Inc.

"Just leave your things in the car for the butler."

"George?"

"Yeah?"

"With all this, what the hell are you doing in the Army?"

He grinned and answered, "I like it."

Even though we were soon settled in our own home in Annandale, Virginia, and caring for our beautiful, new baby girl we named Robin, CeCe and I remained close to the Iversons. We had the chance to briefly meet Post a year later when we were among her invited guests for a gala event in Washington, D.C. The evening began with a formal cocktail reception at her near-by magnificent 25-acre Hillwood estate, which bordered Rock Creek Park and rivaled the most ornate art galleries in Paris.

"You know who that is?" Iverson asked, nodding toward a distinguished older gentleman in a medal-encrusted military dress uniform chatting in a circle of friends.

"No."

"General McAuliffe."

"Nuts McAuliffe?"

"Yes, that's the one."

McAuliffe, who had parachuted into Normandy on D-Day, earned legendary standing for the succinct response he dispatched to a written ultimatum by a German commander whose forces had surrounded the U.S. 101st Airborne at Bastogne, in December of 1944. In part, the German communiqué read: "…There is only one possibility to save the encircled U.S.A. troops from total annihilation: that is the honorable surrender of the encircled town. In order to think it over a term of two hours will be granted beginning with the presentation of this note. If this proposal should be rejected, one German Artillery Corps and six heavy A. A. Battalions are ready to annihilate the U.S.A. troops in and near Bastogne. The order for firing will be given immediately after this two hours term. All the serious civilian losses caused by this artillery fire would not correspond with the well-known American humanity."

Known for never swearing, McAuliffe's response simply read: "To the German Commander, NUTS! The American Commander."

"At least it was a four-letter word," I remember saying to Major General Mason – my pheasant hunting mentor – in Korea when he first told me the "Nuts!" story.

After the cocktail party, we reconvened at a D.C. hotel for a performance by the National Symphony Orchestra and I silently gave thanks to Mason for his dogged tutelage on the finer aspects of classical music and dining with the rich and influential.

Seated at one of several circular, linen-draped tables, CeCe and I were surrounded by the highest ranking Washington dignitaries and insiders of the day. In her late seventies, elegantly dressed and bejeweled, Marjorie Post sat across from us and seemed to know everyone in the room. Graceful and full of personality, she had "merrily weathered" four husbands, including E.F. Hutton, and countless suitors.

"I heard she even owns the Russian Crown jewels," I whispered to CeCe.

I clearly anchored the food chain that night and thankfully, no one pried enough to learn I was just a no-name helicopter pilot from Akron, Ohio. Besides, most people had their attention focused on the honored guests seated just two tables away – President Johnson, his wife, Lady Bird, and their two daughters, Lynda Bird, 21, and Luci Baines, 18.

As the evening of mingling, dining, dancing and drinking came to a close, I came away with one unavoidable conclusion – the Johnson girls sure knew how to party and their father drank like a soldier on leave. These were not skill-sets I was expecting to find in our country's First Family and especially in a public setting. It definitely contradicted the sophisticated and controlled image portrayed in newspapers and on television.

Giving me greater pause was that no one said anything. No one seemed to even raise an eyebrow. It was clear to me, there were unwritten rules for the Johnsons and I had missed that briefing.

Up until that night I had had complete confidence in Johnson's leadership and judgment. Along with my father, we had celebrated the passage of the Civil Rights Act and the Economic Opportunity Act. I had accepted without question the President's decision to increase U.S. troops in Vietnam after he reported three North Vietnamese torpedo boats attacked a U.S. destroyer in the Gulf of Tonkin, an eventually disputed incident.

Feeling too straight-laced and critical for my own good, I put the night behind me. Everybody likes to let loose now and then – even Lynda Bird and Luci Johnson. Besides, even though I had personal opinions about the course our country was taking, my job was to serve its leaders, without resistance or question.

Johnson handily defeated Arizona Senator Barry Goldwater in the 1964 race for president and was inaugurated on January 20, 1965. That same month, on a crisp, clear day, those of us on standby at Anacostia got word the President was out of town and we could practice "touch and go" landings at the White House. *Finally*, I said to myself. After months of training and anticipation, I was buckled into the right seat at the controls of a VH-3A about to make my first landing at the White House. An instructor pilot was in the left seat. I lifted off facing downriver and then made a climbing turn to about 100 feet over the Potomac to head north. Washington National Airport was on my left and the 555-foot tall Washington Monument straight ahead. Skirting to the left of the monument at 45 to 50 knots, I slowed for our final approach to the White House.

Everywhere else in the world I had flown, helicopters were assigned a lower priority than jet or fixed-wing traffic. Being more maneuverable, it was easy for control towers to adjust our altitude and routes. However, if that helicopter had the call sign of Army One or Marine One, it had priority unless there was some other emergency situation.

Three round wooden platforms the size of a dining table for six were placed on the south portico lawn – one for each wheel – by the groundskeepers. As I lined up the helicopter nose facing slightly southeast to let down, I concentrated 99 percent on making a perfect landing and one percent on a phrase used by old-timers back home when they couldn't believe what their eyes were seeing.

"Well, poke me with a stick."

I was less than 100 feet from one of the most historic buildings in the world. I glanced briefly over at the Oval Office windows. Built between 1792 and 1800, every president and his family had lived at the White House since John Adams. What might those walls say if they could talk? My fascination lasted for only the few split seconds the wheels were on the ground before I lifted up to hover and return to the base, knowing I could do the job when called upon.

Even though I had a thousand more hours of flight time than any of the pilots with the Exec Flight, I was still one of the new guys and had to work my way up. We lower-ranked pilots were assigned emergency standby duty at Anacostia instead of any specific missions and used that time to practice our response skills and timing. Those drills would begin with a horn blast launching us into action and was followed by a loudspeaker alerting us as to the nature of the exercise.

We always had five ready helicopters at Anacostia. One week there would be three Army-staffed helicopters and two operated by the Marines. The next week, it would be the opposite. Each helicopter had a specific designation in case of a crisis. One was for picking up the president, and the others were for the vice president, cabinet members, Pentagon officials, and other Capitol Hill dignitaries who were to be evacuated and taken to a secure, classified location. It was our responsibility to transport every key leader in the area to one of four top-secret destinations within 30 miles of the White House in less than 20 minutes.

The decade that was branded "the turbulent sixties" continued to gain steam with the civil rights movement and the Vietnam War. Headlines from 1965 told the story: outspoken black activist Malcolm X is assassinated; Dr. Martin Luther King leads protest march from Selma to Montgomery, Alabama; the first U.S. combat troops, 3,500 Marines, land in South Vietnam; the first mass bombing raid of Vietcong strongholds is launched in June; week-long riot in Watts leaves 35 dead and causes 200 million dollars in damage; anti-war protestors burn draft cards; and in November of 1965, casualties from a week-long battle in Vietnam's Ia Drang Valley number 240 dead, 470 wounded and six missing.

It was an incredibly difficult time to be an American president. Seeming to be in perpetual motion, Johnson was spending more and more time in southeast Texas at his secluded ranch 50 miles west of Austin and 60 miles north of San Antonio. Table talk among the pilots and crew chiefs in the mess hall speculated that Johnson was dodging both the press and the public eye. Still a low pilot on the totem pole and with the Vietnam build-up inching closer to home, I began to think I might not have even one chance to fly the President.

Then, sometime during the summer of 1965, I was sitting

comfortably on a toilet while on duty at Anacostia when the alert horn went off.

Damn!

"This is not a drill," said the announcer over the loudspeaker. "Pick up Volcano immediately."

Volcano was Johnson's aptly designated code name. In all the scenarios I had imagined for my first call to fly the President, I certainly didn't think it would start with me on the crapper.

The crew chief had the engine running by the time I strapped in and positioned the headphones over my ears. Out of the blue, the White House had called for a helicopter to pick up Johnson and take him to Andrews AFB where Air Force One was waiting to fly him to Texas. The only pause in an otherwise rapid pace of activity happened when I looked at the warrant officer in the co-pilot's seat to my left. There wasn't a trace of color in his face and he was doing more random fidgeting with the controls than anything resembling take-off protocol.

Oh great, this was his first official pick-up, too! Two rookies were on their way to the White House and there was no time for a pep talk.

Airborne within 45 seconds, I dared not think of anything but the duty underway and hoped like hell this day would be among my best memories and nothing I wanted to forget.

In less than three minutes, we were on the South Lawn. Collective down, controls centered, force trim on, throttles flight idle. We methodically ticked through the "after landing" tasks, but my co-pilot, whom I will call Leonard, was battling nerves so much that he could hardly talk into the radio.

"Hey, it's okay," I said to him. "Relax."

I don't think he had taken a breath since we had lifted off.

"Just breathe," I coaxed, irritated that I had to add him to my list of responsibilities, "We've got it made."

Shortly, Johnson and his entourage rumbled on board and, for the first time ever, I was flying Army One. Even though I had seen him once in person at the National Symphony Orchestra event, he looked a lot bigger as he brushed pass the cockpit. Offering not the slightest glance our way, I could tell he was steaming about something.

"Don't take off yet," an aide said to me. "The doctor isn't going with us."

The doctor?

Leonard and I looked quizzically at each other and I stole a quick glance into the cabin. The back side of an older man in a gray suit was bent over Johnson doing something to his eyes or face.

"What's happening?" Leonard asked.

I shrugged, just as a call came in over the radio from my commanding officer and Johnson's Army chief pilot, Colonel Jack Tinnin, Jr. After hearing the call from the White House for a helicopter, he had flown up from Belvoir and was circling the tidal basin between Anacostia and the White House.

"You can go back," he said. "I'll go in and pick up the President."

"Well, sir," I answered, mustering a wave of confidence, "The passengers are on board and we're ready to lift off."

Silence.

"Do you copy? The President is already on board."

"Okay," Tinnin said. "Go ahead and I'll follow you to Andrews."

A long five minutes later, without explanation, the doctor scurried off the helicopter and we broke ground headed to Andrews. Leonard was still pale and I figured if he fainted, that would probably be good for us both.

When I landed Army One at Andrews AFB and taxied to the front of Air Force One, the President and other passengers disembarked without comment, obviously unaware of the minor drama that had unfolded in the cockpit. Leonard released a sigh of relief big enough for both of us. While we waited for Air Force One to take off, we got another radio call asking us to look under the President's seat for a contact lens.

Amazingly, the crew chief quickly located the lens and we were instructed to leave it with the Jet Star pilot at Andrews who was flying the First Lady to Texas later that day. As to why they were flying in separate planes to the same place on the same day, I learned that when Johnson found out Lady Bird's hair appointment would delay their departure time he blew a gasket and called for a helicopter.

After I went off duty, I drove back to Fort Belvoir where Colonel Tinnin called me into his office. My height and dark-haired, he was a WWII veteran, still very physically fit and a man of few words.

"Tell me everything," he directed. "Everything. I don't want any surprises I can't explain."

"Yes, sir."

"Start with Leonard. How'd he do?"

"You want the truth?" I asked.

"Yeah."

"Sorry, but I think he should go," I told the Colonel. "I'm surprised he even made it into the unit."

"Okay."

"But the bigger truth is," I ventured, driven by the prospect of having to rely on someone like Leonard in the future and ending up dead, "there are at least five or six other guys here in over their heads and it's the same with the Marines. They don't even have a thousand hours and the warrant officers coming out of Vietnam are carrying the load for majors and lieutenant colonels who I sure as hell wouldn't want flying the President of the United States."

The Colonel thought for a moment while I worried I had said too much and then decided I couldn't hold back now.

"It doesn't make sense," I continued, "having guys just coming through to get their tickets punched, more interested in promotion than being qualified for the job."

"You have a point," Tinnin said, without a hint as to whether or not he concurred.

That experience was the beginning of my long-held perspective that there should be a special military category for White House pilots that encourages them to stay in the unit without fear of surrendering career advancement opportunities if they don't move on within two years. Such a program would make the position a profession in and of itself, eliminate frequent turnovers, reduce the learning curve for new arrivals and result in a higher level of expertise for those flying the president.

Leonard was gone within 48 hours, but not before he sought me out to apologize.

"Hey, don't be sorry," I told him. "You were put in a tough position and you're not alone."

"I couldn't even talk."

"I know," I said, "but we made it."

In early 1966, Johnson ordered half of the Exec Flight to relocate to Randolph Air Force Base northeast of San Antonio to support activities in and around the LBJ ranch for three major reasons: 1) Johnson was spending four to five months a year at the Texas White House; 2) it was easier to hide from the press and public in Texas; and 3) the Army already had a post in the region. The Army's new mission was to provide helicopter support for the ranch, everything west of the Mississippi and all overseas trips. The other half of the Exec Flight pilots was rotated into Vietnam to meet the escalating demand for helicopter pilots. I was included in that group and served from 1966-67. The Marine's HMX-1 unit remained at Quantico, Virginia, where they continued White House service within the northeastern region of the country.

I was among several Army personnel with the unit to receive an unexpected note of appreciation from New York Senator Robert F. Kennedy, who wrote: "Dear Major Boyer: It is with deep regret that I write a farewell letter to the officers and men of the Executive Flight Detachment. President Kennedy, as well as his entire staff, always greatly admired the excellent service of the Presidential Helicopter Unit. Their performance was a source of pride to all who were associated with them – Colonel Jack T. Tinnin, Jr., and the pilots and crews who served with him will always have our greatest respect. Sincerely, Robert Kennedy."

Only a portion of the unit went to Texas. The rest of us got an all-expense-paid ticket to Vietnam. Johnson's decision to downsize and move the Exec Flight haunts me to this day.

"Don't worry," I said, trying to comfort CeCe who had just put our two-year-old daughter to bed. "I'm a maintenance officer. I'll be overseeing the repair of damaged helicopters and nowhere near the front line."

Dead Man's Curve 6

I wish I could tell you about these pilots. They make me sick with envy. They ride their vehicles the way a man controls a fine, well-trained quarter horse. They weave along stream beds, rise like swallows to clear trees, they turn and twist and dip like swifts in the evening....

– John Steinbeck

It's long been said, though not often heeded, "the first casualty of war is truth."

Just as our headlong tumble into the Iraq War in 2003 was based on misinformation and grotesque rationales, so it was in Vietnam. A localized rebellion from 1945 to 1954 against French colonial rule in Indochina spiraled into a civil war between North and South Vietnam before exploding into an international conflict. In December of 1965, Defense Secretary Robert McNamara stated in a memo to President Lyndon Johnson that troop strength in Vietnam must be substantially augmented "if we are to avoid being defeated there." However, McNamara further noted additional deployment of some 150,000 U.S. personnel would not necessarily assure victory. Soon after, General William Westmoreland, commander of American military forces, beefed up the request and called for 250,000 more.

I was part of the build-up, known to us today as a "surge," during what were called the war's "peak years." Before the end of 1967, more than a half million American troops representing the Army, Navy, Air Force and Marines were in Vietnam fighting alongside the South Vietnamese. Casualty reports peppered nightly television news. Based on U.S. losses compared to the much higher figures of the "enemy," we were kicking Charlie's ass and stemming the tide of communist rule. Yet, for all our military might and political dexterity, time was not on our side. Rather, it played into the strategy of a people who had nothing but time to defend their objectives and were impervious to

intimidating behaviors. Unfortunately, our commander-in-chief, President Johnson, was a classic, impatient bully.

Even so, the day in 1966 when I and more than 100 other soldiers boarded a 707 commercial jetliner at Travis AFB in California to fly to Vietnam, I carried not an ounce of doubt about the mission ahead. Simply put: America had a responsibility to protect itself and the world from the evils of oppression and communism. Few questioned the merit of that objective or that the effort involved extreme sacrifice. Even when Senator Ernest Gruening, a democrat from Alaska, publicly challenged Johnson's claim that he was obligated by the commitments of previous administrations to support South Vietnam, I chalked up the "dove talk" as naïve. Along with my family and most Americans, I believed the Vietnam conflict posed a national security threat to America and military action was warranted. In Johnson's 1966 state of the union speech, he encouraged hope for an early resolution by disclosing some 300 private talks had taken place in the past 12 months exploring options for peace with leaders throughout the world.

Hindsight would come with a wrenching, astronomical price tag.

My parents supported the war, but thought it made no sense to send a White House helicopter pilot from the "top of the food chain to the bottom." I understood their concern, but I also knew how desperate the Army was for experienced helicopter pilots and maintenance officers in the war zone. I estimate that about one third of all helicopter crashes in Vietnam were accidental. Different than any previous war, there was an enormous reliance on helicopters. Tragically, that demand put far too many men into circumstances for which they had not been thoroughly trained.

Those of us flying rotary wing aircraft knew that if a pilot could survive for at least 90 days, his chances of staying alive through a one-year tour increased substantially. That is, until the last 30 days, when high confidence could disintegrate into being overly cautious and getting killed in a fatal moment of hesitation. The more a person thought about dying the more vulnerable he became. Combat is all about instinct. There was no time to think about anything other than what we had been trained to do.

Landing at Cam Ranh Air Base on the central east coast of Vietnam in the province of Khánh Hòa, I boldly believed I was prepared for anything the gods of war could hurl my way. The thick, rolling Vietnamese forestlands and serpentine coastline with blue-green waters were beautiful. The climate, on the other hand, was a cat-and-mouse game with torrential rains and sweltering dry spells.

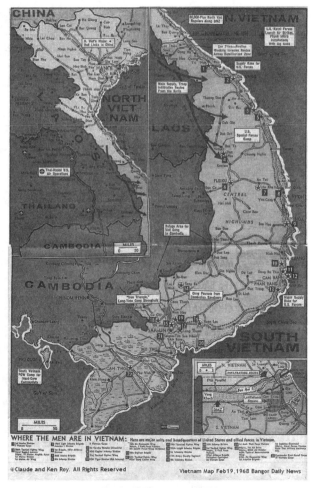

Map of Vietnam, 1968

Me with a Bell UH-1D, An Khe, Vietnam, 1966
(Boyer Family Archives)

Cam Ranh Bay, with its natural deep water harbor, was a major supply delivery and troop rotation area. With the airstrip, the docks, barracks and network of roads and rails, the activity level matched that of a large bustling city. I couldn't wait to get off the plane and stretch my legs. I was tired, constipated and sick of smelling the stench that had built up among my fellow human sardines during our trek across the Pacific Ocean. Such trivial irritations were about to vanish forever, given what was ahead of me and completely outside the limits of my expectations.

Florida – that was my first thought upon deplaning into the dense humidity of Vietnam. If I closed my eyes, I felt like I was standing on a breezy beach just after a rain somewhere along the Gulf of Mexico. That postcard image was obliterated by rumbling truck motors and plane engines, officers barking orders and the familiar chatter of a flight of Hueys arriving from the north. Landing nearby, they deposited departing troops. Some were in body bags and I wagered all the others were wounded even if there wasn't a mark on their body.

War changes people.

Forever.

The next day, I was flown about 100 miles north to An Khe Base Camp. The site of a former rubber plantation, it was located at the base of Hon Kong Mountain, a prominent hill topped with U.S. radar and communication facilities. Just below the radio relay station, soldiers had painted on the hillside a giant replica of the 1st Cavalry Division patch we wore on our left shoulder sleeve. A yellow, triangular Norman shield, it had a black diagonal stripe and horse's head in the upper right portion. The distinctive patch, along with all insignia on our hats, fatigues and belts, had to be darkened with shoe polish to make it harder for the enemy to distinguish an officer, a preferred target.

A ten-square-mile complex, the An Khe base was less than a year old and covered a plateau area with rows and rows of tents and boxy wooden structures with tin roofs. With a military population approaching 20,000, it was a crude, start-up city composed of administrative services, a mess hall, hospital, chapel, morgue, barracks, barber shop, post exchange, supply warehouses and transportation maintenance operations. A local village provided laundry services and a semi-exotic nightlife that, as a new husband and father, held little appeal. By the same token, I didn't judge those who made different decisions. Living with the constant knowledge that at any second your ass could get zapped made booze, drugs and sex a popular way to dial down and escape that pressure. "Sin City," otherwise known as the more sanitary An Khe Plaza, housed bars and brothels under strict Army medical supervision.

A massive airfield, nicknamed the "golf course," had enough space for a 3,300-foot runway and stored hundreds of aircraft ranging from C-130 transport planes to two-seater Bell helicopters. Parked on steel hinged mats to prevent landing gear from getting mired in mud and to also keep the dust down when it was dry, many of the helicopters were also protected from incoming mortar rounds by revetments – U-shaped earthen berms. On average the 1st Cavalry burned 85,000 gallons of fuel a day. A ten-mile defense perimeter with watch towers and land mines was encircled by snarled concertina wire that would measure several thousand miles if stretched out.

My assignment was to command a maintenance company of

about 150 mechanics, tech support people and supply personnel. Besides routine aircraft maintenance, our responsibility was to "repair, rearm and return" helicopters to the battlefield. I also did test-pilot flights to clear aircraft for readiness.

During orientation, every aircraft crewman was given a small fabric swathe with a red, white and blue American flag and the following text written in 14 different languages: "I am a citizen of the United States of America. I do not speak your language. Misfortune forces me to seek your assistance in obtaining food, shelter and protection. Please take me to someone who will provide for my safety and see that I am returned to my people. My government will reward you."

The effectiveness of this appeal depended on who took the time to read it. If in the hands of the central highlands pro-American Montagnards tribe, they cooperated fully. However, if in the clutches of the Vietcong, they either killed on the spot or held their new prisoner as a future bargaining chip. Some men folded the cloth in such a way that only the flag showed and then stitched it on to the back of their flight jackets. I carried mine in a small pouch attached to my belt. Today, it is framed and hanging on my wall, the fold creases forever soiled by the grime of war.

Long before I landed in Vietnam, I knew I had to find my way to a combat command.

"Are you crazy, Major?" the battalion commander responded when I asked for a flying assignment.

"I didn't come here to be some grease monkey supervisor."

"It's a hell of a lot safer."

I shook my head and got an unofficial green light to start snooping around for another assignment. More than military courtesy or adhering to conventional hierarchy, common sense reigned supreme under a host of pressing conditions. So on the QT, only a few days after landing at An Khe, I was negotiating with the commanding officer of the 228th Aviation Battalion.

"I probably have more flight time than anybody here and I know I'm up to the job," I told the colonel, hoping he didn't think I was just whistling in the wind. "So, what are my chances?"

"Pretty good," the colonel answered like a man who had been ready to have this conversation long before I walked into his hooch. "There's another White House pilot here who is, well...not what I would expect."

I knew the man he was talking about very well and even though he was a good aviator, I had heard he didn't want to take flights. In Vietnam, or in any war for that matter, respect was earned through deed and not automatically granted on the basis of rank. He was among those who, for reasons known only to themselves, played it so safe it was hard to not call him "chicken" to his face, but even if I had, he probably wouldn't have cared. For those of us more "gung-ho," there was also a clear contingent of those who weren't. One of the worst things any of us could do was try to delve into another man's mind. Combat altered each of us and that was the one thing we all had in common.

"I've got a mess here at headquarters," the colonel began. "We've got to make things more comfortable. I don't want anybody sleeping in helicopters when the monsoons hit. You help me with that and I'll give you the command you want."

"Just tell me what to do," I said.

"You know anything about cement or construction?"

I couldn't believe it. All those summers of working with Dad and our neighbor had just paid off in spades.

"I sure do. It's how I got through college."

"Okay. You got the job."

The next several weeks, I worked shoulder to shoulder with my men in blazing heat to improve our facilities and give some added comfort to the troops during the rainy season. Besides sidewalks and foundations, we built shower towers made from 55-gallon drums strapped high on concrete and steel pillars. Until then, we had to wait for a healthy downpour for a good scrubbing. If we ran out of lumber or cement, it wasn't beneath us to make a night raid on, for instance, a nearby Air Force supply unit to restock. As I recall, our best cement mixer came from the Air Force along with a few cases of booze, some blankets, and a refrigerator or two.

In early September, 1966, I took command of the 24-helicopter B Company, 228th Aviation Battalion. An assault support

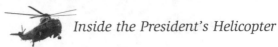

Commanding Officer, B Company, 228th Aviation Battalion
An Khe, Vietnam, 1966
(Boyer Family Archives)

company of about 225 troops, it was made up of pilots, mechanics, gunners and maintenance personnel. I had the best group of aviators the Army could field at the time. Most had flown for about eight to ten years and had earned their seat in a Chinook, each one of which cost about 3 million dollars.

Occasionally, I am asked why most Army helicopters have Native American names. According to a variety of aircraft historians, because U.S. Army aviation began at Ft. Sill, Oklahoma – an area rich with Native American culture – it was considered appropriate to honor that influence with names like Choctaw, Kiowa, Comanche, Iroquois, Apache and Chinook.

No longer a conventional infantry unit, the newly formed 1st Air Cavalry Division joined with the 101st Airborne to literally

debut air assault tactics and protocol that had never been tested in actual combat. For most helicopter pilots, Vietnam was a
dress rehearsal with live ammo and real blood. Our job was to
take the war to the enemy, wherever they were – from jungle
bunkers to rice paddies, from tunnels to ridgelines, from peasant villages to our own backyard. My job was to determine
when, how and where to do that. A typical mission involved
hauling troops, artillery or cargo to hot zones, plus medevac
duties as ordered.

I got shot down my first flight.

In a Chinook with four door gunners and two mechanics, I
was leading a flight of about 16 helicopters to pick up an
infantry battalion 20 miles northwest of An Khe. At nearly
1,500 hundred feet I slowed from 130 to 40 knots and dropped
to 100 feet, ready to let down in a clearing on an otherwise
forested hilltop. Anytime a helicopter flew low and slow it
entered what we called "Dead Man's Curve" and became a sitting duck for enemy attack. Before we could land, machine guns
opened up on us.

"Number two engine is on fire!" shouted the crew chief. "I'm
spraying!"

The door gunners unloaded all they could as he shot foam on
the fire. I shut down the burning engine, cutting off the fuel supply, dropped the nose to increase air speed, turned back toward
An Khe and hugged the tree tops looking for a place to let down
all the while repeating over the radio:

"May day, we're hit, abort mission, we're going down," I
hollered into the radio, my heart hammering. "Everybody okay?!"

"Yeah!" someone called out to my great relief.

We limped along for about four miles at full power before I
spotted a rice paddy big enough to land in. There was another
skirmish underway nearby with troops descending into battle
and they were quickly rerouted to protect us. Two gunships and
two F-4s circled overhead, giving us enough cover to assess
damage. Setting down in about six inches of water contaminated
with Agent Orange, all I had on my mind was figuring out a way
to save my men and the Chinook. I knew if I could get it to
hover, I could get it back to the base.

We stripped the chopper down to bare bones and dumped most of our fuel to get rid of every ounce of excess weight. Leaving behind all our weapons and ammo plus all the crew but one for an incoming Huey to retrieve, I started the remaining engine and lifted up, practically elevating in my own seat to reduce the weight. Able to hold a steady hover, we dipped forward and hugged the deck all the way back to base.

A couple of escort pilots and my crew threw a "survival party" that night in the battalion's small clubhouse and gave me one the biggest ribbings of my life.

"What kind of goddamn CO are you?"

"Couldn't even make it through your first flight."

"And you flew for the fucking White House?"

Someone brought me a half dozen of the bullets that had lodged in the fuel tank of the downed Chinook.

"Be glad nobody had to dig these out of your hide," he said.

"Yeah," I replied and ordered another vodka tonic.

I was suitably intoxicated by the time I got back to the tent I shared with a three-month-old German Shepherd puppy and a rascal of a long-tailed monkey. I was asleep before I hit the cot and back in the air the next day. Close calls were common and often put behind us with a good laugh. And then there were the exceptions.

About a month later, one of my Chinooks had just taken off at the north end of the runway on a night flight from An Khe to Saigon when they were hit by heavy fire from Vietcong infiltrators. The helicopter crashed almost immediately, killing all eight of the men on board. I knew them personally by their first names. Such permanent, instantaneous loss drills hard, fast and deep and, for a fleeting moment, I did what most of us do – wish with all my heart for a second chance. But oddly enough, it's the cruel finality that diffuses the shock. Duty moves us forward and shovels time on the memories we hope to bury, but never quite succeed in doing.

Once we had gunships in the air to secure the crash area, my first task as the CO was to dispatch a team to collect their bodies for transport to a nearby aid station to be processed for shipment home. I also sent personnel to their tents to collect, inventory and pack up personal possessions to send to their families. That assignment also included the unwritten obligation to remove and destroy any items that might add to a family's darkest distress like a stash of hashish hidden in a football or a boot box crammed with porn.

Even in death, we had to have each other's backs.

I still have a photograph of eight pristine white pilot helmets lined up in front of the headquarters monument where I conducted a memorial in their honor. They were the first and only men I lost under my command. The irony still unnerves me that they had dodged death looping in and out of the jungles only to get wiped out taking off from base, doing everything right.

I can't be sure, but it could have been this incident that caused one of my warrant officers with almost 20 years to confess to me that he didn't want to fly.

"Why?" I asked. "That's what you came here to do."

"I'm not good enough and I'm scared."

Memorial for B Company, 228th Aviation Battalion Chinook Crew
Shot down near An Khe, Vietnam, 1966
(Boyer Family Archives)

Being scared was a lame excuse. Part of me admired his honesty. Another part knew such a refusal was grounds for a court martail.

"I don't know..." I answered, definitely alarmed by the thought of having to rely on him.

"Look, let me do re-supply. I can do that."

To my surprise he was volunteering to take the position of a guy who had just been killed and do what I thought was an even more dangerous job – going in with ground troops as a point man in charge of directing helicopters to land, load and take off. Seeing he was still willing to take major risks and "play for the team," I couldn't fault him.

"When you get back to the States," I advised, knowing he had at least 18 years in the service, "it would probably be a good time to retire."

We both knew he had initiated a self-imposed demotion from which he could not recover.

In some ways, the hardest thing for me to take in Vietnam was watching a good man's spirit break. We seemed to dodge more demons than bullets. I brought in two new pilots and went on about my business hoping for at least one day without any surprises.

Wishful thinking.

Not only were there no front lines in Vietnam, we had an added disadvantage of not being able to distinguish friend from foe. Especially when transporting South Vietnamese troops, we were constantly on the lookout for Vietcong moles within their ranks known for tossing grenades into a helicopter as they exited.

During a combat raid over the Bong Son plains near the coast, we had just set down and were offloading South Vietnamese troops when one of the soldiers suddenly fumbled a grenade on the ramp. The instant it hit the floor my crew chief snatched it up and threw it discus style out the back end of the helicopter where it exploded in the air over a rice paddy. Several troops wrestled the infiltrator to the floor, disarmed him, and killed him before tossing aside the man who knew before any of us that he was about to die.

On another flight in the same region, I was putting along at

Me with front line artillery troops near the Laotian border
Vietnam, 1966
(Boyer Family Archives)

MAJ Ed Adams and I (right) near An Khe Vietnam, 1966
Boeing Vertol Chinook CH-47 at work in the background
(Boyer Family Archives)

about 55 knots in a two-seater Bell H-13 Sioux with a piston-driven Franklin engine on the way to check on my troops. I had climbed to a deceptively safe 2,500 feet only to spot a shoulder-fired missile about a mile away speeding straight for my forehead. In a split second, adrenaline flooded my senses, but before I could take evasive action, the thing exploded right in front of me. My only guess, other than divine intervention, was that the enemy had either undershot me or prematurely triggered detonation. Regardless, I dropped the collective, made a diving turn to the right and headed out of the area, burning all my ammo on nothing in particular. Damn – 2,500 feet wasn't even safe anymore.

Rarely did we see the enemy before they attacked. Their ability to maneuver in the dense forests and conceal operations gave them a huge advantage and gave us a reason for Agent Orange. No one disputed its effectiveness as a defoliant. The more pressing challenge was in determining how to safely and effectively apply it. Named for the 55-gallon orange-striped barrels that stored the lethal powder, Agent Orange was used to destroy jungle foliage and crops as well as for clearing landing sights and base perimeters. Its short-term positive effects were indisputable. Its long-term impact was one of the greatest tragedies a country has ever heaped upon its own. Dow Chemical may not have disclosed the hazards to the U.S. government, but together they are responsible for all the men forced to fight for our lives long after we had left the jungles of Vietnam.

In 1966, we had yet to develop an efficient method for helicopters to spread the chemical. When I received orders to organize a distribution test flight that required us to dump Agent Orange out the back of a Chinook, I assigned the mission to one of my crews to give it a try, even though I thought it was a wild-ass idea. When the crew returned to base, they and the interior of the helicopter were completely covered in what looked like white flour.

Had it really been that hard to pour that stuff out the back of a helicopter?

I was asked to try again, so I did the next flight and this time made sure we were all wearing gas masks. The moment the first barrel was tipped out the back, the deadly powder billowed up and was sucked back inside the cabin and through the forward windows. I wrote the mission up as a failure and removed Chinooks as a viable means of distribution. Later, spraying wands were developed for UH-1D helicopters, but for now, B Company was out of the picture and as a result, our exposure was reduced.

An estimated 4 million acres of central and southern Vietnam were dusted with Agent Orange. Its effects on both the land and humans are expected to last up to 100 years. I am among the tens of thousands of Vietnam vets to develop multiple cancers. Eventually declared 100 percent Agent Orange disabled, I have endured both the loss of my own robust health and the loss of countless friends and colleagues. It remains a bitter, rancid pill to swallow.

Among my fonder duties at An Khe was delivering shipments of food and supplies to a leper colony we had adopted on the beach south of Qui Nhon. On one trip we landed on the damp sand between the surf line and a colony of tidy white huts and small buildings. Nestled in lush greenery with banana and coconut trees, it was a peaceful, almost intoxicating paradise setting. Greeted by two French nuns dressed in their traditional habits, my crew and I helped cart crates into a patio area while a few afflicted residents looked on. We made a point of not staring and had been warned about having any contact. I remember a man, probably about my age, with a horribly disfigured face and missing arm. I couldn't tell if he was smiling or not, but I still gave him a friendly nod. There are few diseases as insidious as leprosy.

"Merci, merci beaucoup," said one of the nuns, surveying the boxes. "And coffee, too?"

"A whole case," I happily answered.

She clapped her hands with glee.

"Mind if we take a swim?" I asked.

"No, not at all," she said. "It's a big ocean, major."

Nothing washed away the grit caked to our bodies like a dive into those gently churning aquamarine waves.

In October 1966, the heaviest air strike to date was made on

North Vietnam's panhandle region. U.S. bombers flew hundreds of missions striking radar stations, transportation facilities and storage centers. President Johnson embarked on a 17-day Far East tour, which included a seven-nation conference on Vietnam in the Philippines. Stateside anti-war demonstrations were attracting more publicity with pickets, protest marches, sit-ins and flaming draft cards. Vietnam had become an international time-bomb. Everyone could hear it ticking. And everyone had an opinion, including literary giant John Steinbeck whose own son, drafted by the Army, was serving as a journalist in Saigon for Armed Forces Radio and TV.

Two years before he died at the age of 66, the senior Steinbeck spent six weeks embedded with U.S. troops in Vietnam during the winter of 1966-67. Initially expressing strong doubt about U.S. involvement in the war, he had recently shifted to voicing support for Johnson's policies. As a result of his travels from one end of Vietnam to the other, that viewpoint began to weaken. On assignment for *Newsday*, Steinbeck wanted to see everything, experience all he could short of getting killed, and talk to anyone who could rub two words together. In a nutshell, he wanted to capture the human side of the war and he was the last person I ever expected to spend Christmas with.

I had just finished a mission and was walking off the "golf course" when I looked up to see my CO approaching with a rugged-looking older man, slightly taller than I, and dressed in fatigues.

"Major Boyer," said the colonel, "this is John Steinbeck."

"It's an honor to meet you, sir," I said, shaking his hand and wishing I had a copy of *Grapes of Wrath* handy.

"Same here," he said with a respectful grin.

"I want you to take care of him," the colonel told me, "until he's ready to leave."

Within minutes, Steinbeck and I were leaning against the little bar at the clubhouse swapping stories and buying each other drinks. Adding a seasonally festive touch was a large cut-out of a winking Santa Claus tacked on a nearby wall. Since he was a writer, I expected him at any time to whip out a notepad and pencil, but instead, he just kept asking questions and listening.

My crew and I having a beer and absorbing the wisdom
of literary great John Steinbeck on assignment for *Newsday*
An Khe, Vietnam, Christmas, 1966
(Boyer Family Archives)

"Where'd you grow up?"

"Tell me about your family."

"You married?"

"A daughter, huh? You miss her?"

"Every day," I answered.

I didn't mind the personal nature of the questions as much as I worried that he wasn't getting anything significant from a no-name helicopter pilot. Then he asked:

"How long have you been flying helicopters?"

"Since Korea."

"Can you take me out?"

"Sure," I said, anxious to show off our unit.

"I hear you flew for the White House."

"Yeah."

"So how'd you end up here?"

"Guess it was just my turn."

We sacked out in my tent that night. I don't remember where I boarded my dog and monkey, but I'll never forget lying there in the dark thinking what an amazing and unexpected privilege it was to bunk with a Nobel Prize winner.

The next day, Steinbeck flew along with us on a supply drop and didn't miss a beat talking to other pilots, crew chiefs, door gunners and mechanics. A man of eminent gumption and character, he wrote a letter to President Johnson a few weeks later that included the following: "Dear Mr. President: I have been in Vietnam for about six weeks now... From north to south I have been on every outpost, have flown with Air Cavalry, with Forward Air Control, with 1st Cavalry units... I think I know our men very well now for I have lived with them and have been shot at with them...we have here the finest, the best trained, the most intelligent and the most dedicated soldiers I have ever seen in any army and I have seen soldiers in my time... The restrictions placed on them in carrying the war to the enemy must be and are galling to our soldiers. But they obey. I hope, sir, that in the near future you may find occasion to celebrate these men... Yours with all respect, John Steinbeck"

Steinbeck had been a big morale booster for us, but nothing lifted troop spirits more than United Service Organizations (USO) shows. From 1965 to 1972, the USO staged over 5,500 shows throughout Vietnam. Headliners like comedian Bob Hope, always in the company of a cast of gorgeous women, were greeted with uncontained enthusiasm during the Christmas holidays as were other celebrities throughout the rest of the year.

USO staffers and entertainers came in and out of An Khe on Air Force C-130s. One quiet, overcast day, I had landed a Chinook back at the base just in time to see an incoming C-130 skid into an ammo bunker at the end of the runway. A blaze erupted on the right wing and I knew it was only a matter of minutes before the fireworks started. I ordered my crew to move nearby helicopters and ran to the plane. Surprised to see no one emerging, I figured the doors and rear ramp were jammed so I, along with a sergeant, scrambled on top of the plane to muscle open the hatch. As soon as it popped free, someone from inside yelled, "Thank God!"

"How many?!" I shouted through the smoke.

"Twelve! We've got a USO troupe!"

"Move it fast!" I shot back. "You're on an ammo bunker!"

"We've got ammo on board, too!"

I reached down to grab the first hand I could and hauled up a tiny South Korean woman, then another and another, telling each to "Go! Run! Run fast!"

Within seconds everyone was out and we were all running like hell away from the plane when it exploded, sending a volcanic ball of fire into the air. Not knowing what other surprises might materialize, my Chinook crew and I moved more helicopters out of harm's way. The fire burned for over three hours until there was nothing left but a smoldering tail and wing, and a damn good story to tell over a drink at the clubhouse that night.

Several weeks later, my CO told me to meet him at the parade grounds in ten minutes. I arrived on scene to see an Air Force brigadier general motion me closer. In a brief, no frills ceremony, I was surprised to receive the rarely awarded Soldiers Medal "for heroism not involving actual conflict with an enemy."

C-130 crash scene where I helped rescue a flight crew and USO troupe.
An Khe, Vietnam, 1967

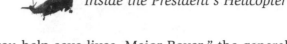

"Not only did you help save lives, Major Boyer," the general said, "but you saved the USO show."

I thanked him for the honor and zipped my lip regarding the insane stupidity of transporting strippers and a band of musicians with crates of live ammunition.

More than a medal that day, I needed a break and decided to take CeCe's suggestion in her last letter to visit her former boss, Bill Porter, in Saigon. A one-time U.S. ambassador to Algeria, Porter was now Deputy Ambassador to Vietnam under Henry Cabot Lodge. Tasked with operating the "rural pacification program" in South Vietnam, he was highly respected and would eventually be chosen by President Nixon to head the American delegation to the Vietnam peace talks in 1971 before becoming Under Secretary of State.

Any concern I had about taking up his valuable time was quickly allayed the instant we met.

"So how's the husband of my favorite assistant?" Porter asked, greeting me outside a fancy Saigon restaurant.

I was in fatigues. He was in civilian attire and looking just as professorial as he had at the wedding when CeCe and I were married in Paris.

"No complaints," I answered.

"Hungry?"

"Always."

During dinner, Porter rivaled Steinbeck with inquiries about operations at An Khe and I didn't mince words about what I thought was working well and what wasn't. We had too many poorly connected, uninformed leaders relying on too many under-qualified and wary troops. I especially took issue with Johnson's hard-line policy of restricting military operations to Vietnam as a strategy to prevent the war from spreading. This only allowed the Vietcong to establish a refuge area along the Cambodian and Laotian borders where they could comfortably hide, treat their wounded, regroup and launch offensives. What Johnson didn't seem to get was that the war had already spread.

My conversation with Porter continued back at his villa where he made good on a promise to connect me with CeCe by ham radio. The instant we heard her voice rise above the static, Porter and I smiled like school boys. But the elation was short-lived.

"Thank God you're safe," CeCe said, and quickly explained that news had just come in about a major attack on An Khe. "I'll call your parents and let them know you're all right."

"How bad was it?" I asked, afraid to calculate all the losses I knew were possible.

"I don't know," CeCe replied. "But please be careful."

"I will," I assured, never figuring I was about to have my work cut out for me on the helicopter flight back to An Khe.

Porter and I talked until about 2:00 a.m. before turning in. When I hooked up with a Huey leaving Saigon the next morning, I was glad I wasn't the pilot so I could grab some shut-eye. I remember strapping in and casually glancing at the flight engineer across from me. He looked like he wanted to say something, but then looked away as we lifted off.

Unknown to me, in the cockpit were two colonels with less than 200 hours each of flight time. I dozed lightly as they headed toward the coast, then climbed to about 5,000 feet. Within seconds after dipping into some large, fluffy clouds, the helicopter started bouncing and rocking. I woke to see the flight engineer roll his eyes in too much of a prayer expression for my comfort, so I made my way to the cockpit.

"How's the weather?" I asked.

"Just some clouds," said the right seat.

"I'm an instrument instructor. I could take the left seat."

"We're fine, Major."

"Okay, it's your helicopter," I said, reluctantly.

But something told me to not budge from where I stood and things went from bad to worse in a heartbeat. Both pilots were completely disoriented. The co-pilot quickly scrambled out of his seat for me to slide in – a dangerous maneuver on its own to do mid-flight. I got control of the helicopter in short order and as soon as we landed at An Khe, I wasted no time reeling off a few choice words.

"Gentleman, screw your rank," I blurted. "Right now, consider me a general. Neither one of you should be flying without a qualified pilot."

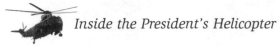
"I sure won't fly with you again," chimed in the flight engineer.

Both men knew they deserved anything I wanted to say to them.

"And if I recommend you be grounded, it's for your own good and the safety of others."

"We know you saved our lives back there," confessed the right-seat colonel.

"I saved my own," I snapped back. "You just got lucky."

When I turned to leave, he asked, "Don't you want to sign the flight log?"

"No thanks. I don't need the time."

Five minutes later, I was standing in front of my tent. It was riddled with shrapnel from the attack the day before. CeCe's push for me to visit Bill Porter may have saved my life and I couldn't wait to hold her and Robin in my arms.

A few weeks later, I met CeCe and Robin for a brief vacation at the balmy terminal at Hickham AFB just south of Pearl Harbor on the island of Oahu. CeCe was as beautiful as ever, but when I reached out to Robin, she clung to her mother. I was stunned. We hadn't seen each other for about seven months. Was that long enough for "Daddy's little girl" to have forgotten me?

Yes.

It took us five long days of a six-day visit to inch my way back to romping about with Robin like the old days. Now two-and-a-half years old, she was talking a blue streak and let me know she had a mind of her own every chance she got. I loved it, all the while knowing I was about to leave again and she wouldn't have a clue why.

I was also unprepared for CeCe's response to my gift of a necklace with three of the bullets recovered from the helicopter I was flying that got shot down. She held up the chain, stared at the bullets dangling in front of her and then looked at me with dismay.

"Why would I want these?"

"I just thought–"

CeCe pressed the necklace back into my hands.

"The last thing I want," she said, "is to be reminded that there are people shooting at you."

As in all wars, families took their own barrage of hits, but the impact of the war on me was miniscule compared to men who were getting Dear John letters, parents getting death notifications, or newborn children who would never know their fathers. But the kids who suffered the most were those in Vietnam who had seen their homes destroyed, members of their families killed and any number of other untold human atrocities.

A few times during my tour I was called upon to airlift refugee children. On one trip, I brought two Chinooks into a clearing 15 miles north of An Khe where about 60 young children and a couple of adult women had hunkered down after being driven from their village. As the small sea of dazed and tearful faces poured on board clutching meager belongings, the children began wailing and pointing out the back of the helicopter. When I asked the crew chief what was going on, he said they were upset about leaving their elephant behind.

We had strict regulations about transporting or hunting animals ever since a general was recently injured and his pilot – in the last week of his tour – was killed in a helicopter crash hunting tigers.

"It's just a baby," yelled the crew chief over the crying children.

It was only a 20-minute flight to the coast, I figured, where support services were waiting to receive the children. If it was a small elephant, maybe we could bend the rules.

"How much does it weigh?" I shouted back.

"Three, maybe four hundred pounds."

"Okay, let it on," I said, caving in.

The joyful cheers of delighted children rippled across the clearing and for one radiant moment, there in the ravaged jungle of Vietnam, everyone was smiling.

Later that spring, sometime after midnight, a runner from headquarters pounded on my tent door and alerted me to an emergency mission. Within minutes, my crew and I were on a solo flight through the inky night on a medevac rescue mission. A mixed-forces platoon was surrounded by about 2,000 VC. They had been in a hellacious fight and had several casualties. My co-pilot was Captain St. Peter. The religious implication was of little note until I discovered a middle-aged chaplain stowaway.

"What the hell are you doing here?"

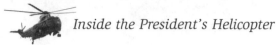

"I thought I could help," he calmly said.

"You don't have to do this," I told him.

"Of course I do," he boldly replied.

There was no turning back, so the best I could do was tell him to stay out of the way. "Puff the Magic Dragon," a C-47 that could shoot a seemingly unending flame of mini-gun tracers, arrived to circle over us and we moved closer to our pick-up point on a hilltop near the Ho Chi Minh Trail, the Vietcong's main supply route.

"Don't you bastards shoot me down!" I shouted into the radio. "Follow me in!"

"You guys okay?" asked the voice on the other end.

"We're great," I answered with sarcastic confidence. "Some chaplain snuck on board and St. Peter is my co-pilot."

As soon as we got close, we were heavily pinged by enemy small-arms fire and had to pull back. I wouldn't let any of my gunners shoot back, otherwise we would light up like a Christmas tree and become an even bigger target. Multiple times we tried to get through – pressing in, drawing fire, pulling up to hide in the clouds and reposition before giving it another go. But the ground fire was so intense and the tracers coming so fast and furious I couldn't find a break. When our fuel ran low, we had no choice but to return to base. I hated leaving without having rescued a single man. I wondered if they had heard us and knew how hard we tried.

Moments later I got word over the radio that U.S. ground troops had penetrated the VC position and were providing reinforcements. Just as I breathed a slight sigh of relief, the most bizarre thing happened on our approach to An Khe. Even though we had both cockpit windows open, the front windows fogged up so bad I couldn't see squat. I yelled for the crew chief to wipe away the moisture. But each time he swiped a space for me to see, it filled in again. The best way to describe our landing in those dark, pre-dawn hours was that we staggered in and grabbed the first open ground we saw.

When we shut down the engines no one moved for the longest time. I was gutted about not getting to the guys who needed to be rescued; dumbfounded by the weird little cloud that had invaded the cockpit; and profoundly proud of the men who trusted enough to fly with me into the perilous night.

Volcano 7

The presidency has made every man who occupied it, no matter how small, bigger than he was; and no matter how big, not big enough for its demands.

– Lyndon B. Johnson

A few months before my Vietnam tour ended the summer of 1967, a forward landing zone on the Bong Son Plains 20 miles north of An Khe sustained a major nighttime attack. Along with several fixed-wing planes, a number of Hueys from other companies were destroyed. There were also substantial casualties. I brought in a pre-dawn flight of troops to help clean up and re-establish security. In the chaos, I heard the pilot I had earlier relieved from his flying assignment had taken cover in a heap of rubble and spent the night there. I was really glad to know he had made it out alive.

After hours of fighting fires, hauling debris and recovering the wounded and dead, I took a C-ration break in my helicopter.

"Boy," said a voice I couldn't quite recognize, "you really know how to live dangerously."

I looked up to see George Iverson climbing aboard.

"And I suppose you're living in some luxury hotel in Saigon," I responded, not blinking an eye. I hadn't seen Marjorie Merriweather Post's son-in-law since leaving Washington, D.C., where he and his wife had briefly bunked CeCe and me in their Maryland mansion.

"Nothing but the best," he answered, grabbing a seat.

"What the hell are you doing here?" I asked.

"Checking on you," he said, with a joking glimmer in his eye.

Iverson, now a Lt. Colonel, had flown in on a Cessna to survey damage and made a point of seeking me out. After he revealed he had orders to go back to the Pentagon, I let him know I had just picked up orders, too. I was headed to the LBJ Ranch where, once I had re-qualified in the VH-3A, it looked like I would be the new senior pilot for the Texas White House unit.

"Congratulations," said Iverson.

"Thanks, but I wanted to go to back to Benning and teach helicopter tactics and advanced infantry courses."

"Well, I've decided to quit," he told me. "I'm resigning my commission and going to work for Howard Hughes."

"Damn," I said with surprise. "Now I know who to call for a job when I retire."

However, as I entered the last 30 days of my command at An Khe, I knew better than to think about life after Vietnam. Allowing a single thought to wander forward meant increasing the odds of losing whatever edge I had managed to hold. So in my mind, the best way to stay above ground was to keep flying like nothing could touch me.

One of my toughest flights, for which I would be awarded a Distinguished Flying Cross, happened on June 29, 1967. The military write-up read, in part: "While serving as aircraft commander of a CH-47 Chinook helicopter during a night emergency resupply mission near Dak To...for three hours, Major Boyer flew his aircraft through hazardous weather conditions and unfamiliar terrain hauling desperately needed ammunition. The weather being below safe operating limits, on numerous occasions Major Boyer was forced to fly by instruments, without visual reference to the ground. He was also forced to fly at a low level, exposing himself to small arms fire which was prevalent throughout the flight route. Despite the hostile fire, mountainous terrain and hazardous weather, Major Boyer successfully completed the entire mission."

Infinite acts of untold bravery occurred every day in Vietnam. Most of us were more concerned about doing our job and whatever it took to protect each other than we were with collecting ribbons and hardware; but every once in while it was a boost to know someone recognized those efforts. While in Vietnam, I earned the Soldier's Medal, two Distinguished Flying Crosses, a Bronze Star, seven Air Medals, an Army Commendation Medal, and, the one I am most proud of – the Army-wide Aviation Safety Award. B Company lost only one helicopter and an eight-man crew during my command – one helicopter and eight men too many.

I slept most of my flight from Vietnam to California. Even though I had an arm-length's worth of personal opinions about how the war was being conducted, I still believed it was a necessary and justified battle and still had confidence in President Johnson's resolve to fight for freedom and human rights.

Most of all, I wanted to see my wife, daughter, parents and brothers, and find my way back to the life I had left behind – if that was even possible. In the process of catching a connecting flight to Virginia out of San Francisco with a couple of other officers and a handful of GIs, we were confronted by about 50 anti-war protestors in the terminal.

"Baby killers!" they chanted, waving crudely painted signs that read, "No More War!" and "Get Out of Vietnam!"

Startled, we stopped in place – a half dozen guys wearing khaki uniforms in a face-off with a bunch of the craziest looking people I had ever seen. We had been warned about possible encounters with demonstrators but were not expecting any action at the airport. It was almost midnight, for God's sake. Plus, for the life of me, I couldn't understand why we were targets. What had we done wrong? They needed to take their beef-fest to the government, not the soldiers.

"You should be in body bags!" screeched a frizzy-haired woman in bell-bottom jeans. Then someone heaved a can of soda at us.

"Fucking draft dodger!" ripped back one of my comrades.

Without a single word, we pressed together and walked toward them with a "kick-ass" attitude. Several cops materialized out of thin air.

"Hey fellas," said one, "don't let them get to you."

"A little late for that," I muttered as we regained our composure and continued on to our gate.

This was my first of many encounters with anti-war protestors in the coming years. I had been away a full year, but it seemed like overnight America had become a different country. Dresses were shorter, hair was longer, and people were angrier. There were race riots in Detroit, teachers on strike in New York and protesters practically camping at the Pentagon. Patriotism was losing its footing at the very time I thought we needed it most.

The fall of 1967, at the age of 38, I was assigned to the 4th Army Aviation Detachment headquartered at Fort Sam Houston in San Antonio. Ten miles to the northeast, the detachment had seven helicopters based at Randolph Air Force Base: three VH-3As, three Hueys and a four-place light observation helicopter we called a "loach."

President Johnson's personal Army helicopter fleet
Randolph AFB, San Antonio, Texas, 1967
(Boyer Family Archives)

On average we had two or three helicopters on continuous standby at the LBJ Ranch, which was a 25-minute northbound flight from Randolph. However, when Johnson traveled on Air Force One, he preferred going in and out of Bergstrom AFB just south of Austin, the state capital.

Also, within this general area were more than two dozen rural properties, owned by either Johnson or his associates, which he frequently visited. Many were remote cattle ranches and few had safe landing sites, given the archaic if not non-existent navigation facilities available to travel about the rolling terrain and having to cope with the unpredictable weather. Most were privately owned destinations and had no adequate emergency or firefighting equipment, no landing-pad lights, no rescue protocol, not even a damn wind sock – just a President who did not want anyone, especially the press, to track his activities.

Some landing sites were marked with circles of painted white rocks, which were harder than hell to find at night or in bad weather. We also had at our fingertips some aerial photographs and a rudimentary matrix on a sheet of paper with time and distance headings linked to a non-directional beacon several miles from the ranch. In short, we flew President Johnson in and around his ranch with fewer navigational aids than we had had in the deepest jungle of Vietnam.

It was a lame-brained way to operate, but this was vintage Johnson. Not only did he often fly under the radar, in my opinion, he also flew without radar when it came to grasping the risks he heaped upon the pilots flying for him in Texas. But, there was no reasoning with "Volcano." He made the decisions. The rest of us were on our own to make it happen any way we could.

As presidential pilots, we meticulously recorded arrival and departure times in our flight logs. Beyond that, whatever happened before, during and after was not officially recorded. Rather, those goings-on were woven into our oral history and rarely discussed outside the walls of the nearest hangar.

For instance, we all knew about a Marine VH-34 that had crash-landed at Camp David during the Kennedy years. No one was killed, the event never hit the news, the wreckage was buried somewhere at Camp David and thus forgotten. This was a minor and easily ignored incident compared to one then-Vice President Johnson sought to cover up.

In 1960, an ally at Brown and Root (prior to its merger with mega-defense contractor Halliburton in 1962) loaned Johnson a plush white Convair CV-240 airplane for use on the campaign trail with Kennedy. After the inauguration, Johnson bought the plane at a bargain price and hired pilots Howard Teague and Charlie Williams. Both men were in their late thirties and highly skilled. On a foggy February 19 night in 1961, Johnson ordered the plane to fly from Austin to his ranch 60 miles away. Although there was a paved and lighted runway, there were no ground control instruments or communications. The lead pilot checked

with the Austin tower and was advised against making the flight. When Johnson learned this, he is said to have exploded and demanded the pilots get the plane to the ranch because that's what he was paying them to do. Teague called his wife to let her know Johnson had ordered them into the air and they might not make it.

The plane crashed into a hillside near the ranch, killing both pilots. Not a word hit the airways until three days later when the news reported a plane was "overdue" at the ranch. Rumors swirled regarding who actually owned the plane and what role Johnson had played. Word was Austin's tower records got lost and insurance payments were accelerated. One thing we all knew for certain, two widows buried their husbands and Johnson went on about his business.

When I reported for duty to the Texas White House unit, I had a vague sense of Johnson's lack of consideration for average Joes like me, but never imagined it to be as bad as it was. A popular Johnson comment circulating to this day reads, "When things haven't gone well for you, call in a secretary or a staff man and chew him out. You will sleep better and they will appreciate the attention."

Speaking for myself and the 22 other pilots in the Texas White House Exec Flight unit, none of us ever appreciated that kind of attention.

Johnson's senior helicopter pilot and my boss in charge of operations was Major Pete Rice. An excellent aviator with a buzz-saw personality, Rice had yet to serve in Vietnam and, understandably, was hell-bent on keeping his position with the White House. This intention was regularly made apparent to me each time Warrant Officer Keith Borck, our instructor pilot, wrote my name on the "get current" board to re-qualify in the VH-3A and Rice would scratch it out. This went on for nearly six months. Years later Rice personally acknowledged that he "hadn't treated me very well."

"It was a tough time," I responded, "but that's water under the bridge."

Rice had a tight relationship with Colonel Jim Cross, Johnson's Air Force One pilot and, in a rare departure from convention,

Me in the cockpit of Army One
White House Executive Flight Detachment
(Boyer Family Archives)

also his military assistant, a job usually held by a two-star general or Navy admiral. Each position – Air Force One pilot and White House Military Assistant – were fulltime responsibilities. For one person to hold both was a lot to ask, but made things simpler for how Johnson operated. Instead of scheduling Air Force One through the White House Military Office, he could bypass that process and go straight to Cross.

In Texas, "a check and balance system" equated to whether Johnson approved or disapproved of an undertaking. It also boiled down to whether or not a pilot was a "yes man" or willing to risk getting replaced, which generally equated to an express pass to Vietnam. Johnson also made sure he took care of those who best served his interests. Cross and I had both been majors when I went to Vietnam and I was surprised to

learn that, in the span of a year, he was now a full colonel and on his way to brigadier general. A quick check with the guys in the hangar revealed when Johnson first pushed to accelerate his rank, the Air Force refused to cooperate. Johnson, in turn, delayed the entire Air Force promotion list. Confronted by a no-win standoff, the Air Force folded.

To call the chain of command at the ranch a bastardized system was an understatement, and I did my best to stay out of what looked like kindergarten politics compared to the issues I had dealt with in Vietnam. Unfortunately, since I fully expected Johnson to run and win a second term, this meant I was a long way from becoming a White House senior pilot and was back to flying "ash and trash." Arguably not the best use of my skills, it did give me lots of down time to reconnect with my family, help them with the move into our new home and get in some local sightseeing.

I was still in orientation training when CeCe introduced me to her Aunt Chip and Uncle Dunning in Austin. Chip was a buoyant, animated woman from Pittsburgh and Dunning was a decorated WWII pilot who had flown C-47s "over the hump," a supply route between India and China. A pragmatic straight-talker, he warned me about my new assignment at the LBJ Ranch: "You're in for a real education about our illustrious president."

Chip and Dunning were close friends with the Coke Stevenson family. The former governor of Texas from 1941 to 1947, Stevenson was highly respected and known as Mr. Texas. In 1948, Stevenson ran against fellow Democrat and then U.S. Congressman Lyndon Johnson for the U.S. Senate. Even though Stevenson finished six percentage points ahead of Johnson in the primary, he lost to Johnson in a run-off by only 87 votes out of the nearly one million cast. Stevenson challenged the results. After some legal maneuvers by both men, the matter was turned over to Democratic State Central Committee and they upheld Johnson's victory by a 29-28 vote. Disgusted, Stevenson subsequently retired and changed political parties. Stories to this day circulate about voter fraud, including 200 Johnson votes that mysteriously had been cast in alphabetical order listing "residents" from a duval Cemetery on the Mexican border.

While fishing with Chip and Dunning on their houseboat moored at Granite Shoals (now Lake LBJ), he mentioned he had briefly been a co-investor with Johnson in a real estate transaction and that his son had shot his first deer hunting on the LBJ Ranch. Chip, a dyed-in-the-wool Republican with a bar-room voice, didn't hold back about how much she disliked Johnson. Once invited to a formal reception for Johnson at the State House in Austin, Chip and Dunning were about six handshakes away from greeting the President and First Lady when Chip made a derogatory remark she would only qualify as a "personal criticism." Johnson heard the comment, walked over to her and ordered her to leave immediately, which she did.

"I have no regrets," she said. "That man needed to hear what no one else had the nerve to say."

Dunning later introduced me to Coke Stevenson's son as one of Johnson's helicopter pilots.

"God bless you," said Stevenson, Jr. with a little more compassion than made me feel comfortable.

Needless to say, I was not anxious to enter the Johnson hornet nest and I also knew I wasn't allowed to fly the President until Rice first approved a check ride. In many ways, we were both reluctant for that to happen. He was protecting his job and I was contented flying visitors and making pre-dawn flights to deliver daily newspapers and White House mail for the President; although, the "newspaper run" had its own brand of peril. Rotating UH-1 (Huey) crews were on standby at Randolph AFB one day, then moved to Bergstrom AFB the next. From there we would pick up from two to three hundred pounds of daily newspapers, mail and government documents flown from Andrews to get to the ranch by 6 a.m. every morning. Easing in from the north at the far end of the airstrip, we knew if the helicopter woke the President, "heads would roll."

Unless otherwise directed, the "newspaper run" crew would settle in at the ranch until Johnson went to sleep that night. Sometimes this did not happen until well past midnight. Once he was sawing logs, we flew to Randolph AFB to have a day off and then start the rotation over.

The LBJ Ranch is situated in the Texas Hill Country and faces

the Pedernales River to the south. Located within a mile west of the farm where Johnson was born, the then-dilapidated 250-acre spread was acquired by him from a widowed aunt in 1951. Through a series of improvements and land acquisitions, he built the property into a 2,500-acre working ranch complete with several hundred head of registered Herefords.

Adjacent to the rambling, two-story house was a hangar for his Jetstar and a VH-3A helicopter and a small mobile home for pilots. Due east was a taxiway to Johnson City Airport, a private 5,000-foot runway built with taxpayer dollars prior to 1960. Behind the house, at the far end of the airstrip, were two single-wide mobile homes for stand-by Exec Flight helicopter pilots, crews and mechanics. Inside the "community trailers," we took turns as "chief cook, bottle washer and airplane polisher," and often passed the time playing cards, watching television, and monitoring three radio networks: the White House, the Secret Service and the aviation flight detachment.

Johnson loved his ranch and the Texas culture where Stetson hats and cowboy boots were commonplace. He spent several

Executive Flight Detachment "community trailers"
East end of LBJ Ranch runway, Johnson City, Texas, 1968
(Boyer Family Archives)

months a year at his ranch with Lady Bird, his two daughters, and any number of staffers and guests. Always intent on showing visitors a good time, he usually added a high-speed tour with him behind the wheel in one of his convertible Lincoln Continentals or, if time was short, a lesser jaunt by golf cart. Some of the dignitaries who visited the ranch included former President Harry Truman, Reverend Billy Graham, President Gustavo Diaz Ordaz of Mexico, Chancellor Konrad Adenauer of West Germany and General William Westmoreland, commander of American military operations in Vietnam from 1964 to 1968.

One of Johnson's closest international confidants and staunchest American allies was Australian Prime Minister Harold Holt. Shortly before his disappearance and presumed drowning in December 1967 while swimming near Portsea, Victoria, Holt flew into Austin. I transported him to the LBJ Ranch where Johnson picked him up in an open-top convertible on his way to lunch at a cattle auction. They were on a tight schedule and the Secret Service directed me to find a place to hide the helicopter near their luncheon site where they would bring Holt for a quick return to his plane. I selected a vacant church property, drew the Secret Service a map and flew off to wait for the Prime Minister to finish his visit with Johnson.

A few hours later, I was waiting in the helicopter when I saw the motorcade with Johnson's convertible sandwiched between two Secret Service cars go whizzing past the turnoff leading to the church. I immediately got on the radio.

"Hey," I said, "you should have turned right at that last road."

"Where the hell," demanded the agent who answered my call, "have you parked the *damn* helicopter?"

Imagining the guy was sweating bullets about having to make a U-turn with Johnson, I answered, "I parked it right where I showed you I would on the *damn* map."

A long and eery silence ensued.

The "agent" was actually President Johnson. Not only was he running the show, but he ran his car into a ditch making the turn with Holt sitting next to him. The two men, along with Holt's noticeably shaken party, walked the short distance to the helicopter where I was ready for take-off. Even though Holt was

laughing it off, Johnson was fuming. I still can't say if his anger was directed at me or the damage to his car. I was airborne too quickly to find out.

As the number two pilot behind Rice, I was sometimes called upon to provide aerial security for special events. On October 28, 1967, President Johnson traveled to El Paso, Texas, to meet with Mexican President Diaz Ordaz and officially transfer about 600 acres known as El Chamizal from the U.S. to Mexico. The rightful ownership of the land had been in dispute since 1895 when the Rio Grande River, the one-time natural southern boundary between the U.S. and Mexico, had rerouted itself and, in effect, stole away Mexican land. An initial agreement had been reached during Kennedy's administration for how to divide the land, compensate U.S. citizens for loss of property, and share in the cost of creating a man-made channel to prevent a reoccurance.

With an American Secret Service marksman in the right door and a Mexican counterpart strapped to the left, we flew about a mile ahead of the slow-moving motorcade looking for anything suspcious. Johnson and Ordaz were in an open limosine.

Before crossing the bridge into Juarez, Mexico, I spotted a civilian man with a rifle on the roof of a commercial building. I pointed him out to the agent on board and peeled off toward the man. The gunman quickly disappeared into the building and within minutes, the Secret Service on the ground radioed back that they had him in custody.

The motorcade crossed the bridge safely, looped through Juarez and came back to stop on the bridge for both presidents to address a gathering crowd. As I circled above, I heard an agent on the ground shout, "Get her! Get her!" In short order, a young woman with a pistol not far from Johnson was apprehended and swiftly spirited away. I never heard any more details related to those incidents nor the outcomes. I don't think either situation made the newspapers. All that mattered at the end of that day was that Johnson, who was rapidly losing popularity, had accomplished his objective and made it back to Air Force One.

One of the most bizarre situations I experienced while at the LBJ Ranch involved Johnson's younger brother Sam Houston

Johnson. I was on standby one afternoon at the airstrip trailers when I got a call from the Military Office at the main house.

"We're sending Sam Houston up to you," said the aide. "We want you to take him to San Antonio."

"Sam who?"

"Sam Houston Johnson. The President's brother."

I didn't even know Johnson had a brother, but soon understood why he was kept under wraps.

My crew and I were in the Huey ready to take off when a Secret Service agent drove up with a tipsy man in his mid-fifties wearing a western suit. As soon as the President's brother stumbled aboard, I started the engine, only to have a voice in my headset yell, "Shut it down! The President's getting ready to drive that way."

We killed the engine and from the cabin heard Sam Houston holler, "What's going on?"

"Ummm," all I could think to tell him was the truth. "The President's going to drive by and they don't want him to see you."

"Fuck him," he slurred. "Get this thing in the air."

"I'm sorry, I can't do that, Mr. Houston."

"Johnson," he corrected. "I'm Sam Houston Johnson."

Sure enough, the President passed by in his convertible on a drive around his ranch with a Secret Service car close behind. He didn't even glance at the helicopter.

Once he was well out of sight we were airborne on our way to Randolph AFB. Then I got another anxious call from the Military Office.

"Do you have Secret Service on board?"

"No," I answered. "Just Sam."

"Oh, shit."

"Is there something I should know?" I asked, hoping this little excursion was about to end.

"As soon as you land at Randolph, have one of your officers take him to a hotel until we can get an agent there."

The last I saw of Sam Houston Johnson was him being driven away by an Army major in his private car. I later learned that once they arrived at the hotel, Sam Houston ordered a bottle of bourbon and made a few phone calls. Next, the President's brother convinced the major to get a better hotel and accompany him to a "soiree in Austin for a little fun." The major alerted the Secret Service and they met him at the party. After all that, Sam Houston still managed to ditch the agents and disappear. I was later privately informed that they had finally located Sam Houston in a Juarez jail where he had been trying to convince Mexican authorities that he was, of all things, the brother of the President of the United States.

Prior to that escapade, there had been an incident in Alexandria, Virginia. Driving drunk, he hit another car, ended up in jail and cost the President a bundle to bail him out. After Johnson's term ended I heard Sam Houston moved to Puerto Rico where he wrote a book called, *My Brother Lyndon*. It was billed as "a candid, witty, and often shocking revelation of the personal and political life of the man regarded as 'the most astute politician of our times.'" I had to agree. Johnson was a master among masters when it came to politics and he knew only one speed – full throttle.

After Johnson attended a memorial service for Prime Minister Harold Holt on December 19, 1967, he met with the Australian cabinet in Canberra. As detailed in his book, *The Vantage Point*, he was asked about Vietnam and writes, "I was certain Hanoi was under great pressure to gain some kind of victory and that I foresaw the North Vietnamese using 'kamikaze' tactics in the weeks ahead, committing their troops in a wave of suicide attacks. I was convinced Hanoi was in no mood to negotiate, and that such gestures as a bombing halt would produce no results until the planned Communist offensive was launched and blunted. Then, I said, they might be willing to talk."

From Australia, Johnson flew to Thailand, then Vietnam and finally westward across India with a stop in Pakistan for a brief meeting with President Ayub Khan. Air Force One, followed by a Pan Am flight of beleaguered staff and press, was barreling toward Vatican City where Johnson wanted to meet with Pope Paul VI to discuss the war. Showing apparent little regard for diplomatic courtesies and protocol, or the duties of a Pope at Christmastime, Johnson also expected helicopters and limousines to be waiting for him when he landed in Rome.

We first heard of this secret trip during a briefing at Randolph conducted by our commanding officer, Pete Rice. He told us he had just been notified by Jim Cross' administrative assistant, MSG Bill Gulley, that we were to immediately get helicopters prepped and onto a cargo plane for the President who had just left on a secret world mission.

The kicker? Even *we* didn't know where we were going. The President didn't want any tip-offs and we didn't know whether to pack swim trunks or parkas. "Pack both," Rice told us. "We'll know more when we're airborne."

With no time to do any advance work, we were running around like bugs on a hot rock finding an available cargo plane, disassembling helicopters and lining up security and support personnel. I told CcCc, "This is why things are so screwed up in Vietnam. Johnson is managing the war the same way – by the seat of his pants."

We flew from Texas to a refueling site in New England, and then across the Atlantic to Terejon, Spain. We landed just ahead of a snow storm and were told to stand by for further direction. A day later, on December 23, we got a green light to fly into Rome, but the visibility at Terejon was below minimum and the Air Force planes refused to take off. It wasn't long until a direct call came in from Gulley at the White House Military Office ordering the pilot to "get those goddamn airplanes in the air."

Rumbling down the runway, I thought of the Convair crash in Texas several years earlier and wondered if we, too, were about to become casualties of Johnson's careless obstinacy. Thankfully, we made it to Rome and were offloading the helicopters just as word got to us that Air Force One was on final approach. Rice realized there wasn't time to assemble even one helicopter in time for the President, so he commandeered a Navy CH-34 with a pilot from a nearby U.S. naval base. Completely unfamiliar with Rome, a postcard hastily purchased from a gift shop with an aerial view of the city became a navigational tool for locating the Pope's residence. The flight blew down power lines, cutting off some of the garden lights. Making matters worse, upon landing, the helicopter uprooted a nearby flowerbed.

It was a colossal embarrassment, a huge waste of time and money, and made even more troubling by a general consensus that this whirlwind, high-pressure four-day gamble by Johnson had yielded no significant diplomatic breakthroughs for Vietnam. Anti-war sentiment at home and abroad only increased.

On March 31, 1968, President Johnson addressed the nation on television, announcing a partial halt to the bombing in Vietnam and the opening of peace negotiations. At the end of this speech, he shocked the entire nation and the world by announcing, "I shall not seek, and I will not accept, the nomination of my party for another term as your president."

The future of the Army's Executive Flight Detachment was – pun intended – up in the air. I had been looking for an opportunity to transfer out of the unit, but now thought it best to coast until a new president was elected and there was a stronger indication as to whether or not I would be the new senior pilot and commanding officer for the unit.

Four days after Johnson made his historical announcement he was in Washington, D.C., making final plans to go to Hawaii for a strategy session with U.S. and South Vietnamese military leaders. The same day, April 4, 1968, our unit and helicopters were on a cargo plane about an hour off the coast of California on our way to Hickam AFB to await the President's arrival when we were ordered to turn around.

Dr. Martin Luther King, Jr. had been shot and killed in Memphis, Tennessee. In the distance, the sun had just set on the Pacific horizon and I felt the promise of a gifted civil rights leader sink with it.

Because we had just refueled at the El Toro Marine Air Base in southern California, we were now too heavy to land. Consequently, we had to dump fuel over the ocean before returning to El Toro and wait for further orders. Upon approach, when the pilot dropped the landing gear, one wheel came down sideways. From inside the cabin, a mechanic pulled up a floor plate and went to work on the wheel mechanism as we circled. Once he thought he had it heading in the right direction, we diverted some 400 miles north to Travis AFB, which was better prepared for an emergency landing. We touched down smoothly and turned our attention to King's assassination.

Johnson spoke for us all that evening when he addressed the American public. "I ask every citizen," he said into the television cameras, "to reject the blind violence that has struck Dr. King, who lived by nonviolence...."

But intense fury and anguish sparked devastating riots from coast to coast. Upwards of 20,000 people stormed through Washington, D.C., neighborhoods, looting stores and burning buildings and homes. The deadly riots came within two blocks of the White House and Johnson ordered some 13,500 federal troops into the area to help local law enforcement halt the violence and destruction.

The year 1968 was well on the way to earning its standing as one of the most deadly and turbulent years in American history. For me, it was anguishing to watch a country becoming its own worst enemy and appear to be deepening its racial divide.

Ironically, that very month, the Texas White House helicopter unit welcomed its first black pilot and the man who became my closest lifelong friend, CW4 Carl Burhanan. In Vietnam he had flown one of the first Sikorsky CH-54 Skycranes to operate in a war zone. Able to lift artillery and aircraft heavier than its own weight, the flying crane was considered the biggest and most powerful helicopter in the world. Before Vietnam, Burhanan had also flown in Europe and for the Alternate National Military Command Center, an underground Pentagon facility near Ritchie, Maryland. Without question, he came to Texas with an impressive history and number of flight hours.

He also came with a warning from what he called "higher up."

"Remember," said his superior, "if you're flying the First Lady or the President's daughters, do not offer your hand to them unless they first reach out to you."

Burhanan took the directive in stride, but knew if a woman was not helped in or out of a Huey they were likely going to fall. So, regardless of etiquette or skin color, he took his chances with Lady Bird and always extended a hand, allowing her the option of his assistance. While she never failed to accept Burhanan's offer, Lady Bird never said, "Thank you." That detachment was an ingrained Johnson trait. Neither Burhanan nor I can recall a single instance where the President, Lady Bird

or their daughters uttered even the slightest expression of gratitude to any of us flying helicopters for the First Family.

As Johnson began preparing to leave office, activity on the
airstrip at the ranch picked up considerably. C-130s made frequent trips to unload cargo into the hangar behind the house.
Those of us watching from a distance could only speculate as to
what was on board. Fragments of stories reached us about
White House furnishings and artifacts, but I honestly had no
concerns about any improprieties until Johnson ordered us to
provide helicopter support for former President Eisenhower,
who was on some kind of archeological dig near Twentynine
Palms, California.

At first, the mission seemed straight forward enough – fly to
the Palm Springs Airport and stand by as a personal taxi for use
as needed by Eisenhower, who lived with his wife Mamie less
than two miles away. I had greatly enjoyed flying Ike with
Walter Cronkite five years earlier in France during the filming of
D-Day Plus 20 and was honored to have a second opportunity. I
lifted off with a crew of three in a Huey UH1-D from the LBJ
Ranch on the last Saturday of April 1968. We had stopped to
refuel in El Paso, Texas, when I got a call from Gulley at the
White House.

"Where are you?" he demanded. "I just got a call from the
President and you're supposed to have that helicopter in Palm
Springs tonight."

"I was told the mission starts in the morning," I explained,
"but I'll be there in a few hours. What's the problem?"

"Ike had a heart attack this morning."

For a few short seconds, I couldn't breathe. Even though I
knew Eisenhower had suffered a major heart attack back in the
middle 1950s, I was having difficulty imagining anything taking
down a man of his stature.

As soon as I got to Palm Springs, I telephoned Eisenhower's
aide, General Robert Schultz.

"How is he?"

"Critical," he answered, "but they think he's going to make
it. He's at March Air Force Base."

"How can we help?"

"Well," he said, "you probably have heard Mamie won't fly."

"Yes, I have."

"So I guess for now, you could do a mail run every morning," he directed, "and stay parked somewhere near the hospital in case you're needed."

Mamie had a suite near Ike at the hospital. After we brought in their daily mail or restocked Mamie's personal supply of champagne, my crew and I hung out in a private room where we watched TV and waited for instructions from Schultz. None of it made much sense until one afternoon, he revealed why Johnson wanted the former president to have a helicopter.

"Ike didn't ask for one," Schultz said, explaining the President had offered Eisenhower a small jet and a helicopter to set a "perk" precedent so he could have the same services set up at the ranch after he went out of office. "We turned down the fixed-wing," Schultz continued, "but took him up on the helicopter for a few weeks just to placate him. We'd have been just as happy to hire a local one to fly out to the dig."

Apparently, Johnson had also contacted Harry Truman with the same offer and Truman turned him down flat.

About three weeks later Eisenhower was strong enough to be transported to Walter Reed Army Medical Center in Washington, D.C. A few days before his departure, Schultz told me Eisenhower wanted to see me.

"What about?" I asked.

"I'm not sure," he said. "Just go on up."

When I arrived at Eisenhower's room on the fourth floor the door was open and he was surrounded by several beautiful nurses. Looking fragile and pale, but with a crafty grin on his face, he was in a robe and slippers standing near a window.

"Major Boyer," he said, "I really appreciate you being out here."

"Thank you, sir."

"And as you can see, I like having the best looking nurses around me."

That was an understatement, I thought, smiling along with the small crowd of giggling young women.

"Now, I'd like you to do me a favor," he said, reaching for a small camera on the bed table. "I want you to take these girls

for a ride in your helicopter for about twenty or thirty minutes, then come back here and hover outside the window so I can take their picture."

It was one of the choicest missions ever assigned to me and we followed Ike's directions to the letter. That same group of nurses also accompanied him on an Air Force hospital plane back to Washington, D.C. Mamie took the train. Sadly, the former Supreme Commander of the Allied forces in Europe and the 34th President of the United States suffered more heart attacks and eventually passed away ten months later on March 28, 1969.

Not long after I returned to the LBJ Ranch, the Democratic front-running presidential candidate, Senator Robert F. Kennedy, was shot on June 5, 1968, at the Ambassador Hotel in Los Angeles after declaring victory in the California primary. He lingered until the next morning before he died. The news burned like a deep wound and all I could think was, "What on earth is happening?"

Out of Sight 8

Johnson always liked company, and one day I got to ride with him in the presidential helicopter. After sprinting several yards to get to the chopper on what was a breezy day, I settled myself into my seat. Johnson took one look at me, took a comb out of his pocket, and handed it over. "Here," he said. "Comb your hair. You're a mess."

– Helen Thomas

By the summer of 1968, I had yet to be cleared by Exec Flight Commander Colonel Pete Rice for a check flight in the VH-3A and had given up hope for any change in the situation. Then, quite by accident, I finally got my chance. Like many unplanned developments at the LBJ Ranch, the rule book got thrown out the window.

I was at home in San Antonio one afternoon when fellow Exec Flight pilot Keith Borck telephoned from his home not far away.

"Major Boyer, Rice just called," Borck said. "He wants us to rent a car and drive up to the ranch to stay with the helicopters so he can take the car to some bash in Austin."

"You know I'm not current," I said.

"The President's in residence for the night," he said, "so don't worry about it."

Borck and I got the car and made the 45-mile trip to the ranch. After we parked at the community trailers, Rice and a warrant officer hopped into the car like two fraternity boys on a Saturday night and sped off. Borck was a tall, lanky man with an understated farm boy way about him. We had barely sat down for dinner with the standby flight engineer and a mechanic when from out of nowhere we heard Johnson's voice come in over the White House net, "Get me my helicopter."

Borck and I looked at each other and burst out laughing. This was going to be interesting. Even though Rice had a radio with him, he was too far down the road to call him back to take the

flight in time to satisfy Johnson. I had flown the President before I went to Vietnam, but was technically ineligible now since I hadn't requalified in the VH-3A. Borck, on the other hand, was one of Rice's regular co-pilots. The recipient of the first Distinguished Service Cross for Bravery in Vietnam, he was seasoned and capable. Without discussion, we knew we were up to the task. Flying a twin-engine VH-3A was definitely safer than the single-engine Huey, not to mention we didn't want to risk catching royal hell from the President and a possible return trip to Vietnam if we showed up in anything less than the best helicopter.

An anxious aide called, demanding, "Get a helicopter over there now and pick him up."

CW-4 Keith Borck and I (right seat) on duty in Texas
(Boyer Family Archives)

"Over where?" I asked.

"He's at Judge Moursund's ranch playing dominoes."

"Where the hell is that?" I asked, realizing it was pitch dark outside and silently inventorying the more than 30 landing sites scattered through the hills around the ranch. Most were hard to find in the daytime, so we routinely did flyovers when the President was away to increase our familiarity. Even then, all the ranches looked alike with random clusters of scrub oak, endless barbed wire fences and intermittent power lines.

"I think I know," Borck offered.

"We're on our way."

At more than 100 mph, Borck drove us in a government sedan down the airstrip to the hangar by the President's house. As soon as he slammed on the brakes, I jumped out, ran to the steps of the helicopter where the flight engineer was waiting, and then stopped.

"Which seat?" I asked Borck.

"Hell, take the pilot's seat."

Jesus. I was about to have my long-awaited check flight with the President of the United States on board. Time to fly again like nothing could touch me.

We lifted off and after a glance at our time and distance sheet, Borck said, "Just head east. It's about 15 miles. I flew over it once. There's a lot of scrub oak, some fences and power lines."

"Thanks," I mocked, at least grateful the cattle were bedded down this time of night.

Without knowing it, I flew near enough to the highway for Rice to see the VH-3A flying in the distance. Rice later said he had heard the call on the radio, stopped the car for moment, but drove on thinking, "Boyer better be able to either fly that helicopter or not live through a crash."

Even though Albert Wadel "A.W." Moursund, in his middle 40s, no longer practiced law, everyone still called him the Judge. As tall as the President, but without an ounce of fat, he co-owned real estate with the Johnsons and was the principal trustee of all their land, cattle, radio and television holdings. Rarely visible, he stayed in constant communication with the President by

either radiophone or a direct line to the White House. Like any upstanding Texan, he was rumored to have a six-shooter in the glove box of his Lincoln and a rifle under the front seat.

We managed to ease our way down into a pasture west of the Judge's house. Johnson quickly boarded along with about six other people. They were in high spirits, laughing and talking, and helping themselves to the galley bar at the back of the cabin. The passengers included a Louisiana senator, a Minnesota businessman and two Secret Service agents, one of whom was Clinton Hill, the agent who had jumped on the back of President Kennedy's limousine seconds after he was shot in Dallas. Anyone who has viewed the tragic footage of the assassination will remember how former First Lady Jackie Kennedy crawled onto the trunk of the car toward Agent Hill who managed to climb aboard, move Mrs. Kennedy back into the seat next to her mortally wounded husband and shield them both with his body as they sped to the hospital.

The flight back to the ranch went smoothly and, using Borck's words, I "greased the landing." We shut down the engines and I slipped off my headset, expecting our passengers to disembark. Nearby, an empty golf cart waited for Johnson. The cabin had transformed into a cozy lounge and no one seemed to even notice we had reached our destination. The flight engineer dropped the forward door and was soon standing at attention at the bottom of the steps. Agent Hill took his position just outside the helicopter. A Marine aide also stepped out and motioned up to me and Borck to cover our ears, just as Johnson's voice rose above the buzzing conversation behind us.

"I don't know if I can vote for Hubert," he blurted. "I know he's my vice president, but he's one dumb son-of-a-bitch. God dammit, I just might have to vote for Tricky Dick."

Now Hill was motioning for us to cover our ears, at the same time stifling a grin. I realized Johnson probably had no idea any other pilot but Rice was at the controls, but one thing we all counted on was if something bad happened when Johnson was drunk, he wouldn't remember the next day. On the other hand, if he was sober, he could send someone packing with a wave of his hand. The night of my check flight, Johnson was smashed, so I was safe. He stumbled badly getting off the helicopter, staggered into the golf cart and promptly rammed it into the front of the helicopter before zipping off toward his house.

Now, even more amused, Hill was demonstrating to us how to cover our eyes.

I couldn't believe any of it. My God, I thought, this is the President of the United States, the leader I served in Vietnam, the most powerful human being on earth and I'm just supposed to ignore all of this?

As soon as the last passenger disappeared into the night, Borck turned to me and said, "We have to agree on two things: We never repeat a word we heard as long as the man is alive and you're now current in the VH-3A."

"Got it," I said, tempted to disclose I had recently changed my party affiliation from Democrat to Republican in time to vote for Nixon in the primary. Instead, I adhered to one of our unspoken creeds to not discuss personal politics.

As check rides go, this had been a dilly and I wager the only one in history to have on board a sitting POTUS (President of the United States). Had it been any other president, I would have followed regulations and flown the mission in a Huey and not a helicopter I hadn't piloted for two years. But confident in our abilities, Borck and I took the risk rather than test Johnson's volcanic temper.

In the final months before the 1968 election to select either Vice President Hubert Humphrey or former Vice President Richard Nixon as our next president, Chief Justice Earl Warren announced he would retire from the Supreme Court. Concerned that Nixon might become president and fill the vacancy with a more conservative justice, Johnson scrambled to fill the vacancy and wanted his longtime friend and colleague, Associate Justice Abe Fortas. Twenty years earlier, Fortas had played a significant role in convincing U.S. Supreme Court Justice Hugo Black to overturn a ruling related to corruption charges by Coke Stevenson, Johnson's senatorial opponent.

A top-ranked Yale scholar in 1933, Fortas hailed from Memphis, Tennessee, and shared many of the same politically progressive viewpoints and sensibilities as Johnson. That close

relationship attracted strong scrutiny by others and forced Johnson to spend countless hours in Washington and at the ranch strategizing and lobbying for the appointment.

One weekend during the summer of 1968, I was on duty at Bergstrom with Burhanan when flight operations called. Abe Fortas and his wife were coming in and Johnson wanted us to fly him to the ranch without anyone seeing us, especially the press. This required us to fly very close to the ground and follow the undulating terrain – otherwise known as contour flying. The Fortas nomination was controversial because, as a sitting justice, he maintained a close "insider" relationship with the President, which, among other issues, many viewed as a breach of confidence between the executive and judiciary branches.

Contour flying was fun for pilots but a rugged ride for passengers tolerating what can be compared to being adrift in high seas.

"I can't believe they're making us do this," Burhanan quietly said to me as we were preparing to lift off. "There's nothing out there but cattle, deer and all of Johnson's friends."

"Doesn't matter," I said, not the least bit tempted to amend a Johnson directive. "That's the mission."

Once the judge and his wife were comfortably on board, we left Austin, swung north of Highway 71 and "got down on the deck" for the 30-minute flight. About halfway to the ranch, Fortas got on the intercom.

"I don't know what the hell you think you're doing," he protested, "but you're scaring the life out of my wife."

"I'm sorry, Mr. Fortas," I explained, "but I'm under orders by the President to make sure nobody sees us."

That was the end of our conversation. However, on the return trip, I decided to "hide out" at 2,000 feet, which I'm sure Mrs. Fortas appreciated.

Not long after his visit to the ranch, following a strenuous Senate confirmation hearing, Fortas asked Johnson to withdraw his name from nomination. After being elected president, Richard Nixon instead nominated Warren E. Burger to be the new Chief Justice of the United States, and he was easily confirmed.

I remember reading about Johnson withdrawing the Fortas nomination and feeling an odd sense of amazement at his failure to manipulate a desired outcome. He was a Goliath among men when it came to making deals and getting his way. He was also equally adept at not getting caught in what I considered extreme behaviors unbefitting a president entrusted with public funds and confidence – the reason I will always hold Johnson in contempt.

One experience in particular stands out.

I was sitting in the dark on the steps of the presidential helicopter at about 2:00 a.m. My crew chief was asleep in the President's chair and the co-pilot was stretched out on the bench seat. We had been parked in a stinking cow pasture for hours on one of Johnson's ranches near Granite Shoals. He and several friends were socializing in the main house about a half mile away and I was trying to figure out how in the hell I had ended up here. It was hot, we were hungry and tired, and so far had managed to not step in any cow pies on our way to relieve ourselves behind a nearby tree.

I was a major in the United States Army and for the first time in my military career I didn't feel as though I was serving my country. I was serving the personal whim of Lyndon Johnson at the expense of my country. And there wasn't a damn thing I could do about it without cutting my own throat.

The glimmer of car lights flickered through the trees and I shouted to my crew to wake up. I stepped into the darkened cabin just as Johnson rolled up in his Lincoln convertible with one of his longtime business associates and a woman friend.

"You take her back to Austin," he said to the man and then elaborated on the quality of her unique personal services.

They all chuckled, then the man and woman got out of the car to board the helicopter and Johnson drove off in a cloud of dust. We dutifully flew the couple to Bergstrom, dropped them off, and headed back to Randolph to get some rest and try to forget what just happened.

Of course, it was impossible to forget such incidents. Whenever I gather with fellow pilots, flight engineers and mechanics from the White House days, the Johnson stories roll like a hit parade.

"Remember," someone says early on, "how Johnson hired those seven new secretaries and at least two could type?"

Then there was the flight where, after realizing the air conditioning had gone out on a VH-3A, Johnson went to the back end of the cabin hoping to find an axe so he could chop out a window for some fresh air. Luckily, there was no such tool on board.

Another time, upon landing, Johnson asked a Secret Service agent to get a "cold" Dr. Pepper to take with him. There weren't any cans in the fridge, so the agent asked the flight engineer to help out. He quickly located a can, poured it into a glass of ice cubes and took it to Johnson at the bottom of the helicopter steps. The President took the glass and promptly dumped the soda and cubes onto the ground.

"I wanted it cold in the goddamn can, boy."

One of our favorite stories came from a mechanic at the LBJ Ranch who was asked by Major Rice to unclog a toilet in one of our trailers.

"Major Rice," responded the mechanic, "they've got a plumber down at the main house. Why can't we use him?"

"No," Rice said, "I don't want to bother them. You handle it."

The mechanic went to work on the pipe leading from the trailer to the septic tank, spilling sewage onto the ground in the process. From over his shoulder he heard someone say, "What are you doing down there, boy?"

The mechanic turned around to see the President standing behind him.

"Pipe's plugged, Mr. President."

"Why don't you use the damn plumber we got down at the house?" he said, and moved on.

Shortly, the mechanic went back into the trailer to see Rice.

"Who were you talking to out there?" Rice asked.

"The President."

"Really," Rice replied, stunned. "What did he say?"

"'Why don't you use the damn plumber at the house?'"

Rice relented and Johnson, contrary to his usual standing, was the hero of the day at the community trailers.

Among the most memorable visitors for me to the LBJ Ranch was General William Westmoreland, commander of military operations in Vietnam until the summer of 1968, when Johnson replaced him with General Creighton W. Abrams. Westmoreland went on to serve as U.S. Army Chief of Staff from 1968 to 1972. A confident man with a striking profile, he was instrumental in developing key U.S. strategies in Vietnam and advocated fighting a war of attrition to wear the enemy down. Johnson was reluctant to supply the troop numbers essential for that objective, fearing the consequences of expanding the war into Laos, Cambodia and China. He took a more moderate approach and hoped somewhere a viable window would open to negotiate with the North Vietnamese.

I flew Westmoreland to one of his last meetings with Johnson at the ranch before the General was relieved of his command and the President left office.

While the two men met at the main house, I waited with my crew in the trailer for a call to transport the General back to Randolph AFB where he would continue on to his next destination. We were told Westmoreland was on a tight schedule and the meeting wouldn't last long. As one, then two, and finally three hours passed, I grew concerned – not because I had anyplace special to go, but because the weather was starting to turn foul. "How does it look?" I asked when I telephoned the Randolph tower.

"Weather about five hundred feet," was the response. "A mile visibility."

No problem as long as we left soon.

We waited 30 more minutes and there was no sign of the General, so I called again.

"How does it look now?" I asked.

"Three hundred and a half mile."

I called an aide at the main house to tell them we needed to get moving if we were going to beat the weather in San Antonio. Within minutes, Westmoreland rushed on board the Huey and we took off. For about 20 miles we flew without contact with Randolph because the hills between the ranch and the base blocked communication.

Then, after several attempts, we connected.

"Right now, weather is below minimum," they reported.

"How much?" I asked, cursing the fickle Texas sky.

"Zero-zero."

"Damn. What about Austin or Dallas?"

"Bad and expecting to worsen."

Initially thinking the mission was a simple pick-up and quick return, I hadn't refueled the Huey at the ranch. Consequently, we had about an hour-and-a-half worth in the tank and were now flying in pea soup.

Hoping to find a break in the visibility, I told the tower at Randolph we were coming in and holding on their beacon. Next, I asked them to turn their strobe lights up for us to make a low approach. At least the clouds were now illuminated.

"Okay," responded the tower. "We'll get the crash trucks out there. Who do you have on board?"

"General Westmoreland."

"Oh boy...."

"I'm turning final," I reported at 3,000 feet and about five miles from the runway.

Then, we heard the General's voice over the intercom: "How bad is it?"

"Visibility isn't very good," I answered calmly. "We're going in low."

"Okay," said Westmoreland without the slightest hint of concern. In that moment, we were just two soldiers – one was doing his job and the other one was staying out of the way.

Holding at about 60 knots, we began a 500-feet-per-minute descent. Once we were about 150 feet above ground with a 15-mile-per-hour wind on our nose, we slowed to about 30 miles an hour and eased downward, still not able to see a damn thing. Finally, the skids hit the runway and we slid about 40 feet, sparks flying, before coming to a complete and blessed stop. I looked at my co-pilot and we both just shook our heads. This was one for the books.

"You down?" asked the guy in the tower.

"Yeah," I answered.

"Everybody okay?"

"I think so."

"Can you taxi?" he asked.

"Hell no, I don't have wheels on this thing and I still can't see shit," I said. "Just get a jeep out here for my passenger and another one for me to hover behind so I can follow it off the runway."

The pat I felt on my back was the hand of General Westmoreland.

"I've flown in a lot of helicopters and that was something."

"Thank you, General."

"Did you learn how to do that in Vietnam?"

I nodded, but I really wanted to say my best training had come from flying half blind in the middle of the night around the Texas Hill Country scrounging for cow pastures.

Westmoreland was forever known as the general who "won every battle but lost a war." Years later, when asked about his perspective regarding Vietnam, Westmoreland was quoted as saying, "Vietnam was the first war ever fought without any censorship. Without censorship, things can get terribly confused in the public mind."

True enough. Different from WWII or even Korea, the Vietnam War had daily reports from the field and political strongholds. Televised images of American casualties streaming into the public consciousness shortened their patience and heightened their expectations regarding U.S. leadership and policy. By the summer of 1968, three-and-a-half years after the troop build-up began, a majority of ever-growing skeptical Americans believed the war was a mistake. Even though Johnson left a commendable legacy of legislative advancements related to, for instance, civil rights, fair housing and space exploration, his deteriorating credibility related to the war in his final year forever contaminated those accomplishments.

As much as I believed in our military superiority, the courageous resolve of our forces, and our rationale for being in Vietnam, I knew if Johnson was managing the war and international relations anything like he was running the LBJ ranch, we were not in good hands. I had watched too many people bleed and die in Vietnam and, for the life of me, it was getting harder and harder to justify those losses.

Many of us who had tours in Vietnam, Korea or even WWII were unavoidably offended every time Johnson referenced his own military service or the small Silver Star pin he always wore

on his left lapel, signifying an act of heroism. Rarely did he appear in public without the pin. It is visible in virtually all photographs from his White House years and even when he was taking the oath of office after Kennedy's assassination, standing beside the grieving wife of a fallen president who had an undisputed distinguished military service record.

The Silver Star is the third highest recognition for heroism, just beneath the Medal of Honor and the Distinguished Service Cross. It is rare and not awarded lightly. According to Johnson biographer and historian Robert Caro, "...it is surely one of the most undeserved Silver Stars in history, because if you accept everything that he said, he was still in action for no more than 13 minutes and only as an observer. Men who flew many missions, brave men, never got a Silver Star."

Johnson's brief military experience began just days after the Japanese bombed Pearl Harbor on December 7, 1941. Congressman Lyndon Johnson volunteered as a commissioned officer in the Naval Reserve. Considered a Roosevelt protégé, now Lieutenant Commander Johnson was asked by the President in the spring of 1942 to travel to the Southwest Pacific Theater and report back on combat conditions. After checking in with General Douglas MacArthur in Australia, Johnson boarded a "battle-scarred" B-26 Marauder on a hazardous bombing mission to observe an attack on a Japanese airbase on the island of New Guinea.

Accounts vary as to whether or not the bomber, the *Heckling Hare*, with Johnson on board, actually came under fire before the generator that controlled the right engine failed and they turned back. The other bombers continued on and encountered heavy enemy fire from Japanese fighter planes. Several men were wounded and one B-26 was shot down. Its entire crew died. Of those aboard the *Heckling Hare*, Johnson was the only one awarded a medal.

For what?

For being there and doing nothing?

Among the Army pilots and crew members at the LBJ Ranch there were multiple Distinguished Flying Crosses, Air Medals and Bronze Stars. Johnson's experience was laughable compared to, for instance, that of Keith Borck.

Official Army records detail how, after his helicopter had been shot down, "...he evacuated the crew to a rescue helicopter. As the helicopter attempted to take off, it was too damaged by intense automatic weapons fire which wounded all the crew members... Borck voluntarily and bravely exposed himself to the automatic weapons fire while administering first aid to his wounded comrades. Then, as a second helicopter returned to affect the rescue, it was struck by recoilless rifle fire and crashed... Borck dashed through intense weapons fire, reached the downed aircraft and, while exposed to the onslaught, tore out plexiglass panels and extricated the crew. For three hours they lay in a wet, muddy rice paddy under constant sniper fire. When hostile strafing prevented a third aircraft from affecting the rescue, he led the men to a more protected area and organized a perimeter defense until an aircraft finally succeeded in effecting their evacuation."

The official military write-up for Johnson reads: "...While on a mission of obtaining information in the Southwest Pacific area, Lieutenant Commander Johnson, in order to obtain personal knowledge of combat conditions, volunteered as an observer on a hazardous aerial combat mission over hostile positions in New Guinea. As our planes neared the target area they were intercepted by eight hostile fighters. When, at this time, the plane in which Lieutenant Commander Johnson was an observer, developed mechanical trouble and was forced to turn back alone, presenting a favorable target to the enemy fighters, he evidenced marked coolness in spite of the hazards involved. His gallant action enabled him to obtain and return with valuable information."

Guys from the trenches had their idea of heroism and Johnson didn't make the cut. We came to the conclusion that MacArthur wanted more support for "his war" from Washington, D.C., and Johnson knew a military honor could help advance his political aspirations. Regardless of the motives, the recognition was viewed as an insult to every soldier who had genuinely earned such an honor – dead or alive.

In hindsight, I suspect our objections related to Johnson's Silver Star would have faded into the woodwork if he hadn't exploited the situation by wearing the pin every day he put on a suit. Admittedly, it did take some guts for Johnson to get on a bomber in the first place, but a real act of real courage would have been for him to get on that same plane a second time. Instead, Johnson returned to Washington, D.C., and relayed details to Congress about the deplorable conditions of the U.S. military in the Pacific, as well as the pressing need for more troops and equipment. He was subsequently made chairman of the Naval Affairs subcommittee in Congress.

A fitting example of Johnson's brand of personal entitlement occurred when I was sitting in the cockpit of one of five helicopters at an airport waiting to transport Johnson and a large entourage, which included the White House press corps. I looked out to see the President walking toward us. We were the number two helicopter on that mission. Army One was parked just beyond us. I caught the attention of my crew chief.

"Let the President know this isn't his helicopter," I told him. "He's flying with Rice."

The crew chief nodded and hurried down the steps to greet Johnson.

"Mr. President," he said, "this isn't your helicopter."

Johnson paused mid-stride, gave him an icy glare and said, "Son, they're all my helicopters."

Standing behind Johnson was UPI reporter Helen Thomas. Known as the "dean of the White House press corps," she was a small, spunky woman and one of our country's most respected journalists. Thomas stifled a smile as we all watched Johnson change direction and head to Army One.

I liked Helen Thomas. She began covering presidents in 1960 with Kennedy and was still on the job when President Barack Obama held his first White House press conference. But unfortunately, in the summer of 2010, some candid comments she had made about the Palestinians and Israel hit the Internet. Her remarks created such controversy that she announced her retirement. Thomas also expressed her regret for having made statements that did not reflect her true beliefs. Regardless, I am among many who will always admire her resilience and determination to fearlessly ask our Presidents the hard questions throughout the last fifty years. How tough was she?

I was in Army One watching Air Force 1 arrive at Homestead and taxi into position for President Nixon to disembark, glad hand a few dignitaries, and then board the helicopter for us to fly him to his home. Members of the press had come in on an earlier flight and when Air Force One appeared to have stopped, several rushed toward the front of the plane. Thomas, however, took an alternate route down the side and around the back just as the pilot gunned the engine to move a few more feet forward. She was blown ass over teakettle.

Someone hollered over the radio for Air Force One to shut down. Before anyone could get to Thomas, she had gotten back on her feet, smoothed her skirt, and marched on to get as close to the President as she could. She probably got the scoop she wanted that day, but we know what part of the story didn't make it into print.

On August 6, 1968, at the Republican National Convention in Miami, Florida, Richard Nixon was nominated for president over California Governor Ronald Reagan and New York Governor Nelson Rockefeller. Maryland Governor Spiro Agnew was selected as Nixon's vice presidential running mate.

"When the strongest nation in the world," Nixon said in his acceptance speech, "can be tied down for four years in a war in Vietnam with no end in sight; when the richest nation in the world can't manage its own economy; when the nation with the greatest tradition of the rule of law is plagued by unprecedented lawlessness; when a nation that has been known for a century for equality of opportunity is torn by unprecedented racial violence; when the President of the United States cannot travel abroad or to any major city at home, then it's time for new leadership for the United States of America."

Three weeks later, all hell broke loose at the Democratic Convention held in Chicago on August 29, 1968. Thousands of antiwar protestors gathered in Chicago to send a message to Vice President Hubert Humphrey who was viewed by most as an extension of Johnson. Mayor Richard Daley dispatched nearly

12,000 police officers and some 7,500 National Guardsmen to keep the demonstrators away from the convention site. With television cameras rolling, enraged protestors clashed with police as they tried to make their way to the International Amphitheater. Bombed with tear gas and beaten back with billy clubs, more than 500 marchers were arrested. Countless people were injured, including bystanders, the police and guardsmen, and several members of the press.

The 1968 Democratic National Convention in Chicago reflected a nation that had reached a boiling point. Humphrey addressed the convention in a futile attempt to calm that rage:

"What we are doing," he declared, "is in the tradition of Lyndon B. Johnson who rallied a grief-stricken nation when our leader was stricken by the assassin's bullet and said to you and said to me and said to all the world: 'Let us continue.' And in the space of five years since that tragic moment, President Johnson has accomplished more of the unfinished business of America than any of his modern predecessors. I do believe that history will surely record the greatness of his contribution to the people of this land. And tonight, to you, Mr. President, I say: Thank you, thank you, Mr. President."

President Johnson did not attend the convention.

One of my last assignments for the LBJ Texas White House was to make a test flight to the roof of the newly constructed Federal Building in Austin's financial district. The exterior of the 162-foot-tall structure resembled a concrete Belgium waffle. Johnson had chosen its top floor for his new 2,100-square-foot executive office, complete with a plush bedroom, dining room, fully equipped kitchen and bullet-proof glass windows. The bathroom had a large marble shower with four showerheads and a wash basin with an embossed presidential eagle and gold-plated faucets.

Just outside the office entrance, near the elevator, was a stairway to the top of the building where Johnson wanted access to come and go in a helicopter. My first thought when I walked onto the roof to survey the surface area was, "This is going to be tight and tricky."

Fortunately, there were no other tall structures in the immediate area. But landing on top of a building, as I had learned during my brief career with New York Airways eleven years earlier, was a lot different than setting down in a field or on a runway. There was far less room for error. A heavy load, a warm day, a gust of wind or simply the unknown could spell disaster. I still had imprinted in my memory a film I had watched in the mid-1950s of a Bell helicopter lifting off from the top of the New York Port Authority. Either an extension power cord or tie-down cable had not been detached and within seconds the helicopter jerked to a stop, the nose dropped, the line snapped and the aircraft plummeted to the ground below, killing all on board.

The roof above Johnson's office was sturdy enough, but the four-foot-high wire mesh guardrail around the perimeter was a safety impediment. If a skid caught in the railing, a helicopter would instantly tip forward and fall helplessly to the earth. All around the building was a bustling city and less than two miles to the northeast was a municipal airport. Given the prevailing winds and air traffic patterns, approach and especially lift-off from the Federal Building was not as simple as it might look.

I made my test flight in a Huey on a clear, windless day. Coming in at 300 feet and not too shallow, I had little room to maneuver. I sat down where I could do a maximum performance takeoff to clear the railing before I was out of ground effect. This translated into using all available power to perform a rapid climb while keeping the air speed down, until I cleared the edge of the building, dropped slightly and then settled before increasing my speed to 45 knots to build altitude. Once I got to 1,000 feet, I dumped the nose and kicked it up to 120 knots to fly back to Randolph.

My recommendation to 4th Army Flight Detachment was simple: "If I were in charge, the Federal Building would not be an option."

I don't know if or how much that helipad was ever used by Johnson. Of course, the office, appropriately decorated in multiple shades of dollar-bill green, saw a lot of traffic. In 1999, the building itself was named after former Democratic United States

Representative from the 10th congressional district of Texas, James Jarrel "Jake" Pickle. A self-described LBJ Boy, Pickle held the seat once occupied by Johnson from 1963 to 1995.

Shortly before the 1968 presidential election, CeCe and I, along with all the other military personnel and White House Communications staff, received invitations on White House stationery, reading: "The President and Mrs. Johnson hope you can join them for an evening fiesta at the LBJ Ranch."

Billed as an appreciation barbeque Texas-style, the outdoor dinner took place at the LBJ Ranch the day after Nixon was elected the 37th President of the United States. CeCe and I arrived at 6 p.m. on the dot and were soon circulating among the some 200 guests awaiting Johnson's arrival.

As parties go, the atmosphere at this gathering drifted from polite chit-chat to idle conversation. In other words, for many of us on that mild fall evening, no matter how loud the mariachi band played, no matter how delicious the food, no matter how strong the cocktails, it was a flat fiesta.

CeCe and I were sipping drinks when Johnson and Lady Bird finally arrived on the scene dressed in casual Western wear. They were smiling and upbeat, shaking a few hands here and there, urging people to enjoy themselves and thanking them for their service. Johnson didn't stay around long enough to make it to the outer fringes of the group where we were standing.

It all felt very hollow to me and when I looked at CeCe, she read my mind and we left.

As we exited the gate and drove onto the narrow concrete weir to cross the Pedernales River, I marveled at how so many of us had spent so much time at the LBJ Ranch without even a handshake from our boss. However seemingly insignificant, General Mason in Korea, General Eisenhower in France and, most recently, General Westmoreland, had all demonstrated they knew such gestures mattered to the rank and file.

I never wanted to set foot again on the LBJ Ranch.

The day Nixon was inaugurated, he allowed Johnson to use Air Force One to fly back to Texas where his minions promptly stripped it clean. Nixon's pilot, Col. Ralph Albertazzie, wrote in his book, *The Flying White House*, that he couldn't believe his eyes when he got the plane back and it was nothing but an "empty larder" Everything was gone – the presidential china personally selected by Jacqueline Kennedy, the silverware, stemware, ashtrays, cigarettes, napkins, towels, blankets, and pillows. None of the items had Johnson's initials or name on them. Rather they were all marked as belonging to Air Force One. Even his special executive chair had been unbolted and taken away.

Now a multi-millionaire, Johnson left the White House with more loot and exit perks than any president in history and because of how he had exploited the Army's White House helicopters, the future of the Exec Flight could not be predicted.

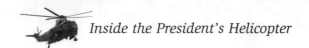

Glory Missions 9

I like to believe that people in the long run are going to do more to promote peace than our governments. Indeed, I think that people want peace so much that one of these days governments had better get out of the way and let them have it.
— President Dwight D. Eisenhower

Even though I had voted for Richard Nixon, much to the disappointment of my father, I was not a fan. In 1968, I would have voted for Mickey Mouse if he were running against a Johnson Democrat.

"Nixon is a crook," my father, now 64, grumbled over the phone.

"I hate to tell you this, Dad," I answered, "but I'm beginning to think they're all crooks."

My parents were now living in Santa Maria, California, north of Vandenberg Air Force Base where my brother, Major Dick Boyer, was stationed with his family and overseeing the construction of Atlas missile sites around the country. Like many new retirees, our parents had abandoned Ohio's harsh winters and stifling summers for sunny southern California. Mom was thrilled to be near her grandchildren and Dad, to keep from climbing the walls, was working at a service station where he could tinker with cars and mess with tires.

By the time Nixon, code-named "Volunteer" by the Secret Service, was inaugurated on January 20, 1969, CeCe and I were still not clear what the Army had in mind for newly promoted Lieutenant Colonel Boyer and the White House Executive Flight Detachment. Everyone at Randolph wondered if the Military Office would order the Pentagon to deactivate the unit and assign the entire mission to the Marines HMX-1 unit at Quantico, Virginia. Four main factors, we hoped, would keep our operation alive: Nixon planned to travel a lot, Army pilots

had more individual flight time than the Marines, our pilot pool was much larger, and we had the most rapid deployment experience for global mobility. Known as "glory missions," these assignments required extensive advance work and mechanics who could partially disassemble a helicopter, pack it on board a cargo plane and then reassemble it for use at various overseas destinations from Thailand to England, Peru to Egypt, and Vietnam to Italy. On average, it took eight hours to disassemble a VH-3A and eleven hours to reassemble. If pressed, we could cut that time in half.

Should the White House decide to keep the Army unit, I was counting on an executive or maintenance officer position, or perhaps that of an instructor pilot. But my highest hope was lodged in becoming the new commanding officer. Rice, as all Army pilots eventually did at the time, was headed to Vietnam, so I thought I was a likely candidate to replace him. That hunch was confirmed when I received orders from Nixon's military assistant, Air Force Colonel Don Hughes, the last week of February to command Nixon's first international trip. The new president wanted to introduce and establish himself as a world leader, and I was determined to prove our unit was up to a task of such magnitude. We all knew Colonel Hughes was paying close attention.

A native New Yorker, Hughes graduated from West Point in 1946 and was assigned to the Army Air Corps, which became the U.S. Air Force one year later. By 1951, he had flown 101 combat missions in jet fighters over Korea and was awarded two Distinguished Flying Crosses, nine Air Medals and the Purple Heart. In Vietnam, he had been an instructor pilot for the South Vietnamese Air Force. Most recently, he had earned a master's degree in international affairs from George Washington University. Hughes was seasoned and smart, and had an authoritative, even-keel manner of communicating. Like General Mason, he would rank as one of my most respected superiors.

There is a longstanding rivalry between branches of the armed forces. Within the White House presidential helicopter fleet in 1969, the tension between the Army and the Marines vacillated between good-natured competition to outright loathing. The Army criticized the Marines for being elitists and the Marines charged us with having no class. We were the grunts and they were the cream of the crop. They were stationed in Washington, D.C., and we were still stuck in Texas. However, in the spring of 1969 and staffed with the best pilots to survive Vietnam, the Army began to earn its way back to Washington, D.C., the hard way – through Vatican City, Nixon's first global mission.

It had been barely a year since the Johnson trip fiasco that had intruded on the Pope's Christmas and ravaged his flower garden. At least I knew what a bad mission looked like.

It became abundantly clear we had a new administration in charge when the White House Military Office notified us of Nixon's trip to Europe three days before we had to leave, gave us an itinerary of the President's schedule, and provided enough information for us to know what kind of clothing to pack.

Parkas.

During the next two days, I selected a crew of 15 mechanics and nine pilots for multiple missions in London, Bonn and Rome. We prepped all three VH-3As and loaded them on two C-5As along with helicopter spare parts, including blades and an extra engine. Both planes were safely on the ground at Heathrow International Airport in England by Saturday, February 22, 1969. The weather was cold and dismal. Once we offloaded and reassembled the helicopters, we took each one up for a five-hour test flight and then sent one to Bonn, Germany, for a meeting later that week.

Nixon flew directly from the States to Brussels, Belgium, where he met with King Baudouin. He later addressed the representatives at the new NATO headquarters, which had moved from Paris in 1967 after President Charles de Gaulle ordered SHAPE and NATO out of France. Also traveling with the President on this trip were Secretary of State William Rogers and National Security Advisor Henry Kissinger.

Our first mission was to fly Nixon about 35 miles west of Heathrow to Chequers for dinner with Prime Minister Harold Wilson. The twelfth-century country estate was England's equivalent to Camp David. By the time Air Force One arrived in

London, the visibility had slipped below minimum and we were unceremoniously grounded by the infamous, enveloping fog.

"I'm sorry," I said to Hughes when he came on board the helicopter, "but we'd never find the place in this fog."

"Don't worry about it," he said, "you can't control the weather. We're putting together a motorcade. See you in Rome."

A tall, lean man with a crew cut in his early 40s, Hughes had been Nixon's military aide when he was vice president and had been with him during the riotous visit to Venezuela in 1958. He was not easily rattled – another indication we had a new administration.

As soon as Nixon was officially greeted by Prime Minister Wilson with full military honors and their motorcade had disappeared into the gray mist, I caught a commercial flight to Rome to make advance preparations for the next two missions. We had one put-down location at the Piazza Quirinale, the residence of Italian Republic President Giuseppe Saragat. The second landing site was St. Peter's Square for an audience with Pope Paul VI.

While I walked each area during a blustery morning on February 25, looking for potential obstacles and determining where to place the half dozen helicopters in the flight, my crew was flying our helicopters in from London. We had also picked up a C-130 from a U.S. air base near Heathrow to transport our spare parts. In the meantime, Nixon had taken Air Force One to France to meet with de Gaulle before he flew to Rome.

The Piazza Quirinale sat atop the highest of the seven hills in Rome and, with a 20-foot-tall obelisk, a fountain and two horseman statues at its center, the space was cramped but adequate. St. Peter's Square is a massive expanse of cobblestone with an even higher obelisk at its center. Located in front of St. Peter's Basilica in Vatican City, the square was suggested as a landing spot by the city's governor general since "recent rains have softened the gardens." During my meeting with him and other officials, including our Secret Service, he didn't hesitate to remind us of Johnson's "unforgettable" trip.

"Are you aware of the visit by your former president?" he asked tactfully.

"Yes, I am," I answered, feeling a flush of embarrassment.

"We were assured your helicopters would not cause any damage if we allowed them to land in the gardens," he continued, leaning forward to hold my attention, "and, as a result, we had a series of, let's say, unusual incidents. We won't have a repeat of that, will we?"

"No, sir."

We exchanged slight, all-knowing smiles.

A U.S. military aide quickly added, "We will land on the spot where we have drawn an X and will not do any damage."

Just as I thought all was going like clockwork, the White House communications people forwarded me an urgent message. Mid-way to Rome, one of the helicopters had picked up ice and ingested a large chuck into an engine, causing it to fail. They had managed to land at a French Air Force base, so we diverted the C-130 to that base to deliver our back-up engine. With the generous help of the French military, our crew swapped engines and was again airborne within four hours.

Army One, Piazza Quirinale , Rome, Italy, February 28, 1969
(Courtesy of Richard Nixon Presidential Library, NARA)

Army One, first helicopter landing in St. Peter's Square
Vatican City, Italy, March 2, 1969
(Courtesy of Richard Nixon Presidential Library, NARA)

Hughes flew with us on both missions in Rome. I especially remember that March 2, 1969, flight into St. Peter's Square with the President and his entourage on board while more than 25,000 people watched. It was a first for any helicopter and as if to make sure we didn't blow even a speck of dust off the ancient statuary or even ruffle the feathers of a single pigeon, Hughes stood at my left shoulder as we gently sat down.

"That's fine," he said, before disembarking.

A few hours later, I sat in the cockpit beneath a darkening sky and watched Nixon and the Pope emerging from the Papal Palace with a small crowd of officials, aides and members of the press. As they approached the helicopter, I caught sight of the previously stern governor general who looked up at me and grinned with welcome approval.

Lifting off, I was surprised by how heavy the tail had become, now loaded with presidential gifts from the Pope – several large crated oil paintings. But the greater concern hit when a flurry of flash bulbs exploded beneath us and, there within a stone's throw of the most powerful religious figure on earth, I thought to myself, "Jeez, I hope those are all cameras and not small arms fire."

With the Vietnam War threatening to burst through neighboring borders, scattered European anti-war protestors managed to dog Nixon wherever possible on the week-long tour. Back in the States, civil unrest was taking root on college campuses across the nation. If Nixon was going to have any impact on world and domestic affairs, he needed as many allies as possible. And fast. I got the sense he had forged some valuable connections on this trip and could only hope, for all of us, that this momentum translated into a more cooperative and peaceful world.

We flew Nixon to Fiumicino Airport where Air Force One was waiting to take him back to Andrews and our two C-5As were waiting for us to pack up for our trip back to the States and a new mission waiting in California. Following Nixon off the helicopter, Hughes ducked into the cockpit.

"Congratulations," he said. "You did a good job."

"Thank you, sir."

"You know what this means?" asked Hughes.

"I think so," I answered, proud as hell of every Army grunt who had busted ass with me on this trip.

"Okay, you'll be hearing from me. We're going to keep you very busy," he said before giving my shoulder a quick tap and hurrying off to Air Force One.

It didn't take long for me to connect by phone with CeCe.

"I saw you on TV," she said excitedly. "You were landing in St. Peter's Square."

"Yeah," I said, downplaying my own jubilance, "it went okay."

"Well?"

"Well what?"

"Do you know if you get—"

"Yes," I told her. "I got it."

CeCe cheered for us both and I felt like I was about to fly across the Atlantic through a sky full of cloud nines.

Because Nixon had a residence in Key Biscayne, Florida, the White House Military Office ordered our unit to relocate to Homestead AFB, located about 20 miles southwest on the Florida mainland. CeCe and I moved to base housing that spring, just 200 miles away from her mother who was now living in Sarasota. We were all glad to be closer to her, especially Robin who, at age four-and-a-half, loved the extra attention only a grandmother can give. When I contacted my parents to give them the big news, my mother was instantly elated and my father, ever the self-proclaimed fountain of wisdom, reminded me, "Don't let it go to your head."

As the new commanding officer of the Army's White House Exec Flight, my immediate responsibilities were to select people I wanted to go with me to Homestead. There we would maintain seven helicopters – three plush VH-3As, three Hueys and a CH-3A we swapped for the Loach we had to leave behind for Johnson's use. Among the nearly 20 pilots I asked to stay in the unit were Borck and Burhanan, as well as three other outstanding pilots. All were decorated combat veterans and hailed from Minnesota, Wisconsin, Alabama and two from Pennsylvania. Major Bill Shaw was confident, methodical and always had a cigar handy to chew on. Always reliable CW4 Bobby Bruce was a rotund cheapskate with a crackerjack sense of humor known for wearing the worst ever thrift store clothing. At age 42, and meticulous to a fault, CW4 Leroy Brendle was our oldest pilot and always delivered.

These five master aviators were just a sample of the many sharp, seasoned and dedicated men I relied on to fly with me in the coming years. We were a mixed bag united in duty, each with an average of 4,000 helicopter flight hours accumulated during the previous 15 years. It remains my supreme honor to have served with them on the battlefield, at the LBJ Ranch and for Nixon and Ford in Washington, D.C.

By coincidence and not because I just went to the top of some list, all of us had last names that started with a "B," except for Shaw. But he was still a fit since his first name was Bill. Maybe we were part of a cosmic force: the first pilot to fly a president from the White House to Camp David and back during "Operation Alert" was Air Force Major Joseph Barrett; the first Army pilot to land at the White House was my ever-studious Fort Sill classmate CW4 Ray Bowers; and in Vietnam, I had commanded not the A or C Company, but the Army's B Company, 228th Aviation Battalion.

Following suit and also new on the scene was Marine Major Jack Brennan, one of Nixon's military aides along with Army Lieutenant Colonel Vernon Coffee and Navy Commander Charles (Chuck) Larson. Under the direction of Air Force Colonel Hughes, all three rotated duty aide assignments and had a number of responsibilities that included military asset support for the President, mission logistics and caretaking the ever-present "football" – a small briefcase that held a series of briefing books and other critically sensitive material essential to making decisions in a crisis such as a nuclear event.

A few years younger and slightly shorter than I, Brennan was born in Massachusetts and graduated from Providence College in Rhode Island. Intelligent, shrewd and dedicated, he was a decorated Vietnam veteran and was promoted to major on the "temporary" list to fill the Marine Aide slot in the White House Military Office. We first connected at El Toro Marine Corps Air Station in Santa Ana, California, in March 1969, to advance a helicopter landing site adjacent to the San Clemente residence Nixon was about to purchase.

What became the Western White House was a ten-room, Spanish-style mansion that sat on about 15 acres above one of the West Coast's premier surfing beaches. Named "La Casa Pacifica" by Nixon, it was located next to a U.S. Coast Guard Station midway between Los Angeles and San Diego with world-wide radio, navigation and communication services. The Marine Corps' Camp Pendleton was ten miles to the south and El Toro ten miles to the north.

After a dinner getting to know each other and outlining our reconnaissance plans, Brennan and I drove to the Coast Guard Station where he picked up the phone at the gate to speak with an unsuspecting petty officer in a nearby office building.

"Hello?" answered the officer.

"Yes," said Brennan, "there are two of us here. Army Lieutenant Colonel Gene Boyer, the President's helicopter pilot, and myself, Major Jack Brennan, Marine aide to the President. We're here to inspect your facility."

"Is that so?" he responded, unimpressed. "Listen, I think you *two* better get out of here."

Brennan continued, explaining that President Nixon was due out to survey progress on the clean-up of the Santa Barbara oil spill and was also interested in moving into the estate next door. Now convinced we weren't jerking his chain, the petty officer came out to check our identification and allowed us through the gate. Once inside the nondescript 20-acre facility, Brennan pointed out a large area with a softball field. It was close to a masonry wall separating the lackluster station grounds from the stately dwelling on the other side.

"What do you think?" asked Brennan.

"Perfect," I answered, certain the space could handle several helicopters.

"Okay," Brennan said turning to the bewildered petty officer. "We'll be bringing five helicopters in here in two days."

"I can't authorize that," the guard stammered. "You'll have to talk to my admiral."

"No problem," Brennan replied, demonstrating in the span of about ten minutes the impressive power of the White House Military Office.

The quiet little Coast Guard installation was about to change dramatically. Within months, two large pre-fabricated administration buildings with offices and sleeping quarters were under construction with a golf cart path leading from the President's new office to his home. A new chain-link perimeter fence was built with manned posts, surveillance security cameras were installed and roving armed patrols were on constant duty. A few key Secret Service agents and other White House personnel were lodged on site. Other staffers and the press were dispersed among local hotels and motels. One continuously available helicopter remained at the Coast Guard station on emergency standby for immediate evacuation of the president if necessary. The rest of us, along with the Air Force One crew, stayed at the "always happening" Saddleback Inn on Main Street in Tustin, just north of El Toro.

The day after we visited the Coast Guard station, Brennan and I continued to reconnoiter on the ground preparing for the Santa Barbara mission. Meanwhile, Burhanan was in the air charting coordinates and landmarks for the President's route the next day. The plan was to pick Nixon up at the Point Mugu Naval Station and then fly Army One about 20 miles northwest up the coast to circle the still-seeping offshore oil derrick before landing on a Santa Barbara beach. There, Nixon would meet with petroleum company officials for a briefing on the oil spill – the most devastating of its kind to date and so catastrophic it would definitively launch the environmental movement. The following year, in 1970, the nation celebrated our first Earth Day.

Because my parents lived near Santa Barbara, I called to tell them I had gotten them clearance to come to the beach where they had a chance to meet the President of the United States.

"Are you kidding?" my father, the ex-union organizer snapped. "Why would I want to meet that SOB?"

They didn't come and I was disappointed, feeling much like I would if they had failed to attend one of my high school football games. I had to admit I was more interested in them seeing me in action as the President's pilot than I was in having them meet Nixon.

After the Santa Barbara landing at the beach, we then transported Nixon about 150 miles back down the coast to San Clemente. Unnoticed by the throng of reporters traipsing after Nixon on March 2, 1969, was an historical first for the White House helicopter fleet – CW4 Carl Burhanan was my co-pilot and the first African American aviator to fly a president. Historical significance aside, we both had our eyes on the weather that day. Heavy rain was engulfing the unfamiliar coastline and visibility was down to a half mile. We were grateful

My favorite co-pilot, CW-4 Carl Burhanan,
the first black pilot to fly for the White House
(Carl Burhanan)

to have two local Marine helicopters, even though we could not see them, leading the way to San Clemente.

"We're getting close," Burhanan said to me as he intently watched the ground below and then checked in with one of the Marine helicopters. "Have you guys landed yet?"

"We have not reached our destination," was the terse reply.

"Then you passed it," Burhanan told them.

"Carl," I said, dismayed, "these guys live here."

"I got it handled," he said, then pointed out a small wharf appearing through the haze below. "Okay, start your turn."

"You're sure?"

"Right here," he calmly assured.

"Okay."

Within seconds we were over the Coast Guard's softball field and setting down. By the time the Marine helicopters turned around and came in to land with the rest of the President's party, Nixon was already off to tour what would be his new home. It was one of several days Burhanan and I would reflect upon for the rest of our lives. We had had a perfect mission and a black man had flown in the cockpit of Army One for the first time, a monumental, unrecorded accomplishment at the height of the civil rights movement. But perhaps most memorable of all, a president had taken time to notice two no-name pilots and say, "Thanks for a nice flight," on his way out the door.

Unknown to me in 1969 and during our five-and-a-half years together at the White House, Brennan was looking for a way to, in his words, "get rid" of the Army's Exec Flight. He revealed that objective in a September 15, 2008, interview with Jonathan Movroydis for the Nixon Foundation Archives, explaining that his reasoning was based on first learning when he arrived at the White House in 1969 that there were Marine helicopters in Washington, D.C., and Army helicopters in Texas that Johnson used for flights between the ranch and Austin.

In the Movroydis interview, Brennan wrongly indicated it was somehow up to him, and not the Military Office Director, to decide the future of what he called "that little organization," saying, "Oh my God, what the hell do I do with them and why are they there?" Brennan also falsely credited the Marines and not the Air Force as the first military branch to fly a president and provide White House helicopter support.

Watching that interview, knowing Brennan had flown on Army One countless times – including what I consider to be our toughest White House flight in Peru – I was shocked by his disdain for the Exec Flight. Even more astonishing to me, was hearing that he had actually submitted paperwork, early in Nixon's first term, to Army Chief of Staff General William Westmoreland recommending our unit's deactivation. Brennan stated that Westmoreland "went to the President and said I (Brennan) was trying to destroy the morale of the Army."

Whether true or not – and I do question Brennan's authority to have submitted such a request – I was oblivious to his intentions while I was at the White House. Instead, during that time, I felt genuine appreciation for what I considered sincere support from Brennan and all of the military aides with whom I served. Had I known what was underfoot, I would have questioned more, assumed less and fought harder for the Army.

To be fair, it probably goes without saying that in our line of work no one ever felt secure or completely comfortable on a landscape that was always shifting and moving. We all had to pick our battles, navigate the politics, and walk that fuzzy line between carrying out assigned missions and working personal agendas at the same time.

The Key Biscayne residence Nixon purchased in Florida was an unremarkable concrete block, ranch-style home without enough land for a helipad. So the Department of Defense built one over the water on pilings. As I had with Johnson, I was realizing more and more that presidential security and convenience spared little expense and heeded few objections. The boundary between the abuse of power and public funds was not well-defined. Still, there was an obvious difference to me between what Nixon and Johnson perceived as presidential necessities. For example, Nixon selected residences conveniently located near military installations. Johnson created a secluded, quasi-military operation at his own ranch. Nixon got temporary helipads and Johnson got a permanent airport.

The "Florida White House" was a five-house compound with space for the Military Office, Secret Service and other government services. In addition to Nixon and his family, controversial friend Charles "Bebe" Rebozo, the son of a Cuban cigar maker and owner of the Key Biscayne Bank, also stayed at the compound. Multi-millionaire industrialist Robert Abplanalp, inventor of the aerosol can spray valve and resident of Grand Cay, Bahamas, was an occasional visitor.

On March 28, 1969, President Dwight D. Eisenhower lost his

valiant battle with heart disease and died at the age of 78 at Walter Reed Army Hospital in Washington, D.C. One of the most admired men in American history, Eisenhower was a brilliant, decisive and courageous leader with an uncommon streak of humility and, as I had personally experienced in Palm Springs, a healthy sense of humor.

During Eisenhower's state funeral in Washington, D.C., Nixon delivered a poignant eulogy. Not far away, Ike's friend and WWII ally, French President Charles de Gaulle, towered over international dignitaries like a human monument to WWII. On April 1, Mamie, ever the skittish flyer, accompanied her husband's body by train back to his family home in Abilene, Kansas.

A second funeral service for the 34th President of the United States was held in a small chapel near the Eisenhower Library before burial in the nearby Place of Meditation crypt. Even in death, Eisenhower communicated his respect for the millions of troops once under his command by selecting the same $80 government-issue casket that had held the remains of so many fellow soldiers.

Former presidents Harry Truman and Lyndon Johnson flew into Salina, Kansas, as did hundreds of prominent government leaders and heads of state from all corners of the world. Between Salina, Fort Riley, and the Manhattan and Kansas City airports, there were at least 50 helicopters shuttling dignitaries. Luckily, the weather was clear. We had issued a routine "NOTAM," or "notice to airman in the area," that there was a five-mile, 5,000-foot secure zone around the funeral site, so there were no unrelated aircraft to contend with.

As soon as Air Force One landed in Salina with the President, Mrs. Nixon and their party, we flew them the final 12 minutes to a huge, fallow wheat field about 100 yards from the chapel. As the ceremony got underway that crisp morning, my crew and I stayed with Army One. Parked near several other VIP helicopters and their crews, we were sharing a pot of coffee with several Secret Service agents when the drone of a single-engine Cessna caught our attention. A small, definitely unidentified plane was coming in to land. Once on the ground, it was swarmed by Secret Service who soon had all five passengers out and searched.

I hurried onto the scene to discover three crying children, a terrified young mother and a ghostly-white Kansas farmer. I had spent enough time in the Fort Riley region years earlier to recognize they were local innocents and not a threat.

"Didn't you get the NOTAM?" I asked.

"The what?" he stammered.

"Never mind," I said, realizing he had likely taken off from a private airstrip behind some barn.

As the Secret Service checked his I.D. and combed through the plane, I tried to calm the family by asking, "So, where are you folks from?"

"Kansas," he nervously said, as the children's sobbing began to subside. "Northeast Kansas. We just wanted to come in and pay our respects."

I felt horrible for them and as soon as I got an all-clear sign from one of the Secret Service agents, I decided the kids might like to see the inside of a helicopter. Their tears dried up and they beamed with anticipation as we walked to one of the helicopters – not the President's. Smiles really broadened when we gave the children some wrapped candy and their parents a few packs of presidential cigarettes and Army One matchbooks. I also wrote each of the kids' names on official seating cards for them to take as souvenirs.

When we went back to their plane, an agent discreetly asked me, "Now what? They're parked in your way."

"So let's unpark them," I said, "and let them go."

"I don't know," he pondered. "We should use them to set an example."

I gave him a questioning look, he shrugged, and the family was soon happily scrambling back on board their plane. I lost count of how many times they said, "Thank you," and thought I had made the right decision to let them go until I realized the guy had been in such a hurry he was taking off downwind.

Damn it.

The doomed little plane was rolling at full speed over the bumpy field well past the point it should have lifted up, getting closer and closer to a grove of trees directly in its path. We all watched helplessly as it bounced along. If I hadn't told him to leave, they would still all be standing here alive and not about to crash.

Then, as if straight from the Jerry Columbus flight school back in Ohio, the agile little aircraft staggered upward, barely cleared the trees and disappeared into the distance.

If anything had happened to that family, I would have never forgiven myself.

Never mind probably losing my job.

Back at Homestead AFB in Florida, base operations was doing its best to accommodate the arrival of our unit. Major Morgan, a young Air Force special actions officer with Hollywood good looks, was assigned to me as a liaison to help us settle in. The base had cleared a hangar for Air Force One and another, next door, large enough for all our helicopters. Located north of the east-west runway, we had an operations room with a direct line to local weather and an area with several bunks.

Additional air support for the President was provided by a top secret aircraft called the National Emergency Airborne Command Post. Even more sophisticated than Air Force One, it was able to stay aloft for extensive amounts of time by being refueled in flight. Rarely in sight, the airborne facility was in constant touch with whomever was flying the President with designated emergency evacuation plans and landing sites for each mission.

I often caught sight of Homestead personnel watching us come and go, and wondered: What were they thinking? Was the Exec Flight an unwelcome intrusion? A welcome distraction? Or maybe just a novelty act? One way or the other, we had done a bang-up job of disrupting business as usual, so one evening I called CeCe and told her I would be home late. We invited Major Morgan to join a few of us at the officer's club for some drinks.

"This one's on me," I said, buying a round for him and my crew at the bar.

"Thanks," he said.

"We appreciate all of your help."

"No problem." Morgan answered, and then with a grin asked, "So what were you doing before you became such a hotshot?"

A couple of other curious Air Force officers listening nearby waited for my response.

"I was in Vietnam."

"Really? Doing what?"

"Flying helicopters," I said, knowing they were expecting me to describe some kind of cushy assignment.

"You get shot at?"

"Got shot down the first day out."

"Oh, great!" roared Morgan. "And now you're flying for the White House?"

We all laughed at my "shortcomings" and I knew the months ahead were going to work out fine between the Air Force and the Army. The first chance I got, I took Morgan, who had flown F-4 fighter jets in Vietnam, on a short helicopter flight and he shared an opinion that meant a lot to me:

"You know, I'd never given much thought to you Army pilots," he said. "I mean, we are the *Air Force,* but now I think these damn things are harder to fly than any jet I've ever been in."

In the spring of 1969, Nixon announced plans to meet with South Vietnamese President Nguyen Van Thieu on the tiny Pacific island of Midway the second week of June. The intent of this first conference between the two leaders was to discuss U.S. troop reduction and a strategy for their replacement by South Vietnamese forces. Nixon's soon to be announced "Vietnamization" program had provisions to diminish the role of U.S. military troops, to provide the South Vietnamese with more modern equipment and weapons, and to increase advisory assistance, shifting responsibility for defeating the Communists from the United States to South Vietnam.

Our unit shipped three Hueys to Hawaii for use by the President before and after his trip to Midway, about 1,300 miles to the northwest. On June 7, we picked up Nixon from Hickam AFB in Honolulu for transport to Waialea Country Club where he spent the night. The next morning it was back to Hickam for him to board Air Force One. The U.S. delegation consisted of Secretary of State Rogers, Henry Kissinger, Ambassador to Vietnam Ellsworth Bunker, Ambassador-designate Graham Martin and military contingents – one of whom was the Navy's

Commander-in-Chief of the Pacific Command, four-star Admiral John McCain, Jr.

The McCains had a long and notable legacy of military service. Admiral McCain's father had also been a four-star admiral and his son, then Naval Aviator Lieutenant Commander John Sidney McCain III, was currently a POW at the "Hanoi Hilton." Shot down during a bombing mission on October 26, 1967, over North Vietnam, he had been severely wounded upon ejecting from the aircraft. He parachuted into a lake and was pulled ashore by North Vietnamese captors who further beat him. McCain was a prisoner of war for five-and-a-half years. That horrific ordeal became the foundation upon which he later built a prominent political career as an Arizona Republican senator. In 2008, at the age of 72, he ran for president, losing his bid to Illinois Senator Barack Obama.

After meeting with President Thieu on Midway, Nixon and his delegation flew back to Hawaii. The next morning he led a two-hour debriefing at Camp Smith, a naval installation located inland about ten miles northeast of Hickam. Parked outside the pristine CINCPAC headquarters building on a graveled helipad, I stood by with Army One and a few other helicopters waiting to transport everyone back to Hickam.

A weird chain of events was launched when Navy aide Chuck Larson casually approached. Average-sized and clean-cut, Larson had been a classmate and best friend of POW John McCain at the Naval Academy in Annapolis.

"I had a meeting with Admiral McCain," he told me. "He wants to be on the President's helicopter for the trip back to Hickam and I didn't want to tell him he's on the number two helicopter, so I told him to talk to you."

"Why did you do that?" I asked with disbelief. "You know I can't do anything."

As the President's senior pilot, my responsibilities were many, including where and when to land, how we refueled, who guarded the helicopters and where my crew and I slept and ate. But the responsibility of the passenger manifest and seating arrangement came out of the White House. The last thing I wanted to figure out was the latest pecking order that determined who needed to be close to the President, who shouldn't sit next to each other, or who belonged in another helicopter. The challenge was a lot like a large family on a long trip in a cramped station wagon. I didn't care who got a window, I just wanted to drive.

"Listen," Larson continued, "a Marine general is going to come ask you if McCain can ride with you."

"You're kidding."

"Just tell him Haldeman is in charge."

"Why didn't you tell him that?" I asked, feeling like we were on some elementary school playground.

"I didn't want to be the one to piss him off," Larson confessed and walked on.

Sure enough, several minutes later, the Marine general drove up to the helicopter in a jeep. I had checked the passenger manifest and determined we did have one empty seat, but still, I had no authority to give it to someone, even if that someone was a four-star admiral.

"What can I do for you, sir?" I asked.

"Can you get the Admiral on the President's helicopter?"

"I'm sorry, General," I said, politely, "but I don't have the authority to make those decisions. I think you need to speak to Haldeman."

"I figured that," he answered, and sighed. "Okay, I'll let the Admiral know."

This is just great, I thought, as he walked away. I was now in the hot seat and hadn't done a damn thing to deserve it. No telling what kind of conversation happened behind the scenes, but it was clear I was the default culprit in the cockpit when I saw Nixon come out of the building. McCain, in a full white dress uniform and a good head shorter, was tagging along behind the President. Known for his feisty demeanor, the Admiral got the President's attention and then pointed up at me. Nixon followed his gaze with a quizzical look and then, upon boarding, asked me if there was room for one more. "Yes, sir," I said to the one and only person who could revise the passenger list on the spot.

McCain boarded, and flashed a smug little smile my way. I thought to myself, "Way to play it, Admiral. My hat's off to you, but my boot wants to plant itself on Larson's butt."

Moonglow 10

No event in American history is more misunderstood than the Vietnam War. It was misreported then, and it is misremembered now. Rarely have so many people been so wrong about so much.
— President Richard Nixon

I lifted my shirt so Nixon's personal physician, Dr. Walter Tkach, could take a close look at a small patch of reddish welts just beneath my ribcage.

"Does it itch?" he asked.

"Like crazy," I said.

"Looks like hives."

"Hives? I've never had hives," I countered and dropped my shirttail.

In his early 60s, Major General Tkach was the former Deputy Surgeon of Pacific Air Forces and had provided medical support to both Eisenhower and Kennedy. A bright-eyed, congenial man, Tkach stepped back and studied my face.

"You nervous about something?"

"Not at all," I replied confidently.

"Must be something you ate then," Tkach suggested.

"Must be."

After all, we were in Bangkok.

Tkach gave me an injection and twenty-four hours later, I was good as new.

Bangkok, Thailand, was the first stop on an around-the-world advance trip we were doing for Nixon, codenamed Moonglow, in honor of the Apollo 11 mission. Six months into his presidency, Nixon was getting hammered pretty hard by the media. Increased U.S. bombing raids were creeping across the Cambodian border. Protest groups were getting larger and bolder in their objections. Morale in Vietnam was plunging. Troop withdrawals were going too slowly. And the world was watching.

In part, intending to engage more support from U.S. Asian

allies to stabilize the Near and Far East regions, Nixon planned an 11-day trip that would begin with the Apollo 11 splashdown in the South Pacific on July 24, 1969. To prepare, he wrote two speeches – one if the return to earth from the first walk on the moon was successful and another if the mission ended in disaster.

The Boyer family had a special connection to Apollo 11. The space craft lifted off on July 16, Robin's fifth birthday. While Command Module Pilot Michael Collins orbited in Columbia above the lunar surface four days later, Commander Neil Armstrong and Lunar Modular Pilot Edwin "Buzz" Aldrin landed on the moon July 20, which was CeCe's birthday. Splashdown occurred on July 24, 1969, my 40th birthday.

I have yet to find a word to describe my emotions the day Armstrong took his "one step for man and one giant leap for mankind." The whole world had to be thinking if a man could walk on the moon, anything was possible. *Anything.* For our family of three, we could not have had better birthday gifts.

After the splashdown, Nixon was headed to the Philippines, Thailand, India, Pakistan and Romania. Several weeks before his departure, I joined a mission advance party of about 20 White House aides and officials aboard Air Force 26000, the Boeing 707 Nixon used as Air Force One. Included in the group was Colonel Hughes, Army aide Vern Coffey, Secret Service agent Bob Taylor, and Ron Walker, the principal advance man. It was the White House's A-Team, which led me to suspect something might be in the works for the President and First Lady to visit troops in Vietnam, but no one was talking.

We moved from one country to the next to inspect travel route options, scout facilities and make arrangements related to security, lodging, communications and transportation. At each destination, a small onsite team was left behind to coordinate details for upcoming ceremonies and meetings.

My checklist required locating a tested fuel source, a hangar with a heavy-duty crane able to lift helicopter parts for reassembly and scheduling guards for the helicopters. I also was responsible for surveying landing sites to make sure they could handle the rotor wash, documenting the safest paths in and out of those locations, and pinpointing the nearest hospital. If possible, especially with single-engine helicopters, we would avoid flying over heavily populated areas. If there were tall buildings or mountains, we increased altitude and performed near vertical ascents and descents to minimize vulnerability. And, of course, we flagged any obstacle like a church steeple, utility poles or the ever-hazardous wires. The scope of considerations was vast and complex, and would have taxed a unit twice our size, but I had confidence in my pilots and crew to get the job done and done well.

In New Delhi, after we took a break to visit the Taj Mahal, I came across a metal smith on the street tooling intricate designs into a large brass tray. The detail of his work was so remarkable I fetched an Army One matchbook from my pocket and handed it to him. Printed on one side was an illustration of the Army One helicopter and on the flip side was the presidential seal. Once he assured me he could reproduce the images, I ordered one for myself and a couple to give as gifts. A colleague at the U.S. Embassy shipped them to me several weeks later. I had one of the trays made into a coffee table which I gave to Nixon shortly after he left office in 1974.

One of the brass trays I had made in India. Exec Flight mechanics made one into a coffee table which I gave to President Nixon after he left office. Summer 1969
(Boyer Family Archives)

Lahore, Pakistan, in the middle of summer was a blast furnace. The asphalt at the airport was close to melting. The A-Team dragged itself through the heat of the day to accomplish a host of tasks only to find out the air conditioning at our hotel was not working. When offered the option to sleep outdoors on mattresses around the pool, we didn't hesitate to relocate. It took awhile to fall asleep in the suffocating air, but we finally managed and were all snoozing soundly when heavy banging noises jolted us awake at dawn.

What the hell?!

Several hotel employees were wandering around the outer perimeter of the pool pounding large metal dishes loud enough to wake the dead. But in this case, they had another purpose – to scare away thirsty cobras eyeing the pool water. I was glad we were sleeping in our clothes. It made it easier to get the hell out of there.

An even more bizarre experience occurred in Bucharest, Romania, where Nixon would be the first American president to make a state visit to a communist satellite country. A briefing officer at the U.S. Embassy told us to be careful as we moved about the hotel where Nixon would stay.

"Most of the people there," he warned, "work for the KGB."

Obviously, I thought, the Secret Service is going to be busier than usual.

After dinner I went to my room ready to sleep off another exhausting day. When I stretched out on the bed and looked up at the ceiling covered with thin wooden planks, I saw several small peep holes. When I stood on the bed to take a closer look, I could make out a camera lens through one of the openings.

When it came to spying, I concluded, the Romanian government could improve their technique. I smiled, waved, turned off the light and went to sleep.

Shortly after we returned to Washington, D.C., we debriefed Operation Moonglow at the White House Military Office. It did not take long to calculate the time-table was too tight to take helicopters beyond Thailand. Still, it was an ambitious mission, one I knew we could handle, and I couldn't wait to get back to Homestead to start packing.

However, before I left for Florida, Brennan, who had not been on the recon trip, approached me with an unusual proposition on behalf of HMX-1. Indicating to me that he thought the Exec Flight's plate was pretty full and the Marines had been pressuring him to do an overseas flight, he asked if I would do him a favor and include them on this trip.

The relationship between the Army and Marine White House helicopter units, especially since we were based about 1,000 miles apart, was best described as compartmentalized. Even though we had the same mission to support the President and White House activities, we had had few opportunities to collaborate and had established some distinctly different operating standards. The Army required at least 2,000 hours of flight time for a co-pilot. An aircraft commander had to have in excess of 4,000 hours. With so many experienced Army helicopter pilots coming out of Vietnam, we had an optimal pool from which to draw. The Marines did not have that advantage so their requirements were less demanding. Co-pilots needed only a few hundred hours and commanding pilots had to log 1,000 hours before taking the stick of a presidential helicopter. It wasn't until 2008 that that basic prerequisite changed to 2,000 hours.

All pilots – no matter from what military branch – agree there is no substitute for experience and the more the better.

White House pilots were expected to be able to fly day or night, in all weather and climates, over any terrain from sea level to mountain peaks. And we had to do it with unflinching confidence and a back-up plan waiting at our finger-tips. Meeting that challenge was a constant goal for both the Army and the Marines.

During my time at the White House, I frequently faced the dilemma of staying with the Exec Flight with little chance for promotion or moving on with assured advancement. For me, I chose to stay where I believed I was most needed and best able to serve. In that same time frame, HMX-1 cycled through four commanders. Two retired as lieutenant colonels, one as a full colonel and the last as a two-star general.

In 1969, the Exec Flight also had the advantage of the Army's unique Warrant Officer program, which produced the equivalent of professional pilots who were part of another system and not as pressured to transfer. Absent the academic background required for a commission, warrant officers functioned as technical experts. Our unit was composed of many decorated warrant officers who had flown in Vietnam and averaged about 3,000 hours each.

Regardless of rank, military branch or personal opinion, flying for the White House was an extraordinary privilege for all of us and there was no greater vote of confidence than having such a high-profile assignment. Consequently, when Brennan told me HMX-1 wanted to be part of Nixon's global trip, I understood the desire. Since Johnson moved the Army unit to Texas in 1966, the Marines had done little flying outside the D.C. area and eastern United States.

"Can they have Apollo 11?" Brennan asked.

Apollo 11 was the first manned flight to land on the moon. The launch from Cape Kennedy, Florida, was scheduled for July 16 and the splashdown in the South Pacific near Johnston Island for July 24. It didn't make sense to pull the mission from the Army unit, which was still stationed in Florida, but the last thing I wanted to do was contribute to friction between the Army and the Marines. If there was less competition and more coordination, I thought, maybe we could get more support at Homestead from the Military Office or, better yet, be moved back to Washington, D.C., where we could rebuild what Johnson had fractured.

"Okay," I told Brennan, "but I wouldn't worry about the take-off. We're right there and Nixon isn't going, just Johnson, but the Marines could fly the splashdown."

"Great," he said, brightening up.

"But there's a problem."

"What kind of problem?"

"They don't know how to tear down their helicopters for transport."

"What do you mean?"

I can still see the red flag that popped up the instant I realized Brennan wasn't as familiar with White House helicopter operations as I thought he was, but I waved it off. He was still learning and I wanted everyone to be happy.

"The helicopters have to be disassembled," I explained, "packed in cradles for shipment, then reassembled and test flown before we can fly the President."

"Yeah."

"I don't think they know how to do that."

"Really?" he said, looking surprised.

"Plus, the Marine helicopters don't have pop-out floats on the sponsons," I added, hoping the picture was becoming clearer, "and we have to fly about seventy-five miles over water."

Brennan fell silent.

"Listen," I reassured, "I think we can still do this, but your pilots will have to fly our helicopters. You have to get your crews down to Homestead now so they can observe and fly out with us. We'll be hauling ass after the launch to disassemble and pack up, then as soon as we get to Johnston Island, we'll reassemble for your pilots."

"Sounds good," Brennan replied.

In my eagerness to create a more positive relationship plus regain status for the Exec Flight, I may have unwittingly played into a Brennan agenda. Knowing what I know now about his desire to do away with us, I would have either flatly declined the request or I would have bargained, perhaps agreeing to include the Marines if Brennan would help upgrade our assets. But I was too much of a straight-shooter to think that hard.

The Apollo splashdown in the South Pacific on July 24, 1969, was a spectacular success. On board the recovery ship, the USS *Hornet*, Nixon was euphoric as he personally welcomed the astronauts who were quarantined in a small trailer. The joint Army-Marine operation to fly the President to and from the ship went off without a hitch and I could not have been more proud of how we had worked together.

On July 26, Air Force One landed in Manila where I piloted Nixon between the Presidential Palace and the Intercontinental Hotel that evening for a meeting with Philippine President Ferdinand Marcos. With the President safely tucked in for the evening, one of my pilots, Bill Shaw, went out for dinner and to do some sightseeing and souvenir shopping. After a couple of

purchases, he handed a dollar bill to a cashier not knowing it was counterfeit and was briefly taken into custody before the police were convinced he was not a thug and released him.

Back at the hotel, where our helicopters were under guard in a parking lot, I had just gone to my room when I heard two gunshots. I stayed put until a couple members of the Philippine Army came down the hall announcing everything was all clear. The most they revealed was that they had shot someone trying to sneak into the hotel. We couldn't be sure, but we had to assume someone was trying to get to Nixon. The story never hit the newspapers and we didn't hear any more details, but that incident, along with Shaw getting tangled up with the local police, quickly became secondary concerns as soon as we heard a monster monsoon was about to slam into us.

The next morning, before dawn, my crew and I scrambled like mad in a torrential downpour to get our helicopters and ourselves on board a C-141 to fly to Bangkok, Thailand, for the next leg of the trip. Once we had slogged onboard and the pilot had plowed through a foot of rain on the runway to lift off, I opened a small envelope Hughes had given me an hour earlier.

"Don't read this until you're airborne," instructed the colonel before hurrying off to join Nixon on Air Force One for their flight to Guam.

I quickly scanned the brief, neatly typed message on a single sheet of paper. I was to direct the pilot to divert our flight to Tan Son Nhut Air Base southeast of Saigon 1,000 miles away. Once on the ground, six people would deplane in civilian clothes: myself, a co-pilot and four of my best mechanics. In no way were we to display any affiliation to the President. The C-141 would immediately continue on to Bangkok with our helicopters and remaining pilots and crew. Navy aide, Chuck Larson, would be waiting to take us by car into Saigon for additional instructions.

Bottom line: President Nixon and the First Lady were headed to Saigon and would have helicopter support. I wasn't that surprised. Being so close to Vietnam, Nixon had to have been considering a visit. He was also intent on making public what became known as the "Nixon Doctrine," a declaration clarifying the United States would continue military and economic assistance to nations struggling against communism, but not again involve American troops in a ground war.

With less than three days to prepare, my first thought was how glad I was that I had been to Vietnam and knew my way around Saigon. My second thought? Even though the city was a relatively secure area with only sporadic enemy assaults, I knew the VC had infiltrated almost every South Vietnamese organization. And it hadn't been all that long ago that a VC mole had pulled a grenade on one of my flights out of An Khe. Plus, during Vice President Hubert Humphrey's visit to the presidential palace in 1967, four enemy mortar shells struck the newly built 95-room structure.

No one could or should be trusted. The palace was now an armed fortress with sandbags in every entrance. A successful mission boiled down to four elements: the right people, reliable equipment, ample authority and a strategic itinerary.

The only way for the C-141 to get clearance to fly into Tan Son Nhut that Sunday morning was to radio ahead that we had an emergency. This set into motion a lot of gyrations on the ground, the most prominent being that of a brigadier general who was in my face the second I stepped off the plane into the all-too-familiar dense, sweltering air.

"I want to see your idiot pilot," he roared. "He better have a damned good excuse for coming in here!"

"Sir, he was under orders."

"Whose orders?" he snapped, eyeing me up one side and down the other.

I leaned close and whispered, "The President's."

The general swallowed whatever he had planned to say next.

"I think you better look inside," I said, motioning to the open door behind me.

He stomped up the steps, stuck his head inside the plane, saw a presidential seal on the front of a helicopter and then turned back to me with a dumbfounded look on his reddening face.

"Any chance you can tell me what's going on?"

"No," I answered. "I'm not even sure myself."

An hour later my co-pilot, CW4 Roy Brendle, and our mechanics were checked into a hotel, and I was on my way to

a meeting at the U.S. Military Headquarters in Saigon. Besides Larson, the only other people who knew about the mission were Westmoreland's successor, General Creighton Abrams, three of his top officers, the U.S. Ambassador, South Vietnamese President Nguyen Van Thieu and a few of his senior officials.

The five-hour mission involved transporting Nixon to Di An, a farmland region about 18 miles northeast of Saigon where the 1st Infantry Division was stationed. While the President was with the troops, Mrs. Nixon would visit an orphanage and a hospital for U.S. wounded. Afterward, the Nixons would join President and Mrs. Thieu at their palace before returning to Air Force One and flying back to Bangkok and on to New Delhi.

We had two-and-a-half days to prepare, hopefully without tipping off anyone that the President was on his way. It was a little like trying to hide an elephant under a rug, but we managed, at least for awhile.

To begin, we needed five secure helicopters for VIPs and at least another three dozen to support the flights. This meant going "helicopter shopping." To disguise our true objective, we were each issued a Department of Defense civilian I.D. so we could pose as Army Maintenance inspectors. Our "inspection" team of six had grown to include two plainclothes Secret Service agents. Escorted by a colonel from Abrams's office, we were driven to the 45th Aviation Battalion in Bien Hoi just outside of Saigon where we met the battalion commander inside his tent. He had been told to expect "visitors" and greeted us with a cordial handshake.

"Hello, gentlemen," he said with a smile that soon faded to a quizzical look as the colonel reeled off a series of directions.

"Mr. Boyer is your boss for the time being," he explained, "and has the authority to order a stand-down until he's finished."

"Are you saying – "

"Yes, he's now commanding this battalion."

I could see the lieutenant colonel growing more suspicious by the second.

"All I need," I offered, hoping to ease the undercurrents, "is a tent and we can begin inspections right away, starting with your newest Hueys from the States."

"Why the newest?"

"We want to make sure," I said, with feigned conviction, "that the helicopters coming out of Fort Worth are meeting contractual assurances and we're getting what we pay for."

We all knew civilians didn't waltz in and take over a military operation, but also knew when to stop asking questions and obediently move on, which is exactly what we did. Once the battalion's crew chiefs, some of whom were just kids, realized we weren't there to criticize them, but rather to help locate threats to the safety and efficiency of their helicopters, we were given red-carpet treatment. Anyone who has ever been shot at understands how important it is to have every advantage going in. By the end of the day, we had inspected almost two dozen Hueys, noting here and there immediate maintenance needs.

That evening while Brendle and I were eating dinner with the battalion commander in the mess hall, a warrant officer strolled past our table, stopped and came back.

"Brendle?" he asked, peering closer. "What the hell are you doing here? I thought you were flying for the White House."

The two men had flown together in Vietnam a few years earlier.

Brendle looked at me and I looked at the commander who now had a dawning grin on his face.

"You want to tell me who you really are?" he asked.

Our masquerade at Bien Hoi was over, but the revelation did not diminish the task. If anything, as the word inevitably spread, it heightened enthusiasm and cooperation. During the next two days, we went over each helicopter inch by inch – one for the President, one for the First Lady, a third as a back-up and two others for additional VIPs. We cut half-inch ballistic blankets to fit around the seats and cover the floor to protect against small arms fire.

I test flew each helicopter for several hours and did extensive check flights with our chase pilots and the co-pilot who would fly the President with me. Brendle, who would transport the First Lady on a separate flight, did the same with an equally qualified aviator. Every pilot was outstanding and handled any curve we threw. We grilled them on suspected VC enclaves in the region and even made several low level passes to see if we could draw any fire. Nothing.

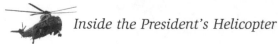

The morning of July 28, two days before the President arrived, I took a jeep into Saigon for a countdown meeting with Larson and the other designated officials at the Military Headquarters. I was expecting to see the same small group I had met with earlier, but instead, there were a half dozen new people in the room, including more South Vietnamese officers and a couple of Navy admirals.

As soon as I could, I took Larson aside.

"Why are all these people here?"

"They want to know what's going on."

I liked Larson, but sometimes it was hard to tell if he was just a good-hearted pleaser or an ass-kisser.

"It doesn't feel right," I told him. "Too many people know what we're doing. I think we should call Bangkok and talk to Colonel Hughes."

"You that worried?"

"We should take every precaution we can," I said.

"Okay," Larson replied, "let's call him."

Once Hughes understood the concern, he hopped on an F-4 and was in Saigon that evening. I suggested we follow the original itinerary until the last minute, and then reverse the order. Hughes approved and said he would notify the President and other passengers 30 minutes before they landed. I would call the audible with the helicopters about the same time.

Back at Bien Hoi in a hangar, I outlined the original plan to the some 100 pilots assigned to our mission, those who would be in the air holding the perimeter and those standing by on the ground. Around the hangar, I had stationed a platoon of MPs to make sure no one came in or out until the flight was completed.

"Just watch me," I instructed. "When I start my engines, you start yours."

Shortly before noon on July 30, 1969, against the insistent advice of the Secret Service to not go to Vietnam, Air Force One landed at the Tan Son Nhut Airport. Hughes let the President know there had been a "precautionary" change in plans, and he would later tell me Nixon took the news with an approving nod as did the Secret Service. I radioed the same course change to my pilots. If Nixon was a target, his exact whereabouts at any one time and in which helicopter he was riding had now become guesswork.

I first flew the Nixons in an unmarked Huey escorted by Cobra gunships over the crowded streets to the palace ten minutes away. There they and other dignitaries met with President and Mrs. Thieu. Fellow passenger, Henry Kissinger, would later recall how "we were whisked from the airport to the presidential palace in a helicopter that seemed to go straight up out of range of possible sniper fire and then plummeted like a stone between the trees of Thieu's offices. I never learned how many times the pilots rehearsed this maneuver or how its risk compared with that of sniper fire."

Kissinger was correct in assuming the vertical take-off and landing was a defensive tactic mastered by those of us who had flown in combat – especially those like me who had been shot down. However, he was not correct in assuming we had rehearsed the landing. I had visited the palace site on foot, saw it was a tight fit for a helicopter and knew the only safe way in

Escorting First Lady Pat Nixon in Saigon, Vietnam, an active combat zone
Bell UH-1D, July 30, 1969
(Courtesy of Richard Nixon Presidential Library, NARA)

and out, sniper worries aside, was straight down and up – a maneuver every helicopter pilot learns early in their training. If any of us had needed to rehearse that day, we didn't belong on the mission.

From the palace, where armed soldiers patrolled the roof and a swarm of helicopters had fighter jets circling above, Brendle flew Mrs. Nixon, along with a cluster of Secret Service agents and reporters, to the Thu Duc Orphanage. They then traveled to the 24th Evacuation Hospital about 20 miles north of Saigon where the First Lady visited wounded American soldiers, sometimes jotting down names and addresses so she could send a note to their families.

Meanwhile, with a sunlit sky teeming with chattering helicopters, I took Nixon on a flight north to visit the 1st Infantry Division in Di An where thousands of soldiers were waiting to greet him. We landed on an abandoned runway at about 4 p.m. Dressed in a blue business suit and tie, the President was accompanied by several dignitaries including General Abrams, Colonel Hughes, Henry Kissinger, Bob Haldeman, Ron Ziegler, Vern Coffey, and Bob Taylor. Members of the press darted about with cameras clicking away. The Secret Service was easy to spot, because they were the only ones not smiling.

Riding in an open jeep over hard-packed red dirt, Nixon spent about two hours in the area touring bunkers, guard posts and helicopter revetments. He awarded three Distinguished Service Crosses and trooped a line of men dressed in helmets and combat fatigues that was about a quarter-mile long. As soon as he got out of the jeep to mingle and talk with the troops a wave of excitement rippled through the hordes of men straining to shake his hand or just catch a glimpse of their Commander-in-Chief.

Everyone wanted to somehow brush up against the President, even the assistant division commander who commented to Taylor that Nixon could use his personal helicopter to fly back to Tan Son Nhut. I was in earshot of this discussion and imagined the general assumed the flight was using local pilots – so why not grab a piece of the action and make a little personal history?

"We have the safest and best crew in Vietnam," began the

President Richard Nixon with 1st Infantry Division, Di An, Vietnam,
July 30, 1969
(Courtesy of Richard Nixon Presidential Library, NARA)

general, "and we'd like the privilege of flying the President back to the airport."

Taylor politely introduced himself as the President's chief Secret Service agent and said, "Thanks for the offer, but that's the President's personal pilot over there and he's spent the last three days pulling this together. I think we better leave well enough alone."

The general nodded and mumbled something about how he was only making a joke. Regardless, I was grateful for Taylor's intervention and knew we had made a positive impression on him regarding our professionalism and the security of the mission.

Nixon left Vietnam elated. Haldeman noted in his diary that the President "was really taken by the quality and character of the guys he talked to, and by reaction really fed up with the protestors and peaceniks."

Getting out of the Vietnam War was on everyone's mind, but for Nixon, it was more about staying under different circumstances rather than a total withdrawal. He believed the United States had an undeniable responsibility to help non-communist countries willing to defend their independence. Knowing when and how much to help ease the struggle of other nations is a challenge that lands squarely on the desk of every president.

Combat deaths in Vietnam numbered nearly 35,000 in 1969, surpassing those killed in Korea. On April 24 of that same year, in our heaviest aerial raid yet, U.S. B-52s dropped nearly 3,000 tons of bombs on enemy positions near the Cambodian border. Two months later, Nixon announced that troop reductions would begin in August. For the men and women put in harm's way to fight for freedom and human dignity, I knew it helped to know our Commander-in-Chief had firsthand knowledge about what they were going through. Nixon's trip to Vietnam was not only good for the troops' morale, but for his as well.

Back at the Tan Son Nhut Airport, before he boarded Air Force One, Nixon thanked me for a good trip. Colonel Hughes also expressed appreciation and gave me a hodge-podge of White House souvenirs for the local pilots and crews in the flight. I wished I had had a crate full of medals instead of cigarettes, matchbooks, lighters and ink pens bearing the presidential seal to hand out, but no one seemed to care what I put in their hand. They might be walking away with a memory about being in a presidential flight, but I was walking away with immense admiration.

I felt tremendous relief watching Air Force One, bathed in the light of a setting sun, take off and bank to the west toward Thailand.

No major glitches. No damage. No hives.

And *no briefcase,* I discovered when I got back to the jeep where I had left my gear. I figured someone in the party had picked it up and it would eventually surface. Even though the paperwork inside was no longer considered sensitive, I was ticked off about it missing. Inside were the names of all the people who had helped with the mission and I wanted to send each one a Presidential Flight Certificate.

Brendle and I, along with the four exceptional Master Sergeant mechanics who accompanied us – Nick Carter, Bill Moore, George Gresham and Amor Miller – hitched a ride on a C-130 the next morning to Bangkok to reunite with our unit for the flight back to Homestead. In the span of two weeks, an American astronaut had taken the first walk on the moon and, in the far-reaching shadow of that magnificent accomplishment, I had helped carve a notch in history, as well, by successfully flying the President into a combat zone – a first in its own right.

My *good-natured* colleague, Navy aide Chuck Larson, later referred to the 1969 Vietnam trip in a letter to me before he left the White House in 1971: "We've served in the sunny comfort of Grand Cay to the dusty, hot, hectic trip in Saigon (where you built your own helicopter with spare parts). You guys are the best in the world and working with you was an honor, a pleasure and in every case, *fun*."

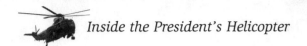

Rare Atmosphere 11

The Chinese use two brush strokes to write the word "crisis." One brush stroke stands for danger; the other for opportunity. In a crisis, be aware of the danger, but recognize the opportunity.
– President Richard Nixon

The briefcase that mysteriously disappeared from the Tan Son Nhut Airport in Vietnam was never found. Luckily, its contents were valueless to anyone but me – unlike the nondescript attaché case that was *always* within the President's reach wherever he went, day or night, awake or asleep.

Except on September 1, 1969.

President Nixon and a full entourage of White House and military officials were in Colorado Springs, Colorado, to attend a meeting of the National Governors Association. Prior to the event, Nixon toured the headquarters of the North American Air Defense Command (NORAD). A vast, underground combat operations hub, NORAD was jointly founded by the U.S. and Canada to defend against nuclear missiles and function as a central coordination facility. Like its Canadian equivalent in North Bay, Ontario, the Cheyenne Mountain command center was equipped to monitor early warning systems and to detect, validate and respond to an attack anywhere in North America.

Brendle and I picked up the President at Peterson AFB just before 2:00 p.m. and led a flight of several helicopters to Fort Carson about five minutes away. Nixon's party included NORAD Commander in Chief, Lieutenant General Seth McKee, Attorney General John Mitchell, Henry Kissinger, Ron Ziegler, and Colonel Hughes. After a brief meeting, the entire group took the eight-minute drive up the hill to Cheyenne Mountain.

Once they were on their way, I noticed the "football" tucked behind the President's chair. The briefcase holding nuclear weapon launch codes and a "playbook" for handling any number of national emergencies was generally the responsibility of

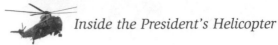
the military duty aide. However, the unusual number of digni-taries on this trip had bumped people around and my best guess was that the "atomic football" had gotten lost in the shuffle.

Within seconds of my discovery, we got a panicked radio call from someone with the President.

"Do you have the football?!" he shouted.

"I do," I calmly replied.

"Can you bring it up? Wait –" he stopped, trying to compose himself, "we'll send a car. No. Is there a car there?"

"Yes," I said, glancing out at a Colorado Highway Patrol cruiser parked nearby.

"Okay, good, good! Get it up here now!"

I snatched up the brief case, ran down the helicopter steps and to the squad car. My entire crew was laughing their butts off and I had to admit it was hard to keep a straight face imag-ining the embarrassing scene that had to have unfolded in the NORAD command center when Nixon's people realized what they had left behind.

Riding up the hill in the cruiser, I wondered what might be inside and hoped the damn thing never had to be opened except for a good cleaning.

The next week the President went from focusing on a worst case scenario in the event of a foreign invasion to celebrating what he termed, "the spirit of understanding and cooperation which binds our two countries." He and the First Lady joined Mexico President Diaz Ordaz and his wife on a scorching hot day for a joint dedication ceremony at the newly built Amistad Dam just north of Del Rio, Texas. Fed by the Rio Grande River, the dam was called a physical and diplomatic achievement by Nixon, "and impressive in human terms, because of what it says about the special relationship which has grown between the people of Mexico and the United States."

President Ordaz echoed Nixon's comments, noting that "amistad" was the Spanish word for friendship. After posing for photographs, the two couples and their guests were soon off to a nearby luncheon.

Parked near the river on a strip of concrete, Brendle and I waited in one helicopter for the President to finish his duties.

Burhanan and his crew were also standing by in a second VH-3A ready to transport additional VIPs back to Laughlin AFB about 15 miles southeast of the dam. Besides being a convenient and secure form of transportation, the White House helicopters also provided a critical mobile communications service. This meant, in a pre-cell phone era, that we endeavored to stay as close as possible to the President when he had no other options for staying in touch with the world.

Preserving that proximity for Nixon on this mission meant maneuvering around a high voltage tower and power lines to land within walking distance of the ceremony stage. It wasn't dangerous, just a tighter space than usual.

Separate from the cockpit, there were four phones mounted on the wall inside the cabin. One was located beside the President's chair, one adjacent to where the duty aide sat across from the President and two for the Secret Service. Through a radio relay, all four were directly linked to the White House switchboard.

When the President's cherry-red phone rang in Burhanan's helicopter while they were standing by at Amistad Dam, the crew chief answered and was surprised to hear a man's voice ask for Burhanan.

"It's for you," he said, handing the receiver to a perplexed Burhanan.

"Hello?" he said, tentatively into the receiver.

"Carl?"

"Who's this?" Burhanan asked.

"Man, I'm glad I found you," said a familiar voice. "I've got some bad news."

The caller was one of Burhanan's buddies and he had somehow managed to track him down through the White House to deliver horrible news. Jim Ervin, one of their closest friends, had been killed in a helicopter accident in Alaska.

"He flew a pipeline into a river bank," he told Burhanan, "and crashed."

Burhanan went numb, thinking of the man who had five daughters and, the last he heard, had convinced his wife to try one more time for a son.

"Carl?"

"Are you saying…he's not here any longer?"

"Yeah, that's what I'm saying."

Burhanan took the news hard. He and Ervin were among the pioneering pilots to fly Sikorsky sky cranes in Vietnam and had navigated myriad perils and hazards. There was no way to justify such a loss or explain how deep the pain burrowed.

By the time Burhanan's passengers started arriving, he had pulled himself together and was in the cockpit preparing for take-off as they boarded. Among the dignitaries were Attorney General John Mitchell and his wife, Martha, whom Nixon described in his memoirs as "vivacious and pretty in a flamboyant, self-amused way" with a reputation for saying exactly what she thought. In other words, she had a big mouth. And as Burhanan was about to find out, if something crossed her mind, she wasn't shy about speaking up.

"Young man?" Martha called to Burhanan from where she stood outside the cockpit window.

"Yes, Ma'am," he respectfully answered.

Martha pointed over Burhanan's head. "Do you see those big wires?"

"I do."

"You'll be careful, won't you?" she sternly cautioned, shaking a motherly forefinger in the air.

"I will," Burhanan coolly assured.

"Good," she said, and promptly boarded.

A few minutes later, Burhanan radioed me to jokingly pass along Martha's warning. We both agreed she was pretty smart for a big mouth. By many accounts, that unrestrained gift of gab played such a pivotal role in Nixon's downfall that he wrote in his diary a full two years before he resigned in 1974, "Without Martha, I am sure that the Watergate thing would never have happened."

Martha certainly had her own radar system and perhaps could have advised NORAD regarding a weakness discovered in its air defense system at Homestead AFB on Sunday, October 5, 1969. The President had spent a few days at his Key Biscayne residence reviewing with Kissinger and other key advisors what

Haldeman described as "plans and ideas, especially about the need to game-plan Vietnam alternatives and start build-up for whatever actions he decides to take."

Air Force One had flown to Homestead and was waiting for me to fly out to Key Biscayne and pick up Nixon once he had finished dinner. Just after 8 p.m., as I started to taxi for lift-off, I caught sight of what looked like a Russian MiG 21 fighter jet landing on the runway in front of me. Once I realized what I thought I saw was actually happening, I said to my co-pilot, as transfixed as I was, "Jesus, that's a goddamned MiG."

Over the radio, I could hear the Air Force One crew screaming for security.

"That's a MiG!" I yelled into my mic.

The tower was going nuts. Sirens went off and a "welcome committee" of jeeps full of armed troops raced toward the camouflaged, supersonic jet now turning onto the taxiway. When it headed toward Air Force One, I thought it was about to open fire on the President's plane and concluded I had better get the hell out of there, especially if this guy had any other delta-winged friends coming in behind him.

Not knowing if I would be called upon to evacuate the President, I was lifting off just as the MiG stopped within only a hundred feet of Air Force Once. The pilot popped the canopy to stand with his arms in the air, sparing me further alarm. Homestead military personnel with weapons drawn closed in and the pilot appeared to be fully cooperating.

Since the Cuban Revolution in 1958 and the country's subsequent conversion to communism, massive waves of immigrants and defectors had found their way to the United States across the 125 miles of ocean that separated Cuba and Florida. Some had come in yachts, others in fishing boats and many more on crude, homemade rafts, but no one had used a MiG. This was a first! And hopefully a last.

I radioed the Secret Service at Key Biscayne to let them know that by the time I picked up the President we would likely have an all-clear to land at Homestead.

A half hour later, I returned to Homestead with Nixon and Kissinger on board. The MiG had been pulled into a hangar

where the base commander now stood with a few other officials by the partially open door. The Cuban pilot was in custody and undoubtedly facing a barrage of questions in some cramped briefing room.

As soon as we landed, Kissinger came up to the cockpit.

"The President wants to see the plane," he said.

Instead of taxiing to Air Force One, I headed to the hangar and shut down. Nixon and Kissinger spent about five minutes looking at the plane and talking with the base commander. I figured the President was making some potent inquiries about how such a thing could have happened.

The President had been in touch with NORAD and was told they had everything under control. As to what was meant by control, I would have liked to have known. The base tower had explained to the commander they had tracked the MiG all the way in, as if that offered a level of comfort. But Kissinger cut through the bullshit.

"No, you didn't," he said. "You didn't know it was a MiG until it landed."

The pilot had flown the entire distance less than 50 feet above the ocean surface and had successfully breached the U.S. air defense system. A lot of people had egg on their faces, but we were all hugely relieved that nothing more sinister than a gutsy man escaping an oppressive society had occurred that day. As a result of the incident, the base was put on continuous alert and opened a new radar tracking facility to prevent a similar event in the future.

Having a Russian-made MiG lollygag into Homestead that day was an excellent wake-up call to re-evaluate how well Florida air space was defended. Not only did the President have a home there, but Cape Kennedy, the Apollo launch site, was just a few hundred miles up the coast. In the past decade, since I had witnessed Sputnik 2 streaking back to earth over the jungles of Venezuela, the space race had accelerated with mind-boggling speed.

Only four months after the first manned landing on the moon, a return 10-day mission was scheduled for November 14, 1969. When I heard we were flying the President and Mrs.

Apollo 12 Launch: watching President Richard Nixon from the cockpit of
Army One, Cape Kennedy, Florida, November 14, 1969
(Courtesy of Richard Nixon Presidential Library, NARA)

Nixon to the Apollo 12 launch site at Cape Kennedy, I was
ecstatic. I still couldn't believe there were footprints on the surface of the moon.

An overcast sky and steady rain had engulfed the Cape by
the time we arrived at 10:45 a.m. with two helicopters carrying
the Nixons. We landed briefly in front of the viewing stands to
allow our passengers, who were all smiles, to button up their
overcoats and disembark beneath a colorful assortment of
umbrellas. As soon as everyone was a safe distance away, both
helicopters picked up and moved to an isolated area well away
from the crowd. We shut down with our noses pointed at the
launch pad. A loudspeaker broadcast the remaining minutes to
countdown and I have to admit, I felt like a teenager at a drive-
in movie, only instead of my Dad's Ford and a high school
cheerleader, I was in a helicopter and Brendle was my date.

"Five, four, three, two, one...ignition..."

I was spellbound watching the enormous flames erupt
beneath the Saturn 5 rocket. For a second or two, the spacecraft
appeared to at first levitate then suddenly accelerate upward

into the metal-gray haze, leaving behind a luminescent contrail. A bolt of lightning deep in the clouds lit the sky obscuring Apollo 12's flight, but the spacecraft continued on, unphased by the extra pyrotechnics. As a boy, I thought I could go anywhere on a bicycle and I now marveled at the ingenuity and technology that could put a man on the moon. Apollo 12, I decided, wasn't just going to the moon. It was rocketing into the future.

Unfortunately, after five subsequent NASA missions, Congress and the American public lost their enchantment with space exploration and the Apollo program ended in December of 1972. Nixon explained the demise by saying, "The argument went, as long as one person on earth is poor, not a dollar should be spent in space. In my opinion, however, exploration of space is one of the last of the great challenges of the American spirit. Space is perhaps the last frontier truly commensurate with America's capacity for wonder."

One thing I was beginning to appreciate about Nixon was that he, unlike me, was an extremely deep thinker. The more I observed him, the more I saw a man who seemed to always be on the job. If he wasn't huddled in some kind of intense conversation with an aide or a visiting dignitary, he was in his seat reading, drafting notes or gazing out the window as his thoughts traveled well beyond what occupied his line of vision. Different than Johnson – who knew how to close up shop and partake in a variety of distractions – Nixon was not a womanizer and he rarely drank. As a result, the inside of the helicopter took on a study hall atmosphere and the wet bar gathered a lot of dust.

As far as I know, Nixon didn't even play cards, though that was not always the case. While stationed on a jungle island in the South Pacific during WWII, Navy Lieutenant Nixon built a small shack and bar where he played high stakes poker and managed to win enough money to finance his successful run for Congress in 1946. He alluded to this history, writing in his autobiography: "I learned that the people who have the cards are usually the ones who talk the least and the softest; those who are bluffing tend to talk loudly and give themselves away."

I couldn't agree more.

President Nixon welcomes former President Johnson and family
San Clemente, CA, August 27, 1969
(Courtesy of Richard Nixon Presidential Library, NARA)

When Nixon did take a break, he strolled on the beaches near his California or Florida home, played the piano, bowled at the White House or played golf. I'm told he was a fair golfer and had a good swing. In 1961, he had a hole-in-one at the Bel Air

Country Club in Los Angeles, an event which he reportedly called "the greatest thrill in my life – even better than being elected."

Nixon especially liked playing golf with celebrities like Jimmy Stewart, Fred MacMurray, Jackie Gleason and Bob Hope, who was a longtime friend with a low handicap and a ready inventory of one-liners like, "Golf is my profession. I tell jokes to pay the green fees."

With the exception of President Carter, a non-golfer, Hope played with every president from Eisenhower to Clinton before he passed away at the age of 100 in 2003. A popular photo of Hope putting a golf ball into an ashtray held on the floor by Nixon in the Oval Office was inscribed by the President: "To Bob Hope. Like me, he nose all! From Dick Nixon."

On January 3, 1970, shortly after Hope returned from his 1969 USO tour to entertain troops in Europe, Vietnam, Thailand, and Guam, I flew Nixon to Hope's Bel Air estate for a round of golf. Brendle and I landed on Hope's private three-hole course, but the two men motored to another course to play, while we waited with the helicopter.

After the President and his fellow ski-nosed, Republican compatriot had departed, a Hope employee brought us a tray of cold drinks. Tagging along behind were Hope's four adopted, pride-and-joy children. Ranging in age from a little tyke to a pre-teen, the two girls and two boys stopped at the bottom of the helicopter steps.

"The President said it was okay," said the employee, smiling up at me where I stood in the doorway, "for the children to see inside the helicopter."

"By all means," I answered, and stepped aside.

The kids bounded on board and did what any children would naturally do – they dipped into a dish of candy and started asking questions.

"What's this for?" asked one, picking up the receiver of a telephone.

"Can we go for a ride?" queried another, plopping down in the President's seat.

"Yeah!" they all chimed in. "Please."

"Sorry, not today," I said, and stationed myself between our inquisitive visitors and the cockpit.

Brendle and our chief engineer filled in as tour guides opening every door, from the galley compartments to the lavatory closet, for the kids to peer inside.

"What happens when you flush the toilet?" one asked.

In short order, all four children, wide-eyed and grinning, were crowded together in the doorway of the cockpit for me to show them how to fly a helicopter.

"It's very important to concentrate," I said, and then asked them to each rub their tummies in a circular motion with one hand, the top of their head with the other hand going the opposite direction, and wiggle both feet. "If you can do that, you can fly a helicopter."

Their gyrations and giggles had us all laughing. Before they left we broke out some give-aways for them to take back to the house. What a great group of kids. I recall thinking how special it was to have entertained the children of the man responsible for boosting the morale of hundreds of thousands of G.I.s around the globe. Bob Hope was more than one of the world's finest comedians, he was an American hero.

I'm certain Hope was also good for Nixon's morale at a time when the President had pressures coming from every direction. The economy was faltering with rising inflation and joblessness; environmental issues had elbowed their way into mainstream consciousness; and the Vietnam War was about to get even uglier.

The Exec Flight was picking up more and more flights and traveling greater distances with fewer assets. In 1969 we had had 1,150 missions compared to 826 missions for the Marines. As we moved into 1970, their helicopters were averaging the same level of activity as the previous year, but our numbers were growing with no assurances for increased resources. Plus, being at Homestead AFB was not the most practical place for the missions that were coming our way.

"Sometimes," I told CeCe, "it feels like we're meeting ourselves coming and going."

Sometime in late January of 1970, after I had dropped a few hints to a couple of military aides, newly promoted Brigadier

Inside the President's helicopter: left to right, Tricia Nixon (Nixon's oldest
daughter), Rose Mary Woods (Nixon's personal secretary), White House
Navy Aide Commander Chuck Larson and President Nixon, 1970
(Courtesy of Richard Nixon Presidential Library, NARA)

General Hughes called to invite me and CeCe up to D.C. for the
weekend.

"We'll do a little socializing," he said, "and talk about the unit."

"Great," I replied, and headed home to give CeCe the good
news. I was more than anxious to make a case for getting the
Exec Flight back to the nation's capital where it had started and
where it still belonged.

CeCe and I rounded up 300 slipper lobsters and caught a
commercial flight from Miami to D.C. General Hughes and the
Military Office hosted a reception for us at the Bolling AFB
Officer's Club located just south of Anacostia Naval Station and
across the Potomac River from National Airport (since renamed
Ronald Reagan National Airport). The conversation was robust,
the lobsters delicious, and the news from Hughes was music to
my ears: "We want the Army back in Washington."

I was ecstatic and so was my unit a few days later when I briefed them in the hangar at Homestead about the plan to relocate to Fort Belvoir by early summer. They had made an extraordinary effort to overcome the negative impacts of the LBJ Ranch years and, at last, their hard work had paid off.

On April 30, 1970, Nixon announced to the American people a military operation into Cambodia aimed at destroying enemy sanctuaries. Termed an *incursion* by the White House, the action involved some 50,000 U.S. and South Vietnamese troops. Despite Nixon's attempts to stress it was not an expansion of the war, the news ignited a rash of anti-war demonstrations. The most violent occurred at Kent State on May 4, 1970. During a confrontation between protestors and armed National Guardsmen, four students were shot and killed. Nine others were wounded.

The campus was not far from where I grew up. It was also where my brother Jack had earned his degree in business administration before going on to the University of Wisconsin and a master's degree in banking. My parents had moved back to Ohio from California and were living in Monroe Falls, only about five miles away from Kent State. The horrific events of that day left us all reeling.

By all accounts, Nixon stood by his Cambodia decision but was unprepared for what he called one of the darkest days of his presidency. The tragedy sparked a nationwide wave of outrage and violence, forcing hundreds of colleges to shut down. As a result of the unfolding civil instability, Nixon cited "matters of state" when he bowed out of a commitment to attend the dedication of the Stone Mountain Monument on May 9, 1970, and sent Vice President Spiro Agnew in his place.

About ten miles east of Atlanta, the Confederate memorial carving was the largest bas-relief sculpture in the world and depicted three Confederate leaders of the Civil War on horseback, President Jefferson Davis and Generals Robert E. Lee and Thomas J. "Stonewall" Jackson, holding their hats over their hearts. The entire carved granite surface measured three acres and had taken nearly sixty years to complete.

Initiated by the United Daughters of the Confederacy, funding for the memorial came from both the federal government and the Ku Klux Klan – a detail unknown to me when I selected Burhanan to fly our Number Two helicopter when we flew Agnew to the ceremonies at the base of the small mountain. Also among the dignitaries was Georgia Governor Lester "Axe-Handle" Maddox. The governor had earned the nickname when

Vice President Spiro Agnew arrives at Stone Mountain Carving dedication
Near Atlanta, GA, May 9, 1970
(Courtesy of Richard Nixon Presidential Library, NARA)

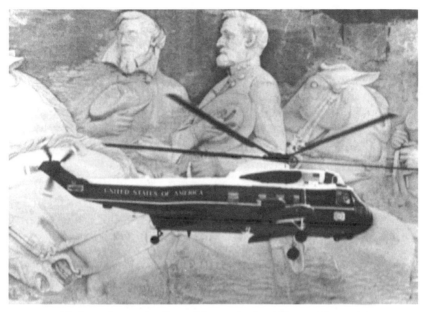

Me hovering at the Stone Mountain Confederate Memorial
Near Atlanta, GA, May 9, 1970
(Boyer Family Archives)

he was photographed in 1964 wielding an axe handle at three black college students attempting to enter his whites-only Pickrick Restaurant. A devout segregationist, Maddox sold his restaurant rather than serve non-whites.

With the festivities well underway at Stone Mountain, a state trooper approached Bill Shaw and me where we were standing near our helicopters. We each had on a pair of our Army-issue sunglasses.

"I like those sunglasses," said the burly man. "How can I get a pair of those?"

"See that helicopter?" Shaw said, pointing to the second helicopter where Burhanan sat on the steps. "If you want a pair you have to go talk to that pilot."

"The black man?"

"Yes," answered Shaw. "He's our supply officer and I'm sure he can help you out."

"Okay, thanks," said the trooper and walked purposely toward Burhanan.

Shaw and I glanced at each other and just shook our heads.

"Your buddies back there," began the trooper when he got close to Burhanan, "sent me over here to see if there was any way I could get a pair of those sunglasses."

"They did?" Burhanan replied, affably.

"That's right," he said, with awkward politeness. "Could you do that?"

"Not normally," Burhanan replied, "but I might be able to arrange something if you give me your address."

"I'd really appreciate it," said the trooper, jotting down information on a scrap of paper.

"When they show up," Burhanan looked at him over the rim of his own fancy sunglasses, "you won't know where they came from."

"Oh, right, right."

The trooper came back to me and Shaw and flashed us a giant grin.

"That's a pretty good nigger back there," he announced. "Is he flying the vice president?"

"Not today, but he has," I answered. "He also flies with me in the president's helicopter."

"I'll be goddamned," he said, shaking his head. "What's this world coming to?"

Burhanan made good on his promise and it wasn't until weeks later that we heard most of the local Ku Klux Klan had refused to attend the event after they learned the invocation would be delivered by a black Baptist pastor. I'm confident, if they had been there, Burhanan would have found enough sunglasses to go around.

We had our own civil rights movement going on.

The next month, the June 1970 issue of *Army Digest* featured a prominent photograph of a smiling Burhanan shaking hands with President Nixon outside a helicopter in Bangkok, Thailand. The accompanying article was titled: *No notice is no problem for Army One: On the Presidential Run.* The author, MSG William G. Jackson, had spent several days shadowing our unit at Homestead, scribbling detail after detail as we prepared for a presidential mission.

"The men who make the helicopter run," he wrote, "from security guard at the gate, through the maintenance, operational, and supply personnel to the pilots and the unit commander, go quietly about the job of making certain that the craft will be ready.

"They have been doing this since the unit began its globe-trotting in 1957...but all this is routine stuff for these men. Yesterday's topic – where to find a home for three kittens owned by one of the crew – is becoming somewhat complicated. Now one of the pilot's dogs has given birth to a dozen pups during the night. Nobody is quite sure whether one of the kittens should be offered to the President when he lands. The discussion is running against it.

"'Usually, the President is on a tight schedule and we don't get to hobnob with any of the VIPs very much, but even so the President finds time for brief talks with some of us,' says Master Sergeant John H. Baker. 'In Bonn, I remember, President Nixon stood in a mud puddle while he talked with me about my job.'"

Master Sergeant Bob D. Simpson, one of our maintenance supervisors, was quoted as saying, "our work is probably the most mind-wracking job in the whole Army. You're always checking and double-checking everything."

Representing our 24-hour military police force was Staff Sergeant Gordon E. Martin who explained, "Everything in sight is suspect to us...everything from a familiar wheel chock that might seem out of place, press cameras, cigarette lighters, even the lipstick tube of some lady in the crowd. But mostly it is the souvenir seekers that need watching. Some of them would literally dismantle that aircraft if we let them get close enough."

We made our own beds, polished our own boots, and swept all the floors; inventoried and ordered our own parts, swapped out all the helicopter components at half-life, stocked the cabin, and used Q-Tips to clean dust from the crevices on the instrument panel; we meticulously logged departure and destination routes, in-flight times, pilots and crew members for each mission, and which aircraft were used; and we drilled and trained any opportunity we got.

Jackson's article concluded with the following: "Now the

rotors turn. Army One rises from the runway and circles off into the night. The crowd disperses. Nobody has come close enough to grab a souvenir."

On May 31, 1970, a catastrophic earthquake struck the north-central coast of Peru and caused a massive portion of the north side of Mount Huascarán, an extinct volcano and the tallest mountain in Peru, to collapse. Different from U.S. mountains, which are mostly granite, the 22,000-foot Mount Huascarán is a composite of ice, dirt and rocks. The resulting landslide was about a mile long and a half mile wide and deep. In less than five minutes it tumbled and melted, picking up more debris in its path as it flowed 11 miles down the side of the mountain at an estimated 100 miles per hour.

A Japanese climbing group, out of harm's way, filmed the cataclysmic event. When the gigantic mass reached a ridgeline, it stalled momentarily, then heaved itself upon the town of Yungay, burying it beneath 50 feet of mud and rock. Only 400 of the some 20,000 inhabitants survived. The estimated death toll for the entire country was nearly 80,000 with 25,000 missing and 143,000 injured.

Named for the region where the quake was centered, the 7.9 magnitude Ancash Quake made headlines around the world. Three weeks later graphic news reports continued to chronicle the devastating impacts and suffering of hundreds of thousands of Peruvians. The disaster so moved the First Lady that she expressed to the President a desire to do more than send aid. Nixon suggested a humanitarian mission to Peru for her to have a firsthand look and deliver additional medical supplies.

While Mrs. Nixon was crafting a plan to go on what would be the most difficult and hazardous flight of my career, the Exec Flight was preparing for a mission to St. Louis. Scheduled for June 25, 1970, we would fly Nixon through the newly dedicated Gateway Arch and land at its base for a ceremonial presentation. The Arch, the tallest of all U.S. monuments, is symbolic of the role St. Louis played in the westward expansion during the nineteenth century. Later, Nixon addressed the Airlift Command at Scott AFB in Bellville, Illinois.

"We are involved in a war," the President told the troops and their families. "We are bringing that war to an end. And we are going to bring it to an end in a way that the younger brothers and sons of those that have fought in Vietnam will not have to fight, we hope, some place in the future. That is the kind of peace we want."

But instead of me being the one to fly Nixon through the Arch, I got a phone call from Brennan announcing a change of plans. Hughes wanted me to take a single helicopter to Peru and fly the First Lady to Hauraz, one of the areas most devastated by the quake.

"You've flown in South America before, right?" Brennan asked.

"Yeah," I replied, "but not in the mountains. How high are we going?"

"I don't know," he said. "You'll have to pick up some maps."

I knew we needed more than maps. We needed to go down early and do a test flight. Fortunately, I did have some high altitude flying experience and, in particular, with excessively high temperatures and poor wind conditions, which can rob enough power from a helicopter to make it unflyable.

I recalled a specific situation when my flight of five helicopters landed to refuel at Kirkland AFB southeast of Albuquerque, New Mexico. The elevation was about 5,500 feet and the temperature pushing 120 degrees. The added weight of full fuel tanks in the scorching, windless heat prevented us from lifting more than a few inches off the ground before being forced to settle down again. The only way we were going to get airborne was to pretend we were airplanes and build ground speed before lifting up.

I radioed the other helicopters to let them know we had to do running takeoffs. We lined up at the end of the runway and one by one "goosed it" until we hit about 30 miles an hour before pulling ourselves into the sky. The tower got quite a show that day and we couldn't have had a better exercise for what was ahead in Peru.

Before heading to South America the last week in June, I assigned Shaw to take the St. Louis mission and selected Brendle as my co-pilot for the trip to Peru. We organized a crew with guards for the helicopter, packed a VH-3A aboard a C-133B

and headed to Panama to refuel on our way to Lima. Unfortunately, the huge cargo plane experienced mechanical problems and I had to call for a back-up. We lost a day's worth of advance work waiting for the second plane, having to unload and reload the helicopter, before continuing on.

When finally landing in Lima, a Peruvian Air Force general with a gruff, all-business attitude greeted us as we deplaned. His attention soon riveted on the four military police I had brought along and the pistols strapped to their sides.

"Why do you have guards?" he asked with a heavy Spanish accent.

"We have to protect the helicopter," I answered.

"We can do that," he assured. "The wife of our president will be on board that helicopter and we are responsible for her security."

"I understand, but the wife of *our* president will also be on board and we are responsible for her *and* the helicopter."

The general thought for a moment and then said, "Okay, but no weapons."

"But that doesn't make any –" I stopped, struggling to find more tactful words. "I'm sure we can work this out."

Relations between the U.S. and Peru were very strained. The Nixons' trip to South America in 1958 when they were mobbed by Peruvian leftists and nearly killed in Venezuela remained fresh in all of our memories. The country's new president, General Juan Velasco, a leftist, had only recently taken office after the overthrow of the former government in 1968. We were walking a delicate line between operating in what we considered a hostile environment and providing support in the form of humanitarian relief and diplomatic compassion. How I responded to the general could set the tone for the entire mission.

"I will have guards inside yours," said the general.

"Between my guards and the helicopter?" I asked, knowing this was unacceptable. "With mine unarmed?"

"Yes."

"I'm sorry, I really want to cooperate, but we have to keep our guards with our helicopter."

"That's not going to happen here," he puffed.

"What if my guys take unarmed positions between your armed guards and the helicopter, which is where we're going to sleep anyway?"

"You are asking too much."

I was tired, hot and had a list of pending responsibilities spinning in my head, so I made the only call I thought I could without jeopardizing the security of the helicopter and safety of the First Lady.

"Very well," I said, backing away. "I'll let the White House know about this development and they may very well cancel the trip."

The general, fully aware there were two planes due in with food, blankets, tents and medical supplies, quickly reconsidered.

"Please, that won't be necessary," he said. "We will accept your suggestion."

"Thank you," I said with an affirming nod. "Now, tell me about these mountains. I understand we're going pretty high. Hauraz is at what – about eleven thousand feet?"

"Yes, yes," he confirmed and we were soon huddled over a map. The pissing contest had ended and international relations were none the worse for wear.

He went on to tell me that in the last few weeks four Marine relief helicopters from a U.S. Navy carrier off the coast of Peru, along with a couple of planes, had crashed trying to navigate the steep ridgelines in the thin, weak air. I hadn't heard about the mishaps, but couldn't fault the pilots, especially those flying the historically under-powered CH-46 Boeing-Vertol models – that, coupled with high altitude and elevated temperatures, made the job demanding for the best pilots and I considered myself appropriately forewarned.

For our mission, we hoped for temperatures no higher than 60 degrees and a good breeze to give the air more body. A warm, windless environment meant the atmosphere was less dense and the helicopter less able to gain its special brand of traction. With so little room for fluctuating conditions, it was easy to get into trouble without warning.

The next morning, with Brendle in the left seat, two mechanics and an MP on board, we flew the helicopter from Lima to

Hauraz, about 120 miles to the north. The weather was in the low 60s with a brisk wind, but the air was still so thin we could not fly any faster than about 80 knots. It was a constant point of tension to increase power without losing rotor RPMs.

As we came up and over a ridgeline with about 10 feet of clearance between us and the thick clouds obscuring the majestic, snowcapped Andes, we were astonished to discover that the entire city of Hauraz stretching ahead of us had been flattened by the quake. Nestled in a high valley with a mixture of verdant sloping hillsides and alpine streams, the city of 35,000 people had not a single building left intact. Roofs and walls were toppled and tipped in every direction.

Approximately one third of the population had perished. Hundreds of tents now provided shelter and Peace Corps teams were working with Peruvian volunteers to sort and clear rubble. Women and children, dressed in strikingly colorful clothing, combed through what looked like a sprawling, urban dumpsite. Here and there, freshly cleaned laundry clung to clothes lines, flapping cheerfully in the wind – a sign of how some were getting on with life and a promise to us that we would have optimum conditions for the First Lady's visit the next day.

The dazed faces of a small crowd broke into smiles as they watched us approach the soccer field that had been cleared as a landing site. But before we sat down I gauged how well we could hover, knowing as long as we could hover, we could fly.

"We've got to be really careful," I told Brendle, as we held steady about 15 feet above the ground. "Really careful."

"Yes, we do," he replied.

Not in all my years of flying before going to Peru nor in those to follow would I be as pressed to apply every skill and instinct I could possibly summon to accomplish this mission. So long as the weather held, we limited our weight to no more than seven passengers, kept our portable oxygen bottles close and carried minimum fuel, we would be fine.

After we powered down, a simply dressed middle-aged man and tiny woman rushed out of the ruins to greet us. Not far behind were a dark-eyed teenage girl and a small boy, the woman's daughter and son. The man was the town mayor and heaped upon us his gratitude for the small amount of provisions we had already collected and brought along. The woman was an American missionary named Evangeline Castillo and she offered her skills as an interpreter. Even though Mrs. Nixon would be accompanied by Army General Vernon Walters who spoke seven languages, we welcomed her services.

"Can my children look inside?" Evangeline asked with a gentle smile and kind eyes.

No doubt the children had probably witnessed things a child should never have to see during the last few weeks and while I didn't hesitate to wrangle with a Peruvian general, I couldn't deny her request.

"Sure," I said, "come on up."

On the ground for less than a half-hour, we taxied into the wind and managed to lift up, heading to Yungay, 2,000 feet lower and five minutes farther north. It was a smooth take-off. We easily cleared the brick and mortar rubble of a large building at the end of the soccer field and swooped over the ridgeline, dropping into the welcome updrafts of the valley below. Unlike Hauraz, Yungay was a lifeless expanse of solidified mud, debris and motionless protruding body parts. The only thing left standing was a 30-foot-tall cross on a nearby hill casting a long shadow over what had become a mass grave. The scope of the deaths and destruction defied belief.

We returned to a freshly graded dirt landing strip that had been carved out for relief flights in Anta Valley several thousand feet below Hauraz. My crew and I washed away the day's tension by joining some local Peruvians for a soak in a nearby natural hot springs cave that was as big as a football field. Stripped down to our underwear, we stewed in the steamy, bubbling waters known for their healing compounds. I remember being mystified by how untouched that huge cavern was by the Ancash Quake. What had kept it from collapsing? One of many sacred sites throughout Peru, this must have had some guardian spirits in the vicinity and we wouldn't mind having them tag along tomorrow – as long as they didn't weigh very much.

Late the next morning, we were prepped and waiting beside the crude airstrip for a C-130 to land with First Ladies Pat Nixon and Consuelo de Velasco. As the plane was not equipped for passengers, Mrs. Nixon sat on a kitchen chair with seatbelts that had been bolted to the floor. General Walters later remarked that the First Lady should have received combat pay.

We watched the plane descend, wings slightly tilting side to side until it touched down. About the time I thought it should be slowing to a stop, it was still rolling and running out of dirt.

Jesus, I thought, *they're going to kill the First Lady.*

Somehow, the plane came to a halt in a cloud of dust and brake vapors within a few feet of the end of the runway and a mountain stream. More remarkably, Mrs. Nixon, wearing a light blue suit and pumps, disembarked with a carefree smile on her face. Soon we were in the air on our way to Hauraz. In addition to our crew and the two First Ladies, our passengers included a Peruvian Army general, a Peace Corps official, General Walters, a Secret Service agent and Major Brennan.

"We'll stay in Hauraz an hour or two," Brennan instructed. "President Velasco is hosting a dinner for the First Lady at the palace back in Lima tonight."

The 15-minute flight up to the Hauraz went as planned with no glitches. While Mrs. Nixon, her party and the press caravan toured the rubble, offering comfort to the local people, my crew and I stayed with the helicopter. Minute by minute, for more than two hours, I watched the afternoon temperature creep upward and the wind die down until the laundry on every clothes line ceased to move.

By the time everyone returned to the helicopter, it was 75 degrees and I was wrestling with whether or not to cancel the flight. Mrs. Nixon's party could get back to the airstrip by car, but it would be a treacherous trip on steep and narrow switch-back roads. And the cars themselves were a god-awful hodge-podge of older, unreliable vehicles with unknown histories.

I estimated the journey would take at least four hours through unsecured terrain – now eerily named The Valley of Death in the wake of the earthquake. Four hours *if* everything went well. Then, once the First Lady got back to the airstrip, she would have to take off in the same C-130 that nearly dumped her in a creek upon arrival.

First Ladies Pat Nixxon and Consuelo de Velasco amid earthquake rubble,
Hauraz, Peru, June 29th, 1970
(Courtesy of Richard Nixon Presidential Library, NARA)

Given those options, I decided that flying was the best one and powered up. Even in the limited space of the soccer field we had enough room to do a running take-off. Once we cleared the collapsed building in front of us we would drop into strong updrafts of the valley below and be on our way. Brendle and I knew it was no time to be overly cautious. As we both had learned in Vietnam, cautious pilots lose their edge and get killed. That wasn't going to happen today. We knew what we had to do and we knew how to do it, even though the margin of error was just this side of nonexistent.

"When I give you the word, pull the landing gear." I told Brendle, not wanting to lose any rotor RPM. "I'll keep it on the ground as long as I can."

We rolled at about 18 miles an hour across the field until we were about 25 or 30 yards from the heap of ruins when I signaled Brendle to pull the gear. The helicopter wobbled lazily into the air and skimmed over the pile of debris with only a few feet between us and an unpleasant outcome. Already bleeding off RPMs, we crept over the ridgeline and the instant the valley floor opened up beneath us, I decreased the collective and dropped us about 200 feet before we got the rotor RPMs back to a comfortable level. Once stabilized, we climbed to about 13,000 feet for the First Ladies to get a close look at Mount Huascarán. From there we flew over Yungay and then back to the dirt landing strip where our passengers reboarded the C-130 for the flight back to Lima.

As Mrs. Nixon passed by the cockpit on her way off the helicopter, she noticed Brendle and me looking at a map. I was already planning how to get out of the mountains and back to Lima as soon as possible.

"I think we need to sign that," she proudly announced to Mrs. Velasco, who was standing behind her.

"Of course," I replied enthusiastically and handed her a pen.

That map is one of my most prized keepsakes, in addition to the photograph of the Nixon's three dogs sitting on the White House lawn that arrived in my mailbox a few weeks later with paw prints and this inscription: "Thanks for bringing our mistress home safely."

The instant the C-130 carrying the First Lady was out of sight that afternoon, we were refueled and in the air pushing the helicopter as hard as it had ever been pushed. Barely getting a 100-foot-per-minute climb rate and holding right at the engine temperature redline, we couldn't crank it past 65 knots. Still, we managed to crawl over another 12-13,000-foot ridgeline, descend to the coastline and head south toward Lima at a blissful and temperate 500 feet above sea level.

Packing up the next day, the Peruvian general who had greeted us upon arrival a few days earlier stopped by to wish us a safe trip home.

White House note of appreciation for the First Lady's safe return from
Hauraz, Peru, July, 1970
(Boyer Family Archives)

"I must tell you," he said, "this visit by Mrs. Nixon has done more to improve relations with our country than anything the United States has done in a hundred years."

"Thank you," I answered. "Maybe we'll see you again."

I did see the general again after he and I had retired in the late 1970s. I was working for Lockheed and he, as the new president of Aero Peru, came to the States to negotiate the purchase of three L-1011 aircraft. I did the briefing and everything seemed in order until a few weeks later when he was caught at the Miami airport with a briefcase full of cocaine and promptly sent back to Peru and a fate of which I have no knowledge.

One person I certainly did not expect to see again was Elena, the daughter of the American missionary woman we met in Hauraz. In 2001, I experienced my first episode of heart arrhythmia and ended up being admitted to a Southern California hospital. Sometime around 5 a.m., a woman in her mid-40s wheeled an electrocardiogram machine into my room. As she wired me up and began asking a few routine questions, I detected a Spanish accent.

"Where are you from?" I asked.

"Peru," she replied.

"Really?" I said. "I've been there. Whereabouts?"

"Well, you've never heard of this place," she said, adjusting a dial. "It's in Northern Peru where the tourists don't go – Hauraz."

"I know where it is. I landed a helicopter there."

Elena planted a hand on her hip and looked at me more closely. "Was Mrs. Nixon on board?"

"Yes," I answered, now looking more closely at her.

"Are you the pilot who let us go inside the helicopter?"

"I must be," I said, flabbergasted.

"Oh my gosh!" she blurted.

"How's your mother?"

"She's still there," said Elena. "We still talk about that day. You know, Mom gave Mrs. Nixon a family bible and asked her to mail it to my brother who was in the American Navy stationed in the state of Washington."

"Did he get it?"

"Yes."

I wasn't surprised. Pat Nixon, as birdlike and fragile as she might have appeared, was one of the bravest, most empathetic and tireless women I've ever encountered.

Elena e-mailed her mother that night and I soon received a letter and a photo of herself in my mailbox. Even smaller and now completely gray, she was dressed in a brilliant-colored long skirt and a royal blue shawl. Smiling sweetly, she gripped a walking stick in one hand and her 4-year-old great-grandson's hand with the other. She wrote:

"This is a photo of my little great-grandson Danielito and myself in my backyard here in Hauraz...his dad, Danny Cano looked just exactly like he does here when you received us in the big Army No. 1 helicopter that morning in June '70 and gave him an orange to eat! I've often thought of you and Pat Nixon's visit to Hauraz in 1970 and I never dreamed of getting in touch with you after these many (31) years. But God often prepares pleasant surprises for his children and I am very thankful for Elena's sake too. She was excited about the book of Julie Eisenhower's that you gave her autographed by the author. Thank you once again for your kindnesses."

I had forgotten about the oranges.

Vantage Point 12

Bill Holloman, a Tuskegee Airman, didn't stop serving his country when his active duty as one of the United States' first African-American combat pilots ended after World War II. He was called back to service in the Korean War and became the Air Force's first black helicopter pilot. He went to war again in Vietnam. During the nearly four decades after he retired from the Army, he served his country in a different way: by teaching younger generations how war and aviation intersected in a way that helped end centuries of racial separation.

– Seattle Times, June 18, 2010

More than any mission, the perilous trip to Peru lingered with me for a long time. In all my world travels I had never seen such widespread resilience and faith in the midst of such anguish and devastation. It was an unbelievable human marvel.

Months later, on one of Nixon's New York City flights, I reflected on the Peru trip as we flew over acres and acres of crumbling, gutted tenements and corner shops where there had once been thriving neighborhoods. Owners had abandoned many of the properties and squatters had moved in wherever they could. But different from the Ancash earthquake that leveled Hauraz, the disaster in New York was manmade.

So much had changed since my flying days for New York Airways 15 years before. These same neighborhoods had been clean and orderly then. People and automobiles moved about with vigor and purpose. Now, many of the formerly vibrant red brick buildings were nothing but vacant shells. Journalists compared the scene to European cities bombed senseless in WWII. New York City had become overwhelmed by joblessness, poverty, crime and blight. And also different than Hauraz, I saw no one scurrying about to clean up and recover.

There was a curious irony in how the inhabitants of a South American city obliterated by an earthquake had pulled together within hours to rebuild. Even before humanitarian support arrived from around the world, they had not waited to be rescued. As we cruised over the slums of New York, I had to ask myself: What prevented that same survival instinct from flooding the dismal streets below us? What made a natural disaster more worthy than a manmade one? Why couldn't residents and shopkeepers and church congregations work together with the government as if their broken neighborhoods had been torn apart by a monstrous earthquake?

There were no simple answers to these questions and, admittedly, things always looked less complicated from the air.

The Army's White House Executive Flight Detachment arrived back at Fort Belvoir the summer of 1970 with six helicopters: three Hueys, one true presidential VH-3A and two lesser-equipped H-3s that the Marines eventually replaced with plush models from their Quantico fleet. I remain convinced that we were brought back to Washington, D.C., because the White House needed both the Army and the Marines to meet the demands and scope of an ambitious and expanding mission. What I thought was now a joint operation would, in the coming years, sadly, eventually become a horse race.

The Army unit still had a long way to go to reach its former capacity, but I had unflinching confidence in our program and pressed the White House Military Office every chance I got for more personnel and better equipment. For instance, I wanted to add two Chinooks and an assembly-line model SH-3A for training use rather than draining off time from the more high profile helicopters. The response was always some version of, "Just call the Marines and they'll provide you with what you need for a mission."

Although not a convenient option, it was logical. During the four years the Army had been away from Washington, D.C., the Marine One contingent within HMX-1 had significantly expanded, with access to about 40 helicopters, and more than 40 pilots supported by close to 430 personnel. Our unit had six helicopters, 17 pilots, about 120 support personnel and would soon be flying just as many missions as the Marines.

No matter how I sliced it, those numbers weren't working for

Army One Senior Pilot, White House Executive Flight Detachment
Washington, D.C.
(Boyer Family Archives)

me or our standards of operations and efficiency. As the commanding officer, I cringed every time we got a mission I knew
needed more resources than what we could wheel out of a
hangar at Fort Belvoir. Getting on the phone to the Marines with

a wish list was a crap shoot. Sometimes the additional equipment and personnel came without question. Other times, I had to negotiate and justify a specific request, and even then I had no guarantees. And as juvenile as it sounds, neither branch liked to depend on the other for fundamentals. We had our own way of doing things and preferred self-sufficiency to dependence. It was generally cleaner and less complicated.

Every time I had to stitch together a mission, I cursed Lyndon Johnson for splintering the Army helicopter unit. By sending half of us to Vietnam and half to the LBJ Ranch, he had succeeded in creating a nearly impenetrable hideout. The tactic all but severed upper-level support for us by our superiors. They weren't about to meddle in a Johnson scheme and kept their distance, knowing the President's helicopters were off limits. As a result, LBJ was able to circumvent certain lines of accountability and do what he did best – make up his own rules.

How Johnson dealt with inquiries from the House Appropriations Committee was addressed by Marine Master Sergeant Bill Gulley in his book, *Breaking Cover*. Gulley had worked as an administrative assistant in the Military Offices for both Johnson and Nixon. Under President Ford, he became the director of the White House Military Office. That assignment raised a lot of eyebrows since Gulley was a non-commissioned officer in a position traditionally filled by a general or admiral. Predecessors included Brigadier Generals Don Hughes, Brent Scowcroft and Richard Lawson during the Nixon years.

"We were asked about helicopters," Gulley wrote in his book, referring back to the Johnson years, "for example – how many helicopters the President had for his own use. He said, 'Tell 'em I have one helicopter. I can only ride one helicopter at a time, so tell the bastards one's all I've got.'"

Johnson's knack for manipulating numbers and hiding assets was legendary, and I welcomed the assumed transparency that came with having the Army unit back in the D.C. area. During the latter half of 1970, the Military Office organized a system that had us alternating weeks with the Marines. We also swapped duties at San Clemente and Key Biscayne, but the Army was still given the bulk of long-distance and overseas missions.

During Nixon's five-and-a-half years in office, he flew by helicopter at least 1,250 times. During Nixon's first term, the percentage of annual presidential missions performed by the Exec Flight climbed from 23 to 52 percent – putting us back on equal footing with the Marines by 1972. However, those presidential flights were less than one-tenth of the total White House missions, which included transporting the Vice President, the First Lady, other government and military VIPs, White House staff, foreign heads of state and the press. Training exercises were usually coordinated with these secondary level flights and the Army logged close to 60 percent of those trips.

It didn't take long for CeCe, Robin, and me to settle into housing at Fort Belvoir in the fall of 1970. We knew the community well and loved being close to the national political nerve center. There was always something happening to call home about and prod my father into one of his mini-lectures about the state of the economy, the Vietnam War or, one of his favorites, Nixon's shortcomings. Robin, now age six, was headed to first grade and besides the numerous demands of motherhood, CeCe busied herself with the Wives' Club activities and volunteering at the base hospital.

Our Fort Belvoir, Virginia, home, 1970-75
(Boyer Family Archives)

As the mid-term elections heated up that same fall, Nixon decided to make his second trip to Europe instead of hitting the campaign trail. The nine-day tour began in Italy where he met with Pope Paul VI. He also visited with the newly freed American hostages who had been taken captive during a hijacking in Jordan by the Popular Front for the Liberation of Palestine. He continued on to Belgrade, Yugoslavia, to consult with President Josip Tito, then to Madrid, Spain, for a meeting with President Francisco Franco. Our unit and a small fleet of helicopters connected with Nixon and his entourage at Heathrow Airport in London the morning of October 3, 1970.

The entire time we were in the United Kingdom the ceiling for the drizzling, gray sky didn't budge from between 500 and 1,000 feet. We first flew Nixon, Prime Minister Edward Heath, Henry Kissinger, Secretary of State Rogers, Brigadier General Hughes and other dignitaries to Chequers for an informal luncheon with Queen Elizabeth II. The 16th century, gothic-style estate is the official country residence for British Prime Ministers and sits in the rolling emerald folds of Buckinghamshire, 20 minutes northwest of London.

Back at Heathrow at 4:30 p.m., the President, the First Lady and a party of some 45 officials, staff and Secret Service officials boarded Air Force One for the next phase of the tour – Ireland, the ancestral home of Nixon's beloved mother and the Milhous family.

As we prepared the helicopters to follow Air Force One, the pilot scheduled to fly the Huey, our only single engine helicopter, across the Irish Sea, sought me out.

"I've got to say something," he quietly said to me.

"Okay," I answered, zipping up my jacket in the darkening, chilly air.

"I don't feel good about taking the Huey a hundred miles over water."

One of my best pilots, his uncharacteristic concern caught me by surprise.

"Are you serious?"

"It's going to be pitch-black out there," he added.

"So?"

"I'm the only one in a single engine and if something happens," he paused, waiting for me to look him in the eye, "and I go down, you'll never find me."

There was no time for discussion or massaging cold feet that were afraid of getting wet. "All right," I replied, walking away. "You fly the H-3 and I'll take the Huey."

"Wait. You can't do that."

"Of course I can. If you're not happy –"

"Okay. You're right," he grumbled, stuffing his hands into his pockets. "I'm not happy, but that doesn't mean I won't do it."

"Good," I said, moving on. "Just follow my lights."

Flying IFR over the Irish Sea that moonless night, I took the lead, tracking radio beacons and handling communications with the local air traffic control center. We flew in a V-formation with three helicopters staggered off to either side. Each honed in on my flashing position lights and we held at 120 knots as we whirred through the darkness. My reluctant pilot anchored the rear and had ample points of orientation to follow.

As I went, so they did, exercising an even higher level of trust – the type that's never automatic, only earned. And with that crew I would have not hesitated to put any one of them out front. Together we had more combined flight time than any White House unit in history and instrument flying was second nature to us. Two hours later, we emerged like bats from a shadowy cave to land safely at the airport in Shannon, Ireland.

The next evening, we flew to the rural and rambling grandeur of the Kilfrush Estate where the President and the First Lady were staying. The hotel-sized mansion was owned by John A. Mulcahy, an Irish-American millionaire and one of Nixon's top campaign contributors. Word was that he, like the Kennedy family, had built his fortune bootlegging liquor during Prohibition. From the Kilfrush Estate, we transported Nixon and key staffers to the secluded, 400-year-old Dromoland Castle 20 minutes away. There the President hosted a reception for members of the American and Irish press.

We waited in the helicopters outside the castle for about two hours. Thankfully, we had access to a toilet through the servants' entrance in the back. Unlike Texas cow pastures, the

Army One at Dromoland Castle
Ireland, October 4, 1970
(Courtesy of Richard Nixon Presidential Library, NARA)

immaculately manicured surroundings were far too beautiful for us to relieve ourselves behind some unsuspecting bush.

Back at the Kilfrush Estate later that night, we parked the helicopters in a lush grassy area, stationed our guards and made ourselves comfortable in the sleeping quarters set up for us in a huge barn. A few of us put on civilian clothes and ventured to a nearby pub to sample Irish culture. Quaint and musty, the crowded establishment was buzzing with pounding music and merriment. We were quite the attraction and I'm not sure whether they or we did most of the gawking. But I'll never forget how the women grouped themselves on one side of the dance floor and the men on the other. It reminded me of high school, except many of these folks were married and several were just plain old and crusty. Yet, one by one, the gents crossed the floor to take a lady for a whirl.

They were the loudest, most cheerful people I had ever met – sipping tea or juiced to the gills. And I know if one of us had sampled one drop of beer, a town crier would have made it headline news. As ready to party as the next guy, we held to the strictest of rules regarding alcohol and flying. No consumption within 24 hours of being on duty – whether a flight was planned or not, and absolutely no indulging during a mission.

Besides enhanced diplomatic relations with several foreign leaders, the trip provided Nixon a secure, secluded setting to be briefed by Kissinger, Rogers, and other officials involved in the Paris Peace Talks. Kissinger later wrote in his book, *Ending the Vietnam War*, that "Nixon met (with us) to consider his cease-fire speech... This meeting could not have been more optimistic."

Nixon's ancestors represented a long line of pacifists and were buried in the Milhous plot at the Timahoe Quaker Cemetery about 20 miles inland from the capital city of Dublin. Local people, some of whom were distant relatives of the President, had cleared away tall grasses at the burial grounds to expose the foundation of a Quaker meeting house.

On the morning of October 5, 1970, President Nixon and the First Lady walked solemnly among clusters of mossy, weathered tombstones until they reached the grave of his great-great-great grandmother. He later addressed the crowd and spoke proudly about how his family had immigrated to America in the 18th century. He also sought to reassure those listening that, "The armies and the navies and the air forces of the United States of America exist for the purpose of preventing war and building peace."

Nixon's desire to be a peacemaker was deeply rooted in that tranquil Irish valley. Although he encountered sporadic anti-American outbursts among the thousands who cheerfully greeted him, he was undaunted and soon revealed to the world his New Initiative for Peace in Southeast Asia.

An embassy aide approached and asked me a perplexing question the afternoon of October 5, 1970. We had just completed a flight with Nixon from Ambassador John Moore's residence in Naas to Dublin, where Air Force One was waiting to fly him back to Washington, D.C.

"What happened with the horses?"

"Horses?" I replied. "What horses?"

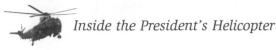

"The ones you scared over a cliff."

My jaw dropped open. "What?"

"Some farmers called the embassy today," he explained in a hushed tone, "and said you ran some prized race horses over a cliff."

"Where?"

"I'm not sure."

"How many?" I asked

"Don't know."

"I didn't see any horses close enough to spook," I assured him, "We were at least above 700 feet all the time. But I guess if they've never seen a helicopter, I suppose we could have set some off."

"I'm not saying you did anything wrong," he said. "I just wanted to hear your side. We'll take it from here."

On one hand, I felt horrible for having caused something so tragic. On the other hand, I damn well wanted to see one of those dead horses. I asked my crew if they had seen any stampeding horses. I got nothing but blank stares and shaking heads. It was a mystery to us all. If we were responsible for such a situation, I wanted the chance to apologize. If we weren't responsible, I did not want someone pointing fingers where they didn't belong.

Weeks later, I found out the United States government paid the farmers some $200,000 to cover the value of the alleged lost horses and, of perhaps even more value, to bury a story that could have tarnished an otherwise productive and influential trip for Nixon.

Besides enlarging the Exec Flight, I also wanted to increase the diversity of our unit. Carl Burhanan was still the only non-white presidential pilot and we both knew black guys returning from Vietnam with lengthy, outstanding flight records who were top-notch candidates. But flying in the obscure jungles of Vietnam was one thing. Flying for the highly visible White House was another. Even though the military had officially integrated nearly 20 years earlier, there were still strong undercurrents of discrimination. To be blunt, a lot of the country and some military leadership weren't ready for a black man to fly the president. (It's important to establish that I never saw the slightest hint of racial prejudice by President Nixon or his family. In fact, they often went out of their way to embrace different cultures and ethnicities.)

U.S. Army CW-4 Carl Burhanan, first black pilot for the White House, shakes hands with Nixon, Bangkok, Thailand.
(*Army Digest,* June, 1970)

White House pilots underwent extensive interviews, tests and training. That process took several months and I personally did the final check flight. Many of our pilots and personnel were recommendations out of Fort Rucker, the center for Army aviation. Some were personal referrals from those already in the unit. Besides high flight time totals and instrument experience, I especially looked for men who had had combat experience. They had a leg up when it came to teamwork and being able to think on their feet and operate under stress.

The second African American to fly for the White House was CW4 Frank Joseph. We first met in the early 1960s when we were both flying for SHAPE and NATO in Paris. An unflappable man, he flew with the steady hand of a stalwart country gentleman. Joseph and his wife, Florence, were even at my wedding. His tour of duty in Vietnam ended around 1969 and I had brought him into the unit at Homestead before we left for D.C. in 1970.

Welcoming U.S. Army CW4 and Mrs. Frank Joseph,
the second of three black White House helicopter pilots, 1970
(Boyer Family Archives)

Flying for the White House had its unique brand of pressure. Yet regardless of experience and training, nothing prepared a pilot for that very moment when the most powerful leader in the world climbed aboard the helicopter and the tower reported, "Army One, you are clear for take-off."

For Joseph, that moment came on October 8, 1970. The President and the First Lady had flown aboard Air Force One to Hunter Army Airfield in Savannah, Georgia. They were met by Governor Lester Maddox and other dignitaries before boarding a yacht for a cruise southward to Skidaway Island. There they participated in a dedication ceremony for the Ocean Science Center of the Atlantic Commission. Before unveiling the architectural plans for the new installation, Nixon spoke about his recent trip to Europe, his newly announced peace initiative and the importance of developing resources from the sea.

In a helicopter we had parked nearby, I waited with Joseph in the cockpit for the President to board for transport back to Hunter AAF. Breathing in the salty Atlantic Ocean air, I glanced at Joseph. He was cucumber cool. Flying was in his blood. He had already bent my ear about his upcoming retirement plans to start a helicopter logging company in the Pacific Northwest. But today, he was flying the President of the United States for the first time. Joseph handled the five-minute flight without blinking.

That is, until after Nixon had disembarked the helicopter for Air Force One and we were watching it taxi for take-off.

"Nice job," I said to Joseph.

He answered with a little nod and an uncharacteristic sniff.

"You okay?" I asked, aware he was struggling to stifle some kind of emotion.

"This was a real honor," he finally said, getting on with business and flipping a few switches. At that moment, I realized it was probably a hell of a lot easier for him to fly the President than it was to acknowledge a personal milestone once thought unachievable because of his skin color.

Joseph did retire about a year later and made good on his dream to start a helicopter logging company. From there, he and his wife moved to Alaska where they operated a supply and shuttle service for hunters and fishermen. He also airlifted daring snow skiers up to virgin slopes high in the mountains. Sadly, like so many Vietnam vets, the lingering effects of Agent Orange ended his life too soon.

A letter Joseph wrote to me in 1995 contains a moving paragraph about how privileged he felt being selected to fly for the White House, adding, "I knew that Carl Burhanan was the first Black Pilot to fly for the President of the United States, and that I would be the second. I also knew that you, Colonel Boyer, were the first Senior White House Pilot with the integrity, conviction and courage to select pilots based on their ability and character and not the color of their skin for this very visible mission. Your ability to select outstanding people, and your management style of fairness while demanding excellence, made the

Executive Flight Detachment the best unit in the Armed Services. During my 26 years of continued Army Service, I had never been in a unit where there was so much trust between all personnel. I had been in what I thought were some very good units, but I had never seen such dedication to the Mission and such loyalty to the Commanding Officer."

In the weeks before the 1970 mid-term election, Nixon hit the campaign trail to stump for Republican candidates in danger of losing to Democratic opponents. On a blustery day midway through October, Nixon left Washington, D.C., with an ambitious multi-stop itinerary during which he addressed tens of thousands of people. He traveled roughly 2,500 miles and made seven appearances in less than 14 hours. It was one of the tightest, most demanding schedules I ever commanded.

October 17, 1970, began with Air Force One flying the President from D.C., to Burlington, Vermont, where he joined a noontime rally for Senator Winston Prouty. A few rock-throwing hecklers appeared on the scene and Nixon cleverly incorporated their right to be heard into his remarks.

"I can assure them," he told the crowd, "that they are a very loud minority, but they are a minority, and it's time for the majority to stand up and be counted...not by trying to shout speakers down, not by throwing rocks, not by bombing buildings, not by shouting obscenities, but I'll tell you how you can be counted: with the most quiet, powerful voice in the world, by voting...."

From Vermont, Nixon took Air Force One to Newark, New Jersey, where I was waiting with Army One and 13 support helicopters. The passenger list included core personnel Haldeman, Ziegler, Rumsfeld, Taylor and Brennan, as well as a rotation of local dignitaries, extra Secret Service support and more press than I could count.

We left Newark shortly before 2:00 p.m. for Teterboro, 15 miles away. There Nixon hooked up with senatorial candidate Nelson Gross, then headed 45 miles south to his next stop – Ocean Grove, an upscale island community with a lot of retired, conservative residents. We landed in a wide grassy area separating the north and southbound lanes of a major boulevard. The

President motored from there to a nearby community center where a couple hundred protestors stirred things up so badly the state highway patrol officers helping us guard the helicopters were called to the scene. This left us with just a few MPs armed with .45-caliber pistols. All the Secret Service agents were also with the President, so I got on the radio to alert my crews.

"Whatever happens," I told them, "you guys have to protect the helicopters."

Sure as hell, as the demonstrators were herded away from the community center, a good hundred of them streamed our way. To my total amazement, a lanky, long-haired man with a small boy on his shoulders came across the boulevard pavement to the grassy divider where we were parked. Before anyone could stop him he grabbed hold of the tail rotor on the President's helicopter and defiantly shook it back and forth.

I practically pushed a young MP down the helicopter steps.

"Pull your weapon," I ordered.

The MP looked at me and then the man and the kid.

"I can't do that," said the bewildered MP. "He has a kid."

"I got it," I snapped and snatched the pistol out of the MP's holster. With the gun barrel pointed upward, I moved toward the protestor who was putting the child on the ground. "If you touch the helicopter again, you're going to jail."

Now carefully contemplating his next move, the man glanced toward the horde of dissidents lining the curb about 50 feet away.

"Do not come on this grass," I shouted to them, "or you will be arrested."

Several of my crew and the other MPs with weapons now drawn eased into position. Reluctantly, the stupidly bold man slowly took the boy's hand and walked away spewing typical obscenities about Nixon and the war. I returned the pistol to the crestfallen MP and relieved him of his job within 24 hours. Hesitation had no place in our flight that day.

By the time the President's motorcade got back to Army One at 4:00 p.m., we were a good 30 minutes behind schedule. The forecasted headwinds had increased from 20 to 40 knots and would gust in our face all 140 miles between Ocean Grove and

Lancaster, Pennsylvania, where Nixon was due at a rally for Governor Raymond Broderick.

When he boarded, the President was remarkably composed considering the chaos outside and paused to calmly suggest to me, "I hope we can make up some time."

"Mr. President," I replied, "the winds are stronger than we expected, but I'll try. We'll have to fly low so it's going to be bumpy."

"Okay, do what you can," he said.

As soon as we were airborne, I instructed the other helicopters, which were lighter and faster, to fly ahead, land and offload their passengers before we got there. This would save time once we were on the ground. We barreled over Philadelphia at about 500 feet. Every time we inched slightly higher the winds picked up and the air got choppier, so I would drop down hoping to smooth out the ride. A few minutes before landing at the Lancaster Airport, Brennan hollered over the intercom, "Slow down! Slow down!"

I immediately pushed down the collective and pulled back on the stick. "What's wrong?"

"Damn," he declared flatly. "Too late… Just go on in."

We sat down on a taxi ramp at about 5:00 p.m. and rolled on to an airport apron close to a special platform where a podium protruded above a jubilant mass of about 15,000 people. I dropped the door for Nixon to walk down the stairs, but when he went by the cockpit I noticed he was wearing an overcoat and holding a briefcase. Odd, I thought, since it was a balmy, warm evening and I had rarely seen him carry a briefcase.

Haldeman followed, commenting to me as he passed, "You *used* to be the President's pilot."

Judging by the smile on his face, I knew he wasn't serious, but didn't understand until Brennan stopped to explain.

"When I told you to slow down," he said, "the President had just gone in the toilet. Then you hit that last big bump and he fell against the door while he was going and it opened and he…he got his pants wet."

"Oh geez," I said, feeling a flash of guilt. "Sorry."

Normally, Nixon had a spare suit on board, but that wasn't

the case this time. From the cockpit, I could see him in the distance at the podium, delivering his speech with unwavering confidence, despite being the only one in the whole state wearing a coat. From surviving the mobs in South America more than a decade earlier, to enduring the constant battering of demonstrators wherever he now traveled, to weathering an unexpected mishap aboard his helicopter, he definitely had an admirable way of persevering in a good-natured way.

When Nixon returned to the helicopter, he grinned at me and said, "You were right. That was a rough flight."

It did not go unnoticed that a side benefit of that extra breezy day was that the President's trousers dried before his next appearance.

An hour later, we landed at Olmstead AFB where Nixon caught Air Force One to Green Bay, Wisconsin, to participate in a political function at the Austin Straubel Airport. From there, he motored to the Brown County Auditorium to honor Green Bay Packers Quarterback and longtime Nixon supporter Bart Starr. The President was back in Washington, D.C., by midnight and, I am guessing, made a mental note to never again travel without an extra suit.

I liked contingency plans. They were essential to dealing with unexpected twists and unforeseen events. The fewer elements left to chance, the smoother the flight, and, the better for everyone – passengers and crew alike. Maybe that was the reason Hughes called and told me to put HMX-1 Commander Lieutenant Colonel Richard Kuci in my co-pilot's seat.

"You're just picking up the President from Andrews," he told me over the phone, "and taking him back to the White House."

"Okay," I answered with a curious tone to my voice. About two months earlier, I had done the same flight with Kuci, only in reverse order. It was our unit's first Washington, D.C., mission since moving back and Kuci had taken the right seat with me for what I termed my refresher course. The ten-minute trip went flawlessly and truth be told, either one of us could have probably done it blindfolded.

"I'm interested in what you think," Hughes said.

"About what?"

"Let's just say, we've noticed you two don't fly the same."

"Are you asking for a check flight?"

"Yeah, something like that."

"You know," I told him, "he probably has less than a thousand hours. I've got almost five thousand. That makes a difference."

"Well, maybe something will rub off."

Kuci was a tall, sturdy man from Pennsylvania, deeply religious and known for his short temper. A decorated Vietnam veteran, he handled the routine flight perfectly from Andrews to the White House. Easy up, steady in flight, easy down. I could not offer Hughes any insights other than Kuci's agitating habit of jiggling his knees up and down. The closer the President got to the helicopter the faster he pumped and the more tempted I was to ask, "Where's the fire?" Fortunately, once airborne, those jitters subsided.

Hughes never did elaborate on the issue, but I knew people were talking and I would hear snippets of opinions here and there about the differences between us and HMX-1. What that meant was for others to discern one way or the other on their own. Our focus remained on doing our job to the best of our ability. It was also important to help others, like General Hughes, become familiar with the intricacies of how we handled missions.

Like most pilots, Hughes loved flying. So much so, that on one of our advance trips in a Huey, he joined me in the cockpit.

"How long," he asked, "do you think it would take me to qualify in one of these?"

"About a hundred hours," I answered. "I can set you up with one of my pilots."

"Let's do it," he said, grinning ear to ear.

Several months later, Hughes soloed with a Warrant Officer instructor pilot at Fort Rucker. He was a remarkable aviator. During his career, Hughes was awarded pilot wings from the Republic of Korea Air Force, Taiwan Air Force, Republic of the Philippines Air Force, and the Royal Thai Air Force, but he is likely the only Air Force general in history to earn Army Aviator wings flying a helicopter.

Hughes took his share of ribbing about his Army wings and I remember congratulating him, saying something like, "Now you should be able to really fly."

In actuality, we were honored to have such an accomplished and respected man go through our program.

At the end of 1970, American troop strength in Vietnam had dropped to about 340,000 and the Strategic Arms Limitation Talks (SALT) between the U.S. and the U.S.S.R resumed in Helsinki, Finland. On the domestic front, President Nixon signed the Organized Crime Control Act pledging "total war against organized crime." William Ruckelshaus became the first director of the newly formed Environmental Protection Agency and Nixon signed the ground-breaking National Air Quality Control Act. The North Tower of the World Trade Center was topped out, making it the tallest building in the world, and Elvis was still King.

President Nixon confers with Secretary of State William Rogers
during British Prime Minister Edward Heath's visit, December 18, 1970
(Courtesy of Richard Nixon Presidential Library, NARA)

During his first term as President, Nixon seemed to always be on the move and rarely spent a weekend at the White House. If he wasn't at Camp David, he was at Key Biscayne or at the Western White House in San Clemente, California. Cross-country missions to provide helicopter support were routine for both the Army and the Marines. With three to five helicopters in those flights, our routes depended on the weather and where we could land to refuel. The trip from Washington, D.C., to San Clemente was about 2,500 miles long and would take from 18 to 22 hours of flight time over a two-day period. Texas was our usual midway stopping point where we put the helicopters under guard and found a nearby economy motel with clean sheets and hot showers for the night.

Other times, we would grab a four- to five-hour nap break inside the helicopters during a refueling stop at either an Air Force base or a commercial airport that had a ready supply of tested jet fuel. Even though we had a 600-mile range, to keep our weight down, we rarely filled our tanks. Usually, the Military Office called ahead to alert a particular base that we were on our way and on a priority mission, and not to disseminate that information. Other times, I made arrangements over the radio.

White House helicopters were automatically granted preferential treatment wherever we went. However, every once in a while the guy in charge decided he had to make a statement about who was in control. After all, who did we think we were, waltzing in from out of the sky acting like we owned the place?

A landing at Maxwell Air Force Base just west of Montgomery, Alabama, turned out to be one of those situations. The head of base operations, a nameless colonel, had his own idea about what constituted a priority on his watch. For him and his strutting rooster attitude, it was a fleet of B-52 bombers currently being fueled and we could get in line.

"We'll get to you as soon as we can," he told me over the radio after we had landed.

"I don't think you understand," I said. "This is a White House mission and we're on a tight schedule. Those B-52s are not on a combat mission and there is no reason to make us wait."

"Sorry, you don't have priority here," he responded, turning up the heat.

"You're making a mistake on this." My warning bounced off him like a ping-pong ball tossed against a wall.

"Like I said, we'll get to you as soon as we can."

I had a couple of options. Since we still had about an hour of flying time, we could have backtracked to a civilian airport in Montgomery or headed south to Fort Rucker. Time-wise and fuel-wise, I thought both choices were a waste of resources. I certainly had enough cause to contact the Military Office and bring in the Air Force Chief of Staff, but that felt excessive. Even though I was pissed off, the colonel did outrank me and I did not want to make any enemies. I just wanted to get our tanks filled and move on.

I figured Ralph Albertazzie, the senior pilot for Air Force One, would be the perfect person to do a little intervention work. As soon as I explained the problem, adding that I thought it best to deal with the situation in-house, he told me, "Don't worry. I'll handle it."

I assumed Albertazzie would call base operations at Maxwell and enlighten the colonel. Instead, he contacted an Air Force general at the Pentagon. The next thing I knew, I was standing by the helicopters with my pilots and mechanics on the edge of the runway when we heard a siren approaching. A car sped onto the scene with a two-star general inside scrambling to get on his uniform.

Damn, I thought, Albertazzie really knows how to pull strings. The disobliging colonel arrived in time for the general to relieve him and order personnel to start refueling us immediately. I don't know what happened to the Air Force colonel who wanted to show an Army light colonel who was boss, but we were soon back in the air. The experience demonstrated to me how swiftly friends in high places could exert their influence. I didn't know it then, but the time was coming for me to cultivate my own connection at the Pentagon if I had any hope of saving the Exec Flight.

In 1971, Lyndon Johnson's memoirs, *The Vantage Point*, were published. After reading his perspective on the years he served as the 36th President of the United States, my viewpoint remained unchanged – he had done more harm than good. But as vantage points go, how any of us sees a situation depends on where we are sitting.

For me, that place was the cockpit of the President's helicopter.

Nap of the Earth 13

The time has come for political campaigning – its techniques and strategies – to move out of the dark ages and into the brave new world of the omnipresent eye.

– H.R. "Bob" Haldeman

"We're in a hell of a snow storm," I reported over the radio to the White House, "but I think we can get on top of it."

I was leading a flight of four or five helicopters from Washington, D.C., to the El Toro Marine Corps Air Station in California. We had just refueled in El Paso, Texas, and were following the Mexican border westward. Nixon was due to fly west on Air Force One the next afternoon and as long as we managed to get through the narrow, fast-moving front between us and San Clemente, we would have the helicopters ready for him when he landed.

Out of El Paso, the visibility had been a good 15 to 20 miles, but as night fell, we could see dense storm clouds boiling up on a low ridgeline to the west. Fixed-wing pilots in the area advised air traffic controllers we would have smooth sailing once we got above 8,000 or 9,000 feet. I radioed the my other pilots to hold back while I went ahead. Climbing upward, I hoped we could hurdle the worst of the storm and at least make it to our refuel stop in Phoenix, Arizona. There we would shut down for the night, get some rest and be at El Toro the next morning with plenty of time to clean the helicopters and prepare for Nixon's arrival.

An impenetrable wall.

That was the only way to describe what I found at about 10,000 feet. Planes reported they were being driven to at least 20,000 feet and then still getting bounced around. Although we weren't picking up any ice, it would have been foolish to push the helicopters any higher. Convinced we couldn't go through, under or over the front, I got back on the radio to the nearest control tower.

"It's a no go," I told them. "I'm sending my guys back to that border patrol station to land."

"Before you do that," a voice crackled in my headset, "you might try going a few miles south to see if you can get around it."

Flying in rain or snow always made it harder to climb and descend, and more difficult for radar to track us. Preferably, each helicopter would have its own control tower contact to keep us from running into each other. If we were on instruments and also looking for breaks in a storm system, it was very difficult to do both well when my attention was moving in and out of the cockpit. I would much rather fly doing one or the other.

But if it was possible to do an end-run play on this obstinate weather system and avoid a late arrival, I was willing to try – even if we had to venture a few miles into Mexico.

"Okay," I copied, "I'll give it a shot."

I turned south and told the rest of the flight to go back to a border town and orbit while I scouted for a through passage. Flying at about 500 feet and barely able to see more than a half mile ahead, I pursued anything that looked like a break. Much like a wayward prospector on the desert chases mirages looking for water, we pressed on through the darkness hoping to get lucky. Clouds have a way of playing games. Sucker holes can appear out of nowhere and entice us with a quick glimpse of the earth below. But as soon as a helicopter dipped into the opening, a dense, foggy vapor would close in and obliterate what had looked like a clear path. At that point, there was no choice but to pull up, get back on top of the clouds and rely on our radar altimeter to find land ahead for us to make an approach.

Five, then ten, then twenty miles we traveled into Mexico. Nothing. I became so intent on finding our way around the system, I briefly forgot we had penetrated a foreign country's airspace. Then, visions of former President Johnson's younger, wayward brother Sam Houston's unanticipated stay in a Mexican jail flitted through my mind.

Getting back meant radioing the others to circle back to the border station town. They found an empty, snow-covered parking lot and put down. I came in about fifteen minutes later just as a county sheriff's deputy rolled up in his cruiser.

"You fellas lost?" he asked me after I dashed through a flurry of snowflakes to his car door.

"No," I replied with a glint of good humor, "just taking a coffee break."

The deputy glanced past me to study the closest helicopter with its presidential seal. "You're not regular military, are you?"

"We're from the White House."

If the deputy and that little town had had a red carpet, they would have rolled it out for us right then and there. Instead, they opened up the local diner where we warmed our fingers around steaming cups of coffee and filled our stomachs with the tastiest food a half-awake cook at a greasy spoon could rustle up.

By midnight, word had spread hither and yon about the President's snowbound pilots. The diner filled with curious locals eager to strike up a conversation, asking questions about the helicopters or what Nixon was really like, and tossing in a political opinion or two. As unplanned events go, this was one of my favorites – having the chance to mingle on the spur of the moment with ordinary, hardworking Americans. The absence of pretense and subplots was as refreshing as the six inches of unseasonable snow falling outside.

We all need a good grounding now and then.

By dawn, the weather had cleared enough for us to take off and we scrambled into the air knowing we were hard pressed to have the helicopters ready for Nixon when he touched down later that day. As it turned out, without a second to spare, everything was in order when the President boarded Army One at El Toro for his flight to the Western White House, except for two things – we hadn't had the chance to change from our flight suits into our presidential uniforms, and we also hadn't had time to wash and polish the entire exterior of President's helicopter. Only the keenest eye would have noticed, upon takeoff, the surface opposite the side where Nixon entered still bore the residue of one hellacious trip across the southwestern United States.

For the President and all those circulating around him, it did not matter how our helicopters got to where they needed to be or who was flying them. What did matter was that when Nixon

Other duties as assigned: Standing at attention in the doorway of Army One,
I was soon called upon to assist with starting the golf cart for the First
Family, San Clemente, California, January 5, 1971.
(Courtesy of Richard Nixon Presidential Library, NARA)

needed us, we were there and ready to go – reliable and orderly. The hallmark of superior service was to run a seamless,
worry-free operation, causing as little distraction as possible. We
had to be automatic and predictable, with a level of consisten-
cy that allowed for countless factors, none of which we wanted
to ripple an otherwise still pond. Our passengers had far greater
interests and demands to address.

As to who those passengers were and on what presidential
flights they flew, manifests for each helicopter and Air Force
One flight are included in President Richard Nixon's Daily Diary
archived at the Nixon Library in Yorba Linda, California.
Meticulously maintained by his staff, this itinerary record provides minute-to-minute entries ranging from when he ate breakfast or called one of his daughters to meeting with a head of
state or traveling from one place to another. This official document

is an excellent companion paper to the Exec Flight and HMX-1 flight logs that specify which helicopter was flown and the names of the aircraft commander, second pilot and chief engineer.

During Bob Haldeman's nearly four-and-a-half years as Nixon's chief of staff, he kept an even more detailed diary of events, developments, personal thoughts and conversations with the President and top level advisors and aides. Those personal observations were published in his book, *The Haldeman Diaries,* in 1994 after his death the previous year. Nicknamed "The Brush" because of his distinctive crew-cut, Haldeman also had an 8mm movie camera I believe Nixon gave him, instructing, "Use this any chance you can."

And that he did.

From China to Italy, the Soviet Union to the Philippines, from Hawaii to New York, Haldeman captured the Nixon presidency in motion. He filmed both the significant and the insignificant: Nixon meeting with world leaders, staff huddling in the oval office, demonstrators being carried away by police, Tricia Nixon's wedding, public speeches, extravagant banquets, ceremonial toasts; the arrival of the annual Thanksgiving turkey, children singing, soldiers saluting, Big Ben, the Eiffel Tower and the pyramids of Egypt. There are also dozens of aerial shots from Air Force One and the presidential helicopter as varied as the California coastline, the Rocky Mountains, and a farmer's grassy field where someone had mowed, "Hi Nixon" for a fly-over greeting.

On May 29, 1971, Haldeman had his camera aimed out an Army One window as we flew Nixon from Stewart AFB in Newburgh, New York, to Target Hill field on the north side of West Point. Kennedy had been the last president to visit West Point nine years earlier. Nixon's trip to participate in commencement week ceremonies was his first visit as President.

It was also my first trip to the United States Military Academy. Swinging around the outer perimeter of the campus located on the bluffs of the slow-moving Hudson River, we had a tremendous view of Constitution Island on approach. We floated by the magnificent landmark granite chapel in all its medieval splendor. In the distance, to the west, were the sweeping lines of the cemetery. Sporting varying shades of gray, the tombstones – from modest to elaborate – appeared to have fallen out of formation from the "long gray line," the phrase used to describe the human chain of all West Point graduates. Somewhere in those deceased ranks was one of the most flamboyant military leaders in American history – General George Armstrong Custer. He was also probably the most famous alumnus to have finished at the bottom of his class.

Then there were those one-time cadets who didn't finish at all and were expelled before becoming a "ring-knocker" – a well-known military slang term referring to the over-sized, gold class ring graduates wore as a symbol of their achievements and fellowship. Within the ranks of the expelled was raven fancier Edgar Allen Poe, "Turn on, tune in, drop out" advocate Timothy Leary, and the bulk of the Black Knights 1950 undefeated football team after participating in one of the academy's worst cribbing scandals ever. Many of those players were picked up by colleges in the Ohio University conference and, although nameless faces to me, I remembered taking a few hits on the field that had what I called a West Point sting.

Nixon and his party, including Haldeman and his 8mm camera, departed the helicopter to join the throng of dignitaries and military officials decked out in full dress uniforms. General Hughes passed by the cockpit and was out the door before I could catch his attention to tell him thank you for the chance to fly into West Point.

I sat in Army One, near the four other helicopters in our flight, soaking in as much of the experience as I could. There was a consuming mystique about West Point. Founded in 1802, it produced many of our country's most prominent military leaders. The most notable being Ulysses S. Grant, Dwight Eisenhower, Omar Bradley, George Patton, Anthony McAuliffe, Douglas MacArthur, William Westmoreland, Creighton Abrams, Jr., my current boss Don Hughes and my respected mentor and classical musical enthusiast, George Stanhope Mason. However, with the onset of WWII, West Point could not keep pace with the growing demand for military leadership and other programs throughout the military were established like the Officer

Candidate School, ROTC, Ranger School, Airborne and Special Forces Training.

Throughout my military career and beyond, I have interacted with countless military leaders in multiple branches of the military. Can I say that a West Point officer is superior to those who have achieved rank by other means? Not always, but they certainly had skill sets that made it easier for them to climb ladders faster. They also had a much better feel for combat tactics.

Nixon made his way to a reviewing stand well out of our sight to address the some 3,700 cadets and their proud parents following the Parade of Colors. We waited on the Target Hill field for about two hours. In the meantime, we could hear the drums and trumpets of a disciplined military band drifting over the academy's 16,000 acres to the surrounding forested hills. Celebratory voices filled the public address system and the President delivered a speech declaring, "Now at last, we have the end of the American role in this war clearly in sight...and it is my highest hope that the great majority of you standing before me today will never be called upon to serve in any war at all."

With the President back on board Army One, I lifted off from West Point very pleased with a clockwork mission and honored to have brushed up against the "long gray line." That continuum included a formidable contingent of aviators beginning with Army First Lieutenant Thomas Selfridge. A classmate of MacArthur, he graduated the same year the Wright Brothers made their first successful flight at Kitty Hawk, North Carolina. Five years later, at the age of 26, well-respected for his forward-thinking enthusiasm for powered flight, he was test flying dirigibles and balloons for the Aeronautical Division of the Army. In September of 1908, Selfridge was invited to fly as a passenger with Orville Wright at Fort Myer, Virginia, in our government's first "fixed-wing asset."

Designated Model A, Serial I and developed and built by the Wright brothers who had won the $25,000 contract from the U.S. Army, the plane had had several successful solo test flights before Wright and Selfridge climbed aboard. Not long after they were airborne, a crack in the right propeller launched a wave of

vibrations so violent that the aircraft lost control and plummeted to the ground. Wright survived his injuries, but Selfridge was killed and became the first U.S. military aviation fatality. The Selfridge Air National Guard Base in Harrison Township, Michigan, bears his name.

When I think back to the warm spring day in May when President Nixon spoke to the West Point Cadet Corps about "duty, honor and country," I am reminded of the extreme raw courage it takes to be among the first, from Selfridge at Fort Meyer to Armstrong and Aldrin on the moon. Like West Pointers, pilots were also part of a long line – one that arched beyond the stars.

Two weeks later, the Nixon administration was dealt an unexpected blow by the *New York Times'* decision to publish an excerpt from what would become known as The Pentagon Papers. The 7,000-page study commissioned by Robert McNamara, Johnson's Secretary of Defense, was a study of American involvement in Southeast Asia from WWII to 1968. Study participant Daniel Ellsberg, disillusioned with what the study uncovered, decided to make it public. A lot of the material was "top secret" and in Nixon's own words, became what "was the most massive leak of classified documents in American history."

The impact of this development launched a tidal wave of concerns at the National Security Agency, State Department, CIA and the White House. In his memoirs, Nixon writes, "Publication of the Pentagon Papers was certain to hurt the whole Vietnam effort."

The papers focused on the policies and decisions made by Kennedy and Johnson that had led the U.S. into Vietnam and the failure to fully disclose to the public increasing military involvement in Southeast Asia. In the months following there were court battles, media campaigns, conspiracy charges, investigations, presidential demands and a break-in. A group of White House-led administrative staffers known as "The Plumbers," because their job was to "plug leaks," broke into the office of Ellsberg's psychiatrist hoping to find more information about his motives and any further related plans. Nixon claimed that he knew nothing about the break-in, but supported the tactics under the circumstances. That event was the start of a downhill slide for the President who would eventually be drummed out of office three years later. At the time, no one had the slightest inkling that something so farfetched could happen.

Nixon's schedule loosened up enough in June of 1971 for CeCe, Robin and me to take our first vacation in years. CeCe had heard so much about Grand Cay that I put out the word to associates in the area that we were on our way to the Bahamas, and for once, the trip would not be business related. Bob Abplanalp somehow heard about our plans and allowed us to use his seaplane to fly out to a small beachfront hotel on one of the islands he owned. One evening he joined us for dinner and on another day he took us on a tour of his massive private aquarium. Robin, who was almost seven years old, was enthralled. Huge outdoor steel tanks, partially sunk into the ground, contained a colorful array of local sea creatures and plant life. It was one of the many indulgences of a man who was pulling in something like $50 million a year later, Alplanalp was a primary funder for the Nixon Foundation and Library.

CeCe, Robin and I walked the beaches, swam in the ocean and went boating. I especially remember one evening of dancing in a hotel lounge. After CeCe and I had danced, Robin, still in her little girl swimsuit, demanded I dance with her, which I did. It wasn't long until she decided it was more fun to dance alone and whirled the night away as we watched with delight. It was a long overdue dream vacation.

On June 24, 1971, Nixon was scheduled to travel to Indianapolis, Indiana, and from there I would fly him about 50 miles south into the state's heartland and the town of North Vernon in Jennings County. The purpose of this trip was for him to participate in a dedication event for an historical marker honoring his beloved mother, Hannah Milhous Nixon, who had been born on a nearby farm.

The day before, we did a routine recon to assess the landing site at the high school in North Vernon. From there, the President would motor to the Jennings County Courthouse for the commemoration ceremony, and then, I assumed because I

had no other information, we would fly him back to Indianapolis for his return trip to Washington, D.C. Orders out of the Military Office were for me to locate the cemetery where Nixon's great-grandparents were buried, in case he wanted to fly over the site. Another pilot and I hooked up with a local official who offered to help us find the gravesite. We drove around following his hunches and best guess directions from whomever he thought to ask, traipsing through several different small graveyards tucked here and there about the sweeping countryside.

After several hours, with sweat trickling down our backs, we finally found ourselves standing in the overgrown grasses of Hopewell Cemetery. About ten plain, barely hip-high tombstones protruded above the weeds that covered a space less than a half acre in size. A cluster of trees stood nearby. Scouting for a landmark, I saw nothing distinctive that would set this patch of ground apart from any other from the air. It was all a patchwork of undulating farmland for miles and miles.

When I notified the Military Office that the cemetery was in ruins and extremely difficult to see anything from the air, I was told to forget about it. So, I did.

The next afternoon, as Nixon, Haldeman, Indiana Governor Edgar Whitcomb and Secretary of Agriculture Clifford Hardin boarded Army One at the Indianapolis Municipal Airport, Brennan let me know there had been a change of plans. The President still wanted to fly over the cemetery.

"Oh, boy," I thought to myself and launched a Huey from our flight with the pilot who had been with me on the advance trip the day before. "Go down there," I told him, "find it and orbit over the site so I can hone in on you."

Our scheduled flight time from Indianapolis to North Vernon was 35 minutes with a specific arrival time. On the flight south, I heard from the Huey that he thought he had it, then no, then maybe now, then can't be sure, until finally he radioed, "I think we're on it."

My relief lasted only a few minutes when I joined the Huey just in time to hear him say, "Damn, I'm not sure now."

I worked the best details my memory could muster and went into my own circle pattern, straining to sort one patch of land from another. Had we been given the green light the day before, we would have done a flyover on our way back to Indianapolis to fix our bearings. But now, imagining the President with his face practically pressed against the glass of his window, waiting to catch site of his ancestor's final resting place, my co-pilot and I nearly bumped heads looking every which way.

Nixon had a strong connection to his family roots and I knew flying over just any cemetery wouldn't do. So we made another, bigger circle.

Joshua and Elizabeth Milhous had come to Bigger Township from Ohio in 1854. They established the "Sycamore Valley Nursery" and were devout members of the Quaker community. One of their sons, Frank Milhous, eventually had his own farm where Nixon's mother was born. Also buried in the Hopewell Cemetery were Francis Demint Smith and two of her 28 children. In 1868 she and her husband, a newly emancipated slave, were taken in by the Milhous family. The President had remained in touch with one of their descendents who lived in Columbus, Indiana.

"If you can't find it," Haldeman said into my headset from the phone he had picked up in the cabin, "just go on over to the high school."

I felt terrible about disappointing the President, thought about making another pass, but instead elected to get him to his destination on time.

After we landed in the high school parking lot where a crowd of some 700 greeted the President with cheerful faces and waving hands, Haldeman stuck his head in the cockpit.

"That was a horrible performance," he charged. "We've decided to go back by motorcade and not use you."

I was speechless. As he hurried down the steps, I wanted to fire back, "I told you guys it was too damn hard to see from the air!"

But instead, I privately seethed, muttering under my breath, "This is bullshit."

I assigned two helicopters to fly motorcade coverage and as soon as the President was on the road back to Indianapolis, I flew on ahead, getting more steamed by the minute. I wanted to throttle Haldeman for making me a fall guy and using the failed tombstone search to change the mission. It was uncalled for and every stiffening muscle in my body said that if I let this pass uncontested I could look forward to a repeat strike.

I called one of my master sergeants at the motel where we were lodged, had him pack my bags and check me out. Still in my presidential flight suit, I managed to catch a commercial flight back to Washington National and called ahead to General Hughes' office at the White House to ask for a meeting before he went home for the evening.

"What's going on?" he asked over the phone.

After I unloaded about how I had been blamed for crap Haldeman had pulled, Hughes told me he would call him to get his input.

"He says it's all a misunderstanding," Hughes told me when I got to his office at the White House. "The plan never was for you to fly the President back to Indianapolis. They had decided to go by motorcade a few days ago, but had kept it secret for security reasons."

"That so?" I said, dissatisfied with the explanation.

"Yeah," Hughes said with a little shrug. "When I told him how angry you were, he told me you need to learn to take a joke. He was just kidding."

"He was dead serious," I countered.

"And he told me to convey to you his deepest apologies."

I paused and took a deep breath. I could take a joke as well as the next guy, but not one that came across with such undeserved condemnation.

"So, just forget about it," Hughes advised, with a grin. "Not too many people get even a half-assed apology out of Haldeman."

That I could believe. I left Hughes' office realizing it was best to keep my mouth shut, but nothing was going to keep me from again standing up for the diligence and competence of my unit. If we screwed up, I could take it. On the other hand, if we had not earned the demerit, I would always have something to say.

No question about it. Haldeman was a sharp-tongued taskmaster. The President's daughter Julie Eisenhower in her book, *Pat Nixon: The Untold Story*, recalled the concern she shared with her mother about Nixon's growing dependency on Haldeman following the 1972 elections, and wrote: "Much of the sensitivity and thoughtfulness we saw in my father was squeezed out by the time Haldeman, overworked and with far too many details to attend to everything himself, parceled out orders to his young aides. Increasingly, loyalty was demanded of all, not judgment."

In early 1973, a large new staff lodge was completed at Camp David. Different than the former facility, the "Laurel" building had two dining areas instead of one. The spacious executive dining room had cathedral ceilings and huge picture windows. A second, much smaller room was nearby with a single table and about six chairs. Shortly after the facility opened, the President's doctor, General Tkach, several military aides and helicopter pilots were eating in the larger space when one of Haldeman's young, up-and-coming assistants notified us that he wanted us to use the smaller room. As I understand it, Haldeman didn't want to take the chance that lower ranking personnel might overhear sensitive conversations, but he hadn't considered the logistics of jamming us all into such a cramped space.

For my part, I was accustomed to confined places and had "dined" under much worse conditions. It remained such an honor to fly for the White House I would have probably eaten on the back porch if told, unless it was snowing. However, sitting elbow to elbow for a meal – or in some cases even standing to chow down – infuriated everyone. The duty aide, Lieutenant Colonel Bill Golden, contacted the Military Office to advise of the new directive. Word soon traveled and after Nixon did a site visit, Haldeman's rules were lifted and we were allowed back into the executive dining room. As for eavesdropping on any sensitive conversations, one thing Haldeman had forgotten to take into account is that most helicopter pilots have lousy hearing. So if there was an exchange of privileged information within earshot, we missed it and posed no threat to national security.

Years later, sometime in 1978 after I had retired and Haldeman had been released from prison for the role he played in the Watergate cover-up, I gave him a lift in my car after a social gathering of former Nixon personnel. Even though it had been only a few years since we had been at the White House, it felt like decades had passed.

"I seem to remember," Haldeman commented to me as we drove, "that you and I did quite a bit of bickering."

"Yes, we did," I agreed. "I don't think we had the same sense of humor."

"You were a pain in the ass," he replied, "but the best pilot we ever had."

"I'm not sure you can have one without the other," I said, and we exchanged friendly smiles.

In retrospect, Haldeman was the right guy for the job as Nixon's chief of staff. He was much more a gatekeeper than he was a politician, and could not have been more dedicated to serving Nixon. I gained even more respect for him when I read his diaries and discovered we shared the same opinion regarding Rumsfeld and his propensity for what Haldeman described as "slimy maneuvers."

Admittedly, a person had to have a thick skin to operate in Washington, D.C. Deals were being cut everywhere – over lunch at Camp David, in the Oval Office, on the beach at Key Biscayne or even in the back of a helicopter. I've seen hundreds and hundreds of confidential VIP huddles and, like the rest of the world, relied on the newspaper or evening news for details. Although, I do remember once being invited by Nixon to participate in what he termed "an historic event."

Our unit was on standby at San Clemente when we were summoned at about 5:00 p.m. on July 15, 1971, to take Nixon, Henry Kissinger and key White House staffers and press on an unannounced flight to the NBC Studios in Burbank, California. They wanted to leave within 30 minutes. The flight of five helicopters would take about 25 minutes, but I had no idea where we would be landing. I quickly dispatched a Huey with Nixon's assistant press secretary Tim Elbourne and Secret Service agents to fly ahead and locate a safe landing site.

When we were about 15 minutes out, Elbourne radioed me to stall as long as I could. They had people removing light poles from a parking lot along with the vehicles parked there to make

President Nixon press conference
Helicopter hangar, Camp David, Maryland
(Courtesy of Richard Nixon Presidential Library, NARA)

space. I couldn't believe it. They were actually unbolting poles, disconnecting the electricity and moving them out of the way. I slowed down and was able to stretch the flight by about ten minutes.

With Burhanan as my co-pilot, I gave the go-ahead for a few of the Marine helicopters we had picked up for the mission to go in and land. On what looked to me to be a normal approach by the other helicopters over a residential area into the NBC Studio lot turned out to be too low for a couple having sex on their apartment balcony. Besides the rude intrusion, the rotor wash blew things around pretty good. Fortunately, I brought the President in from another direction.

After we landed and shut down, I was surprised when Nixon stopped by the cockpit and braced for a comment about what he might have accidentally seen.

"I want to invite you and your crew to witness an historic event," he instead said, with Kissinger standing behind him. "You're going to be in the audience when I make this announcement to the world."

I was mystified and had no idea about what was to happen.

I positioned guards at the helicopter before Burhanan and I, along with a few other crew members, followed the Presidential party into the television studio.

During the past two years, Kissinger had been secretly involved in a series of what Nixon described as "complex, subtle and determined diplomatic signals and negotiations" with China. Nixon felt a viable strategy for ending the Vietnam War involved using Chinese leaders to persuade the North Vietnamese to participate in a peace agreement. The advantage for the Chinese would be normalized relations and expanded trade.

The big announcement was short and sweet – if that's possible with international politics and a pledge to "build lasting peace in the world." During a live broadcast to the nation, Nixon announced his acceptance of an invitation by Premier Chou En-lai to visit the People's Republic of China in the coming year. It was a stunning development and remains a critical turning point in world history for softening tensions between global super-powers.

From the studio, Nixon motored to Perino's Restaurant to celebrate with Kissinger, Haldeman, Ehrlichman, Ziegler and special consultant John Scali. About two hours later, they met us at the FBI helipad in Los Angeles for the trip back to the Western White House. I watched Nixon move toward us as if he was walking on air. Upon boarding, he again stopped by the cockpit.

"Did you see it?" the President asked.

"Yes, sir, I did."

"What did you think?"

"I think it's absolutely great," I replied, tickled that the President of the United States had asked for my opinion.

"Good," he said, clearly pleased himself and then settled into his seat.

It was a momentous day for the President and the world, as well as the amorous couple on a top floor balcony who had been so rudely interrupted. Strangely enough, they filed a harassment claim against the Marines, which would be quietly settled.

Flying as close to the ground as we did, and usually at a leisurely speed, made it possible for passengers to get an excellent view of any scenery. The President and First Lady's seats faced each other with a small table between them and a large plexiglass window to the side. On numerous occasions, the President sent word to the cockpit to slow down or make a turn for a closer look. But there were those few times when we made sure the President didn't see what we saw.

Two particular instances stand out for me.

The first occurred after Nixon had spent two days in the Grand Teton National Park in Moran, Wyoming, and went boating on Jackson Lake with his daughter Julie. We had just lifted off and were headed back over the lake toward Fanning Airport in Idaho Falls, Idaho, to meet Air Force One when I spotted ahead to our left a naked woman floating on an air mattress about a quarter mile offshore from a wooded area. As soon as she started waving with unmistakable exuberance, I knew she had been expecting us. I immediately broke left to conceal her under the helicopter as we flew over.

The pilot in the number two helicopter came on the radio to say, "Hey, you missed a good sight."

"No, I saw her," I answered, "but the President didn't."

My headset filled with so much chatter between the other helicopters that I couldn't make out a single word and didn't much care since the object of their ogling was rapidly disappearing behind me.

A second delicate situation snuck up on me when I was flying Nixon at about 300 feet along an isolated ocean beach on Oahu in Hawaii. There were four other helicopters following when I saw ahead of us near the surf-line a small cluster of people and a couple of movie cameras planted on tripods in the sand. The instant I realized the man and woman on beach blankets were nude, I ordered the flight to break left with me and we managed to spare all of our passengers a bird's eye view of someone filming a porn movie.

Again, a flurry of chatter ensued, but I was the one exhaling relief for dodging what would have been an embarrassing incident for the President. Sometimes flying so close to the earth had distinct disadvantages, but mostly the exact opposite was true.

Nap of the earth flying was a rush for me. Every sense was engaged and the element of surprise only added to the thrill. Helicopter pilots develop an exceptionally intimate connection to the ground and that closer contact makes for some spectacular encounters with Mother Nature. I have hovered in the mist above Niagara Falls, traced the sparkling Colorado River through the Grand Canyon, followed the meandering line of the Snake River from Idaho Falls to Jackson Hole, Wyoming, circled Libby Dam with a light snow falling and all but nuzzled a pristine, cascading Rocky Mountain stream as I climbed above a forested ridgeline.

Flying for the White House had its fair share of perks and pressure points. No two flights were ever the same and the unpredictable rarely failed to disappoint.

Damage Control 14

*If it hadn't been for football and the fact I got my leg broke and
had to go into the movies to eat, why, who knows, I might have
turned out to be a liberal Democrat.*

— John Wayne

Ten years old. That was the age of the eight VH-3A presidential helicopters in 1971. Concern regarding the number of flight
hours they were accumulating and their life span became a
growing topic of conversation. As a result, midway through that
year Nixon's Military Assistant General Don Hughes called a
meeting to gather input from the Exec Flight, HMX-1 and the
White House Military Office.

Two helicopters were candidates for replacement: the Army's
Chinook CH-47 workhorse manufactured by Boeing-Vertol, and
Sikorsky's CH-53 Sea Stallion in use by the Air Force, Navy and
Marines. Both models had been placed into service about 1967
in Vietnam for rescue and supply missions. Each shared the
same capacity for carrying 30 to 55 passengers or 24 litters,
depending on the configuration. The Chinook was 10 feet longer
with a service ceiling of 18,500 feet. With a slightly longer range
of distance, the Sea Stallion was six feet higher, but with a lower
ceiling limit of 16,750 feet. Weight characteristics were compa-
rable and maximum speed for both was 170 knots.

The most significant difference between the two was their
rotor systems. The Sea Stallion had a single six-blade rotor head
and a smaller tail rotor for anti-torque. For the last two years,
because I had had to borrow back-up Marine CH-53s for our
larger missions, I was very familiar with how it flew and where
it made sense to use it.

Conversely, the Chinook had a large set of three-blade tandem rotors, which made it the more stable and easier to fly of
the two, especially when we were flying on instruments. With the
forward blade spinning counterclockwise and the aft turning the

opposite direction, the air flow was better dispersed and generated far less rotor wash than the Sea Stallion.

Furthermore, the CH-47 had a more spacious cabin with about 8 to 10 inches additional head space, which made it comfortable for those onboard. A VIP configuration could accommodate at least 18 passengers plus a four-man crew and four Secret Service agents. An option to the traditional aft side door was easy access through the back and up a ramp.

I loved the CH-47. It was a great combat helicopter – reliable, versatile and, in my opinion, superior to the CH-53 when it came to what was best for the White House. Consequently, I was highly disappointed when I got a call from the Military Office letting me know they had decided to go with the CH-53. Given what I knew about the advantages and disadvantages of each model, I came to the conclusion that the best helicopter for the mission had fallen victim to partisan politics. Additionally, the Marines had more equipment and people with clearances in the CH-53, which left the Exec Flight without much leverage.

On paper, after the numbers were crunched, the decision made sense.

Me with U.S. Army BG James "Don" Hughes during an award ceremony
for the White House Executive Flight Detachment
Ft. Belvoir, Virginia, September 17, 1971
(Boyer Family Archives)

A few weeks later, I received a small plastic scale model of the Sea Stallion from Sikorsky, painted with the fleet's distinctive green color and bearing the presidential seal. Well, I thought, at least I know what I will be flying in a few years and did not give the situation much more thought. There were plenty of other things to keep me busy – like Nixon's trip to Montana the last week of September in 1971.

The trip's countdown meeting on September 24 was held at a motel near the Glacier International Airport north of Kalispell, Montana. Nixon would land in Air Force One the next day about noon. As to where he went next, a local newspaper headline read: "Only His Pilot Knows for Sure."

The article speculated as to whether or not the President would "actually examine from the ground the massive Libby Dam project...White House spokesman continued to insist that the President would merely fly over the project, but said he would be in Montana for about two hours."

Keeping the public guessing about Nixon's itinerary was a common security tactic of the White House. However, in this case the strategy rang a little hollow since the Army Corps of Engineers had work crews at the dam site scurrying to construct two landing pads on the right dam abutment. If that weren't enough, they were also installing a press area and telephone jacks next to one of the pads. So no one really had to wonder what the President's pilot knew for sure – Nixon will land at the dam.

I would first fly him to the Libby Dam construction site on the Kootenai River for a tour before he headed to Portland, Oregon, for an informational briefing on the West Coast dock strike.

The next day we would fly him by helicopter from Walla Walla, Washington, to the Hanford Atomic Energy site on the Columbia River, which housed the world's first full-scale plutonium production reactor. The plutonium manufactured at the site was used in the first nuclear bomb as well as in the bomb detonated over Nagasaki, Japan. Ironically, Nixon's next stop on this trip would be Anchorage, Alaska, for a meeting with Japanese Emperor Hirohito on his first trip to America. Popular opinion at the time was that the visit was a goodwill gesture by

Nixon to soothe the Japanese government for his failure to consult with them regarding U.S. plans to broaden relations with China.

The final Kalispell countdown meeting the night before Nixon arrived included about 20 people handling communications and logistics. I ticked off a list of routine considerations about the number of passengers, number of available seats, time and distance calculations, and contingencies in the event of inclement weather.

Someone mentioned the front page of the local newspaper had a great article welcoming the President. Along with photos of Nixon, Montana Democrat and Senate Majority Leader Mike Mansfield and Governor Forrest Anderson was a stock photo of me in the doorway of a VH-3A. Wow! The President and a no-name helicopter pilot, on the same page. This I had to see.

Dressed in civilian clothing, I bundled up against the harbinger chill of winter and walked across the street to a small drugstore to find *The Daily Inter Lake* newspaper on a rack not far from the check-out counter. Sure enough, there was my picture, in the lower left-hand corner with a nice little write-up about being the pilot of Army One: "Lt. Col. Boyer, 40, is a master Army aviator with almost 16 years of helicopter experience and 5,000 hours (of helicopter time) under his belt." My Ohio upbringing was also mentioned. It was a proud moment and I probably would not have paid any attention to the grungy, long-haired man pressed against the counter talking to the young female clerk if I hadn't overheard what he said.

"I know we can get the helicopter," he said softly to her. "We know the route."

I froze like a statue bent over the newspapers, with my back to the pair, waiting to hear more, but the conversation volume dropped too low for me to decipher anything else. Damn pilot ears. Still, I heard more than enough. I casually left the newspapers behind and headed back to the countdown room where I went to alert the agent in charge.

After explaining what I had just witnessed, I summed up by saying, "I think it bears looking into."

He agreed and within less than a minute had rounded up a few other agents and a couple of sheriff's deputies. I remember thinking to myself as we hurried back to the drugstore that I was the only one without a weapon, so I positioned myself at the back of the hastily assembled posse.

As soon as one of the agents confronted the young hippy and began searching him, he blurted out a stream of objections.

"What the hell are you talking about?!" he shouted. "I never said anything about any helicopters."

"We have someone who says otherwise," the agent responded.

The eyes of the young woman behind the counter were as big as saucers and it was clear to us all they were hiding something.

"Who says otherwise?" demanded the fuming man as he was being handcuffed.

"Him," the agent said calmly and pointed at me.

The guy glared at me from beneath a scruffy mane of hair.

"So, who's he?"

"The President's helicopter pilot," replied the agent.

Game over.

The militant hippy was arrested, his female friend grilled for more information and the commune where they lived, just a mile south of the Canadian border, had some unexpected visitors. A mound of anti-war publications was found in his beat-up car. At the compound, several automatic weapons, including a machine gun, were confiscated, and a couple of military deserters were also apprehended.

A deputy sheriff told me the group was known to local officials and he wasn't surprised to learn they were planning some kind of event. Whether or not they would have acted on the threat I overheard he could not say, but no one wanted to take any chances.

By the next day, the dust had settled and I finally purchased some extra newspapers to share with relatives. The only complication turned out to be a sneaker snow storm that forced us to skirt north to get the President to the dam construction site. As a result, we arrived a little late and by the time Nixon and Mansfield paired up to dump a ceremonial load of cement, it had hardened up and was unpourable.

That was a complication we could all live with, not to mention have a good laugh.

Back at Belvoir the next week, the "Kalispell Hippy" story got a lot of airtime in the hangar. It was also the time period that CW3 Ron Bean first flew with me as my co-pilot on a presidential mission. An average size man with light brown wavy hair, Bean knew how to laugh long and hard. He was one of the few men I've ever known who could always turn any negative into a positive, and was an excellent addition to our unofficial "B Company."

Burhanan was the first to give me a heads up about Bean being Exec Flight material. On one of our cross country trips with four White House helicopters, I had made a point to stop by Ft. Sill, Oklahoma, to interview Bean and take him up for an orientation ride. I experienced a good surge of nostalgia flying in over the field where I had learned to fly a helicopter and had first soloed in a little two-place Bell H-13. Even though it had been almost 20 years since evading premature death, I could still feel the pulse of adrenaline as if it had happened just yesterday. I had lost track of my flight instructor through the years, but knew he would be more than slacked-jawed if he knew I was now the Exec Flight's commanding officer.

A brigadier general greeted us at a Fort Sill hangar and made some good-natured comments about us being there to steal one of his best pilots, so I opened one of the helicopters to let anyone with military I.D. take a quick tour.

"I can't believe you're doing this," he said to me.

"It's owned by the taxpayers," I said. "Just don't let anybody steal anything."

Soon, hundreds of gawking GIs were streaming through the helicopter and snapping photographs with crew members. Remarkably, not even a book of matches came up missing.

For our first White House mission together, Bean and I flew Nixon about an hour northeast from the White House to the John W. Rollins estate in Wilmington, Delaware. Rollins was hosting an evening reception for the Republican National Committee's "Salute to the President" fundraising dinners. Our passengers included Attorney General John Mitchell, Senators Bob Dole, Hale Boggs and William Roth, along with regular passengers like Ziegler, Brennan and Tkach.

The estate was in the country and we had plenty of room to land. Not long after Nixon and his party disembarked, Bean and I grew anxious about the low-level clouds closing in on us as night fell.

"What do you think?" he asked me.

I was familiar with the air space, knew there were no obstructions, and had confidence in the air traffic control system to support us. "We'll probably be on instruments all the way, but think we'll be okay."

"Sounds good," he replied, confidently.

We lifted off with limited visibility and inched our way through the black night, adding ten minutes to the flight before touching down at the White House. A decorated Vietnam War vet, Bean performed flawlessly and proved himself worthy of his new assignment. I saw in him then what his home state of Louisiana saw when they elected him to the State Senate in 1992 – a competent, level-headed man.

Shortly after noon on December 12, 1971, I picked up Nixon from the White House for a routine flight to Andrews AFB. After we landed, the President boarded Air Force One, which was waiting to take him on a five-hour flight to the Azores for a meeting with French President George Pompidou on international finance conditions. Just as Air Force One lined up for take-off, I got a call from the pilot, Colonel Ralph Arbertazzie.

"There's a deer on the runway," he announced.

"Where?" I asked.

"At the far end."

Next to a small forested area, the runway was well-fenced and heavily guarded, but somehow a doe had managed to breech that security. I squinted into the distance, hoping to spot the unwitting intruder.

"Just get the damn thing off the runway," snapped Albertazzie, who was known as a stickler for taking off and landing on time down to the second.

"Okay," I answered, as I lifted up, certain members of the press on Air Force One were already taking notes.

At last, all that time spent herding cows out of the way for LBJ in the Texas Hill Country had finally paid off. Although there was a lot of firepower in the area, no one wanted to see the deer hurt, so I came in from one side and eased close enough for her to head toward the hangars. As soon as ground personnel were able to corner the doe there, I backed off.

"Okay," I alerted Albertazzie, "make it quick."

"Thanks," he replied and did exactly that.

A small article in a D.C. newspaper, titled: *Deer on Runway Delays President*, read: "The helicopter that brought President Nixon from the White House to Andrews Air Force Base today was called on to do double duty as an aerial cowboy when a deer wandered onto the runway in front of the presidential jet… Mr. Nixon's plane got off four minutes late."

I have no doubt Bambi's mother was safely returned to the forest with bragging rights for having stopped a very big bird in its tracks and escaped from some kind of weird flying creature.

The press loved peppering the news with such anecdotes, but perhaps none grabbed more attention for an Exec Flight helicopter than an incident that occurred on December 28, 1971.

We had just landed at the Key Biscayne helipad for a Head of State arrival with Chancellor Willy Brandt of the Federal Republic of Germany. That ceremony generally included a red carpet, an honor guard, a band, a horde of press and any number of officials in the President's welcoming party. In this case, that party included Secretary of State William Rogers, Ambassadors David Kennedy and Kenneth Rush, Haldeman, Ziegler, and Hughes.

As Brandt prepared to disembark and before we dropped the airstair door, a member of the honor guard unrolled the red carpet, secured the end with tape just outside the helicopter and stepped to one side. As we waited for Nixon to arrive on the scene, I asked my co-pilot if it was clear to let the door down.

"All clear," he said.

I gave the flight engineer the go ahead sign to release the lever and lower the door. At that same time, a gust of wind caught the end of the carpet and it flopped to one side. The attendant hurried back to re-secure it just as the stairs came down on top of him. He crumpled into a ball holding his head with white gloved hands. The press had a field day snapping

Whoops! Preparing for President Nixon to welcome
German Chancellor Willy Brandt, Key Biscayne, Florida, December 28, 1971
(Courtesy of Richard Nixon Presidential Library, NARA)

President Nixon welcomes German Chancellor Willy Brandt after the
red carpet mishap. Key Biscayne, Florida, December 28, 1971
(Courtesy of Richard Nixon Presidential Library, NARA)

photographs as the guy crawled out, brushed off his clothing
and got back into position.

Following the ceremony and after Nixon and Brandt had
walked into the house about 30 yards away, Hughes darted on
board the helicopter.

"What happened?" he asked.

"We didn't see the guy sneak back to fix the carpet," I
explained, "and we bounced the door off his head."

"Was he hurt?"

"No, he told us he was okay."

Hughes sighed and turned to leave saying, "Thank God the
President didn't see it."

"I know," I said, glancing at the throng of scattering press,
"but he'll probably see it on the news tonight."

As predicted, every television station ran the story that night
and the incident was forever memorialized on a TV program

called *Famous Bloopers of the 20th Century.* I don't know if the President ever found out about it, but the story did make its way to HMX-1 Commander Kuci and he took the opportunity to have a little fun with me a few weeks later.

Before then, on December 31, 1971, we flew Nixon from Key Biscayne to Homestead where he boarded Air Force One for a New Year's Eve flight back to Washington, D.C. We had the helicopters in the air soon after for our seven-plus hour flight back to Fort Belvoir and arrived about midnight. Just as we had stretched out to get some needed sleep after a longer than usual day, my phone rang. Chancellor Brandt had been promised a helicopter ride from his vacation residence in Sarasota, Florida, to the newly opened Disney World just outside of Orlando.

Don't kill the messenger, I reminded myself and replied, "No one told me anything about this. What's our pick-up time?"

"Nine a.m."

"Okay," I said, not wanting to waste any more energy jawing. "We're on our way."

During the nearly 1,000-mile trip *back* to Florida, we rotated pilots, allowing each of us to grab a two-hour nap. The sun came up and we put down in a park near the beach property where Brandt was staying. He soon boarded with a party of at least ten dressed in Florida casual clothing for the hour flight to Disney World. After we landed in a special closed-off area of a parking lot near a hotel, Brandt leaned into the cockpit.

"Would you like to join us?" he asked with an inviting smile on his rugged face.

"I'm sorry Mr. Chancellor," I answered, already dreaming of the freshly turned-down beds awaiting us inside the hotel. "We have some...some maintenance work to do. But thank you and enjoy yourself. We'll be ready for you when you come back."

By the time we returned Brandt to Sarasota and cruised back to D.C., I had traveled approximately 3,500 miles and accumulated nearly 30 hours of flight time in a 48-hour period. All in a day's work.

A few weeks later, with the red carpet blooper incident far from my mind, Kuci and a few of his crewmen arrived unannounced at my Fort Belvoir office with a large matted and framed photograph of the door mishap in Key Biscayne. Several clever phrases were neatly handwritten around the print, such as: "Bullseye: Army 1, Air Force 0," "Avon Calling," "Excedrin Headache #86," "We didn't promise you a rose garden," "OK, Top, if he can't get it up, we'll go with it down," and the obvious "Welcome Aboard Army One!"

I thanked Kuci profusely for his extraordinary empathy and generous offering, and promised to place the artwork in a most prominent location – my closet. All kidding aside, he confessed he had come close to making the same mistake himself. The lesson for us all was to always double and triple check clearance for the door from now on. As a result, there were no repeat episodes.

Moving into the fourth year of his first term, Nixon's trip to China the last week of February 1972 greatly enhanced his chances of being re-elected. Efforts to improve relations with the People's Republic of China were among Nixon's most productive diplomatic accomplishments as a world leader and peacemaker. Also significant were similar achievements in the years to come with the Soviet Union and the Middle East.

On the evening of February 28, 1972, my crew and I were in Army One waiting inside an Andrews AFB hangar along with 10,000 people dressed in heavy winter coats. Nixon was arriving back from an unprecedented weeklong visit to the People's Republic of China where he had met with Communist Party Chairman Mao Zedong (Tse-Tung), Chinese Premier Chou En-Lai and countless other Chinese officials. It was the first trip by a U.S. president to the PRC to meet with leadership who considered us to be far more foe than friend.

It had been dark for several hours by the time Air Force One taxied into the hangar. As soon as the President, the First Lady, Kissinger and a stream of other beaming VIPs deplaned, everyone went crazy cheering and applauding. Smiling ear to ear, Nixon walked to a podium where Vice President Spiro Agnew gave opening remarks and then relinquished the spotlight for the President. Bright lights glared, television cameras rolled and the beaming crowd riveted on Nixon. He began by expressing appreciation for the support of U.S. government leadership and

President Richard Nixon returns from historic trip to China
Andrews Air Force Base, February 28, 1972
(Courtesy of Richard Nixon Presidential Library, NARA)

the hardworking members of the press who had made it possible for the American people "to see more of China than I did."

With an undertone of cautious optimism, the President continued, "When I announced this trip last July, I described it as a journey for peace...peace means more than the absence of war. In a technical sense, we were at peace with the People's Republic of China before this trip, but a gulf of almost 12,000 miles and 22 years of noncommunication and hostility separated the United States of America from the 750 million people who live in the People's Republic of China, and that is one fourth of all the people in the world."

Flying for the White House often placed a helicopter pilot somewhere in the vicinity of international developments, but this situation was different – we were about as close to world history as we could get. First invited by Nixon into the NBC studios when he announced his trip to China and now, waiting for him to board Army One for the quick hop back to the White House, I felt a tremendous sense of pride and privilege.

An agreement between the two nations was outlined in a document called the Shanghai Communiqué. Both assured each other that, despite obvious differences, they would work together to normalize relations, reduce the risk of war, and expand the exchange of cultural and scientific assets. Also, the U.S. acknowledged that Taiwan was part of China and would begin withdrawing military troops as progress was made.

On that cold February night, Nixon seemed bigger than life and appeared to be easily cruising toward a second term. The Paris Peace Talks were about to resume, the last U.S. combat forces would soon leave Vietnam, inflation was coming under control, unemployment was dropping, and the Democrats didn't seem to have a worthy contender in the ranks.

That same winter, Brigadier General Don Hughes transferred from his position as Nixon's military assistant to that of Vice Commander of the 12th Air Force at Bergstrom Air Force Base in Austin, Texas. His successor was Air Force Brigadier General Brent Scowcroft. A Utah native, Scowcroft had an understated, purposeful personality, but was less accessible than Hughes. Not nearly as hands on, he seemed more comfortable delegating responsibilities to lower ranking military aides.

About the same time Scowcroft joined the Military Office, I was struggling with nagging afterthoughts regarding plans for the CH-53 Sea Stallion to replace the existing fleet. I had now seen the helicopter in action enough, along with feedback from other military personnel, to conclude the rotor wash was going to be too strong for the White House grounds. Even the Navy had trouble doing water rescues. If they hovered too close to their subject, the helicopter could literally drive a victim beneath the surface.

Attempts to convince the Military Office to further investigate the matter and at least make a test landing and take-off at the White House were unheeded until I practically cornered Scowcroft at Camp David one morning.

He patiently heard me out and then said, "We've already spent over eight million on this contract. It had been pretty embarrassing if we had to cancel it."

"It's going to be even more embarrassing," I said, "if you

can't put it on the White House lawn after you paid for it."

"All right," he replied, thoughtfully, "go ahead and make the arrangements and let's find out for sure while the President is gone."

When I telephoned Kuci to ask him to meet Scowcroft and me at Anacostia with a CH-53, he was unenthused, but agreed.

"You're sure?" he asked.

"If I'm wrong, I'm wrong," I offered.

"I guess we'll find out," he answered.

I wanted to say to him, "Dick, I know you're smart enough to have figured this out, too, so why are you giving me a hard time?" But I kept that opinion to myself. I knew the Marines had a lot riding on this contract. I didn't want the White House to find out the hard way that they had to choose between not using their new helicopters or having to remove several massive trees, many of which were planted by former presidents.

On the other hand, if I was mistaken, I would never hear the end of it.

We alerted the White House Secret Service and groundskeepers that a non-presidential helicopter was going to do a test landing on the South Lawn. With Kuci in the right seat, me as his co-pilot and Scowcroft standing in the cockpit doorway, we followed our regular path and put down in the usual spot on the South Lawn. Scowcroft and I stepped out into the frigid air to have a look around.

The canvas awning protruding from the south portico was torn off its frame and tree branches were everywhere. Three groundskeepers in complete shock were standing near the small red fire truck parked about 40 yards away. We had broken off enough branches to fill three dump trucks.

"I've seen enough," Scowcroft said, and climbed back on board and we lifted off to return to Anacostia.

No one said much of anything. Scowcroft was stone-faced, Kuci focused on his flight duties, and a single question churned inside of me: How can so many smart people be so stupid?

The contract was cancelled that week and plans set into motion to develop the Sikorsky Sea King D to replace the White House fleet of VH-3As. Those helicopters remain in service today.

Kuci was rotated out of the HMX-1 unit in June of 1972 and ultimately earned the rank of major general. To my surprise, the Military Office asked me to keynote his departure dinner at the Quantico Officer's Club. In the room of close to 100 well-wishers, I had the chance to rib Kuci about his jittery legs and boast about all the money I had raked in playing poker with the Marines at Anacostia. On behalf of the Army's Executive Flight Detachment I commended him for his service to the White House and wished him every success in the years to come.

The new HMX-1 commander was Marine Colonel Jim Perryman, a tall, confident man who came to the White House like the rest of us – through Vietnam.

In May of 1972, Nixon continued his campaign for global peace by being the first U.S. president to visit Moscow. Under the leadership of Leonid Brezhnev, General Secretary of the Communist Party, the Soviets signed a number of agreements with the United States, including a treaty on antiballistic missile systems and a blueprint for a joint space mission.

The Watergate break-in was just weeks away and I've never been able to fathom what made that move such a good idea when so much was working so well for Nixon. But then, such stunts were part and parcel of the political arena – all in a day's work for the high and mighty. Paranoia about what the other side might be up to came with the territory. I had heard from reliable sources that Johnson even bugged Nixon's campaign plane in 1968.

What Nixon knew about Watergate and when, I'll leave to the historians. I was as much in the dark as the rest of the American public as we watched events unfold during the last year of Nixon's doomed presidency. What did stick with me about the entire ordeal was that it was not so much the immorality of the burglary, but how inept Nixon was at covering his tracks. In the end, along with a host of others, he was ill-equipped to handle the impacts of a second-rate burglary. Consequently, getting caught was not the main issue. Lying about it was.

And so it was, that on June 17, 1972, five men were arrested while breaking into the Democratic Party headquarters housed at the Watergate complex in Washington, D.C. One of those men was James McCord, a former CIA agent employed by the Republican National Committee. Three days later, the head of the Democratic Party filed a million-dollar civil lawsuit against Nixon's campaign staff, charging them with "political espionage."

The day before the break-in, Nixon was at the White House. He hosted a Cabinet meeting, had an inner circle discussion related to welfare reform legislation, met with Mexican President Luis Echeverria Alvarez, and then departed for Florida on Air Force One on Friday afternoon. They landed at the Grand Bahama Island Auxiliary Airfield where Nixon transferred to Army One for a 20-minute flight to the Grand Cay residence of Nixon's friend, Bob Abplanalp. The President spent the next day swimming and boating.

On Sunday, June 18, 1972, the day after the Watergate burglars were arrested, I picked up Nixon and BeBe Rebozo from Grand Cay and flew them to the President's Key Biscayne home. Nixon flew back to D.C. the next evening. Everything about that weekend was routine and unremarkable.

Little did we know....

During the second week of July 1972, the Democratic National Convention nominated South Dakota Senator George S. McGovern for president and Missouri Senator Thomas Eagleton for vice president. Less than three weeks later, Eagleton withdrew after it was learned he had received psychiatric treatment several years earlier for what was termed "nervous exhaustion and fatigue." Former head of the Peace Corps, Sargent Shriver, succeeded Eagleton on the ticket.

In mid-July, I had one of my most personally memorable flights. I was at the El Toro Marine Corps Air Base when a call came in from my stand-by pilot at San Clemente.

"We just got a call for a Huey," he said, "to give one of the President's guests a lift."

"Okay, I'll send –"

"Uh, sir?" he interrupted. "You might want to take this one yourself."

"Why do you say that?"

"It's John Wayne."

I didn't have a favorite John Wayne movie. I liked them all and I especially liked what he stood for. "The Duke" was an unrestrained patriot, defender of the American way and an unwavering supporter of the Vietnam War. Long recognized as a steadfast conservative, he had four years earlier starred in the film, *The Green Berets*. Considered by most critics as an over-the-top glorification of the war against communism, the movie functioned well as a platform for Wayne's personal perspective.

Still, flying over to San Clemente, I was powerless against the little flutter in my stomach. I was about to meet one of the most beloved and well-known actors of the 20th century. My orders were to take him to a golf course about 15 miles east where he would meet an associate to sign a contract of some kind, and then bring him back to have lunch with the President. I set down on the helipad shortly before noon next to the Western White House and was about to power down when I looked up to see Wayne, all six feet four inches of him, jogging toward us.

I remember thinking how odd it was to see him without a cowboy hat and a six-shooter strapped to his side. As soon as he was onboard we headed to the golf course and landed in a parking lot next to the club house. A younger man with a multi-page document scampered out to the helicopter. Wayne met him on the helicopter steps where he sat for a short discussion.

"I'll wait while you make the changes," he said, and the guy with all the paperwork ran back into the club house.

As much as I wanted to gush about how much I admired Wayne or ask for an autograph, my crew and I stayed in the background, not wanting to bother this larger-than-life icon. About the time I thought we would have no personal interaction other than a cursory greeting, Wayne approached me where I was standing in the cockpit doorway.

"Mind if I take a look inside?" he asked, motioning to the cockpit.

"No, not at all," I eagerly responded. "If you want, go ahead and sit in the co-pilot's seat."

"Okay," he said, and eased his large frame into the compact seat.

I glanced into the cabin to see my crew chief and co-pilot watching intently, as taken by his interest as I was.

"So exactly how do you fly one of these things?" he asked.

"Well, it's a little tricky," I said, and settled in next to John Wayne for a mini-flight instruction course. Nodding with each piece of information I offered, he could not have been more down-to-earth and considerate.

"Your feet control the tail rotor blades," I said, pointing to the pedals on the cockpit floor.

"Okay," he replied, taking a closer look.

"The cyclic stick controls the main rotor blades," I continued, "and the collective takes care of the blade pitch."

"Did you fly helicopters in Vietnam?" he asked.

"Yes."

"Pretty tough?"

"Sometimes."

"So what do you think about the war?"

A deluge of thoughts and memories streaked through my mind: the worst images of the brutality of war; the anti-war protestors spewing disgust at the airport when I returned from Vietnam; the drunken voice of LBJ coming from the shadows of some Texas cow pasture; the skinny man shaking the helicopter tail rotor in Ocean Grove; and Kalispell with its compound of draft dodgers plotting to harm the President.

Like John Wayne, I was anti-communist and believed in fighting for our freedom at all cost, but I was having my doubts about how best to do that.

"What do I think about the war?" I repeated, pondering how best to capture my viewpoint. "We went in with the wrong strategy. We should have been given the chance to win it when we could have. But now, with all the anti-war protesting and politics, it's time to get out and cut our losses."

Wayne gave me a contemplative look just as the man with all the paperwork dashed on board to steal his attention and I busied myself preparing for take-off. Once Wayne finished signing the document, the man hurried off and the crew chief closed the helicopter door.

Wayne didn't budge from the co-pilot's seat.

"Any chance I could stay here for the flight back?" he asked.

If there was someone who could have said no to John

Wayne, I didn't know who it was. It certainly wasn't me. No, I was the guy who helped position a headset on the world's greatest western movie star and showed him how to push the button on the cyclic so we could talk during the 10-minute flight back to San Clemente.

"That was great," he announced as soon as we landed. "Really great. Thanks a lot."

"You're welcome," I answered, watching him exit and walk over to Nixon who had driven up from the house in a golf cart.

Spending time with John Wayne, personal politics aside, was one of the best short hours of my life. About a month later, as a gesture of his appreciation, he invited me and CeCe, a few Nixon staffers and some people I had never met for an evening dinner cruise on his yacht, *The Wild Goose*. A converted WWII mine sweeper, it was moored in a San Pedro harbor off the coast of Los Angeles and accommodated about 20 people. We sailed south, almost to Newport Beach, watching the sun slip from a cloudless sky and disappear beneath the horizon.

I have always appreciated how unaffected John Wayne seemed to be by his fame and how thrilled he was to play the role of helicopter co-pilot. He did a much better job than I would have done climbing on a horse pretending to be a cowboy. In fact, I did ride a horse once while we were stationed in Texas and ended up with such a sore butt that I decided to leave that pastime to the experts. Every man should know his limits, but not let them get in his way.

Four More Years 15

I remember when I first came to Washington. For the first six months you wonder how the hell you ever got here. For the next six months, you wonder how the hell the rest of them got here.
— President Harry S. Truman

March 23, 1972, was a Sunday. I was on double standby at Belvoir – waiting for either a call from the White House or one from CeCe who was expecting our second child.

"It's time," was all CeCe had to say and I was back at the house to drive her the short distance to the base hospital. Curtis Christopher Boyer arrived in perfect form with long and lanky arms and legs.

"That boy," the doctor quickly commented, "is definitely going to be over six feet tall."

CeCe came from a tall family, but none of us expected Curtis to eventually top out at six foot seven inches. That was a family record and a basketball coach's dream.

The day before the 1972 Republican Convention in Miami at the end of August, I flew to Homestead AFB with several helicopters to advance the trip. With me was Major General William Maddox, the Director of Army Aviation at the Pentagon. We had met several months earlier after General Hughes, about to leave the Military Office, advised me to build an upper level alliance to gain more support for the Army's helicopter unit.

During the past three-and-a-half years, the Exec Flight had gone from flying 23 percent of the presidential flights to just over 50 percent, even though we still had less equipment and personnel than the Marine unit. To help rectify that situation, Hughes had advised me to connect with Maddox. One of the most decorated Army aviators in history, the general had more than 4,000 helicopter combat hours in Korea and Vietnam and, among countless awards, had earned eight Distinguished Flying Crosses, four Silver Stars, five Legion of Merits and 127 Air Medals.

"Maddox needs to know more about what you guys do," Hughes said, handing me a crisp white envelope. "Here. Give him this. It's an invitation to a state dinner at the White House."

Now, armed with a little grease for the wheels and determined to enlighten the powers that be about the scope of our work and need for additional assets, I made my way to the Pentagon just across the Potomac River from D.C.

Upon arriving at Maddox's tidy outer office, I introduced myself to the colonel who was his chief of staff and explained the purpose of my visit.

"Let me get this straight," the colonel said. "You work for the White House and you're here because you need help?"

"More like guidance."

"This is a first," he said, with a baffled smile. "Okay, but the General is in a meeting and –"

"I'll wait."

Nicknamed the "Gray Ghost" because of his distinctive mustache and head of thick, silver hair, Maddox was a pilot's pilot. He was outgoing and in constant motion. It was a privilege sitting down at his desk and having his ear, which I proceeded to bend enough to test anyone's patience.

"So that's the story," I wrapped up. "Nothing's been the same since Johnson split us up, took over and told the Army brass to mind their own business. Now, it's a constant battle to keep the Marines from squeezing us out. We deserve this mission and I want to save it, plus, we're damn good at it."

"I have to tell you," Maddox said, leaning forward, "we've wondered about you guys and how to connect without pissing somebody off."

"How about if I set up an orientation at Belvoir for you?"

"That would be great," he replied, and we shook on it.

"I'll get things set up this week."

Maddox fanned the envelope from Hughes. "And tell General Hughes thanks for the invitation."

I had barely gotten back to my office at Belvoir when I got a telephone call from Maddox's aide.

"Colonel Boyer," he said, "we may have a problem with this invitation to the White House dinner."

"What kind of problem?"

"The General's wife is Japanese."

"That's fine," I assured him, "there's always lots of different people at these things."

"Well, she's the daughter of the Japanese ambassador to the United States."

"Excellent."

"On December 7, 1941."

The day the Japanese bombed Pearl Harbor.

"Oh, damn," I responded with a dawning breath. "I guess I better run that by General Hughes and get back to you."

Hughes promptly waved off any concerns and thought such a development would make an interesting topic of conversation at the dinner.

During his Exec Flight orientation at Fort Belvoir, we briefed Maddox on the unit's operating procedures, mission protocol, training regime and warrant officer program, which received high praise. His son was an Army aviator warrant officer. Maddox toured the hangar and our maintenance and supply facilities, looked at our security system and asked a lot of questions about how we did what we did before I took him up in one of the VH-3As.

Flying over the outskirts of Washington, D.C., with a man of Maddox's caliber and history was better than having John Wayne beside me. We shared a common heartbeat about helicopters, thrived on the camaraderie, swapped story after story and were soon making plans for him to grab some stick time on our next trip to Florida.

Top rate. That's how Maddox described the Army's Executive Flight Detachment and I was beyond grateful to have him in our corner. A short time later he put out some directives that resulted in the replacement of our Huey single-engine Bell D models with six twin-engine N models – three for the Army and three for the Marines.

As long as progress had that kind of balance between the Exec Flight and HMX-1, I felt secure about the unit's future at the White House. My objective was to never "get rid" of the Marines, as Jack Brennan had wanted to do with the Army. I

believed having both branches serving the White House provided just the right mix of competition and capacities to elevate helicopter support from excellent to superior.

When we were assigned the mission to fly Nixon at the Republican Convention the last week of August 1972, I gave Maddox a quick call to see if he wanted to tag along. I didn't have to ask twice. We went down to handle the advance work the day before Nixon was scheduled to arrive in Miami. The weather forecast was good, we had ample equipment and all scheduled air taxi routes were under 15 minutes over familiar territory. The prevailing concern, from the Secret Service to every Nixon aide, was figuring out how to minimize security risks for the President and the First Family.

Anti-war, anti-Republican, anti-Nixon activists had converged in droves on Miami. I heard estimates of there being more than 10,000 protestors around the convention hall. Nixon wrote in his memoirs, "...frustrated demonstrators attempted to set fire to buses filled with delegates. They slashed tires, pelted delegates with rocks and eggs, and marched on the hall wearing their own gas masks and brandishing night sticks."

Going back to my years of flying in and out of combat zones, I relied on what I thought was more effective than a gunner hanging out a door or a bulletproof fuselage – knowing when, where and how to fly. The entire city knew Nixon was on his way to the convention by helicopter so we had to do what we could to confuse people regarding his activities. Normally, the President was the last to land and the first out of any location. In this case, I readied three helicopters and inserted the presidential seal and number "1" placard in the outside window slots for each one.

The Associated Press described the strategy in an article titled, "Security fake-out veils Nixon arrival at convention:"

"President Nixon and members of his family flew by helicopter to the convention hall last night under a cloak of unusually tight security precautions. All helicopters bound from his home in Key Biscayne to a closed-off parking lot behind the convention hall all bore the bright orange number "1" on their bows... Also on the nose of each craft was the presidential seal. Anyone on the ground would have been unable to detect which of them carried the First Family.

"Inside the helicopters, passengers received strict orders to keep shades drawn over all windows. A newsman who has been traveling in official aircraft for 10 years could not recall such similar precautions.

"The first helicopter to land carried 11 newsmen and photographers and three Nixon aides. They arrived behind the hall and breathed in gas fumes unleashed earlier against demonstrators. The newcomers were handed moistened towels to relieve their discomfort.

"When the Nixons arrived, the President led his family into the glare of television spotlights and cameras, walking slowly and smiling all the while – seemingly mindless of the fumes."

Fortunately, the maneuver worked like a charm and that night, amid an unprecedented outpouring of unbridled respect and confidence from the convention floor – with General Maddox seated somewhere near the rafters – Richard Nixon and Spiro Agnew were nominated for a second term. The President's acceptance speech covered issues related to domestic policy, the economy, Vietnam, foreign affairs and disarmament, and concluded with trademark comments from the man who wanted more than anything to be known as a peacemaker.

"I ask you, my fellow Americans," spoke Nixon, "to join our new majority not just in the cause of winning an election, but in achieving a hope that mankind has had since the beginning of civilization. Let us build a peace that our children and all the children of the world can enjoy for generations to come."

The week after the convention, Nixon addressed the Watergate break-in situation by announcing to the nation that White House counsel John Dean had conducted an investigation and concluded that administration officials were not involved in "this very bizarre incident." In the years to come, many questioned if that investigation even took place. As the 1972 Election Day grew closer, the Nixon White House was starting to unravel due in part to two Washington Post reporters: Carl Bernstein and Bob Woodward were about to help transform the Watergate burglary into Nixon's Waterloo.

The Exec Flight had our own "unrelated" Woodward – Chief Warrant Officer Edward "Woody" Woodward, another highly decorated Vietnam War veteran pilot. He had joined the unit in 1971 and flew as my co-pilot on about a dozen presidential missions. Woody was methodical and alert, and when he climbed into the cockpit, there was no dividing line between the man and the machine.

After I retired in 1975, we lost contact with each other until his son, Marine Colonel Greg Woodward, an Iraqi War veteran, contacted me in late 2008. Just a teenager when his father joined the White House detachment, the younger Woodward wanted to learn more about his father, who had passed away unexpectedly in 1991 at the age of 51 from a heart attack. Woodward had tracked me down through the Nixon Library and made contact by phone to see if I knew if his father had ever flown the Last Flight Helicopter on exhibit at the library. After a quick check of the flight log, I was able to confirm that he indeed had.

Colonel Woodward, his wife Paige, Carl Burhanan and I soon met for lunch at the San Clemente Inn. I was instantly impressed with his devotion and humility. When he talked about his father, I could see the deep love he held for him and an aching desire to learn more about his time as a White House pilot. Burhanan gave Woodward an Army Exec Flight unit patch with the presidential seal on it like the one his father had worn on his flight jacket.

A couple of months later we met again at the Nixon Library. I had made special arrangements for Woodward to sit in the very seat of the helicopter his father had flown. He was wearing a Marine flight jacket with the Army Exec Flight patch from Burhanan sewn onto the upper sleeve. I was struck by the symbolism that simply illustrated the mutual respect and combined contribution to military aviation by both the Army and Marines.

Greg sat in the co-pilot's seat of helicopter 150617 for a long time, asking question after question, smiling like a kid, imagining what it had been like for the father he had lost too soon to have been in that very spot.

Army Chief Warrant Officer Edward Woodward would have

Marine Col. Greg Woodward sits with me in the cockpit of Army One, the same seat his father, CW4 Edward "Woody" Woodward, occupied as one of my Exec Flight co-pilots. Richard Nixon Presidential Library and Museum, Yorba Linda, Spring 2008
(Paige Woodward)

been very proud of his son, Marine Colonel Greg Woodward, and his grandson, too, recently commissioned as a second lieutenant in the Marine Corps.

The end of September 1972, I commanded the flight that took Nixon to the base of the Statue of Liberty located on Liberty Island, a 12-acre island at the entrance to New York Harbor. We picked up the President and the First Lady at the Newark Municipal Airport in New Jersey for the five-minute trip. Circling the statue gave us all a fantastic view of the magnificent gift of friendship given to the America by France in 1886.

Without warning, a White House cameraman with a large movie camera squeezed into the cockpit between me and Bean, my co-pilot, and began filming our approach. I believe that was the first time an official photographer had documented a flight from that vantage point. Helicopter pilots always had a ringside seat and it was great to know what we saw was going to be seen by others.

Thousands of people were gathered below for a ceremony to dedicate the new American Museum of Immigration. We landed

on a wharf at about 2:45 p.m. It was a bright, sunny day and one of the first public appearances in quite some time where we thought Nixon would not be heckled by protestors, since access to the island had been so well controlled.

As it turned out, six anti-war demonstrators materialized right in front of the President as soon as he started his speech. They chanted the slogans displayed on the signs they held up for the television cameras, "Stop the bombing!" and "Stop the War!"

The surrounding throng of celebrants fired back with, "Four more years! Four more years! Four more years!"

Nixon raised a calming hand as security hustled away the dissenters.

"Thank you, ladies and gentlemen," Nixon said into his microphone. "I would only suggest that on your television screens tonight, in addition to showing the six here, let's show the thousands that are over here... A few moments ago, as we got off the helicopter, four little girls were there in native costumes to greet us. One of my aides pointed out the helicopter window and said, 'That one is Italian and this one is Polish and this one is Ukrainian and this one is German.'

"Let me just say," Nixon continued, with the election more than a month away, "that every one of us is proud of his national background, but I say instead of referring to someone, 'He is Italian, he is German, he is a Pole, he is a Ukrainian,' let's say, first of all, 'He or she is an American....'"

On Election Day, November 7, 1972, Nixon and the First Lady were in San Clemente. He started the day by motoring to a local elementary school to cast his vote. A few hours later, I transported the President, the First Lady and key staffers from the Western White House Compound to El Toro where they boarded Air Force One for the five-and-a-half hour flight back to Washington, D.C.

Before midnight, Eastern Standard Time, President Nixon made a televised statement to the nation regarding his re-election. He had taken every state but the Democratic stronghold of Massachusetts and defeated South Dakota Senator George McGovern by the fourth largest margin of victory in presidential election history. I had voted for Nixon, had confidence in his leadership and, like a lot of people, was hoping the whole Watergate thing would go away, especially since, in the world of hardball politics, the incident wasn't all that unusual anyway.

Another four years for Nixon meant the Army and the White House might want to keep me on as the Exec Flight commander, to which I had no objection. I worked long hours under weighty pressures, but loved the job enough to stay as long they would keep me. CeCe and the kids were thriving at Fort Belvoir and we were grateful for the security that came in knowing there wasn't a move for us in the near future.

No surprise, my father didn't vote for Nixon, but he had softened enough to finally agree to meet the President if I made the arrangements. After all, his son had been flying the man around the world for the last four years. That opportunity came on December 20, 1972, the day Woody and I flew Nixon from the White House to Bethesda Naval Hospital for his annual checkup and back.

Landing on the South Lawn, I could see my parents, now in their middle sixties, dressed in winter overcoats with CeCe, Robin and a White House escort standing near the entrance to the South Portico. Dad looked like he was going to a funeral, but Mom had a faint little smile on her face. I was reminded of a photograph in a newspaper article they had sent me the year before. They were visiting a couple of old friends near Athens, Tennessee, and someone had tipped off a local reporter that the parents of a White House pilot were coming to town. On what I guessed must have been a slow news day, Mr. and Mrs. George Boyer were interviewed and photographed sitting on a sofa holding glossy pictures of Army One. Dad had the same "going-to-a-funeral" expression on his face, not because he was in any kind of agony, but because neither he nor Mom was comfortable being in the limelight.

The article headline read: "Parents of presidential pilot visit in McMinn" and my mother made it clear to the reporter that even though they were talking about just one of their sons, "We are proud of all of our children."

As Nixon, his doctor and duty aide Colonel Bill Golden exited the helicopter, I pointed out my parents to Woody.

Mr. and Mrs. George Boyer (center) of Akron, Ohio, have been visiting in the home of Mr. and Mrs. Miles Hughes (extreme left and right) in the Clearwater Community. The Boyers are the parents of Lt. Col. Gene Boyer, who is the Army One presidential helicopter pilot for President Nixon. The group hold several pictures of Gene during trips with the presidential party. (See story) (Photo by Sue Jolley)

Parents of presidential
pilot visit in McMinn

Mom and Dad in the middle with friends, expressing pride in the
accomplishments of all three of their sons, Athens, Tennessee, 1972
(Boyer Family Archives)

"Dad's not much of a Nixon fan," I told him. "I hope he doesn't say anything embarrassing."

Woody looked at me like that was an odd concern for a smart-ass like me to have.

I saw Golden lean close to Nixon as they approached the Boyer contingent, obviously briefing him on the unexpected welcoming party. Nixon nodded and then graciously extended his hand first to my mother and then to Dad, CeCe and Robin. The handshake looked like it went well and after a brief exchange, Nixon continued on into the White House.

The somber look had lifted from my father's face and I could not wait to hear what he thought.

"He's got a good grip," Dad told me back at our house.

"What did he say to you?" I asked.

"'It's a pleasure to meet you,'" said my father.

"And 'Thanks for stopping by,'" added my mother, "and 'You must be very proud of your son. He's an excellent pilot.' I told him thank you and that we were proud of all of our sons, and that was it."

"Great," I replied, adoring my mother's unyielding devotion to the three rambunctious boys she had kept alive with cabbage. "I'm sure glad you could make it."

Dad wandered away from my inquisition, remarking, "I can see how he might grow on you. He's got a tough job."

That short-lived encounter was the first and only time my parents even got close to a president and I was surely more proud of making that happen for them than they were of having a son fly for the White House. The elation of that day doubled after meeting Woody's son, Greg, some 37 years later and being able to tell him that his father was with me when *my* father met the President, so I guess that made us family, "Even if you are a Marine," I kidded.

Woody, along with dozens of other Army pilots who flew for the White House, exemplified the best of the best. Nixon acknowledged that level of performance in a December 15, 1972, letter to General Brent Scowcroft, my boss at the time:

"I would like you to extend to Lt. Colonel Boyer," Nixon wrote, "and his flight detachment my thanks for their outstanding support over the past four years. We have logged many hours together, across the United States and around the world, and each flight has added to my respect for their professionalism and their spirit of service.

"In the rush of everyday business, it is often easy to overlook those who provide support under the most exacting of standards. We are deeply grateful, however, to the officers and the men of the U.S. Army Executive Flight Detachment for their dedication, loyalty, and service. Mrs. Nixon, and all the members of our family, join with me in extending to the members of

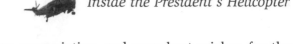

the detachment our appreciation and very best wishes for the holiday season."

The day after Christmas in 1972, former President Harry Truman died at the age of 88 at the Research Hospital in Kansas City, Missouri, from "afflictions of old age." President from 1945 to 1953, "Give 'Em Hell" Harry was a favorite of my father's. Dad liked his straight-forward attitude and barbed wit. We flew Nixon from Richards Gebaur AFB near Kansas City to Mill Creek Park in Independence, Missouri, which was just a couple of blocks from the Truman Library where the 33rd President of the United States was lying in state. Nixon paid his respects by placing a wreath at the foot of Truman's coffin and expressed his personal condolences to the family. LBJ, now the only living former chief executive, also attended.

Inauguration Day was picture perfect and only slightly marred with sporadic clusters of outbursts from protestors. CeCe and I watched the oath of office and parade on television, and then got gussied up to join Burhanan, Master Sergeant Julian Hill and their wives for dinner at the Key Bridge Hotel in Arlington, Virginia. From there we would take a ten-minute drive to one of the inaugural balls in D.C.

The city was teaming with the rich and powerful. In the afterglow of a jubilant day, we gathered on the sidewalk outside the hotel, impervious to the chilly night air. As the only one of us wearing an officer's dress uniform, I teetered on the curb, straining to locate the limo we had hired.

Suddenly, a tall, round-bellied man in a tuxedo, a bolo tie, snakeskin cowboy boots and a cream-colored Stetson pushed past CeCe to tap me on the shoulder. He was about 60 years old and his breath reeked of alcohol.

"How about fetching my car?" he slurred.

Damn. Johnson must have a third brother, I thought.

"What?" I asked with such surprise that he took a closer look at me, then the gold braid on my shoulders and finally, the array of medals pinned on my chest.

"Guess you ain't the valet," he declared.

I shook my head and pointed to a young man in a less adorned uniform standing behind him. "There's your man."

He turned, and without saying another word, staggered away, leaving us to have a hell of a good laugh.

Since the Truman funeral, Lyndon's Johnson's health had deteriorated and he was too ill to attend the inauguration. Just two days later, at the age of 65, he passed away from a heart attack at his Texas Ranch. He had been found dead by a Secret Service agent in his bed with a telephone in his hand. It's anybody's guess as to who he might have been talking to or trying to call. It was rather ironic for a man who was a master at working the phone lines to have died with a phone receiver in his hand.

Much different from Truman's funeral ceremonies, Johnson's body was brought back to Washington, D.C., for a full state funeral. Nixon noted in his memoirs that this was the first time in years we did not have a living former President. During a special Cabinet meeting that same January, he talked about the presidents who had died in their sixties – both Roosevelt's, Coolidge and now Johnson. Nixon had just had his 60th birthday and remarked, "It looks like the sixties are the dangerous age! I don't have any fears for myself in that regard. Whatever happens will happen. The important thing is that each of us has to approach each day as if it might be our last day here."

The President presented each Cabinet member with a leather bound desk calendar covering what he thought would be their next four years together from January 20, 1973, to January 20, 1977. Printed beside each date was the amount of days left in his administration. Unimaginable for all, somewhere along about day 555, the remaining became irrelevant.

The same day Johnson died, a Vietnam peace agreement was signed in Paris by representatives of the U.S., the Vietcong and North and South Vietnam. Key provisions included a cease-fire, withdrawal of American forces, dismantling of U.S. installations, and the release of all prisoners of war within two months, as well as the peaceful reunification of North and South Vietnam.

Henry Kissinger had made several secret trips to Peking, Moscow and Paris during the last year and signed the peace agreement on behalf of the United States. His travels and whereabouts were frequently known only to an exclusive few to prevent unwanted interference in the process of delicate negotiations.

Upon one of his return trips to the States from Paris, I was on standby when I got a call from the Military Office to meet Pat Nixon at Andrews AFB. She was coming in by car. The request had a few unusual conditions.

"This is a secret mission," an aide instructed. "Take her in a Huey, no co-pilot, just a crew chief, and –"

"Did you say no co-pilot?" I asked, not believing my ears.

"The fewer people, the better," he said firmly. "We want you to hide out until Kissinger lands. He'll be in a small jet. And then take them up to Camp David."

"Sorry, I have to stop you, again," I interrupted. "It's flat out not safe to fly the First Lady alone. We have to have that back-up."

"And we can't risk anybody leaking this," he firmly said.

I couldn't have been more bewildered. I had never known any of my pilots or crew to be loose-lipped. Hell, we got most of our news like everybody else – from the newspapers and TV. As far as I was concerned, Kissinger could be flying in from any number of places – from Europe, Asia, outer space or even a tryst with Hollywood actress Jill St. John. We did our job regardless and kept the details within the unit. In fact, I remember a crew chief disclosing the awkwardness he felt after being asked by Kissinger on a flight with St. John to turn down the cabin lights.

"I wonder what people would think if they knew he was with her?" he wondered aloud.

"It's none of our business," I answered, and that was that.

So the request to fly the First Lady and Kissinger in a helicopter with only one pilot made me say to the aide on the other end of the phone line, "This doesn't make any sense."

"Those are the orders," he replied.

"Okay."

I maneuvered a Huey between two hangars at Andrews and soon welcomed Mrs. Nixon and a Secret Service agent aboard. We kept the doors open, hoping to keep the rising temperature from making us too uncomfortable. While we waited, the First Lady, who never smoked in public, quietly puffed on a cigarette, then another and another. I was also a smoker at the time, so when she ran out, I had some to share.

"Thanks," she said, "I didn't think we'd be here this long."

And I said to myself, "And I thought I'd have a co-pilot."

When an obviously weary Kissinger finally boarded, I took off for Camp David. I had flown by myself hundreds of times, but didn't like bending the rules on that day. In retrospect, I wished I had taken one of my warrant pilots and dressed him in a sergeant's uniform to pose as the flight engineer. Fortunately, I completed the mission as ordered, without incident, but with a few choice words churning inside for the person who thought having someone in the left seat was optional. Or even more worrisome, that whoever that might be thought we posed a security risk worthy of overruling my objections.

Somebody needed their head examined. Meanwhile, if it ever happened again – which it didn't – I had a back-up plan and we could never have too many of those.

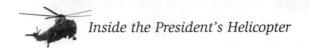

Shark's Point 16

"The trouble with free elections is you never know who's going to win."

– Soviet Premier Leonid Brezhnev

"There's a curious little house off 21st Street," began the May 23, 1973, article in the Fort Belvoir newspaper. "Its dimensions are 4'x5'x5'. Flies buzz in and out of the windows and spiders have a field day on the walls...the mistress of the house tries to keep things in order, but she's only 52 inches tall."

The playhouse I built and CeCe decorated for Robin was featured in *The Castle*, a base publication that kept us all up to date on local developments. Beneath a headline that read: "Flies and bugs love Robin's doll house," the reporter described the bright yellow curtains, wall-to-wall carpeting, three "Lilliputian" chairs and a white picket fence.

"What the house lacks," wrote the reporter, "can always be made up in daydreams."

At the age of nine Robin hosted a full season of tea parties and played surrogate parent to our toddling son, Curtis. Sometimes, the neighborhood boys were invited in, but, as Robin explained, they were not allowed to "play rough or walk away with any of the furnishings."

Just ten minutes away by air was another house with the same rules, but keeping order at the White House was rapidly slipping away from its number one resident.

"We have had in four months," Nixon would write in his memoirs, "more problems than most second term presidents have in four years."

The Watergate scandal was building momentum hour to hour. By the end of April 1973, a tangle of circumstances had forced the resignations of chief of staff Bob Haldeman and domestic policy assistant John Ehrlichman. White House counsel John Dean was fired. Soon after, a Democratic-controlled

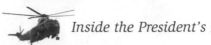

The playhouse I built for my daughter Robin.
Fort Belvoir, Virginia, 1973
(Boyer Family Archives)

Senate committee opened hearings to investigate all parties involved, including the President. Popular opinion remains that if the Republicans had controlled Congress, Watergate would have turned out very differently and Nixon would have served a full second term.

Inflation was climbing to its highest point in two decades and rapidly overtaking the Vietnam War as the prevailing national crisis. Still, in the wake of the newly signed peace agreement, Nixon had ordered continued bombing of North Vietnamese strongholds in Cambodia and Laos. This was to ensure key assurances would be met, not the least of which was the end of Communist military operations along the border still threatening South Vietnam and the safe return of U.S. military and civilian POWs. News of the bombing outraged many, including congressional leaders, who viewed it as unnecessary aggression, and only serving to prolong the war.

Between late January and the end of March 1973, some 600 American POWs were finally released and returned home. Representing every branch of the military, they had been held – many for years – in more than a dozen detention camps under unspeakable conditions scattered in and around Hanoi. Nixon invited all of the returning POWs to a dinner May 24, 1973, on the South Lawn.

President Nixon welcomes South Vietnamese President Nguyen Van Thieu
San Clemente, California, April 1973
(Courtesy of Richard Nixon Presidential Library, NARA)

Staged beneath a massive yellow and orange tent getting pounded by a warm, spring downpour, the event was one of the largest and most elaborate functions ever held at the White House. Aluminum canoes were filled with iced champagne, there was a gourmet menu, and music was provided by Les Brown's "Band of Renown." Among the celebrity guests were John Wayne, Sammy Davis, Jr., Jimmy Stewart, Joey Heatherton, Irving Berlin and Bob Hope, who couldn't resist announcing to the crowd numbering more than 1,280, "This is the first time I've played to a captive audience."

Nixon's comments were more serious. He clarified his decision to resume bombing in December 1972, adding, "all of us would like to join in a round of applause for the brave men that

took those B-52s in and did the job, because as all of you know, if they hadn't done it, you wouldn't be here tonight."

The President went on to ask all the gentlemen to rise and then said, "Tonight, as President of the United States, I designate every one of the women here, the wives, the mothers and others who are guests of our POWs, as First Ladies. Gentlemen, to the First Ladies of America."

The POWs presented a plaque to the President that read, "Our leader – our comrade, Richard the Lionhearted" for his "fortitude and perseverance under fire."

On that stormy evening, I'm sure the President was oblivious to the torrential rains as he basked in the light of their gratitude and admiration. It would be one of the last such validating moments of his presidency.

That same day, with two VH-3As and a back-up H-3, I was slogging through multiple weather systems along the eastern seaboard on our way down to Homestead to be ready for Nixon the next day when he arrived on Air Force One. I had wanted to leave a day earlier and avoid the brunt of the storm, but the Military Office didn't share my sense of urgency and held us back a day.

Again, somebody over there needed his head examined. Throughout my life I have never regretted leaving early, even for a burger at dinner time. But I have regretted leaving late and this trip, sadly, would prove the point more than any other.

The ride was bumpy, but nothing we couldn't handle. A greater concern arose upon hearing from Fort Benning that the two Chinooks I had requested to join the flight couldn't get off the ground. The weather was too intense. Unlike the Marines who had more helicopters in their unit, the Army still had to pick up needed additionals wherever we could. In this case, we knew we had to shuttle the Secret Service for shift changes on Grand Cay and always needed to be prepared for unexpected guests of the President.

Coming in to land at Homestead I had an uneasy feeling about being short on assets and hoped the Chinooks would somehow make it to relieve the load on the VH-3As. If not, we would do what we always did – make it work with a back-up plan.

Unique to this particular flight was having Marine Major Dave Pirnie from HMX-1 as my co-pilot. He had come along to learn the ropes flying Nixon in and around Key Biscayne and the Bahamas. Pirnie was an attentive, capable pilot with a quiet disposition. I sensed no tension between us. We were just two guys doing our jobs.

The weather in Florida on Friday, May 25, 1973, was fairly clear with no precipitation, but Georgia was still wrestling with thunderheads and tornado warnings. Fort Benning let me know they would keep trying to get the Chinooks out, but it didn't look good.

When Nixon arrived from D.C. we took him to Key Biscayne where he spent the night and then, the next day, at about 1 p.m., we flew him to Grand Cay where he went fishing with his family, BeBe Rebozo and Bob Abplanalp. The hour and ten-minute flight we had performed more than a dozen times before with the President on board was uneventful.

On May 26, 1973, well after dark on a moonless, misty night, Pirnie and I had just flown Nixon's chef from Grand Cay to Walker Cay about five minutes away when we overheard a chilling exchange on the Secret Service network.

Ron Bean's helicopter, carrying a replacement shift of seven Secret Service agents and a three-man crew, had crashed into the water on approach to Grand Cay.

My stomach hardened into a burning knot. I immediately took full control of the helicopter and the radio, and flew to the location known as Shark's Point – a name well-earned because the ocean was frequently teeming with sharks. Luckily, that wasn't the case on this night.

Also on board with me was the White House duty aide Army Lieutenant Colonel Bill Golden. A competent, even-tempered man with a keen wit, Golden was a West Point graduate and had served two tours in Vietnam – the first in 1964 as the senior advisor to the First Battalion, Vietnamese Airborne Brigade, and the second, six years later, as the operations advisor to the Vietnamese III Corps Headquarters in Bien Hoa. Golden squeezed into the cockpit between me and Pirnie to help look for signs of the downed helicopter.

The Abplanalp property on Grand Cay had two landing sites. The primary pad, for the President and other VIPs, we used only during daylight hours. A second area, located at the back of the island, was where we dropped off and picked up support personnel. After-dark trips were especially hazardous because of poor lighting. As a result, we worked out an arrangement with the Secret Service to turn on a strobe light, place three portable lights around the pad, and use the headlights of one of their jeeps to help guide an incoming helicopter. The conditions were not ideal, but far superior to those under which we had flown LBJ around the pasturelands of central Texas.

On this Memorial Day evening, just as Bean was approaching, a fire alarm sounded in the main house where the President was staying. The Secret Service agents waiting for us jumped into a jeep and drove some 200 yards away to investigate. In the process, and on the way to what turned out to be a false alarm, they left behind only the strobe light. The helipad was barely a foot above water and surrounded by scrub trees, making it even more difficult to illuminate the landing site.

In the darkness, with just a single light upon which to fix, Bean was hard-pressed to adequately judge his altitude. Even though he had not flown into this site, his co-pilot had done so several times and dutifully relayed data from the radar altimeter. Unbeknownst to either of them, that instrument was not functioning properly.

Bean turned his landing lights on and off several times, sweeping them horizontally and vertically, attempting to get his bearings. Each time he did so, he encountered "backscatter," a condition caused when a dense haze reflects the light source resulting in the loss of any contrasting environmental features. This phenomenon is one reason automobiles are advised to travel with their headlights on low beam through the fog.

Standing near the landing site, planning to get a lift to Grand Bahama Island, was renowned White House photographer Ollie Atkins. According to a May 28, 1973, article in Washington, D.C.'s *Evening Star and Daily News,* Atkins reported he saw the helicopter make a low pass over the pad and then turned for what appeared to be a final approach. Atkins ducked behind some bushes to avoid the rotor wash.

With a lethal combination of poor lighting, instrument failure and a degree of pilot error for not having aborted what was a questionable approach, the helicopter suddenly hit the sea about a quarter mile away. Within seconds, before floatation equipment could be activated, it rolled onto its back and began taking on water.

"I heard a swishing noise," Atkins said, "like water being poured on hot pavement, and then the motor stopped."

Hearing cries for help, Atkins used his walkie-talkie to alert the Secret Service. Everyone, including the crew chief and co-pilot, were knocked senseless with the exception of Bean who was able to dislodge a door and launch a rubber raft. Ingesting an untold amount of jet fuel, he dived over and over into the oily darkness to pull people out of the aircraft.

Miraculously, Bean succeeded in rescuing all but one agent and later received the Secret Service's highest award for heroism. We all knew without a doubt that had it not been for Ron Bean, everyone would have likely perished. Unfortunately, for the rest of his life, Bean endured related health complications, had two kidney transplants and never flew again.

The first thing Golden, Pirnie and I saw through the mist upon coming to hover over the inverted helicopter were several men clinging to the exposed underside rocking in the gentle ocean waves. Within a couple of minutes, two Navy frogmen were on site and Secret Service agents were arriving in small boats. I notified Homestead to launch our standby H-3 and contacted operations at Fort Belvoir to send down our third VH-3A.

By the time I landed at Grand Cay, all the survivors were out of the water and being treated for shock in one of the bunk houses. Golden briefed Nixon on the crash shortly before midnight and later recalled, "It was a very brief after-action report. I told him everybody had been recovered, but there was one fatality. It was a very sobering moment for us all."

The Chinooks arrived very early the next morning to transport everyone, including the body of the agent who had drowned, back to Homestead. After those involved in the accident had departed, I stretched out on the bench seat in the helicopter and tried to close my eyes, hoping to finally get some sleep before

flying the President back to his home on Key Biscayne later that day, May 27, 1973.

I was sick.

I was mad.

I ached for the family who would be getting the worst of calls.

Had we become complacent? Was I getting too cocky? Did I need to roll some heads? Should I resign?

How would all of this affect the President? I hated knowing the Exec Flight had added weight to the enormous burdens he already carried.

I should have pushed harder to get our own Chinooks and better prepped Grand Cay so there was radio contact between the helicopter and the landing site. If the Benning helicopters – able to land and taxi on water – had made it, they would have taken the Secret Service shift change flights.

I should have not delegated landing lights to the Secret Service per the LBJ years, or at least done a better job of impressing upon them how critical the lights were.

We should have had crash support on the ground at Grand Cay.

Mostly, I thought I should have refused the assignment until we had our full contingent of helicopters and personnel to advance and support the trip. And I should have insisted against the wishes of the Military Office that we spend the bucks to ensure such precautions.

Lying there, hearing the surf lap the shoreline, asking questions I couldn't fully answer, it was unfathomable to me that we had had thousands of missions without incident under much more demanding circumstances and now this. As the senior pilot for the White House and the unit's commanding officer, I felt tremendous guilt, but also knew a fair amount of repsonsibility rested squarely in the lap of the Military Office.

There was plenty of blame to go around, but I didn't want to play games, which would undoubtedly exacerbate the situation and perhaps propel it into the Oval Office. Given the magnitude of the problems that consumed him, this was the last thing Nixon needed to deal with, if he could have done so at all.

When the President boarded the helicopter that afternoon for the flight back to Key Biscayne, Nixon offered no clue as to what he thought about the accident. However, word traveled to me that he had taken the accident very personally and talked about how it wouldn't have happened if he hadn't come to the Bahamas to escape.

Nixon ordered an investigation and, as far as I know, never returned to Grand Cay while he was president.

Oddly enough, I looked forward to the accident investigation, hoping for the opportunity to explain some of the challenges faced by the Exec Flight. When I testified before the Army's Aviation Safety Board about a week later in Washington, D.C., I answered questions as succinctly and honestly as possible. I described the uniqueness of a White House assignment, where we had shortages and how we managed to do what we did. The most delicate topic I addressed was explaining to a probing panel of examiners the difficulty with being ordered to break protocol and against our own best judgment: "do it because that's what the President wants."

And finally, in no uncertain terms, I conveyed my unwavering respect for Ron Bean, his years of superior service and his unfaltering heroism.

The board spent weeks interviewing all parties involved with the accident, conducted an operations site visit, and consulted in depth with Sikorsky regarding the maintenance history of 150612. Three causal factors were summarized in the Technical Report of U.S. Army Aircraft Accident. Their conclusion read, in part:

1. "Based on all findings and components tests performed, it is concluded that a pre-crash error of approximately 300 feet was introduced by the R/A (radar altimeter) unit due to: Failure of the blower motor and the resulting increase in R/A operating temperature.

2. "On the night of the accident, there was inadequate provision for lighting the landing site. This is considered to be a major causal factor.

3. "The pilot assigned the mission had not previously flown into this landing site day or night. The assigned co-pilot had landed at this site previously in a VH-3A helicopter during daylight hours. The fact that the pilot had to rely on the co-pilot and

briefings for landing site might have contributed to a higher work load on the approach."

I agreed with the first and second findings, but took issue with the third point suggesting pilot error. A substantial number of our flights, many with the President on board, required us to fly into areas where we had never landed. That skill was a core expectation and one of the reasons I brought in pilots who had flown combat missions in Vietnam. Both of my Distinguished Flying Crosses were for nighttime rescues into locations I had never seen and hoped to never see again. We had all been trained to assess landing conditions and locales well enough to make the call as to whether or not an approach was prudent. We also relied heavily on reconnaissance flights and advance ground work to reduce the need and expense for rehearsal flights.

I had flown with Bean in near zero visibility and we both knew when he hit the water that night it was because he was operating on bad data. One positive outcome as a result of the investigation was that the unit picked up two Chinooks and an SH-3A to use for training.

The Shark's Point accident, our only mishap in the unit's 18-plus years of thousands and thousands of flights, reminded us we were not infallible. Still, the incident was erroneously cited by some as the reason the Exec Flight was deactivated three years later in 1976. Among the few who have perpetuated this falsehood, again to my dismay, is Jack Brennan. He reinforced this perspective in the September 15, 2008 oral history interview he did for the Nixon Foundation Archives, stating "when the investigation concluded, it showed that the Marines' unit did everything by the book perfectly, and the Army slacked off, cut corners and did things differently."

Brennan's spurious account still burns me to my core and I have long pondered, without much success, what drove him to make such claims. The Marines had not been part of the Army's investigation of the accident. If any official comparative study had been done, believe me, I would have heard about it at the time.

It is worth noting – not intending to heap undue criticism on the Marines, but to keep reality in check – that HMX-1 has suffered greater losses of life and equipment. In addition to the one non-fatal accident at Camp David during the Kennedy years, they had at least three major crashes during the 1990s. The most catastrophic happened in southern Maryland, in May 1993, when an entire Marine crew perished in a VH-60N White Top that had flown President Bill Clinton the day before.

The cause of that accident generated significant controversy. Preliminary reports theorized the helicopter had been fired upon by an alien or unidentified craft. Later, some attributed the accident to the incorrect installation of two load-demand spindle pins. Others believed the helicopter went down as a result of an electromagnetic pulse weapon based at the Army's nearby Blossom Point research and field testing facility.

Accidents happen to the best of us, no matter which military branch. For Brennan to be so condemning of the Army's Exec Flight for the Shark's Point tragedy is an undeserved slam against all helicopter pilots who have given their lives in the line of duty from Korea to Vietnam, from the Iraqi War to the White House. Each branch of the military has their share of missteps and tragedies. We also have moments when we outperform the other such as when I was called by the White House on June 21, 1973, to do something that was unheard of – relieve a Marine HMX-1 flight.

Soviet General Secretary Leonid Brezhnev flew into Andrews AFB on Saturday, June 16. At the time, I was providing helicopter support for Nixon in Key Biscayne where he was polishing plans to begin Summit II the following Monday. Before meeting with the President, Brezhnev traveled to Camp David to recuperate from his long trip.

On the morning of June 18, a beaming Brezhnev motored from Camp David to the White House where Nixon was waiting with a jubilant crowd waving American and Soviet flags. The President included in his welcoming remarks, "The hopes of the world rest with us at this time in the meetings that we will have."

Nixon and Brezhnev, along with a steady procession of government officials from both countries, spent the day in meetings at the White House. The following afternoon, after another full schedule of appearances and a ceremony to jointly sign an agreement of cooperation between the U.S. and U.S.S.R. in the

fields of science and education, the two super-power leaders boarded the presidential yacht *Sequoia* for an evening cruise on the Potomac River.

By the time the presidential party returned to the Anacostia boat dock, it was about 8:30 p.m. Brezhnev was visibly fatigued and the weather was growing more unstable with dense clouds rolling in from the southwest. Nixon, Brezhnev and their aides hastened on board Marine One and took off for Camp David. In the group of several helicopters also in that flight was one of our new Chinooks. Army CW4 Benjamin Epps was the pilot. A towering man with the character of a southern gentleman, Epps was directed to transport Soviet national security personnel. He had to wonder who was running the show when he found himself with only one passenger – a confused looking KGB agent on board a helicopter with room for 55 people.

"He didn't know what was going on," Epps later told me, "and we weren't much help. I didn't either."

As the flight approached the Catoctin Mountains, the visibility degraded so badly that the Marine One pilot radioed Epps to proceed to Camp David and check the weather. He managed to get over the helipad but caught only a brief glimpse before the clouds closed in, making the site too dangerous for a landing. As a result, the President's flight was diverted to the designated alternate site – a school soccer field in Thurmont, Maryland, about a 20-minute drive southeast of Camp David.

Colonel Golden was the military aide accompanying the President on board Marine One and had been told by Nixon when he boarded, "Go direct. Don't wait for the press. Don't wait for anybody."

Now, as they orbited above the soccer field waiting for a motorcade to drive down from Camp David to meet them, the President's patience ran short and he said to Golden, "I told you not to wait for the press. Now, land us. And don't ever disobey me again."

The last comment was very uncharacteristic of Nixon and caught Golden by surprise until he realized the overly dramatic command had been for the benefit of Brezhnev's watchful eye; although when it came to barking orders, the Soviets were in a league of their own. Golden immediately relayed the order to the cockpit, "Get this sucker on the ground now!"

The Marine pilot did what I would have done – he dispensed with protocol to put down in an unsecured zone, because that's what the President wanted, and landed without adequate security in place on the ground. Vehicles from Camp David soon whisked away Nixon, Brezhnev and other members of the presidential party, which included the head of the KGB, a translator, personal physicians, several administrative personnel, and a large contingent of American and foreign press. Epps deposited his lone KGB agent on the soccer field and flew back to Davison Airfield at Fort Belvoir, leaving behind Marine One and several accompanying HMX-1 helicopters.

The next day, I got the call from Gulley in the Military Office.

"I just heard from General Scowcroft," Gulley said. "He wants you up at Camp David."

"What's up?"

"They're having some problems," he replied.

"So I've heard."

"You're going to take over the mission."

Damn. What the hell was going on? There must be more problems than what Epps had described to me. Relieving a commanding pilot in the middle of a mission was never done unless something was terribly wrong. In all my years with the White House, I had never known it to happen.

I rounded up Epps to be my co-pilot and Sergeant Mike Hughes as crew chief, briefed them on what little I knew, made sure we had overnight gear, and ordered maintenance to pull 150617 out of the hangar. We were airborne within about 20 minutes, flying into crappy weather and an unknown situation unfolding in the Catoctin Mountains – where the two most powerful leaders in the world were addressing some of the most critical issues of our time.

Mile by mile, we groped our way up a familiar ridgeline through fast-moving clouds into Camp David and put down on the helipad. The Marines' number one helicopter was parked nearby and took off before our blades stopped spinning. Since the accident in Florida the previous month, the departure of one

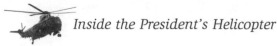

of my best pilots and the excruciating ordeal of the Army investigative hearings, the Exec Flight had flown only a couple of routine missions. Being called up to Camp David was an enormous boost to our confidence.

It soon became obvious from everyone we encountered in the hangar that something major had gone awry and we were expected to take over without so much as a ripple of a complication.

"Whatever you do," cautioned Golden, "just don't screw up."

Our first task was to expand our communication network so the KGB could monitor our airwaves. Apparently they had not been linked in to their satisfaction and the mix-up with the flight the night before had generated some heated outbursts.

While Brezhnev took Nixon for a white-knuckle drive around Camp David in the new Lincoln Continental gifted to the Soviet leader by the Ford Motor Company, Sergeant Hughes scrambled to rewire our communication system. He replaced cables, reset frequencies, swapped out antennas and distributed hand-held Secret Service radios to the KGB. I concentrated on inventorying assets and organizing the remaining Marine helicopters for the 35-minute flight back to D.C. the next day. A formal treaty ceremony was scheduled for the East Room of the White House at 3:30 p.m. Nixon would refer to that agreement for the prevention of nuclear war as the "most difficult and significant subject negotiated at Summit II."

But between that event and Camp David there were two complications: a sky in turmoil and a last-minute request by Brezhnev to fly over the Eisenhower Farm in Gettysburg.

"If we're going to make a 3:20 arrival time," I told Golden shortly before our departure, "and still fly over the Eisenhower Farm, we will have to leave at 2:35 instead of 2:45."

"Okay, I'll have everybody here by then," he assured.

Getting Nixon, Brezhnev and the other passengers to the helicopters on time was like herding cats. Apparently, Brezhnev first emerged from his cabin and upon not seeing Nixon went back inside. Then Nixon stepped out, didn't see Brezhnev anywhere in sight and went back into his cabin. Miraculously, White House staffers helped the two finally find each other and tactfully hurried them on board Army One in time for us to lift off on schedule. Visibility was moderate, the rain was pouring and the thunder and lightning action about to strike at any time.

"Nasty," Epps said, summing up the weather in one word.

I had dispatched a Huey ahead of us to orbit over the Eisenhower property where a beacon had been activated so we could home in on its location. Brezhnev was seated in the President's seat and Nixon was in the First Lady's as we pushed southeast through intermittent clouds into the lush, green expanses of Pennsylvania. Traveling at 135 knots – near the aircraft's red line – we streaked over the modest farm house at 300 feet. Normal cruising speed was 120 knots. While our distinguished passengers caught a blurred glimpse of Mamie standing on the front porch happily waving, I focused on the graphite-gray squall line approaching from the southwest.

"Let the President know," I alerted Golden, "we've got some rough stuff ahead."

I picked the lightest spot in the sky and plunged into the dense cloud. We were at about 500 feet now and although we were flying with reduced visibility, I knew exactly where we were at all times over the familiar terrain. Wrestling against the turbulence, I held us as steady as possible as a heavy shower of hail pelted the helicopter so fiercely that it sounded like gunshots and chipped paint off the sponsons and nose.

We muscled through the front in less than two minutes, but had to stay on instruments all the way into D.C. I had ordered all of the other helicopters in the flight to hold back and let us land first. We shot a modified approach over National Airport which was where I first caught sight of the ground. From there, I turned out over the Potomac, headed north, then proceeded to the Washington Monument, banked right and followed our normal route safely onto the South Lawn of the White House.

We were two minutes ahead of schedule.

Sergeant Hughes opened the folding door between the cabin and the cockpit just in time for me to see Brezhnev, white as a ghost, inching by. Nixon followed, but he looked more like a kid who had just hopped off a merry-go-round ride. Grinning ear to ear, he thanked us for the lift, prompting Epps to say, "I think he got a kick out of that."

President Nixon and Soviet General Secretary Leonid Brezhnev
arriving at the White House, June 21, 1973
(Courtesy of Richard Nixon Presidential Library, NARA)

Given the hairy ride Brezhnev gave Nixon in the Lincoln the day before, I suspect the President entertained at least a passing thought about "turnabout being fair play."

Close behind Nixon was Lieutenant General Sergei Antonov, the imposing head of the KGB. He briefly ducked into the cockpit.

"Colonel Boyer, that was a terrible flight. "

I glanced up with a start, instantly relieved to see he was smiling. I grinned back.

"I suggest" he added, "you stay off the vodka."

I nodded, suddenly wondering how the hell the head of the KGB knew my name. Then, before my imagination took me too far astray, I remembered it was engraved on the crew name plate hanging inside the cabin where he had been sitting.

I never got the full story about what had happened with Marine One on the Brezhnev flight up to Camp David, other than they had not had a perfect landing.

True perfection is impossible.

A second vote of confidence for the Exec Flight came about a month later with my annual efficiency report bearing the signatures of Brent Scowcroft and Richard Nixon: "LTC Boyer has clearly demonstrated that he possesses every attribute required for senior command. In addition, he has proven that he can perform under the most severe cases of strain and duress without degradation of performance. He has accomplished his dual functions of commander, Army Executive Detachment and Presidential Army helicopter pilot in absolutely superior fashion. His performance has earned the personal plaudits of the entire White House staff and the President. LTC Boyer should be promoted to Colonel *now.*"

Working at the White House, a place where few military personnel have the chance to serve, had taken me off the traditional advancement track for nearly ten years. It was the only mentionable downside of my job. As a result, I didn't meet the mandatory criteria for the rank of colonel as required by the U.S. Army Transportation Corps. Even though I had one of the hardest jobs an Army aviator and commanding officer could have, the assignment didn't translate to a requisite like having a diploma from the U.S. Army War College or the Command and General Staff College.

The only way I could make full colonel was if I had high-ranking support and the Transportation Corps would accept the recommendation. Even then, such a move could create its own brand of controversy, as discovered the summer of 1973. *The Washington Post* caught wind of a bid for Brennan's promotion to Lieutenant Colonel and published an article titled: "Marines Upset at Nixon Move to Promote His Military Aide."

"A presidential nomination," began the *Post* staff writer Michael Getler, "to promote an active duty Marine Corps officer working for the White House was strongly opposed by the top Marine generals and has caused widespread resentment among hundreds of Marine majors and lieutenant colonels...once approved, Marine Corps spokesmen say, (Major Jack Brennan) will jump over 1,100 more senior officers."

The article further explained, "Officers familiar with the situation say the Marines have been leaned on by the White House since last year to promote Brennan. 'Every general I know,' said one officer, 'including [Marine Corps Commandant Robert E.] Cushman, [Deputy Commandant Earl] Andersen and the rest opposed it. We were leaned on and then bypassed,' he explained, after selection boards in August 1972, and March, 1973, declined to promote Brennan.

"The Marines say there is a precedent," read the concluding paragraph, "for such action. In 1968, former President Lyndon B. Johnson promoted his Marine aide, Haywood R. Smith. 'That also caused hate and discontent,' says one officer, 'and there are still a lot of guys around who remember it.'"

Brennan, the only White House military aide to start and finish with Nixon, was eventually promoted to lieutenant colonel in September 1973. His job was demanding and unforgiving, and without fail, like every other aide, he worked extremely hard. While serving as ex-President Nixon's chief of staff in California, Brennan would resign from active duty in 1975. Shortly before moving back to Washington, D.C. in 1980 to start his own consulting business with former Attorney General, John Mitchell, he would be promoted to colonel in the Marine Reserves.

I never attained the rank of full colonel. With each year I spent flying for the White House, that likelihood faded, but it remained my choice to keep doing what I loved and what I was good at. I have no regrets.

A Gift Between Peacemakers 17

"When Moses was alive, these pyramids were a thousand years old. Here began the history of architecture. Here people learned to measure time by a calendar, to plot the stars by astronomy and chart the earth by geometry. And here they developed that most awesome of all ideas - the idea of eternity."
— Walter Cronkite

Leaks, wire taps and secret tapes. They all came with Watergate.

The red carpet for Brezhnev had not even finished rolling up when, on June 25, 1973, former White House counselor John Dean began his five-day testimony before a Senate investigation committee led by South Carolina Democratic Senator Sam Ervin. Nixon responded with frustration and anger, and believed Dean was "recreating history in the image of his own defense." He would further write in his memoirs, "I did not see it then, but in the end it would make less difference that I was not as involved as Dean alleged than that I was not as uninvolved as I had claimed."

The objective of what became known as the Ervin Committee was to inform the public about developments and facts related to Watergate. Ervin was an intense, surgical thinker with a propensity for waggling his finger and sounding like a scolding father. He and Nixon frequently clashed over what was in the best interest of the government and the nation. Ervin wanted full disclosure. Nixon wanted discretion. Arguments for and against both perspectives were easily made, but there was absolutely nothing cut and dried about Watergate.

The same day Dean began testifying, the House of Representatives agreed to a Senate bill cutting off funds for U.S. bombing in Cambodia. Nixon saw this as interference in his ability to enforce the Vietnam peace agreement. He vetoed the bill but agreed to a modified version that went into effect a short time later.

The nation was tired of Vietnam, was about to be consumed by Watergate and, before the end of 1973, would be struck by an oil embargo imposed by the Organization of Petroleum Exporting Countries (OPEC) in response to the U.S. support of Israel in the Yom Kippur War. Gasoline shortages spread across the country and prices at the pump jumped as much as 30 percent.

On July 12, 1973, Nixon was diagnosed with viral pneumonia and admitted to Bethesda Naval hospital. Midway through his ten-day stay, he received word from his chief of staff, Alexander Haig, that a former Haldeman aide had revealed to the Ervin Committee staff that the White House had an audiotaping system. Nixon had once considered erasing most of the tapes, but now it was too late. He hoped they would serve more to defend and explain his choices than they would to incriminate him.

That optimism rapidly faded.

News that the White House was bugged made us all wonder who was bugging whom. Air Force One pilot Colonel Ralph Albertazzie addressed this concern in his book, *The Flying White House*. As did I, Albertazzie had a phone in his residence at Andrews AFB, directly connected to the White House military switchboard. Suspicions grew for him when Generals Hughes and Scowcroft began calling him on a separate Pentagon line or public phone when they wanted to ensure privacy. He further conveyed in his book that he was even more convinced "after passing along a confidential word to Lt. Col. Gene Boyer." Albertazzie continues, "The next thing I knew I was called on the carpet by General Dick Lawson [Scowcroft's successor] for what I had said – privately to Boyer, a longtime friend. That really bothered me. Then I remembered Lawson had told me earlier, in no uncertain terms, that he had 'the means' to monitor everything. I am sure now, given all the suspicion pervading the White House during the Watergate period, that we were all monitored. There were too many 'private' conversations that were later, in some context, reported."

When I read Albertazzie's account, I couldn't remember the details of the conversation he mentioned, but know we certainly had had our share of discussions about Brennan and how difficult it was to get a read on whether he was friend or foe. However, I was troubled by Albertazzie's belief that I had somehow violated his confidence when I hadn't. I didn't like wading through a lot of the political crap that got stirred up between the Military Office and those of us who flew for the White House, but it was impossible to ignore the undercurrents. So after the incident with Albertazzie, I also stopped using my White House phone for anything but the most essential, brief calls.

As the ugly side of Watergate – from the West Wing to the corner coffee shop – spilled into our laps, we were all coping with variations of amazement. I had once flown for a President I considered unworthy of the job, but Nixon was very different from LBJ. I viewed Johnson to be obsessed with personal and financial gain at the expense of anyone who got in his way. And that included all 50 states and any number of foreign countries. In my opinion, Johnson was a lousy leader and overly crude. On the other hand, Nixon was a better leader, an astute scholar with a fair share of Quaker sensibilities. What he lacked in personal charisma he made up for with a bull-headed fortitude to do what was best for the nation and the world.

Nixon lost his way with Watergate. It was like he was standing with one foot on the dock and one foot in a drifting row boat. The dock symbolized a new way of conducting the business of politics with more transparency, more accountability and definitely more scrutiny by the press. The row boat represented the old system once so heavily anchored with deals, favors and shady deeds. The "end" would never again so easily justify the "means." Nixon lost his footing and fell face first into a sea of public disgrace. For me, hardly a day passed during his last year that I didn't ask myself, "Where the hell was Sam Ervin when Johnson was president?"

Much has been written about Nixon's last year at the White House, his mood swings and drinking. I did notice an understandable downturn in his usual upbeat demeanor, but I was mystified by future accusations that he abused alcohol. In the five-and-a-half years that I flew him on 451 missions, I can recall only one time he took advantage of the galley bar. It was during a Florida flight with his confidant BeBe Rebozo on board. After we had put down on the pad at Key Biscayne, Nixon stopped by the cockpit. His cheeks were flushed and Rebozo was standing behind him.

"I want you boys to know," he said with the vigor of a long-time chum, "if you ever need a girlfriend, BeBe has tons of them!" He promptly turned on his heel and exited the helicopter. Rebozo raised his eyebrows, shook his head and followed.

As soon as the cabin was empty, I said to my co-pilot, "What the hell was that about?"

He shrugged, as mystified as I by the peculiar behavior, so I went back into the cabin to check with the crew chief.

"Did the President have something to drink?"

"Yes, sir," he said. "Two martinis."

"You're kidding."

"No, sir," he replied. "I think it's the first time I've ever seen him drink."

"I know it's the first time for me," I told him.

Nixon's history of non-consumption aboard Army One prompted me to jokingly comment, during the restoration of the Last Flight Helicopter in 2005, that to keep the interior truly authentic, there needed to be a lot of dust on the liquor bottles. However, an argument could certainly be made that I had done my part to drive Nixon to drink with a few of the flights we had.

One such trip began at Camp David on a brutally cold winter night preparing for a flight back to the White House. Concerned about picking up ice, I checked air traffic control at Andrews for the latest weather conditions. The freezing level was reported to be at almost 6,000 feet, well above the altitude we typically flew. With Nixon on board, we took off on instruments and began climbing over the ridgelines blanketed by total darkness. Carl Burhanan was my co-pilot. We were barely two minutes into the half-hour flight when I glimpsed tiny crystal specks collecting in the corner of the windshield. I quickly checked the front of the sponson over the right front wheel and saw nearly a half-inch layer of ice had already formed. This meant ice was also building up on the rotors and other surfaces.

"We've got ice," I said to Burhanan, wondering how the weather report had gotten so screwed up.

"I see that," he answered.

Ice comes on extremely fast and is an instant hazard for two main reasons: it obstructs normal air flow over the blades restricting lift, and adds weight, which reduces power. Without power and lift, a helicopter transforms into an elevator going down and a pilot's butt cheeks experience what we call the "pucker factor."

Flying at 60 to 65 knots, trying to keep the rotor RPMs up, we began losing altitude. The helicopter shuddered. I counted fractions of passing seconds hoping to get beyond the ridgelines and over the small valley near Thurmont so we could descend. Burhanan kept an eye on the windshield and the sponson to his left. I was glued to the instrument panel – the air speed indicator, artificial horizon, temperature gauge, radar altimeter – poised for the first sign that we could drop into the valley and warmer air.

Finally, after a minute that felt like half a lifetime and before we were out of preferred options, we were over the valley and promptly dropped about 500 feet. The ice started to break off and hoping to shed the build-up, I shook the helicopter like a dog that had just come in out of the rain.

"This is Army One en route to Hotel," I radioed Andrews. "Picking up ice at 2,000 feet, descending near Thurmont, Maryland. Advise other air traffic."

"Roger," Andrews responded. "Do you need help?"

"Negative," I said, just as we broke through the clouds to see a scattering of twinkling house lights. "We are now visual at 1300 feet and will proceed VFR to Hotel."

"Roger, copy that."

"How the hell," Burhanan muttered, "could they have missed that system?"

I had held my breath so long, I could barely answer, "That was too close."

We followed a highway back to D.C. and landed safely at the White House, which was gloriously aglow in the darkness. When Nixon and the other passengers filed past the cockpit, they gave us small, wordless nods acknowledging they knew we had pulled out a few tricks on this trip.

Even though the most perilous part of that otherwise routine flight lasted less than five minutes, it occurred to me that sometimes flying IFR meant flying *Instinct* rather than flying *Instrument* Flight Rules. I made a report to the Military Office about getting bad weather information. For anyone who wanted more details, I gave credit to some power other than a control tower who was watching over us that night.

By October 1973, Nixon was moving toward his own brand of disaster. The coming weeks delivered several major blows. Vice President Spiro Agnew resigned on October 10 and pleaded no contest to income tax evasion. Gerald Ford, a soft-spoken, one-time All-American football player, Navy veteran and congressman from Michigan, was sworn in as his replacement before the end of the year. In what became known as the "Saturday Night Massacre," Nixon ordered the firing of Watergate special prosecutor Archibald Cox on October 20; Attorney General Elliot Richardson and the Deputy Attorney General William Ruckelshaus refused and resigned in protest.

More than twenty impeachment resolutions were in process on Capitol Hill, several of which were introduced in the House of Representatives on October 23. That morning Nixon was at Camp David (he had motored up the day before) and I flew him back to the White House. He stayed there for about eight hours and then was taken back to Camp David by car. Nixon's travels and use of aircraft shifted noticeably during this time. We went from a regular schedule of one-time high visibility trips to various parts of the nation and the world, to more frequent, almost erratic jaunts back and forth between the White House, Camp David, Key Biscayne and San Clemente.

For instance, after I had flown him back to the White House on October 23, he motored back to Camp David that night. HMX-1 returned him to the White House on October 24, then back to Camp David on the 25th, then to the White House on the 26th for a full day before flying back to Camp David that evening for a weekend stay. After he had returned to the White House, he took a car up to Camp David three days later and I flew him back on October 31. The passenger manifests were also indicative of the changing times. They now consisted of the

President, his doctor, a military aide, two Secret Service agents and an occasional family member. Gone were the high-ranking U.S. officials and array of dignitaries.

From where I sat in the pilot's seat of Army One, Nixon appeared to be more alone than ever.

The President also began using cars more for trips formerly handled by helicopters. Besides dealing with the gas shortage, I figured many of these trips were attempts to escape under the radar and hide from the intense stress or even to go off in search of ways to manage those pressures. He was also enduring mounting calls for his resignation and intense examination by "the opposition" regarding his personal finances, campaign contributions, tax returns and use of government funds. In a Q & A session at the annual conference of the Associate Press Managing Editors Association in Orlando, Florida, on the evening of November 17, 1973, Nixon attempted to calm the tumult threatening to unhinge his presidency. His remarks declaring he had never profited from public service were broadcast live on national radio and television.

"People have to know," he said with terse conviction, "whether or not their President is a crook. Well, I'm not a crook. I've earned everything I've got."

Among the many issues addressed, he explained that he was making new efforts to conserve energy and had refused to allow a back-up plane to follow him in Air Force One on this trip.

"If it goes down," he kidded about Air Force One, "they don't have to impeach."

The financial histories of Nixon's close friends, Bob Aplanalp and BeBe Rebozo, were also investigated. Among the government agencies involved in that effort was the Federal Deposit Insurance Corporation. Amazingly, my twin brother, Jack, worked for the FDIC as a bank examiner and was assigned to Rebozo's bank in Key Biscayne. Years later, after the dust had long settled, he confided in me that they had discovered no improprieties and found it to be a sound financial institution.

I had no problem accepting Jack's word. He was good at his job and always went the extra mile. An excellent example of the integrity he brought to his work involved a struggling bank in

Watts, an impoverished Los Angeles neighborhood that had suffered greatly during race riots in the mid-1960s. Jack spent three months with the failing institution helping it reorganize its books and operating practices. This undertaking so strengthened the bank that it not only became viable once again, but thrived.

On November 17, 1973, Nixon attended the AP Press Conference at Disney World in Orlando, Florida. Afterward, Air Force One brought him back to Homestead AFB. When he boarded Army One for me to fly him to Key Biscayne, he was accompanied by Alexander Haig, Ron Ziegler, Pat Buchanan, Bill Golden, his physician and other aides. More and more, the mood following a public appearance carried little of the jubilance once so detectable in the chatter of the President's party as they settled into the cabin for take-off.

It was a strange time. Everyone in the Exec Flight had a lot to say about the slide we felt was underway, but we kept it mostly to ourselves.

In the midst of the near-volcanic developments with Watergate in the fall of 1973, the Middle East Crisis heated up, driving a wedge between the recently improved U.S. and Soviet relations. Israel was under siege from Syria and Egypt and losing the war. The U.S. launched a massive airlift to resupply Israeli forces, which helped to turn the tide. The Russians had sided with Syria and Egypt, though those relationships had begun to sour. Nixon sent newly appointed Secretary of State Kissinger to Moscow, while Nixon concentrated on trying to put out fires sparked by the Watergate investigation. As history would bear witness, he just as well could have been using gasoline for that task.

In his resolve to demonstrate restraint related to energy conservation and use of public assets, Nixon did not use a single White House helicopter during the months of December and January, and flew only a couple of times in February of 1974. Consequently, and with the help of the Christmas holidays, our workload lightened enough for CeCe and me to take the kids to Florida for a long overdue vacation at her mother's house in Tampa Bay.

I hadn't been water skiing in years and, at the age of 44, didn't consider myself pasture material. However, the instant I took a bad angle into a wave and flipped flat on my back, I knew I should have given the pasture option more thought.

The pain, shooting down my leg from my lower back, was excruciating. With the help of friends, I was pulled out of the water and taken back to my mother-in-law's home. It hurt to wiggle even a toe. As awful as I felt, I kept telling myself the injury would heal and I would be fine in a few days.

I was wrong.

After a few weeks of bed rest back in Fort Belvoir, nothing had improved. I consulted Nixon's doctors, Tkach and Lucash, and they made arrangements for me to meet with surgeon Lieutenant Commander John Burkhart at Bethesda Naval Hospital.

"There's a blockage of some kind," he told me, "pressing on your spinal cord."

"Can you fix it?" I asked.

"I don't know," he replied. "We won't know until we get in and take a look."

Surgery was scheduled for early February, which meant taking medical leave from the Exec Flight. Facing the looming prospect that my flying days for the White House might have ended on Tampa Bay behind a ski boat, I did the only thing I thought made sense – I ignored the worst and expected the best.

The most likely candidate to succeed me as commanding officer was Major Bob Shain, a new arrival from Hawaii who, unfortunately, had not yet accumulated the mandatory 300 hours to qualify in the VH-3A. As a result, I designated Burhanan as the unit's number one pilot and asked the two of them to work together to get Shain his flight time.

Before I went into surgery, a hospital administrative staff person stopped by my room to discuss options for retirement. I was just a few months short of the 20-year mark.

"We can make it possible for you to retire on a 100 percent disability," she explained, "with full retirement benefits."

"Thanks for the information," I said, "but let's not get ahead of ourselves."

All along, even though the pain could drop me to my knees,

I refused to see any outcome other than being back in the right seat of Army One. Thankfully, Dr. Burkhart reinforced that belief shortly after I woke up from surgery.

"I found a two-inch fragment of a calcified disk," he told me. "It had broken off and was jammed into your spinal cord blocking the nerve canal."

"Okay," I answered, blurry-eyed.

"The good news is," Burkhart continued, "it was a very simple fix. We just pulled it out and the even better news is you can expect a full recovery."

That full recovery took more than four months of conditioning exercises, agility tests and re-qualifying in the VH-3A. I couldn't have asked for a better doctor than Burkhart and we got to know each other pretty well as I inched toward clearance to resume my former duties. He asked that when I was back in the air I would give him a call the next time I had a night take-off from the White House. An amateur photographer, Burkhart positioned himself on the Virginia side of the Potomac River that evening to take a time-lapsed photograph of the presidential

A photo of one of my take-offs from the White House taken by my back surgeon – Lieutenant Commander John Burkhart, Bethesda Naval Hospital, 1974
(Boyer Family Archives)

helicopter leaving the White House. Our lights created a glowing C-shaped path against the darkened sky made by our turn toward the brightly lit Washington Monument reflecting on the surface of the Potomac.

Burkhart had the photograph framed and presented it to me with this inscription: "To Gene Boyer – who could rise from my table *without* Army One." It was an awesome gift and remains one of my most prized possessions.

Fortunately, I was cleared to return to full flight status with no restrictions in time for Nixon's historical trip to the Middle East, which was also the first state visit by a U.S. president to the countries of Egypt, Saudi Arabia, Syria, Israel and Jordan. Naturally, political opponents and the pundits theorized that Nixon was embarking on an elaborate expedition to revive his credibility and deflect impeachment. Like Kissinger, who had spent many grueling months negotiating disengagement between Syria and Israel and broadening diplomatic relations between Egypt and Israel, Nixon had much more complex and far-reaching objectives.

He wrote in his diary the day before departure: "All I must do is to do everything possible to see that we leave a structure on which future presidents can build – a structure based on military strength, diplomatic sophistication, intelligence, and, of course, a strong strain of idealism, which will lead to progress despite some rough waters through which we will have to pass toward our goal of a permanent peace in that area."

For my part, I was acutely aware that we were all headed into a volatile and peril-ridden corner of the world, and the Exec Flight had but four days to prepare. We placed five helicopters – three VH-3As and two VH-1Ns – onto three C-5As for transport out of Dover, Delaware, to Cairo, Egypt. Unique to this mission, one of the Hueys was outfitted with a medical team, operating room equipment and surgical supplies. I didn't know it at the time, but Nixon was again suffering from phlebitis. An inflamed vein in his left leg had caused such swelling his doctors warned of a possible blood clot that could break loose at any time. If it reached the President's lungs, he would likely experience a fatal embolism.

Self-described as being "lame," Nixon was determined to not allow anything to disrupt the trip, swore to secrecy those who knew of the condition and reportedly cared for his leg by regularly wrapping it in warm towels and staying off it as much as possible – none of which I saw happen.

"Nixon came out of the palace," duty aide Bill Golden later told me, "to meet with someone in a building just 200 yards away. We wanted to put him in a car, but he refused, insisting he walk. We were afraid he would go down right there."

Nixon managed to complete his Middle East trip without medical incident, but less than five months later private citizen Nixon was hospitalized in critical condition at the Long Beach Memorial Hospital Medical Center for internal bleeding complications following surgery for blood clots.

But for now, in the middle of June 1974, two months before the resignation none of us dreamed would happen, Nixon was intent on improving relations between the U.S. and the Middle East. He also hoped to broker greater stability between Israel, the Palestinians and Arab nations. Critical to that goal was to eventually bring the Soviet Union – which had supplied some arms and economic aid to Egypt and Syria – into the dialogue. I was aware the Egyptian government believed the Soviets had not fully delivered on their promises of support, so the U.S. was the new gift-horse. With generous assurances from Nixon to Egypt for technical and financial assistance, former anti-American sentiment in the region was rapidly receding.

Still, the threat of a terrorist act or an assassination attempt loomed large and we all knew Nixon was taking a hell of a risk with plans to travel into Cairo in an open motorcade, journey some 140 miles by train to Alexandria and fly by helicopter to visit the pyramids.

Besides the five helicopters we brought over from the States, we picked up additional aircraft based on the USS *Inchon* anchored in the harbor at the west end of Alexandria on the Mediterranean. We were also using several Egyptian Air Force Russian-made helicopters with which we shared a huge hangar at the airfield northwest of Cairo.

Carl Burhanan will never let me forget that when we arrived in Cairo there weren't enough rooms at the Hilton and he was among the crew who spent the night on a nearby Nile River houseboat – a very plush houseboat, I have to add. Burhanan suffered through another unexpected development when I assigned him to do some advance work in Israel. Because Israel had no diplomatic relations with Egypt, he couldn't use his passport, which now had an Egyptian stamp, to enter their country. Consequently, we had to first send him to the U.S. Embassy in Athens, Greece, to pick up a modified passport so it appeared as if he was coming straight in from the States.

The pyramids were barely visible from the top floor of the hotel and while most people saw the Great Pyramids of Giza, one of the Seven Wonders of the Ancient World, I saw sand. Acres and acres and acres of sand.

Nothing was harder on a helicopter. If it got into the intake, the grains would erode the compressor fins, pass through the combustion chamber into the turbine blades and destroy them. Finer sand would make its way into the bearings and the oil and hydraulic systems, eating up any other moving parts from seals to gears. The result would be mechanical failure or worse – a catastrophic event. Even the forward edge of the rotor blades would suffer. One way or the other, the helicopter engine would need to be completely rebuilt.

To better understand the power of sand, we need look no further than Operation Eagle Claw – the failed hostage rescue mission that took place the last week of April in 1980. The top-secret plan to free 53 Americans held hostage at the U.S. Embassy in Tehran, Iran, seemed to have planned for every contingency but an unexpected sandstorm.

On November 4, 1979, Iranian revolutionaries took over the embassy and demanded the U.S. return the overthrown former Shah of Iran who had been allowed into the States for cancer treatment. President Jimmy Carter approved a joint military operation to rescue the hostages. The mission was led by U.S. Army Major General James Vaught and included Army Colonel Charles Beckwith, in charge of ground assault troops; Marine Lieutenant Colonel Edward Seiffert, commanding a squadron of

eight helicopters; and Air Force Colonel James Kyle who oversaw the fixed-wing air support.

The first stage of the complex mission began on April 24, 1980, when six USAF planes took off from Masirah Island, Oman, and successfully navigated the sandstorm to land at a remote, temporary airstrip in southern Iran. They carried assault troops and helicopter fuel for the incoming eight Navy RH-53D Sea Stallions launched that evening from the USS *Nimitz* anchored in the Indian Ocean.

En route, the eight helicopters, flying without radio communication to avoid detection, encountered the unforeseen sandstorm and had to abandon their formation to avoid hitting each other. The unraveling of the mission began when one helicopter was forced to land with a cracked rotor blade. The crew was picked up and the flight continued on toward the staging area. Then a second helicopter developed erratic instrument readings attributed to its exposure to the hot and gritty air and had to turn back to the USS *Nimitz*. Six helicopters, the minimum number for carrying out the next phase of the rescue mission, managed to arrive late to their destination, but sand had so infiltrated the hydraulic system of one, it was now inoperable.

Left with only five of the original eight Marine helicopters and more than 90 minutes behind schedule, previously manageable complications became insurmountable. The plan, according to ground commander Beckwith in his book, *Delta Force*, to pick up "fifty-three hostages, Delta, the DOD agents, and the assault team and their three hostages freed from the Foreign Ministry Building" for a total of 158 people could not depend on what he called "the eccentricities of choppers." Beckwith had no option but to send a message to President Carter recommending they abort the mission and he agreed.

But the sand was not finished with Operation Eagle Claw. Just before 3:00 a.m., one of the helicopters lifted up to make room for a C-130 to take off. Stirring up a massive dust cloud, the pilot became disoriented, banked left and struck the plane. An explosive fire quickly spread. Tragically, eight men were killed.

The failed attempt to rescue the American hostages has been cited as a major reason for Carter losing his bid for a second term against Ronald Reagan the following November. The hostages would eventually be released on January 21, 1981 – more than a year after they had been seized and the day after Reagan took office.

Sand. In this case it did more than mess with a flight of helicopters. As I had learned in Egypt, flying in the Middle East was synonymous with "flying in sand." I don't think it's a stretch to say on April 24, 1980, it had triumphed and changed the course of history.

My advance work in Cairo preparing for Nixon's arrival on June 10, 1974, included a meeting with General Hosni Mubarak, the Commander of the Egyptian Air Force and future president of Egypt. His term of office would span from 1981 to present day. Shortly after I checked into our hotel, one of his aides drove me to their headquarters about 15 minutes away. The streets of Cairo, one of the most densely populated cities in the world, were congested, grimy and not for the faint of heart. Every class of people – from hollow-faced beggars in rags to wealthy businessmen in crisp Western shirts and slacks – jammed the sidewalks. A countless number of dingy buses belched impurities amid a chorus of constantly honking horns. Apparent in all the chaos were symbols of a richly woven culture. The first chance I got, I thumbed through the history books in the hotel gift shop to learn more.

My initial impression about Mubarak was that he just wanted to keep track of the President Nixon's helicopter pilot, but after a few cordial words, I was convinced he also wanted this trip to be the success we all envisioned and that we had everything we needed to accomplish that. He spoke excellent English and, as a fixed-wing pilot, he had several aside questions about flying helicopters.

Mubarak's first concern was to find out how we were getting along with the Russians at the hangar where we were reassembling our helicopters. I let him know I had asked an Egyptian officer to make introductions so I could express appreciation to them for making space for us. Minutes later, we were all looking over one another's aircraft as fellow pilots and touting various features. I was honored by an invitation to fly their "Hind" gunship and let them know I hoped I would have time to do that and then proceeded to boast a bit about having recently flown General Secretary Brezhnev.

"We're doing great," I said, moving on to my biggest worry – shoulder-fired surface-to-air missiles. "What about the SAMs? My briefing papers say there are thousands in the area."

"We're collecting them now," he said, "and putting them in locked storage until after President Nixon's visit, but, of course, we can't account for them all, so I have a recommendation."

Mubarak suggested we not take a direct flight path from Alexandria to the pyramids. Rather, we swing a few miles out over the desert, staying low and away from the Nile delta. I agreed on the tactic, but still made a private subterfuge plan to change the route slightly at the last minute as an added assurance.

"I'm also concerned about the sand."

"I have a unit preparing to build a temporary helipad at the pyramids."

"What kind of pad?"

"Blacktop," he replied, "with room for several helicopters. Will that work?"

I concurred with pronounced relief. The news was music to my ears and it would play like a symphony for my mechanics.

Mubarak assigned his aide to accompany me on a flyover along Nixon's proposed motorcade course from the airport to the Qubba Palace in Cairo. From there, we traced the 140-mile train route up through fertile delta farmlands to Alexandria and then touched down briefly at the Ras el-Tin Palace, one of Sadat's official residences where President Nixon and the First Lady would host a Western cuisine dinner. An ornate, rambling Islamic building with fenced grounds, the palace was situated within sight of the sparkling blue Mediterranean. About 20 miles to the east was the similarly classic Maamura Palace where Sadat and his wife were staying.

Next, I made the hour flight southwest back to the pyramids. Circling around the massive structures built 2,500 years before Christ was as breathtaking as it was mind-boggling. I couldn't begin to fathom the feats of engineering and science involved. Minimally, there had to have been thousands of miles of rope, the brute force of hundreds of thousands of people and more fulcrum and pry-bar action than at any other time in the history of the world.

One evening at the Nile Hilton, while passing through the lobby, I noticed a smartly dressed, middle-aged black woman standing nearby. She looked familiar and as I moved closer she glanced up and I saw the twinkling, inviting smile of celebrated songbird, Pearl Bailey. A self-taught singer who dropped out of high school to pursue a vaudeville career, she had been named the "ambassador of love" by Nixon in 1970 and frequently appeared in USO shows.

"Pearl Bailey?" I asked, extending my hand.

"Yes, I am," she answered and took my hand for a gentle squeeze.

"I'm a big fan," I said, and promptly couldn't think of a single song for which she was known. Songs like *Baby, It's Cold Outside; Ain't She Sweet;* or *Bill Bailey, Won't You Please Come Home*. "What brings you to Egypt?"

"I'm on tour. How about you?"

"I'm here with President Nixon. I'm his helicopter pilot."

"How wonderful. I've met him, you know?"

"I think I knew that," I said, still dazzled by her bubbly radiance.

"My husband and I were about to have dinner," she said. "Would you like to join us?"

"Sure," I replied, probably a little too eagerly. "May I bring along one of my pilots? He's the first black pilot to fly for the White House."

"Oh, of course," she answered. "I'd like to meet him."

The four of us talked for about two hours covering where we were raised, how we met our spouses, what our children were like and stories about the White House where she frequently entertained. I was amazed by her warmth and overflowing appreciation for the military. Before moving on, we exchanged contact information and she later sent me a copy of her autobiography, *The Raw Pearl*, in which she wrote, "To Gene and Family – In all love and truth – Pearl." Not long after, we received *Pearl's Kitchen: An Extraordinary Cookbook*. It was inscribed, "To Gene and *mostly* his mate. ☺ Warm Pots, Pearl."

The cookbook became a Boyer family favorite with chapter titles like "All Burners On" and "I Don't Iron Dust Rags." Recipes included fried apples, hard-shell crabs in beer, greasy greens and corn fritters. But more than the recipes were stories from her past and perspectives about life, such as, "God gives each of us a stove. Some people light one burner at a time, and thus slow down on their cooking and on their lives. God gave me a stove and said to me, "Cook on it." He did not tell me what to cook or how much. My feeling is that I must keep that stove forever warm, and that for as long as it is possible for me to do so, I should keep all the burners lighted... I cannot let myself go cold to humanity, cold to everything but Pearl."

Pearl Bailey did a lot more for the world than sing, prompting President Ford to make her a Special Ambassador to the United Nations in 1975.

Nixon flew into Egypt on Air Force One on June 12, 1974. The weather was scorching hot and there wasn't a cloud in the sky. Traveling with him were the usual folks – the First Lady, Kissinger, Ziegler, Haig, Scowcroft, his personal doctor and secretary, photographer Ollie Atkins, General Richard Lawson and a horde of Secret Service agents and members of the press.

President Sadat met the Nixon party at Cairo International Airport before they joined the 180-car motorcade that delivered them to Qubba Palace 45 minutes later. The crowds along the way were estimated to be close to one million. Nixon described the jubilant scene as the "most tumultuous welcome any president has ever received."

In the distance, able to reach the President in less than five minutes, one of our helicopters circled ready to respond in the event of an emergency.

"This is a real welcome from the heart," Sadat would tell Nixon as they embarked on a series of meetings, photo opportunities, gift-exchange ceremonies and cultural festivities. The train ride the next day was even more impressive as rivers of cheering people flowed into open spaces along the tracks to catch a glimpse of the two presidents on their way to making history. The entire experience was a far cry from what we had become accustomed to in the United States. Nixon had his supporters, but the opposition had grown immensely in the last year. I couldn't remember the last time he had made a public appearance without the intrusion of a protesting faction. It wasn't unreasonable to think the welfare of the President of the United States was more at risk at home than in the Middle East.

Once the Nixons and Sadats reached Alexandria, they threaded their way by car through the dusty, nearly impassable streets to the Ras el-Tin Palace. Sadat, who had had some recent heart problems, wanted to travel on to the Maamura Palace for perhaps an afternoon catnap before Nixon, after resting his swollen leg, would later join him. Both presidents would return that evening to Ras el-Tin for a dinner prepared by White House chefs.

Somewhere along the line, a Chief Executive decision was made, and I was called in to fly the Sadat party to Maamura, then return to Ras el-Tin to pick up Nixon, Kissinger and other U.S. officials to take back for a business meeting. Afterwards, we flew the President's group back to Ras el-Tin, only to return to Maamura a short time later to retrieve the Sadats for a reciprocal dinner hosted by the Nixons at Ras el-Tin.

My crew and I had the chance to chow down in the palace kitchen which was bigger than most houses. I can't remember what was on the menu, but it was delicious. Our last flight of the evening was to transport the Sadats back to Maamura where he graciously thanked us for the lift service through the day. I got the sense he was thinking, "I could get used to this."

We then headed out to the USS *Inchon* to sack out for a few hours.

The next morning, in the company of several other helicopters full of officials, security and the press, we flew the Nixons and Sadats out to the pyramids, circled the location at about 400 feet and then sat down about a half mile away on the newly black-topped helipad. I joined the dozens of people who poured out of the helicopters to get a closer look at the pyramids named for Kings Cheops, Chephren and Mycerinus. I didn't stray far from Army One and Doctor Tkach was never far from Nixon.

As photo opportunities go, few compared to this nearly windless day on the Giza plateau. Even my pilots and I got into the act, snapping a few quick shots of ourselves in front of the

Army One, Egypt, June 14, 1974
(Courtesy of Richard Nixon Presidential Library, NARA)

pyramids. We hadn't been on the ground long when Military Assistant General Lawson approached me with some very startling news.

"President Nixon," began Lawson, "has given your helicopter to President Sadat."

"What?" I replied in an overly protective tone regarding #150617. "This is my best helicopter. He can have one of the others."

Lawson gave me an "end of conversation" look and I resisted the urge to kick a cloud of sand into the air. What made #150617 my best helicopter? Nothing in particular, other than I seemed to have a stronger attachment to it since we had been together for so many memorable flights. Thankfully, a decision

Presidential mission to Egypt, June 14, 1974
(Boyer Family Archives)

was made to give #150615 to Sadat, but Lawson let me know that Kissinger, upon hearing my objection, said, "Tell Boyer if he is not careful, we will give him away, too."

I ended up staying in Egypt for a few days after Nixon left to determine training and support requirements for the VH-3A we

President and Mrs. Anwar Sadat (left) and First Lady Pat Nixon and
President Richard Nixon Egypt, June 14, 1974
(Courtesy of Richard Nixon Presidential Library, NARA)

were handing over to the Egyptian Air Force. During that time I
had the chance to fly a couple of Russian helicopters – the
extremely agile Mil Mi-24 Hind gunship and the huge Mil Mi-6
Hook transport capable of carrying up to 65 troops along with a
five-man crew. I was surprised to discover the Hind was more
maneuverable and powerful than our Huey Cobra and had the
added advantage of being able to carry a seven-man infantry
squad plus the crew. On the other hand, sitting in the cockpit of
the Hook was like riding in the cab of a semi-truck. Nothing
seemed to work smoothly and just hearing the grind of the
engines made me think the steering and hydraulic systems were
on the verge of collapse. A monster of a helicopter, it ran as
crudely as it looked, but like the Hind, was still very powerful.
Suffice it to say, the Russians favored function over form.

I also worked with Mubarak personnel to write an "after
action" report for the Military Office verifying that Egyptian
pilots and their organization were qualified to fly the helicopter.

"Pilot training is excellent," I wrote in the report to General Lawson, "and consists of only the top personnel. Pilots expected to fly the VH-3A average over 2,000 hours helicopter flying time. Many of the pilots are connected with the current program of supporting President Sadat. I have flown with several of their pilots and consider them excellent... I am convinced that several weeks training, to include 15-25 hours flight time, on two of the Egyptian pilots by USAEFD instructor pilots would be more than adequate for the anticipated mission."

I also included in the report a plan for training engineers and ground personnel, stating that they needed to be "more detailed due to the difference in their S-61 and the VH-3A. The primary difference is the power plant; the S-61 has a Rolls Royce engine while the VH-3A has a General Electric engine... It would appear that the in-country technical assistance of Sikorsky Aircraft is essential and the most economically feasible to ensure the success of this mission. The Egyptians anticipate a flying hour program of 200-250 hours per year. This is approximately one half of ours. Thus, the Special Periodic Airframe Rework (SPAR) program will be 18-24 months. This reduced flying hour program should assist in the training of ground and engineer personnel."

To augment a Sikorsky team, I recommended a few Exec Flight personnel remain in Egypt until their arrival and that two Egyptian Air Force pilots and six mechanics be immediately trained in the United States to form a nucleus for the future Egyptian training program.

Working with the Egyptian Air Force was extremely gratifying and our report was so well received by Lawson and the Military Office that, as late as a chat in 2009, he mentioned to me how impressed he had been with the document.

Leaving Egypt, I felt we had left #150617's sister ship in excellent hands. Nothing proved that sense of confidence more than when I was invited by Clayton International in 2009 to be the keynote speaker at a roll-out ceremony in Atlanta, Georgia. They had just completed a year's worth of work refurbishing #150615 to return it to the Egyptian government where it had not stopped flying since being gifted to Sadat in 1974.

In a pristine hangar at Clayton International, I was able to walk through the helicopter – freshly painted the color of desert sand – which I had not seen in 35 years. The American and Egyptian flags hung in the background. Several banners had captions that read: A Gift Between Peacemakers – President Nixon – President Sadat.

A cluster of Egyptian officials, including Egyptian Air Force Major General Mahmoud Gamal, were present in the audience and it was my extreme privilege to recount to them the events of June 14, 1974, and how that singular encounter between two unlikely allies had changed the course of history. Gamal and I also sat together at a table and autographed photographs of Nixon's trip to Egypt for a string of people eager for a souvenir of that unforgettable day.

"I want you to keep in mind," I said to those gathered, "that even though the helicopter that flew Nixon away from the White House the day he resigned is the most well-known helicopter,

Me (far right) next to Egyptian Air Force Major General Mahmoud Gamal,
U.S.Navy Captain Greg Wallace and an unidentified Egyptian pilot.
Clayton International rollout ceremony for refurbished VH-3A gifted to
President Anwar Sadat by President Nixon in 1974, Atlanta, Georgia,
May 14, 2009
(Boyer Family Archives)

yours has the most colorful history. It was used by JFK, LBJ and Nixon before going to Sadat and later Mubarak. I can't even begin to imagine how many heads of state have flown on 615 during the last 35 years. You have a real prize. It belongs on a pedestal."

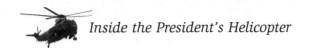

Turning Final 18

"The thing I want more than anything, and strive hard for is to stay the same on and off stage. Many people are so different onstage. Then there are those who never get off."

– Pearl Bailey

Less than two months after Nixon's triumphant trip to Egypt, on the evening of August 8, 1974, the telephone rang at my Fort Belvoir home while CeCe and I were having dinner. I had a sobering sense of dread about what I was going to hear on the other end of the line. It seemed to take forever to walk from our dining room table to the bedroom where the cherry-red phone directly connected to the White House switchboard sat on a nightstand. I lifted the receiver to hear the familiar but uncharacteristically subdued voice of Lieutenant Colonel Jack Brennan. He was direct and succinct, the unspoken undercurrents of disbelief flowing uneasily between us.

Brennan told me that at 9:00 p.m. the President would address the nation from the Oval Office on television. I could barely concentrate as the realization of what was unfolding filled me with dismay. *It was actually going to happen.* One-and-one-half years into his second term, Richard Milhous Nixon, the 37th President of the United States, was about to become the first chief executive in our country's history to resign. It was an excruciating time for everyone struggling to understand the bizarre and too often compromising nature of politics, power and public service.

More details from Brennan: The President would leave Washington, D.C., in the morning. I was to have Army One on the South Lawn of the White House by 8:30 a.m. where I would completely shut down the engines and wait for the President, his family, a small group of aides, his doctor, two Secret Service agents, and the White House photographer for transport to Andrews Air Force Base. There they would board Air Force One

and take off for San Clemente, California. I was to expect luggage. No members of the press would be among the passengers. The President planned to meet with the White House cabinet and staff before departure. The transfer of power to Vice President Gerald Ford would take place at noon, Eastern Time. Nixon wanted to be somewhere over the country's heartland when that happened.

"How's it going down there tonight?" I asked Brennan, trying to imagine the atmosphere at the White House.

"It's terrible," he said solemnly, and we both knew it was going to get worse.

Before Brennan hung up, he let me know that Nixon had asked him to accompany him to San Clemente. He didn't know what that meant for his career, but he had agreed to go. Unlike Brennan and the rest of Nixon's personally appointed staff, my position as commanding officer and chief pilot for the White House was not threatened by Nixon's departure. Yet, with 20 years of military service, I was suddenly wondering if I should retire or maintain active duty status by staying on with incoming President Gerald Ford. After all, my job as a White House helicopter pilot had afforded me one extraordinary opportunity after another – to witness a multitude of monumental historical events and countless behind-the-scenes happenings. On the other hand, I did wonder what would life be like to not be on call 24 hours a day. Except for a one-week vacation and a hospital stay for back surgery, I had taken no time off during five-and-a-half years of flying for Nixon. So, along with Brennan and an undetermined number of others struggling to sort their thoughts in all the turmoil, I also had trouble sleeping the night before he said goodbye.

CeCe and I watched Nixon's speech that night on television. For all of those who were outraged by Nixon's behavior during the Watergate scandal, there were some, like myself, who were also saddened by his collapse. I remember thinking how terribly unfortunate it was for everyone – from everyday citizens to world leaders – that the President of the United States had come to be in such a position.

About 5:00 a.m., I gave up getting any rest and got out of bed.

Routine duties and tasks kept me going because my heart sure wasn't ready for the task ahead. One immediate decision was to choose a co-pilot from the 28 outstanding men under my command. I didn't hesitate to dial Burhanan's phone number.

"We have a flight leaving," I told him. "We'll be shutting down on the South Lawn at 8:30."

"Is the President's going out?"

"Yes."

"I saw him on TV last night."

There was a long pause. Neither of us really knew what to say, so I started outlining the mission the press memorialized as "Nixon's Last Flight." Normally upbeat and talkative, Burhanan would say little the rest of that humid, hazy day that was already taking on a funeral-like pall. We would meet at the hangar in about an hour.

I next telephoned Sergeant Major Julian Hill at home and asked him to alert maintenance to prepare the helicopter. The flight engineer on duty was Sergeant William Robinson. He was the third member of our crew and would appear for all time standing at attention at the bottom of the helicopter steps in the photographs capturing Nixon's last dramatic moment as president.

Dressed in my army-green presidential summer flight suit, I hugged my tearful wife good-bye, swallowed my own churning emotions and made the five-minute drive in my Volkswagen bug to the hangar. Generally, not many people show up for dawn take-offs, but by 7:00 a.m., after we had rolled out #617 and performed our safety checks, most of the some 150 personnel assigned to the Exec Flight were there to see us off. It was an incredible and forever appreciated display of solidarity.

Before we taxied onto the runway, I made a final call to Brennan to assure him the mission was in good shape.

"We're on schedule," I said. "How are things on your end?"

I heard him take a deep breath before confessing he was worried and not sure the family was going to be able to hold it together. I shared his concern for the First Family along with my crew and even myself.

"This is Crossbow Six," I radioed, "requesting taxi take-off clearance."

"Cleared onto runway thirty-two for a west departure," responded a steady voice from the Davison Army Airfield tower at Fort Belvoir, "Winds two-eighty at ten."

Like so many other trips, we lifted off heading west and climbed to about 500 feet to follow the meandering Potomac River. Flying east, we passed Mt. Vernon, Washington National Airport and Anacostia Naval Station. Upon approaching the White House (code name "Hotel"), we heard from Washington National Airport's control tower when we were about 200 feet from the Washington Monument.

"Report turning final to Hotel."

I answered, "Roger, Crossbow Six turning final to Hotel."

Descending, we cleared the South Lawn's wrought-iron fence for Burhanan to align us with an orientation mark on a nearby tree trunk. Foot by foot, he guided me in, until we touched down on three large wooden disks about 120 feet from the White House south portico. It was a perfect landing, executed far more from habit than any choreographed exhibition for the hoards of television cameras aimed in our direction. As we shut down the engines, Sergeant Robinson opened the forward and aft doors – forward for the VIPs and aft for staff and the Secret Service.

It was an incredible, unprecedented sight. The fire truck always on scene with a crash crew seemed slightly farther away. The normally vibrant red carpet being rolled our way appeared a little less bright. The normally vacant south portico balcony was lined with people, including the kitchen staff, dabbing their eyes with handkerchiefs. Massive crowds had collected both inside the White House grounds and outside stretching as far as the Washington and Lincoln Monuments about a quarter mile away. Media people were everywhere.

Of my more than 100 landings at the White House, I could not recall a time when at least one photographer or press rep was not present. Since the Kennedy assassination, it had become standard policy for pictures to be taken of even the most uneventful flight – just in case the unthinkable might happen again. On all trips with a president on board, except those between the White House and Andrews Air Force Base, there were typically two chase helicopters carrying Secret Service personnel, members of the White House press pool, and additional staff often filming us in flight. Sometimes, with visiting dignitaries, there could be up to eighteen aircraft in a flight.

Robinson helped Nixon's valet Manolo Sanchez and his wife, Fina, load luggage at the back of the helicopter before, eyes glistening, they took their seats in the cabin. Robinson would later tell me how surprised he was to see a joint military Honor Guard in full dress uniform assemble along the red carpet and how embarrassed he was to stand with them in "my old khaki uniform" waiting for the President to board. Neither of us had even the slightest notion that he would continue to accompany Nixon through all time as *that* square-shouldered soldier standing at the bottom of the steps welcoming Nixon aboard Army One with a crisp and final Army salute. Wearing a spotless white Marine uniform, Brennan came on board for a cursory confirmation regarding the mission. Everything was going according to plan.

In an upstairs hallway at the White House, President Nixon and his family exchanged parting words with the residence staff. To the housekeepers, waiters and valets the President related how he had visited with royalty and government leaders around the world in magnificent palaces and houses.

"But this," Nixon said, with mounting pride, "is the best house because this house has a great heart, and that heart comes from those who serve in it." Nixon went on to express his confidence in knowing they would attend to the new President and Mrs. Ford with the same care. He then shook hands with each person and walked to the elevator with his family.

To hide her eyes reddened by tears, Mrs. Nixon had started the day wearing dark glasses, but removed them for the President's farewell to the White House administrative staff and his Cabinet in the East Room. His speech was televised and, as he would later reveal in his memoirs, "the emotion in the room was overpowering."

While Nixon was often portrayed as shrewd and insensitive, I knew him to be a considerate man who seemed to struggle

deeply for perspective. One thing for sure – he along with most of the nation was searching for answers.

Each time I hear the words he spoke the day of his resignation, I am struck by the contrast of how Nixon came into the White House as a seasoned and headstrong politician, and left surprisingly free of that demeanor despite the tumultuous forces that had driven him from office. I detected no posturing, no heaping blame, and no plea for sympathy during those final days. He admitted errors in judgment and seemed sincere in wanting to share the benefit of that experience in his parting words as President of the United States:

"...Always give your best," he told the nation, "never get discouraged, never be petty; always remember, others may hate you, but those who hate you don't win unless you hate them, and then you destroy yourself."

Besides the President and the First Lady, their daughter Tricia and husband, Ed Cox, the Army One passenger manifest on August 9, 1974, included Manolo and Fina Sanchez, Brennan, Nixon's appointments secretary Steve Bull, the President's physician Major General Walter Tkach, Press Secretary Ron Ziegler, Nixon's personal secretary Rose Mary Woods, and two Secret Service Agents. Daughter Julie and her husband, David Eisenhower, would stay behind for now.

As the boarding began, I could not remember a time when so many people had so little to say. Dr. Tkach stopped by the cockpit to rest a hand on my shoulder.

"I can't believe this is happening," said Nixon's longtime physician. "I can't believe it's ending this way."

"Yes, sir," I replied.

Tkach had also been Eisenhower's physician and, ironically, was among those standing on the White House lawn on July 12, 1957, when the first presidential helicopter, an Air Force three-seater Bell UH 13-J, landed for an evacuation training.

Next on board was Ollie Atkins, the White House photographer. He positioned himself just inside the doorway to take pictures of President Nixon, the First Lady, the Vice President and Mrs. Ford, Tricia and Ed, and Julie and David now walking toward the helicopter. At the bottom of the steps, Nixon and

Ford firmly shook hands. Mrs. Nixon and Mrs. Ford embraced, kissing one another on the cheek. The exchange was brief and gracious, and mimicked what could have just as easily been the end of a casual summer lunch together instead of a transfer of world leadership. As the Nixons climbed the steps, Burhanan and I heard cheers of support from the crowds. Mrs. Nixon continued on inside the cabin, giving me a grateful, gentle-hearted wave and smile as she passed.

Just outside the doorway, at the top of the steps, the President stopped and turned to face the multitude of people spilling out of the White House, the thousands of curious onlookers encircling the grounds, and the nation watching through the collective eyes of a huge conglomeration of television cameras. Nixon raised his right arm and gave a full, sweeping salute followed by his signature dual-fisted V-for-victory gesture. Of the hundreds of times I had watched Nixon stand on those steps to bid farewell to a foreign government, greet a ceremonial gathering, or acknowledge American troops and citizens, I had never seen him gesture with such spirit and purpose. Richard Nixon was leaving office, but I had the undeniable feeling that he wanted us to know it wasn't because he was a quitter.

As the President stepped inside Army One, I nodded to Burhanan to start the auxiliary power unit, which he followed with the number one engine. Robinson came on board, closed the forward door, secured the folding door between us and the cabin and took his seat next to cockpit. I started number two engine and as the power came up, released the rotor brake thinking to myself, "This better be good because whatever we do is going to be on television *forever.*"

When we picked up to hover, the tail started dropping and my heart stopped. The extra luggage had weighted us down and I had to make a much slower, groaning turn on take-off. Then again, everything felt heavy that day. The President and Mrs. Nixon would both note this "awful, ungodly sound" in their accounts of the day. But as far as all the cameras could see, the lift-off was smooth and unremarkable.

"The emotion of the moment," Nixon would later write in his memoirs, "saying goodbye to so many friends, left me drained,

From inside Army One, Betty and Gerald Ford bid farewell
to First Lady Pat Nixon and President Nixon on his last day in office.
August 9, 1974
(Courtesy of Richard Nixon Presidential Library, NARA)

President Nixon waves farewell
to the nation from the steps of
Army One. August 9, 1974
*(Courtesy of Richard Nixon
Presidential Library, NARA)*

empty. At first no one spoke. Then as the helicopter lifted off, I heard Pat say to no one in particular, 'It's so sad...so sad.'"

Twelve minutes later, we landed at Andrews Air Force Base. Seeing Air Force One ready for flight and the large gathering crowd, the finality of the situation began to settle in. I wasn't even sure from where the tears came. After all, I still viewed myself as a no-name helicopter pilot and was certainly not even close to being any part of Nixon's inner circle. Yet, I had just witnessed an outpouring of more emotion at the White House than I had ever seen for any issue or event, other than the Kennedy assassination. I think now that while most of the world saw a national tragedy, I was witnessing a human tragedy and simply didn't realize how attached I had become to the Nixon family and the, admittedly flawed, man who impressed us all by not caving in that day.

Before Nixon exited the helicopter at Andrews, he paused at the cockpit.

"Stop that. Stop those tears," he said to us, then pointed to all the people waiting outside. His jaw tightened, seeming to deny what had to be a pending deluge of untold and restrained emotions. "I have to walk over there."

With a poignantly deliberate job-well-done pat on our backs, he disembarked, perhaps privately thinking what I would have been thinking: "I should have destroyed those tapes."

Just after noon on August 9, 1974, Chief Justice Warren E. Burger administered the oath of office to Gerald R. Ford in the East Room of the White House. They stood with the new First Lady, Betty Ford, at the podium bearing the presidential seal where Nixon, flanked by the former First Family, had only hours earlier delivered his farewell speech.

On that day, Nixon became the first United States president to resign from office and Ford earned the distinction of being our first and only unelected vice president *and* president. Just eight months earlier he had been serving as a representative from Michigan's fifth congressional district and now, through a sequence of unbelievable events, he had become our "accidental" president. For some, that unique achievement painted a portrait of a reluctant leader coping with a steep learning curve.

I saw Ford as an earnest, fair-minded, and even-tempered man.

Included in his first remarks to the nation as President, Ford declared, "My fellow Americans, our long national nightmare is over... Before closing, I ask again for your prayers for Richard Nixon and for his family. May our former president, who brought peace to millions, find it for himself. May God bless and comfort his wonderful wife and daughters, whose love and loyalty will forever be a shining legacy to all who bear the lonely burdens of the White House."

One month later, Ford's popularity plunged when he announced his pardon of former President Richard Nixon. Many considered this to be a blatant, premeditated act of cronyism. While Ford eventually received a Profile in Courage Award from the John F. Kennedy Library in 2001 praising his actions, that future acceptance was a scarce viewpoint in 1974. Personally, I thought Ford's decision was appropriate. I didn't believe the consequence of leaving office fit Nixon's offenses, so someone had to provide him a measure of relief. That man was President Ford.

The day after Nixon's resignation, the White House Military Office ordered both the Army and Marine helicopter units to scout landing sites at Ford's Alexandria, Virginia, home as well as a vacation house located on a ski slope in Vail, Colorado. The Alexandria house was on a dead-end street with a lot of trees and wires making it barely accessible by helicopter. Ford planned to stay there for about ten days while Nixonites vacated the White House. It was a squeeze to get a helicopter to that house, but we figured out how to land in the street if necessary. Fortunately, that need never arose.

Vail, Colorado, presented a different challenge. I took a Huey out to recon the area just in time for an early dusting of snow. It seemed the only level areas I could find were roof tops and there was nothing big enough for a helicopter. Every other surface was slanting one way or the other, meaning that if we did manage to land near Ford's house, we had a good chance of sliding downhill. The best option was to make a hovering pickup, which I could not recommend for the President of the United States.

My first flight with President Ford on board Army One was a

routine hop from the White House to Andrews AFB. Many of the old faces were gone – the most notable being Air Force One pilot Colonel Ralph Albertazzie and Jack Brennan. Brennan was very loyal to Nixon and had worked diligently in the final days of the presidency to unearth some eleventh-hour ploy to ward off impeachment. I specifically remember a request that has grown more unusual to me through the years.

"I want you to bring me all of your flight records from the Johnson years," Brennan told me over the phone not long after we had returned from Egypt the summer of 1974.

"What for?" I asked.

Brennan explained the Democrats were accusing the President of profiting at the taxpayers' expense. We both knew Nixon's "questionable" activities didn't come close to what Johnson got away with. I didn't hesitate to comply and agreed to testify at any type of hearing if necessary.

My first sergeant, Julian Hill, and I boxed up files from my office and, without making copies, I drove them to the White House and left them in the Military Office for Brennan. No hearing took place, I was never called to testify and when I tried to retrieve the files before I retired about seven months later, they were nowhere to be found, then or ever again. The loss of those records left a regrettable and major void in the history of the Army's Exec Flight.

Ford's new Army aide was Major Bob Barrett and the Navy aide was Lieutenant Commander T. Steven Todd. Military Office director Air Force General Richard Lawson was on his way out and his assistant, Marine Master Sergeant Bill Gulley, was steadily gaining power on his way to an unprecedented appointment as the Military Assistant to the President.

If I were to point to any shortcoming in Ford it would be that he was too trusting. Coming to the Oval Office without ample time to build a proven and well-suited body of advisors and staff, Ford had to scramble to fill the ranks. This meant that the President, known for a clumsy stumble here and there, made what I considered some missteps in selecting members of his administration, the most notable being Donald Rumsfeld and Dick Cheney. The lasting impacts of their ever-controversial

political careers have yet to be fully recorded. However, we do know the most unforgivable and devastating imprint was their alignment with President George W. Bush to lead the U.S. invasion of Iraq on March 20, 2003 – an insane war that should never have made it out of the Oval Office.

Ford biographer and journalist Thomas DeFrank wrote in his book, *Write It When I'm Gone*, "His White House staff was an uneasy amalgam of old-timers, like Bob Hartmann, his congressional counselor and *über*-speechwriter, and new recruits like Chief of Staff Donald Rumsfeld and his young deputy Dick Cheney, whom Hartmann disdained as the 'praetorians.' For all Ford's geniality, the constant internecine warfare between factions got in the way of policymaking."

With every passing day after Ford took office, uncertainty grew regarding the Exec Flight's future. Ford and Rumsfeld, about to be named Secretary of Defense, were both Navy men. Cheney had no military experience, but was solidly aligned with Rumsfeld. When the music stopped and everyone grabbed a seat, the Army found itself without an influential voice in the Military Office.

Long after Ford left office, I had dinner with a trusted Ford staffer who maintained a close relationship with him until he died on December 26, 2006. On the condition of anonymity, he confided to me that he had talked with the former President about his White House Military Office and the deactivation of the Army's flight detachment. I have never forgotten what my friend said about the Ford administration he called "a lot of good old boys working together to enrich their friends."

In regards to Gulley being his military assistant and the deactivation of the Exec Flight, he told me: "The President said he went along with it all and that he wished to hell he'd never done it."

Ford had to have had a mountain of thoughts about what he could have done differently. I know I certainly did, but it was comforting to at least know the Exec Flight was included in his reflections.

A tribute essay written by Henry Kissinger for *Newsweek* following Ford's death recalled: "After Nixon told Ford of the decision to resign, Ford's first call was to me. He invited me to continue in office and asked what I thought needed to be done immediately. I told him that from a foreign-policy point of view, it was important that he establish himself immediately to be in charge...."

President Ford took Kissinger's advice and, in 1974, embarked on an ambitious international get-acquainted tour.

One of my first missions for Ford outside of Washington, D.C., was a flight on October 21, 1974, out of Davis-Monthan AFB in Arizona, through Nogales, Arizona/Mexico, to Magdalena, Mexico, about 50 miles to the south. Together with Secretary of State Kissinger, Ford met with Mexican President Luis Echeverria and his Foreign Minister onboard Army One for the brief trip south of the border – a border plagued by drug trafficking and illegal immigrants. Ford, like Nixon in his early days, was going about the business of making face-to-face connections with other world leaders. Discussions also included subjects related to migrant farm workers, oil exports and territorial control of ocean waters and resources.

It was an unusual trip in that it started inside U.S. boundaries with a foreign head-of-state and progressed into a foreign country. We executed the mission precisely as designed. Yet, with the change of administrations and a lack of confidence in the emerging leadership, I began to sense a nagging desire to retire and move on. I had been flying for the White House for more than a decade with more presidential helicopter missions than any pilot in history. Maybe it was finally time to leave.

But not until the Exec Flight made a little more history.

CW3 George Baker was the third of the three black Army aviators who flew with us. Joining the Exec Flight shortly before Nixon left office, he had had two tours in Vietnam, had more than 2,000 flight hours, and was a solid, methodical pilot with a big heart. I remember my first time with Baker in the cockpit. As soon as President Nixon boarded, Baker got the jitters and kept stalling out the engine. I finally punched his shoulder and he got the message – all he needed to do was what he knew how to do and start the damn engines, which he promptly did.

On October 24, 1974, Baker and I had a mission to take Ford

U.S. Army CW3 George Baker made history with CW4 Carl Burhanan
as the first pair of black pilots to fly a U.S. president, November 24, 1974.
(Baker Family Archives)

from Chicago's O'Hare Airport to the small town of Melvin,
Illinois, about 100 miles to the southwest. If a flight took us to
one of our pilot's hometowns, I'd make sure he was my co-pilot.
In this case, a large portion of Baker's family lived in Chicago
and I made arrangements with ground security for them to be
at one of our stops.

In Melvin, Ford participated in a ceremony to honor Congressional Representative Leslie C. Arends for his 40 years of public
service. The President included some amazing statistics in his
comments that afternoon. When Arends entered Congress in
1935, about the time I turned six years old, the Federal budget
was $6 billion and now was $305 billion, the Federal payroll had
climbed from $780,582 to $2 billion, and the Department of
Defense budget had ballooned from $29 billion to $507 billion.
Those one-time overwhelming figures from 1974 look like pocket change now in 2010.

Following the event in Melvin, we flew Ford to Meigs Field Airport on Northerly Island along the southern border of Chicago Harbor (now Monroe Harbor). From there, the President would motor to a United Republican Fund Dinner. Once the Secret Service and press helicopters had landed, Baker and I put down Army One at 5:40 p.m. on a helipad at the end of the runway. It was a clear, windless day in the "windy city." We taxied toward a crowd of some 200 hundred people, mostly gathered behind a four-foot-high cyclone fence. Between them and us was a small cluster of dignitaries which included Chicago Mayor Richard J. Daley, dressed in a smartly tailored suit and tie. A stocky yet imposing figure in form and reputation, Daley had held that office for almost 20 years. Although a frequent target for charges of corruption and racism, he held his standing as one of the nation's most powerful political figures until his death in 1976.

As we taxied closer, preparing to shut down the second engine, I realized Daley was looking up at Baker with an odd, quizzical expression on his bulldog face. I glanced at Baker only to discover him grinning ear-to-ear and waving toward Daley.

What the hell was he doing?

I looked back at Daley tentatively raising his hand to lazily wiggle a few fingers at Baker. Then I saw behind the puzzled Mayor about a dozen of Baker's relatives in a sea of otherwise white faces waving like a small forest in a windstorm. About the same time, Daley turned to see the proud relatives who were there to welcome the co-pilot for Army One. The Mayor awkwardly tucked away his hand and I postponed a good laugh with Baker until all the VIPs were off the helicopter and safely on their way.

"Did you see his face?" I asked, about to cave into another fit of laughter.

"Not really," Baker answered with a chuckle. "I was looking at my family."

"Well, let me tell you," I continued, "he didn't know what the hell to do. But you just kept waving so I guess he figured he didn't have any choice but to wave back. Damn, that was funny."

We had about three hours of free time in Chicago, so Baker

invited me and the rest of our crews to an authentic soul-food dinner at a nearby restaurant. The place was packed, the food piled high, and the music bounced off the walls. Several of Baker's relatives strolled table to table, pointing out to complete strangers the handsome black man in the olive green flight suit who was flying for the White House.

While I couldn't begin to fathom the deep significance of such a symbolic accomplishment, I was proud to have played a key role, along with the U.S. Army, in bringing black helicopter pilots to the White House. In 1974, my assumption was that we had successfully dismantled enough barriers of prejudice and discrimination to make it possible for many more deserving minority pilots to follow.

I was wrong.

According to Carl Burhanan, a charter member of the United States Army Black Aviation Association, along with fellow Exec Flight pilots now deceased, Frank Joseph and George Baker, they remain the only black aviators to have flown the President of the United States. Additionally, Burhanan continues to hold the distinction of the only black pilot to have commanded a presidential mission and that was more than 35 years ago.

A call came in one evening from the Military Office to fly President Ford from the White House to Andrews AFB and I decided to do something that was long overdue. I assigned the mission to Burhanan and Baker, knowing full well I was placing an all-black crew in the cockpit of Army One. Burhanan had been flying with me since the LBJ days and he had command-ed more than a dozen presidential flights when I was out for back surgery. I had also flown enough with Baker to know he was equally up to the task. They dutifully headed out in a VH-3A and I waited on pins and needles with other unit personnel in my office to welcome them back. We were confident the flight would go off without a hitch and that was exactly what happened.

Burhanan later reported to me that after he and Baker dropped off Ford at Andrews AFB and then landed back at Fort Belvoir, they shut down the engines and looked at each other with amazement. In the dim light of the cockpit, they wordless-ly acknowledged what had just happened. For the first time ever, two black men – who had struggled through untold acts of racism and the rigors of a jungle war to become White House pilots – had just flown the President of the United States as the aircraft commander and co-pilot for Army One.

"We had tears in our eyes," Burhanan said. "It was a memorable day."

But that day became memorable for me in another way when, a couple of weeks later as I was passing through the Military Office at the White House, an office staffer took me aside.

"All I'm saying," he quietly said, "is that there was a discussion."

"What kind of discussion?" I asked, trying to contain my exasperation. Not once had I been criticized or advised on who I put in a helicopter cockpit.

"I can't say," he answered, glancing around, "but it was passed down that you check with us before you do it again."

Why? So the Military Office had time to alert the press and give these guys the recognition they deserve? I decided that that response would not be appreciated. Anything else I could think of included a stream of profanity, so I simply nodded and moved on.

"It" was placing two black pilots in the cockpit of a presidential helicopter. "It" was something, as the Exec Flight commander, I would do again if given the chance. "It" was something that shouldn't even be a topic of discussion. I never learned at what level that special talk took place, but I had enough instinct by this time to conclude the President wasn't involved. Rather, the message came from his "handlers" who were far above my pay grade and the matter was closed, whether I wanted it to be or not.

But I would never forget.

On January 8, 2000, at the age of 65, George Baker passed away from cancer caused by Agent Orange. I attended his funeral at Fort Rucker, Alabama, and his internment at Arlington National Cemetery, Plot 66, 0, 5318. From where I stood, I could see the helipad at the Pentagon to the east across the Jefferson Davis Highway. The location seemed fitting for a man who had been part of the unique trio that had taken helicopters to a new altitude at the White House – however brief and unheralded that trip.

In addition to incidents like the one that occurred with

President Ford Page 2

PRESIDENTIAL (ARMY ONE) FLIGHT LOG

DATE	ROUTE		TIME			CREW			AIRCRAFT	
	FROM	TO	OFF	ON	ENR	A/C	PILOT	CE	TYPE	N
29 Oct 74	Andrews AFB, Maryland	Hotel	2357	0006	00:09	MAJ SHAIN	CPT FRYE	MSG ORTIZ	VH3A	614
31 Oct 74	Hotel	Andrews AFB, Maryland	1320	1330	00:10	LTC BOYER	CW3 RHODES	MSG BREON	VH3A	617
3 Nov 74	Andrews AFB, Maryland	Hotel	0058	0109	00:11	LTC BOYER	CW3 BAKER	SSG HUFFER	VH3A	617
14 Nov 74	Hotel	Andrews AFB, Maryland	0732	0742	00:10	LTC BOYER	CW3 OVNIC	SSG WOMACK	VH3A	617
15 Nov 74	Andrews AFB, Maryland	Hotel	0105	0115	00:10	LTC BOYER	CW3 OVNIC	SPC STEAD	VH3A	617
17 Nov 74	Hotel	Andrews AFB, Maryland	0931	0939	00:08	LTC BOYER	CW3 OVNIC	MSG BREON	VH3A	617
24 Nov 74	Hotel	Andrews AFB, Maryland	1945	1955	00:10	CW4 BURHANAN	CW3 BAKER	SSG CASE	VH3A	617
30 Nov 74	Hotel	Philadelphia, PA	1140	1250	01:10	LTC BOYER	CW4 RANSOM	SSG EAST	VH3A	614
30 Nov 74	Philadelphia, PA	Hotel	1613	1709	00:56	LTC BOYER	CW4 RANSOM	SSG EAST	VH3F	614
10 Dec 74	Hotel	Andrews AFB, Maryland	1407	1414	00:07	LTC BOYER	CW4 RANSOM	SPC FLOYD	VH3F	614
14 Dec 74	Andrews AFB, Maryland	Hotel	2344	2353	00:09	LTC BOYER	CW4 RANSOM	SPC FLOYD	VH3F	614
14 Dec 74	Martinique Airport	Meridien Hotel, Martinique	1710	1715	00:05	LTC BOYER	CW4 ADAMS		VH1N	553
15 Dec 74	Meridien Hotel, Martinique	Leyritz, Martinique	1255	1312	00:17	LTC BOYER	CW4 BURHANAN		VH1N	553
15 Dec 74	Leyritz, Martinique	Meridien Hotel, Martinique	1514	1536	00:22	LTC BOYER	CW4 BURHANAN		VH1N	553
16 Dec 74	Meridien Hotel, Martinique	Martinique Airport	1243	1250	00:07	LTC BOYER	CW3 OVNIC		VH1N	553

U.S. Army CW4 Carl Burhanan made history with CW3 George Baker as the first pair of black pilots to fly a U.S. president, November 24, 1974. (*Army One Flight Log*)

Burhanan and Baker, the Ford people were downsizing and White House helicopter missions were on the decline. Even with all the advancements the Exec Flight had made in the last five-and-a-half years, I could still sense the ground caving in beneath us. Toward the end of 1974, I admitted to CeCe, "I think it's time to retire. I've had enough."

After years of practically raising our children on her own, CeCe didn't offer the slightest hint of disagreement. As to when and how I would leave the unit, I wasn't sure, but figured the pieces would fall into place soon enough.

The morning of the first day of December 1974 was overcast, bitterly cold and windy. Several icy thunderstorms were rolling around the area producing moderate rain showers. The Military Office called to tell me to take an unscheduled flight up to Mount Weather, Maryland, about 30 miles to the west of Washington, D.C., and search for a downed aircraft. TWA Flight 514, a Boeing 727 inbound from Columbus, Ohio, had disappeared in the Blue Ridge Mountains on approach to Dulles International Airport. Seven crew members and 85 passengers were on board.

I was next informed, and adding to the gravity of the situation, that the plane had likely gone down near a "hard point" – a top-secret government installation near the Pennsylvania border. The underground facility, built between 1954 and 1958, was an evacuation site for the President and other high-ranking authorities to be safely sheltered and still run the government in the event of a nuclear incident.

The cavernous facility, unknown to all but a select inner circle of military and government officials, had a 35-ton blast door which was about five feet thick and took several minutes to open and close. Designed to accommodate several thousand people, it included a hospital, residential quarters for 2,000, dining and recreation areas, a television studio and self-contained water and electrical power systems. Following its discovery by the public as a result of the TWA crash, Mount Weather transitioned its 435 acres to include many above-ground service and training facilities and expanded to an "all-hazards" mission under the direction of the Federal Emergency Management Agency.

Within minutes, CW3 Art Ransom had one of our Chinooks powered up and ready to go.

"What are we looking for?" Ransom asked.

"A commercial airliner went down coming into Dulles," I said, a little uneasy about the weather myself. "It looks pretty bad."

We found decent visibility low to the ground and followed a winding, narrow strip of highway through a wooded area up the hill until we hit a thick cloud bank and had to pull back. For about half an hour we endured 40-mile-an-hour winds trying to get to the crash location at about 1,700 feet on the west slope of Mount Weather, only to have to turn around and try again. Once we managed to glimpse a massive swath of severed barren trees, it was soberly apparent the doomed 727 had hit the ground hard.

"We can't get in," I radioed, "but can confirm the crash is behind the security gates."

"Roger. We understand," answered the voice in my headset. "We're getting firsthand reports from the ground."

"Ambulances are taking casualties to the school down the hill," I said. "I don't think there's anything we can do."

"Agree. You can head out."

No one survived the crash. Wreckage covered an area about 900 feet long and 200 feet wide. The National Transportation Safety Board found fault with both the air traffic control system and the pilot, concluding that the controller gave inadequate clearance and the pilot should have determined an unrestricted descent over mountainous terrain was unsafe for the weather conditions. A communications breakdown caused the death of 92 people.

Years later, I found out one of the passengers was newly retired U.S. Army General Roscoe Conklin Cartwright, age 55. Nicknamed "Rock," he belonged to another unique trio of African-American military pioneers. As the third black man promoted to Brigadier General, he followed U.S. Army General Benjamin O. Davis, Sr. and his son, U.S. Air Force General Benjamin O. Davis, Jr., who was the first officer to get wings from the Tuskegee Army Air Field.

Countless men and women of color have since walked upon and beyond their hard-fought paths to shape a diverse U.S. military population. Women have also made enormous strides through the last 40 years. News of the first all-female crew to fly a Marine One mission to the White House the summer of 2009 produced mixed emotions for me. While I applauded the accomplishments of Marine pilot Major Jennifer Grieves, I couldn't help but throw up my hands and ask, "What the hell took so damn long?"

By the end of the third month of Ford's presidency, he had traveled more than 130,000 miles. During his speech at the United Republican Fund Dinner in Chicago, Ford underscored this accomplishment by commenting, "I happen to believe a President of the United States, if he has conviction and dedication, if he believes in the principles and the policies, ought to get out and try to sell them."

Ford's initiative took him to Tokyo, Seoul, Britain and Vladivostok. In Washington, D.C., the President played host to Canadian Prime Minister Pierre Trudeau and West German Chancellor Helmut Schmidt. Topics of conversation rotated from trade agreements to the energy crisis, from inflation to the state of the global economy – all the while seeking to establish "a new day" for America.

Ford's international outreach efforts in his first few months were anchored by a trip to Martinique on December 15, 1974, to meet with President Valéry Giscard d'Estaing. More than making a personal connection, the two new presidents hoped to find some common ground on how to better work with the Arabs, with whom France was historically aligned, and, hopefully, to find a way to bring down oil prices and thus end the gas shortage.

The island of Martinique is part of the Windward Islands, the southern group of the Lesser Antilles in the West Indies located in the eastern Caribbean. Colonized in 1635 by the French, the island has mostly been in their possession ever since. Some 450 square miles in size, the heavily forested and mountainous landscape is dominated by the still-active Mount Pelée volcano to the north where, in 1902, the most disastrous eruption of the 20th century killed more than 30,000 people.

We brought down three VIP N model Hueys on a C-5A the day before Ford arrived on Air Force One. I made one of the helicopter test flights along the coastline. The rich soil and densely humid climate produced lush vegetation and brilliant arrays of exotic flowers. The crystal turquoise sea reminded of me of my bush pilot days doing oil survey work in Venezuela some 15 years earlier. I remembered flying alone in a little three-place Hiller along the northern jungle shore when I spotted a giant manta ray, a good 18 feet from wing-tip to wing-tip, cruising just beneath the surface. Mesmerized by its graceful power and meandering course, I followed it for about ten minutes, impressed by its carefree nature, thinking we at least had that in common.

Getting the flight ready for Ford in Martinique, those earlier carefree days seemed like a lifetime ago and were made even more distant by the irritating attitude of an uncooperative French general. I'd spent enough time in France to know how to defuse and negotiate the generally harmless arrogance of the French military. But on this mission, either because he was a cut above that norm or I was low on patience, things got touchy as soon as we met at the Martinique Airport.

"I thought I explained to your superiors," he abruptly announced, his French accent absent any trace of charm, "we don't need your helicopters. We have our own."

"I'm sorry," I replied, courteously, "but our helicopters are specially equipped with communication equipment and –"

"I am sorry you do not understand," he pressed. "We want your president to ride in our new models."

"Again, that's not possible," I replied, feeling a surge of heat creep up my neck.

"We insist."

"We don't put our president on foreign helicopters."

He gave me a hard look. "You can make an exception."

"I can't negotiate a national security policy," I firmly stated.

"Very well," he unhappily conceded.

Round One: Boyer.

The next skirmish dealt with the matter of where we were going to land and in what order, and I wondered what advance man from Ford's office had neglected to iron out that big wrinkle. The President and members of his party were staying at the Meridian Hotel five minutes from the airport. The hotel's helipad, about 100 yards away, had room for only one helicopter. The general and I agreed that if both presidents were coming into the hotel, Giscard d'Estaing's flight would briefly land for him to disembark, then his helicopter would depart for Army One to come in with Ford.

Round Two: A respectable draw.

Air Force One arrived at Lametin Airport on Martinique about 5:00 p.m., Saturday, December 14, 1974. Both Presidents addressed the crowd during the welcoming ceremony and together reviewed the troops. Before dinner, Ford, Kissinger and Secretary of Treasury William Simon joined the French president, his foreign minister and other dignitaries for a cruise on Giscard d'Estaing's yacht. Later, they enjoyed a folk ballet performance by a local dance troupe.

The next day, at 12:55 p.m., Army One and our two sister U.S. helicopters joined a French flight for a 20-minute trip north to the Leyritz Plantation. Recently converted to a hotel, the eighteenth century agricultural estate was located among pineapple, sugar and banana plantations in the eastern foothills of Mount Pelée. The weather was perfect and the scenery breathtaking as we cruised above scattered colonial-style settlements with an overabundance of church steeples. At the plantation there was plenty of room for all eight helicopters to land in an open field.

Ford, Kissinger and Giscard d'Estaing went swimming and then lunched together in the hotel dining room. About two hours later, the presidential parties returned to their respective helicopters for the flight back to the Meridian Hotel. Army One lifted off first with Ford. As prearranged, Giscard d'Estaing's helicopter followed and passed us en route to put down on the hotel's helipad. I held back until Giscard d'Estaing's car drove away, then began our approach expecting the French helicopter to start up its blades and lift off.

It didn't budge.

I pulled up and went into an orbit over the bay.

Still, the French helicopter remained in place.

I radioed my guy on the ground who told me my favorite French general didn't seem interested in moving the helicopter.

"Can you get him on the radio?" I asked, tightening my jaw.

"I'll try," he said as I circled the bay again.

Someone from inside the cabin picked up the phone to check in with us on behalf of Ford.

"The President wants to know what the problem is."

"They're playing games on the helipad," I replied, imagining Ford had seen enough of the bay and its quaint seaside villages. In less than a minute, I again heard from the cabin.

"The President said, 'Well, do something about it,'" he told me just as the general's voice crackled over the radio and we were heading into yet another orbit.

"Colonel Boyer?" the general asked.

"General, I have been authorized by the President of the United States," I boldly said, fully aware I had no such explicit authority, "to direct you to move that helicopter immediately."

"It will be a few moments."

"Move it now," I snapped, "or we will fly straight to Air Force One and leave this goddamn French Island. Do *you* understand *that*?"

"I believe..." he said, slowly stretching out each word, "it is leaving now."

Round Three: President Ford (without his knowledge).

I lost count of the number of times we had to loop the bay that afternoon, and the number of times I had muttered to myself, "This is bullshit." I hoped Ford and Kissinger were having better luck negotiating with the French than I had had. Ford hosted a dinner at the Meridian that night and singer Sarah Vaughn performed.

By the third day, when I picked up Ford at the hotel to take him back to the airport for a departure ceremony at 1:00 p.m., I sensed the jubilant mood, so evident upon his arrival in Martinique, seemed to have faded. I definitely felt more tension and once again had to track down the general for a conference regarding exit plans.

Everything seemed straightforward enough. President Giscard d'Estaing would wait at the airport for us to land in Army One. We would shut down and the two presidents would join an honor guard and "troop the line." A military band would play both countries' national anthems. Everyone followed cues and hit their spots, until midway through the "Star Spangled Banner," an apparently "lost" French helicopter fluttered noisily onto the scene to land, drowning out the music and distracting everyone.

Unbelievable.

Ford may have gotten off to a bumpy start in Martinique, but I knew I had just experienced a bumpy end to my career as a White House helicopter pilot. I had lost more confidence in the Military Office, knew there were serious maneuvers underway to extract the Army, wanted to spend more time with my growing family, and, perhaps above all, the job had become much more an ordeal than a pleasure. It was time to get off stage.

My last flight for the White House was on January 2, 1975. The flight log reads: FROM: Andrews AFB; TO: Hotel; OFF: 1849; ON: 1858; ENR: 00:08; AIRCRAFT COMMANDER: LTC BOYER; CO-PILOT: CW4 BURHANAN; CHIEF ENGINEER: LITTON; AIRCRAFT TYPE: VH3A; TAIL NO: 616.

After we landed at the White House that final day, I joined President Ford on the South Lawn where he graciously acknowledged my years of service.

"Any plans for what you're going to do next?" he asked.

"Look for a job," I replied, and we both laughed.

"Well, good luck to you and your family," added the President before walking into the White House.

For the last time, as the President's senior pilot, with Burhanan to my left, I lifted off, turned away from the White House aglow in the night, crossed over the south fence and headed toward the Washington Monument before going into Fort Belvoir. An unexpected surge of nostalgia overtook me and a colorful, blurred, kaleidoscope of memories whirled inside my head. It was as bittersweet a moment as I would ever endure.

I recommended newly promoted Lieutenant Colonel Bob Shain to be my successor. Burhanan and a few other "old-timer" warrant officers were staying on as well. I was certain that as a team they would preserve the integrity of the unit and execute a seamless transition to a new commander.

My retirement party was held at the Officer's Club at Fort Belvoir. The banquet room was packed with family, friends and

My last White House flight. President Gerald Ford wishing me well in retirement as co-pilot CW4 Carl Burhanan looks on. January 2, 1975.
(Boyer Family Archives)

colleagues from the Army and the White House. CeCe was stunning in an orange floor-length dress and there was a large cake sculpture of a VH-3A on the head table. Mixed in with a generous dose of salutations were several gift presentations which included a wooden poker table bearing the presidential seal, made by the Exec Flight mechanics, and a "timed-out" presidential helicopter tail rotor blade from Sikorsky.

Among the many letters of congratulations from past and present colleagues was one from U.S. Army Major General William J. Maddox, now the commanding officer at Fort Rucker.

"...I would like to express deep appreciation to you," wrote Maddox, "not only for the excellent cooperation and military support you have rendered to me personally, but for your much broader contribution to the Army aviation program as a whole. You operated in a most challenging position as the principal helicopter pilot for the President of the United States and as Commander of the Executive Flight Detachment. Throughout this assignment you brought great credit to the Army through your personal skill and the high professionalism which your Detachment demonstrated on all occasions. This period was one of substantial turbulence which required of you a high degree of diplomacy as well as flexibility and determination. Your previous outstanding service resulted in your selection for this most demanding and prestigious assignment which you have completed so well."

With each gesture of recognition or words of praise, I winced inside, thinking I should have found a way to do more to save the Exec Flight from Rumsfeld's inevitable chopping block.

After-Action 19

"Don't be afraid to challenge the pros, even in their own back yard."

– Colin Powell

In the wake of a massive evacuation by sea and air, the Vietnam War ended unceremoniously for the United States on April 30, 1975, when the South Vietnamese capital of Saigon fell to the North Vietnamese. The long-divided country reunited under Communist rule and became known as the Socialist Republic of Vietnam. It was not the outcome any of us had envisioned a decade earlier and no matter how hard people tried to spin and rationalize the failures, it was still a loss for the United States – a country accustomed to winning.

According to the Vietnam Helicopter Pilots Association (VHPA), from May 1961 to May 1975, 46,681 helicopter pilots flew in Southeast Asia. Representing all branches of the U.S. military and including pilots from Australia, New Zealand, Korea and the Republic of Vietnam, 2,202 of those aviators lost their lives along with 2,704 non-pilot crew members. Army helicopter pilots who flew in Southeast Asia totaled 37,500, Marines 4,500, and the Air Force 2,000. Of those killed in action, 1,869 or 85 percent were Army and ranged in rank from warrant officers to a major general. Their average age was 25.5 years and the average tour length was less than five months. Among the dead were White House pilots Captain Dale Dwyer and Chief Warrant Officer "Dusty" Rhodes who had flown for President Lyndon Johnson in Washington, D.C., prior to his moving the Exec Flight to Texas.

Close to 12,000 helicopters served in Vietnam and as documented by the VHPA, Bell helicopter built 10,005 Hueys from 1957 to 1975 with 9,216 UH-1s going to the U.S. Army, 79 to the Air Force, 42 to the U.S. Navy, 127 to the U.S. Marine Corps and the remainder to other countries.

A total of 7,013 Huey UH-1s, almost all Army, flew during the Vietnam War. Nearly half of those were destroyed. Army UH-1 flight hours between October 1966 and the end of 1975 totaled 7,531,955 and 1,038,969 for the Huey Cobra. The final tally for helicopters destroyed in the war was 5,086 out of 11,827, one of which was a Chinook from my unit that was shot down near An Khe. All eight men aboard – all courageous, unsung heroes – perished.

Vietnam robbed us of sons and daughters, fathers and mothers, husbands and wives, and brothers and sisters. It ravaged a distant country and severely eroded our standing in the global community. The price we paid in resources and human life was catastrophic, but at least in the spring of 1975, the recovery and healing – in excruciatingly tiny increments – could finally begin.

CALIFORNIA BOUND

Midway into 1975, CeCe, the kids and I were well-settled into our new Palos Verdes home in California. The large, ranch-style house, complete with a pre-requisite backyard swimming pool, Jacuzzi, and built-in barbeque was nestled on a hilltop with a magnificent view of the Los Angeles Basin and Pacific Ocean. I had a civilian job working for Hughes Helicopter as their Director of Marketing for the Middle East and Africa. It was my responsibility to identify helicopter markets, to supervise a small group of personnel and to network with in-country consultants. A few years later I left Hughes for a similar position with Lockheed Aircraft Service representing the L-1011 Tri-Star, a wide-body, passenger jet airliner. Chronic back pain that had been building through the years forced me to resign in 1979, but about two years later I returned to work as a consultant for Royal Jordanian Airlines. I also partnered with Carl Burhanan who had formed Oasis Aviation and Petroleum, an aircraft refueling company, to set up the world's first credit company for jet fuel.

During the late 1970s and early '80s, I made about 40 trips to the Middle East and Africa, which included Oman, Jordan, Egypt, Saudi Arabia, Iran, Iraq, Kuwait, Algeria, Morocco, Tunisia, Sudan and all of the Arabian gulf states. I had the chance to interact with prominent "wheeler-dealers" such as

Jordan's King Hussein and wealthy businessman Muhammed Awad bin Laden, Osama Bin Laden's father, who was nothing like the terrorist mastermind of 9/11. All together, I had close to a billion dollars in sales during my post-Army career.

The money was good, the work enthralling and the California weather was great. Unfortunately, the travel demands took me away from my family even more than when I was at the White House. As many of my colleagues will attest, holding a marriage together in our line of work comes with a lot of heartache and unfavorable odds. Four years after moving to California, CeCe and I divorced. Neither of us remarried and we remain close friends.

I next saw Nixon after he had resigned in the spring of 1975. That meeting with the former President was prompted by a chance encounter with Julie Eisenhower on a commercial flight with my family from Washington, D.C. We were on our way to our new home in Palos Verdes, California. I caught sight of Julie, then in her late twenties, sitting alone five rows behind us, wearing dark glasses. Several Secret Service escorts sat nearby. Upon recognizing me, she asked me to meet her at the baggage claim area, which I did.

I introduced Julie to my wife and children and then asked, "How's the President?"

"He has good days and bad," she said, clearly not wanting to elaborate.

Nixon had nearly died a few months earlier as reported in a November 11, 1974, *Time Magazine* article: "Last week, less than three months after he was forced to resign the presidency, Nixon lay in critical condition in Long Beach Memorial Hospital Medical Center. The cause was internal bleeding in the wake of sudden surgery for blood clots in his left leg and lower abdomen. It is thought that the anticoagulant drugs he had been taking had caused a tendency toward prolonged bleeding, and he went into shock."

"I have a gift for your father," I said, hoping to lighten the conversation.

Julie brightened. "What kind of gift?"

"Before I retired, I had my mechanics build a coffee table out

of a brass tray from India with the presidential seal on it. It's covered with smoked glass."

"Oh, he'll love that," Julie happily responded and gave me Brennan's phone number to make the arrangements. "He'll be so glad to know his favorite helicopter pilot has moved to California."

Several weeks later, Brennan helped me lug the mahogany coffee table from my car into Nixon's office – a pre-fabricated room beside his Spanish-style home. When we opened Nixon's office door, I saw the President, casually dressed, busy writing at his desk. He quickly put down his pen and came around to grab my hand and briskly pump my arm. Nixon looked more fragile than I was expecting but seemed to be in good spirits.

"This is really nice," he said, examining the table. "I'll put it in the library I'm building."

Two weeks later Nixon invited me and CeCe to a VIP reception at his home. Shortly thereafter, I borrowed a four-place helicopter to fly him to billionaire publisher Walter Annenberg's estate in Palm Desert. He and Nixon had been friends since the 1950s. In flight, with his wife Pat, and a Secret Service agent sitting behind us, Nixon watched the rolling hills dotted with scrub pine sweep underneath us and I hoped we were both thinking the same thing: "Just like the old days."

LIGHTS OUT

In 1976, the Ford administration was downsizing White House operations, which included reducing the size of the presidential helicopter fleet. Basically, there were two options – scale down both the Exec Flight and HMX-1 or eliminate one or the other. I supported the first choice. By retaining a joint military operation, there would remain an important check and balance system for monitoring the scope of the mission and ensuring superior service and equipment management.

But it didn't matter what I thought. Then Secretary of Defense, Donald Rumsfeld, and Ford's Chief of Staff, Dick Cheney, favored deactivating the Army's unit. Also supporting that tactic was Ford's newly named Military Office Director, Marine Master Sergeant Bill Gulley and Jack Brennan, who offered this perspective

Sometime private pilot for former President Richard Nixon.
(Boyer Family Archives)

during his September 15, 2008, interview for the Nixon
Foundation Archives: "So it was recommended," said Brennan,
"and approved that the Army unit be disbanded which I had tried
to do for a long time. The blame is kind of on now, 'Oh, Rumsfeld
did it.' Actually, it was Dick Cheney. Dick Cheney was (Ford's)
Deputy Chief of Staff at the time. Dick Cheney recommended
strongly to his pal, who was Rumsfeld and Secretary of Defense,
that the Army unit be disbanded and it was disbanded."

The final campaign for deactivation began in the spring of
1976 when Rumsfeld's Special Assistant, Alan Woods, produced
an "Analysis of White House Helicopter Support" for the
Department of Defense. The report recommended HMX-1 be the

single manager of the White House helicopter fleet and that they develop their own implementation plan.

Woods stated in a May 18, 1976, memo to Gulley: "This analysis indicates that we can free over 100 military spaces and achieve a net reduction of seven helicopters [from 22 to 15] now required for White House support, if we consolidate this mission in one organization under the Marine Corps and eliminate the Army."

Curiously, the analysis did not include White House helicopter usage numbers from 1970, 1972 and 1974 – years that more favorably reflected the Exec Flight's performance. Additionally, the running assumption throughout the document was that the Exec Flight and HMX-1 were interchangeable in depth of experience and range of expertise, which I knew was not the case.

On May 27, 1976, President Ford sent the Exec Flight's death-blow letter to Rumsfeld stating: "In accordance with the study conducted by the Department of Defense, I have determined that the present two-unit helicopter operation provided in support to the Office of the President is excessively costly in terms of personnel and equipment. I have decided, therefore, that this mission should be consolidated in one organization under the Marine Corps and the Army Executive Flight Detachment disestablished... The Army Executive Flight Detachment has fulfilled a vitally important role with total dedication during the past years and I would recommend that their outstanding service be recognized by means of suitable individual and unit awards as appropriate."

Rumsfeld sent a subsequent memo to the Secretaries of the Navy and Army on June 8, 1976, directing, "In order to insure the continuity of helicopter support during this period, the Marine Corps implementation plan should be coordinated with the Military Assistant to the President, the Army and the Secret Service."

Outgoing Exec Flight commander and my successor, Lieutenant Colonel Bob Shain, delivered a handwritten note to his troops on June 14, 1976, stating: "President Ford made the last flight on Army One. At the completion of the flight on the White House lawn, the President asked me to convey to every member of the Executive Flight Detachment his sincere appreciation for your long and faithful service to the White House and to him personally. Robert A. Shain."

The Department of the Army awarded outgoing Exec Flight personnel with Distinguished Service medals, but according to Burhanan, "We didn't hear much of anything from the White House or the Department of Defense."

Shain left the unit at the end of August, 1976. Burhanan, as its logistics officer, stayed on for another month with about ten enlisted men. When he turned out the lights on September 30, 1976, he moved on to a new assignment with the Army's Rotary Wing Priority Air Transport Flight to fly Army generals and other VIPs.

"I was there long enough to fly one mission," Burhanan said, "about two weeks, and decided to retire."

For Burhanan and me, along with others associated with the Exec Flight in its final days, it remains our firm belief that personal agendas and military branch affiliations, more than logic and reason, contributed to the demise of the unit. The people in charge worked the numbers and special interests rather than considering "the big picture." Regrettably, this was and is how business is often conducted. However, from 1958 to today, the White House helicopter support mission has remained virtually unchanged. Helicopters provide an emergency evacuation service and function as an air taxi for the President and Vice President, their families, and selected press, key staff and advisors. Most trips take from 5 to 20 minutes. In the years following the 1976 demise of the Exec Flight unit for the purpose of reducing the White House helicopter fleet from 22 to 15, HMX-1 has increased the size of its presidential squadron to include 35 helicopters. Personnel support has more than doubled.

WINNIE THE POOH FOR PRESIDENT

I left the Army and Washington, D.C., with mounting cynicism and a declining faith in our government leaders. That disillusionment made it easy to accept one of my first missions as a civilian helicopter pilot for Disneyland the fall of 1976. Winnie the Pooh was campaigning for President of the United States

Me with Winnie the Pooh's campaign staff, Pooh-litical Convention,
Anaheim, California , October 22-24, 1976
(Boyer Family Archives)

against Republican incumbent President Gerald R. Ford and the
Democratic candidate, one-time Georgia Governor James Earl
"Jimmy" Carter.

The race was on between a football player running on his
record, a peanut farmer running on grassroots values and a cud-
dly golden bear loved around the world who believed if something hurt, we should stop doing it and think of another way. It
was a most refreshing change in venues. My candidate was an
easy choice and I publicly renounced my former political affiliations to become the official pilot of Pooh Chopper One.

Representing the Children's Party, the Pooh for President
Campaign, in partnership with Amtrak, Disneyland and Sears,
kicked off a cross-country Whistle Stop Tour in Chicago on
September 25, 1976. Sidetrack rallies were staged in Omaha,
Denver, Salt Lake City, Reno, Seattle, Portland, Sacramento,
Oakland and San Francisco before the big Pooh-litical
Convention in Anaheim on October 22-24, 1976.

During the month-long tour, according to Press Secretary

Tigger, Pooh and his running mate Piglet wanted to "lick" the high price of ice cream, deliver an educational message on the electoral process, and ask children to keep the country clean. He further cited the strong ecology program in Pooh's home forest of Hundred Acre Woods and his belief that the energy crisis could be solved by replacing light bulbs with lightning bugs.

"Pooh is true blue," said Tigger. "Hurrah for the red, white and Pooh."

Hughes Aircraft loaned Pooh a Hughes 500-D, a four-place helicopter for me to fly him from Disneyland to Hundred Acre Woods. Being rather stout, Pooh was a tight fit so we removed the back seats in the cockpit for him to lie on his stomach and wave out a side window to the crowd assembled for the send-off rally. A marching band, cheerleaders, Disney officials and Pooh campaign strategists Kanga, Eeyore and Owl all added to the fanfare by joining in the Pooh-rade.

Once the Children's Party candidate bid farewell to his supporters, we lifted to a hover and did a little aerial dance, tipping backward and forward, dipping left to right, then spinning in circles before whisking Pooh off to the Hundred Acre Woods.

The peanut farmer from Georgia beat the football player from Michigan on November 2, 1976. Word from the Woods was Winnie the Pooh received 26,000 write-in votes, one of which was mine.

A few weeks later, to the delight of Robin and Curtis, the entire Pooh entourage trekked up to our house for an appreciation celebration. For a short time, the Boyers' were the "happening place" in the neighborhood. I even received a special invitation to attend the opening of Disneyland's Space Mountain, along with six of the original Mercury astronauts.

The Disneyland Aeronautics and Space Administration (DASA) summons came from Ludwig Von Drake, Director of Flight operations, and read in part: "We know your envious friends and relatives won't believe it, so we have included the enclosed badge. It, along with your starry eyes, should prove to anyone that you will be among the first to experience Space Mountain. Wear your badge anywhere. Wear it to work. Wear it at play. If you are really proud (and not too bright) you can even wear it in the shower. But don't drown in your ecstasy. Your preparation has just begun...."

GOLD-PLATED HELICOPTER

Today, as an 81-year-old, no-name helicopter pilot, 55 years after getting a pair of shiny wings pinned on my chest, if there is anything I know about, it's helicopters. I know what they can do and, perhaps even more importantly, what they cannot or should not be expected to do.

In early 2005, I began following a Department of Defense contract to replace the existing White House fleet with 23 new VH-71 foreign-made helicopters. In the wake of the September 11, 2001, terrorist attacks, the White House and Pentagon were doing a lot of scrambling related to upgrading security. The plan, as undertaken and supported by President George W. Bush, Vice President Dick Cheney and Secretary of Defense Don Rumsfeld, became a "mission creep" nightmare. According to a July 2009 Congressional Research Service report, its author, Ronald O'Rourke, Specialist in Naval Affairs, issued a memorandum to accelerate a previously submitted Fleet Operational Needs document by HMX-1. The urgency to replace an "aging" helicopter fleet by 2007 steadily gained traction.

Was it time to upgrade the fleet? Yes. Was the VH-71 program the best option? *Definitely not.* Did the project land in a Pentagon sinkhole of ballooning costs, multiplying specifications and schedule delays? Sadly, yes.

At first, I just shook my head and thought: Here we go again – smart people doing something dumb. Competing for the contract was United Technology Corporation, parent to Sikorsky Aircraft, and Lockheed Martin Corporation, who was aligned with its European partners, Italy's Agusta and Britain's Westland. Now AgustaWestland, an Anglo-Italian helicopter company owned by Italy's Finmeccanica, it subsequently merged with Bell Helicopter to be the principle subcontractor for Lockheed, my former employer and a company that, as of 2009, had never built a helicopter.

On January 28, 2005, a Navy aviation acquisition executive announced the contract had been awarded to Lockheed Martin on the basis of its assurances that it could better meet the time limits and at a lower cost. I was among those critics who questioned Lockheed's capacity compared to Sikorsky, as well as the decision to use foreign companies to not only build but also supply and provide maintenance in the future. I saw ahead a quagmire of logistical and security problems. But of even greater concern, a closer look at the base model EH-101, compared to Sikorsky's proposed S-92 – an updated version of their Blackhawk – raised serious questions about this being the right helicopter for the job. From all I could see, the Navy, the Marines, the Department of Defense and the White House were working numbers and political agendas rather than focusing on a few basic common-sense factors, the most compelling being: Can the VH-71 Kestral, at operational weight, land and take off from the White House South Lawn without doing damage?

No. The rotor wash is too strong for the space. But, just like in 1973 with the ill-fated selection of the CH-53 Sea Stallion, no one seemed to be addressing that fundamental question.

The total acquisition cost in 2005 for the new White House helicopter fleet was estimated to be $6.5 billion. Within three years it had nearly doubled to $11.2 billion. By January 1, 2009, that figure reached $13 billion. The escalating price tag resulted in a Nunn-McCurdy breach requiring the Department of Defense to notify Congress whenever a defense acquisition exceeds a cost overrun threshold. Excuses were plentiful, as was the finger-pointing with charges that the Marines kept changing their minds and the Secret Service wanted more bells and whistles. Extremely disturbing, but no shock to me, many believed the contract was a payoff by the Bush administration to the Italian government for supplying the U.S. with forged documents proving Iraq was producing weapons of mass destruction, thereby, justifying the "shock and awe" launch of the Iraq War on March 26, 2003. I couldn't be sure one way or the other, but it was sure "quacking like a duck."

Shortly after President Barak Obama was sworn into office on January 20, 2009, I feared that, with all the more pressing issues piled on his desk in the Oval Office, the VH-71 contract might go unnoticed. Insiders were having heated conversations and industry publications were covering developments as they unfolded, but I thought the general public had a right to weigh in on where $13 billion of our tax dollars were headed. The projected cost per helicopter was a mind-boggling $400 million each – roughly the same amount the government had paid for Air Force One, a Boeing 747 jetliner.

The more I learned, the more difficult it was to stay quiet. I wrote letters to California Senators Dianne Feinstein and Barbara Boxer, Secretary of Defense Robert Gates and President Obama detailing my apprehension about what had become known as the "gold-plated helicopter." I received no response. My next step was to email Peter Baker, a reporter at *The New York Times* who had briefly interviewed me a year earlier to confirm that Army One and not Marine One had flown Nixon off the lawn the day he resigned.

In my January 30, 2009, email to Baker, I contended the need for the VH-71 helicopters was exaggerated, misrepresented the actual scope of the mission and would be a waste of time, money and resources. "There are many superior helicopters," I wrote, "that can fill out a fleet...and there are existing models that can be modified to serve the President and not compromise his security, comforts and communication needs."

Baker picked up the story and two weeks later, on February 16, 2009, his article, "Obama Confronts a Choice on Copters," ran in *The New York Times*: "WASHINGTON – President Obama has slammed high-flying executives traveling in cushy jets at a time of economic turmoil but soon he will have to decide whether to proceed with some of the priciest aircraft in the world – a new fleet of 28 Marine One helicopters that will each cost more than the last Air Force One... The Obama administration now must determine if the project is essential to national security and if there are alternatives that would cost less."

The *Times* article set into motion a global discussion and, according to Obama's Press Secretary Robert Gibbs who appeared on CNN's *American Morning* with John Roberts, that dialog now included the President. Regarding the prospect of putting the contract on hold, Gibbs said, "The President, when he read the story in the paper about ten days ago, we were on the airplane. We talked about this. We were both surprised that the airplane that we were on, which is huge, cost as much as the helicopter...."

That same week, I was interviewed by CBS and NBC television news, and *The Huffington Post*, as well as the *Congressional Record Weekly* on March 10, 2009. My message did not waiver: Somebody wants to build a magic helicopter and they don't even know if it can land at the White House.

On February 23, 2009, President Obama met with Capitol Hill lawmakers for a Fiscal Responsibility Summit in the Executive Office Building. At the closing of the event, Obama participated in a question and answer session and fielded comments from his former presidential opponent Senator John McCain on the subject of cost overruns by the Department of Defense.

"Your helicopter," noted McCain, "is now going to cost as much as Air Force One. I don't think that there's any more graphic demonstration of how good ideas have cost taxpayers an enormous amount of money."

Obama responded with assurances that he had already talked to Secretary of Defense Robert Gates about a thorough review of the "helicopter situation," adding, "The helicopter I have now seems perfectly adequate to me. Of course, I've never had a helicopter before – maybe I've been deprived and I didn't know it."

The President went on to say he viewed the VH-71 program as "an example of the procurement process run amok."

Within two months, Gates recommended the VH-71 program be terminated. On May 15, 2009, Ashton Carter, a Department of Defense acquisitions executive, released an Acquisition Decision memo directing the program be cancelled. That same day, the Navy issued a stop-work order and on June 1, officially terminated the main contract. Even though "separation" costs to get out of the contract amounted to more than $500 million, sometimes the best option is to cut one's losses, regroup, bring in fresh viewpoints and re-evaluate the mission. In this case, I like to think I played a small part in the Department of Defense doing just that, regardless of the number people associated with the VH-71 procurement process who may now view me in a less than favorable light.

THE ORANGE COUNTY REGISTER
THURSDAY, FEB. 26, 2009

Creators Syndicate, Inc.©   **Local 10**

MIKE RAMIREZ / INVESTOR'S BUSINESS DAILY

Political artist's interpretation of the ill-fated
VH-71 Department of Defense contract for a new helicopter fleet.
*(By permission of Michael Ramirez and Creators Syndicate, Inc.,
February 26, 2009)*

FROST/NIXON

The opportunity for Burhanan and me to be in the *Frost/
Nixon* movie began with a telephone call in 2007 from a
Hollywood wardrobe department to me at my Huntington Beach
home south of Los Angeles. Movie director Ron Howard was
making a film about Nixon's post-presidency interview.

"I got your number from the Nixon Library," said a pleasant
female voice on the other end of the line. "I understand you flew
President Nixon off the lawn the day he resigned."

"That's right," I answered.

"We need to make a flight suit for a movie and I was wondering if you had any old ones we could use as a sample."

"Sure, I think I have the original suit."

"*Really?* Can we borrow it?"

"Yeah," I told her. "Just give me some time to dig it out."

After locating the uniform buried in a bag in an old foot locker, I took it to nearby Los Alamitos Joint Forces Training Center base to get it cleaned and have the presidential seal and other authentic patches reattached.

Soon after, one of Howard's representatives called to get more information regarding my memories of Nixon's last flight. When he learned both Burhanan and I lived in the area, he asked if we'd like to be in the movie.

"You bet," I said. "Sounds like fun."

Howard's movie was based on the Tony-award winning play by Peter Morgan, which had been adapted from James Reston Jr.'s book, *The Conviction of Richard Nixon: The Untold Story of the Frost/Nixon Interviews*. On the *Frost/Nixon* set at the Nixon Library, Burhanan and I even had our own trailer dressing rooms with personalized name plates next to Frank Langella starring as Nixon and Kevin Bacon as Brennan. Langella had perfected Nixon's moves and mannerisms and I was not surprised to learn he had won a Tony for his stage portrayal of the president I had flown on 451 missions and came to know privately in the years before his death in 1994.

As the filming came to an end that day, an unspoken melancholy welled up inside of me. Just a stone's throw away stood the modest kit house where Nixon had been born in 1913 and not far beyond, nestled in a garden setting, next to his beloved wife Pat, was his gravesite marked with a headstone that read: "The greatest honor history can bestow is the title of peacemaker."

Naturally, I was curious as to how Nixon would be represented in Howard's film. Would he be further demonized for his undisputed offenses as "Tricky Dick?" Would there be any counter-balancing regarding the many commendable contributions of his presidency? And what about that jubilant, little-known post-production party I hosted for the Frost entourage at

Army co-pilot Carl Burhanan and I on the set of *Frost/Nixon*
with film producer Ron Howard, Autumn, 2007
(Robin Boyer LaFerrara)

my Palos Verdes home after he'd finished taping the interview?
What a scene that would be on the big screen – right down to me
fishing Frost's swim trunks out of the pool the morning after.

Leading up to the actual interviews the spring of 1977, there
was considerable buzz in the media and among those of us who
had been part of the Nixon White House. We were all speculat-
ing how Frost, a perceived lightweight talk show celebrity,
would handle the former president and world leader who had
long since proven himself a formidable master communicator.
In the three years since resigning from office in 1974, Nixon had
not been held to account in any forum for his role in Watergate.
While the Attorney General and several second-term campaign
staff and key White House advisors were indicted, convicted
and imprisoned for crimes ranging from attempted burglary to
obstruction of justice, he had been promptly pardoned by

Carl Burhanan and I with actor Frank Langella as President Nixon
on the set of *Frost/Nixon*, Autumn, 2007
(Robin Boyer LaFerrara)

President Gerald Ford and thereby avoided prosecution and direct public examination.

I believed Nixon's desire to be interviewed was motivated by a compulsion to tell his side of the story, to set the record straight no matter how incriminating, and perhaps to somehow offer an explanation or even an apology that might shift public opinion away from thinking he was nothing but a "crook." I personally didn't think Watergate should solely define the man I watched end the Vietnam War, bring home the POWs, open trade with China and impede Russian expansion in the Middle East.

Frost had managed to pique Nixon's interest by raising $600,000 – twice the amount offered by CBS and Mike Wallace – and then locked up the rights with a final promise to share profits. For all the projecting by pundits prior to their meeting, no one came close to imagining how unguarded and revealing Nixon would be with Frost, who also earned praise for his probing inquiry and disarming technique. It was a remarkable, in-depth exchange and obviously one worth celebrating, which I quickly gathered upon getting a call from Brennan at our Palos Verdes home.

"Listen, I'm with David Frost and company," said Brennan.

"Really?" I replied with surprise.

"They just finished taping with the President," he said, getting charged up, "and they want to go some place for a steak

After the White House, our home in Palos Verdes, California, 1976.
(Boyer Family Archives)

and a swim so we're headed your way. Can you open the bar?" Brennan was going through a divorce at the time and had spent several weekends at our place so he knew the lay of the land and the size of the pool.

"Yeah, sure," I answered, then hung up, alerted CeCe and ran to the store for some rib-eye steaks.

Neighbors would talk for years about the day the Frost motorcade of dark sedans arrived on our street. Some called to ask, "What the hell is going on?" A few others invited themselves to the party. One was the first to go skinny dipping.

Besides working the grill and pouring a lot of drinks, I spent time chatting with Frost. He was about ten years younger than I and infinitely more charming. I don't think it was an exaggeration to say he and his team of about eight men and women were euphoric. He had taken a huge risk with the amount of money invested in the project and was now boldly confident it had paid off. Apparently Nixon, in the final session, had finally opened up with uncharacteristic candor to admit transgressions related to Watergate and detailed why he did what he did when he did it.

I was among the more than 45 million people who would later tune in to watch the four historically unprecedented 90-minute interviews about a month later. For me, there were no new revelations regarding Watergate. After all, I had had a front row seat for the unraveling of Nixon's presidency. What did surprise me about the interviews was how introspective Nixon became when an unrestrained Frost asked, "In a sense, do you feel resignation is worse than death?"

"In some ways," Nixon responded and then continued at length with a casual ease as Frost sat across from him patiently listening along with those of us glued to our TVs. "I didn't feel it in terms that the popular mythologists about this era write...that resignation is so terrible that I better go out and fall on a sword and take a gun and shoot myself or this or that or the other thing. I wasn't about to do that."

David Frost's Nixon interview after-party at my house lasted well into the night. Most everybody got pretty smashed and ended up in the water, clothed and unclothed. The last I saw of

Frost, he was leaving the pool area with just a towel. I found his striped swim trunks the next day lying eight feet deep and thought to myself, "That Limey knows how to have a good time!"

The *Frost/Nixon* movie premiered the last week of November 2008 at the Samuel Goldwyn Theater Academy of Motion Picture Arts and Sciences in Los Angeles. Burhanan and I were there, occasionally introducing ourselves as the pilots who flew Nixon off the lawn the day he resigned.

"That was in Marine One, right?" was a common response.

"No, Army One."

"Army One?"

"Yes," I answered, "we flew for the Army."

"I had no idea it was the Army."

"That's okay," I said, "most people don't."

British talk show host David Frost (left) relaxes with former President Nixon's chief of staff, Colonel Jack Brennan, at my Palos Verdes home after they had finished taping the famous Frost-Nixon interviews. April 1977
(Boyer Family Archives)

Burhanan and I were extremely impressed with Howard's interpretation of the *Frost/Nixon* interviews. The actors were incredible and the story kept us on the edge of our seats. However, we were miffed to discover all the footage shot of the two of us in the cockpit of Army One had ended up on the cutting room floor. Only those of us there that day would know the very pilots from Nixon's last day in office were actually sitting in the helicopter when Frank Langella so artfully imitated the President's famous farewell gesture at the top of the steps.

Even then, our disappointment was short-lived. We were used to being invisible.

The Last Flight Helicopter

The VH-3A Last Flight Helicopter, is the world's most recognized helicopter. Not a year has passed since August 9, 1974, that I do not see news coverage of President Richard Nixon's resignation and Army One lifting off from the South Lawn of the White House. I had spent a lot of time with #150617 and much like the oft-romanticized tendency of boat captains, race car drivers and airplane pilots to feel a bond with the machine itself, I didn't realize the depth of my connection to #617 until it was almost too late to save it from a scrap heap.

That undertaking started with an inkling of an idea in 2001. Each time I saw footage of Nixon's resignation, I found myself wondering what had happened to the helicopter. My initial calls to a variety of resources revealed that #617 had been decommissioned in 1976 and used by the Secret Service for training. Then, a few years later, it was sent to the Davis-Monthan Air Force Base boneyard near Tucson, Arizona, and destroyed. Wanting absolute proof, I continued turning stones until someone remembered hearing that a Marine colonel had recognized #617's historical value and arranged for it to be trucked to an Army depot in Indian Gap, Pennsylvania, with hopes that it might be restored. From there, it went to the USS *Saratoga* Museum Foundation, but due to a lack of funding, the air frame sat in a parking lot for more than a decade, cocooned in white plastic at the Quonset Point Air Museum in North Kingstown, Rhode Island.

My quest to rescue #617 took hold during an interview I did for a television special honoring outgoing NBC news anchor Tom Brokaw. On November 26, 2004, *Dateline* NBC presented *Tom Brokaw: Eyewitness to History*, a two-hour documentary focused on the most significant events and social trends of Brokaw's 40-year career as a television broadcast journalist.

Beginning with Brokaw's account of the turbulent events of 1968, which he called a "big blur," the documentary traced highlights from the Vietnam War and President Lyndon Johnson's decision to not seek re-election; the assassination of Reverend Martin Luther King, Jr. and the devastating riots that

followed; the assassination of Senator Robert Kennedy; the defeat of Minnesota Senator Hubert Humphrey by former Republican Vice President Nixon to become the 37th president of the United States; and, of course, Watergate. Brokaw reflected on the infamous break-in and ensuing political scandal, calling it a "constitutional crisis." He further drew upon the memories of *The Washington Post* investigative reporters Bob Woodward and Carl Bernstein, former Nixon aide Ron Ziegler and Hillary Rodham Clinton who, during the Watergate years, was a young, unmarried Congressional legal counsel involved in the investigation.

"All of us from the most senior to the most junior of the staff," Clinton recalled, "felt the enormous obligation to get it right. But the end result was that when the House Judiciary Committee passed the articles of impeachment, it was a vote that the country accepted."

Again, what were the odds that I, that kid from Akron who couldn't fathom a world beyond football and girls, ended up among those asked by NBC to share recollections of Nixon's last day in office? But there I was with powder on the nose I had broken nearly a dozen times, in a makeshift Hollywood hotel studio, speaking about my observations in the final moments of his presidency.

"The mood inside (the helicopter) was unbelievably bad," I told the young man interviewing me. "The First Lady said, 'Oh, it's all so sad, it's so sad.' Everybody else had nothing to say, absolutely nothing."

I went on to describe how, after landing at Andrews AFB near Air Force One waiting to carry Nixon into exile, he told Burhanan and me to "stop those tears." My narrative account played over video of Betty and Gerald Ford escorting the Nixon family from the White House down the red carpet to Army One. I left the interview honored to be included in the Brokaw tribute, but while others watched footage of "just a helicopter" taking off from the South Lawn, I saw an historical artifact that should be on display in an aviation museum.

Shortly after the Brokaw special aired on national television, I was contacted by a high school student in Kansas. Her history teacher had assigned her the task of tracking down Nixon's helicopter pilot. During our brief correspondence, her questions about my service and the helicopter motivated me to once and for all determine if #617 was salvageable. With encouragement from the Nixon Library and Birthplace Foundation, I started making phone calls and soon found myself in an unexpected turf war. All four branches of the military had a tie to the famous helicopter. The Navy developed it, both Army and Marine aviators had flown it, and Air Force generals had been directors of the White House Military Office during most of its service.

A key participant in the effort to recover #617 was Nixon Library curator Olivia Anastasiadis. A small woman with short dark hair and bright eyes, she has a dynamo personality and, most importantly, enough patience to put up with me. A critical step involved determining if the helicopter was worth restoring. Working through personal contacts and with Anastasiadis' dedicated assistance we gradually established contacts with Saratoga and Quonset Point folks along with the National Museum of the Marine Corps (NMMC) at Quantico, Virginia, and Navy Inventory Control Point personnel in Philadelphia. In July 2005, struggling to keep my enthusiasm in check, Anastasiadis and I finally boarded a plane bound for Rhode Island.

When I laid eyes on what appeared to be nothing but a dusty, giant elongated marshmallow on wheels parked among several old Navy trucks, my heart sank. To my heartbreaking dismay, it had been severely cannibalized. Nearly every major exterior component was missing, including the tailboom, gearbox, rotor blades, main transmission blades, engine and airstair doors. It was hard to hold out hope for there to be anything worth restoring inside all that plastic. While Anastasiadis and an accompanying official looked on, I pulled out a pocket knife, sliced open the sheeting over the door and climbed inside.

Disappointment transformed to elation. The interior was absolutely pristine. The upholstery, carpeting and furnishings were clean and unmarred. Although the cockpit was missing various components, the cabin looked exactly as it had the last time I was inside some 30 years earlier. Cigarette butts, at least that old, were still in the ashtrays. I was standing inside a virtual time capsule. Within a space smaller than most living rooms, this "skywitness to history" had carried four sitting presidents, numerous heads of state, and hundreds of high-ranking U.S. military and government officials. I had even flown it in and out of the mysterious and peril-ridden Bermuda Triangle more than a dozen times without incident.

In my mind, the Last Flight Helicopter did not belong to the Army, the Marines, the Navy or the Air Force – it belonged to the American people.

"How does it look?" asked Anastasiadis.

"Great." I answered, helping her inside. "It's perfect. Nothing's changed."

The next steps were clear: We had to convince the Navy to release custody, find another VH-3A for parts and line up March Field and Air Museum (MFAM) to help restore it for display at the Nixon Library in Yorba Linda, California, about 50 miles to the west. But first we had to get #617 from Rhode Island to MFAM in Southern California. All things considered, it was a tall order.

Anastasiadis went to work writing a restoration plan for the NMMC to review and approve. In addition to demonstrating our deep commitment to the project, she outlined stipulations related to security, a restoration team and an outdoor display design. We also gathered letters of support from interested parties such as Nixon's daughter Julie Eisenhower and his former head of White House communications, Herb Klein. Other supporters included my former boss, General Don Hughes, Congressman Duncan Hunter, Senator John Warner, and Ron Walker, a Nixon chief advance man.

With the promise of another helicopter to cannibalize from Davis-Monthan AFB and an agreement with MFAM's executive director, Patricia Korzec, for her to oversee restoration, we reached an agreement with the Navy to release #617 to the Nixon Library. All the lobbying, negotiating and downright wrangling had taken about three months. Everyone was excited about getting started, but no one had the funds to pay for transporting what remained of the helicopter from Rhode Island to California.

Then I remembered a conversation I had had at the MFAM's 2005 Annual Holiday Party for supporters and volunteers. Out of the crowd of about 350 people, a friendly couple in their mid-forties approached me with a question.

"Did you used to live on Colonel Row at Ft. Belvoir in Virginia?" the unidentified woman asked.

"Yes," I answered, "during the Nixon years."

"Well, I was Robin's babysitter," she said with a broad smile. "My father was also an Army colonel. Your wife even did my make-up for my junior prom."

"And she did a great job," said the man beside her. "I married her."

Amazed at the small world we live in, I jokingly took credit on behalf of my children and former wife for their marriage. Her husband was Air Force Brigadier General James Rubeor, commander of the 452nd Air Mobility Wing and head of the C-17 long-range, cargo transport aircraft at the Air Reserve Base.

Now, nine months after that meeting, I telephoned Rubeor to ask a favor.

"General Rubeor," I said when he answered, "this is Gene Boyer. We met at March's Museum Christmas party."

"Right," he answered. "My wife was your babysitter."

"That's right," I replied. "Listen, I've got a special situation and I could use your help...plus, you owe me a favor for helping the two of you get together back at Belvoir."

He laughed and assured me he would happily look for a way to get #617 out to MFAM. Within a short period of time, Rubeor called about a cargo flight to Iraq. The plane was returning empty, so they could pick up the helicopter on their way back. To spare me and Anastasiadis a cross-country trip to Rhode Island to sign the NMMC release, we made arrangements with Jack Brennan who lived in Rhode Island, to handle the paperwork on that end.

Under the supervision of Colonel Gary Pennington, #617 arrived the first week of October 2005 at March Field on board a C-17 and was soon safely stored in a hangar where dedicated volunteers began the arduous job of restoring it to display quality. Like me, a relic in my own right, the aircraft's flying days were over. My Marine counterpart, retired pilot and former HMX-1 commander Lieutenant Colonel Dave Pirnie, and I personally removed the plastic from the helicopter. I remember thinking, "This is going to take a miracle to properly restore it."

Nixon's Last Flight Helicopter during restoration process.
March Air Reserve Base and Museum, Riverside, California, 2006
(Boyer Family Archives)

Our "dream team" was led by Rudy Lerma, a former Air Force security specialist and the head of restoration work at MFAM. Within the ranks of some 150 pairs of helping hands – many of whom were military veterans – were retired Sikorsky - qualified mechanics Steve Tynan, Manny Ornelas, Carl Pease and Dick Van Rennes.

"It's history and we were chosen to do it," Lerma told a *Los Angeles Times* reporter and added he was eagerly awaiting the day he could take his two grandchildren to see the aircraft. "And I'll tell them, 'You know, I worked on that helicopter.'"

The work became a labor of love and pride, and we were

Me speaking at the Grand Opening of the Last Flight Helicopter
at the Nixon Presidential Library and Museum, July 1, 2006
(Robin Boyer LaFerrara)

able to raise about $50,000. The special mix of paint – a combi-
nation of Army green and Marine green – was acquired by Gerry
Tobias, a retired Sikorsky executive. We hoped to have #617
ready for public viewing on Nixon's 93rd birthday in January

Nixon's grandson, Christopher Cox, and I celebrating
the restoration of the Last Flight Helicopter
Richard Nixon Library and Museum, Yorba Linda, California, July 1, 2006
(Courtesy of Richard Nixon Presidential Library, NARA)

2006, but that schedule proved to be too ambitious and the timeline was extended six months. During that time, from a set of rotor blades to a cabin phone, we relentlessly scavenged for missing parts.

After at least 1,500 hours of sanding and painting, muscling and detailing, the helicopter was ready to leave MFAM for the Nixon Library. We recruited the able assistance of Carl Cortez, president of the Vietnam Helicopter Pilot's Association's Southern California Chapter, to coordinate the ground transport and a crane for a pre-dawn move. Once at the library, Lerma and Tynan oversaw the attachment of the rotor blades, and

Nixon Library curator Olivia Anastasiadis (in doorway) and I answering helicopter questions from a fifth grade tour group. Richard Nixon Library and Museum, Yorba Linda, California, March 18, 2010
(Jackie Boor)

Former Nixon Army Aide Colonel William "Bill" Golden and I
aboard the restored "Last Flight" Sikorsky VH-3A
Richard Nixon Library and Museum, Yorba Linda, California, July 2009
(Jackie Boor)

With my family on my 80th birthday
Son-in-law Guy LaFerrara (left), granddaughter Aryn, the birthday boy,
son Curtis, daughter Robin and grandson Ryan, July 24, 2009
(Boyer Family Archives)

preparations for a "permanent landing" ceremony kicked into high gear.

July 1, 2006, was a clear, blistering hot day. Parked on a concrete pad, surrounded by 50 waving American flags and less than 200 feet from Nixon's birthplace and gravesite, the Last Flight Helicopter exhibit was opened to a crowd of several hundred, including Nixon's grandson Christopher Cox, local politicians, former pilots and crew members, and my family. A band played "The Stars & Stripes Forever," a Marine honor guard presented the colors and small cannons showered #617 with red, white and blue streamers and confetti.

Nixon Foundation chairman Donald Bendetti spoke about the helicopter's historical significance and President Nixon's personal connection to the aircraft. "He set records throughout the globe in his quest for peace," said Bendetti. "Now, the helicopter he used will keep watch over these historic grounds for generations to come."

It was a day I thought would never come but, piece by piece, hour by hour, we had managed to pull it off. As I mingled with the flow of people now making their way through the cabin, I watched them studying the layout of the cockpit, imagining the President and First Lady in their respective seats and wondering aloud what issues visiting heads of state might have discussed in flight. They asked me question after question about my years as a presidential pilot. The more I reflected on the many missions I had flown, the more I realized that this very helicopter was now embarking on perhaps the most important one of all – transporting young and old alike back in time for decades to come without even leaving the ground. The Last Flight Helicopter had become a true *magic* helicopter.

What were the odds? How had a lanky, bull-headed kid, born on the advent of the Great Depression, who didn't even like flying kites manage to find his way into the cockpit of the president's helicopter? As usual, I had no answer other than the simple, unpredictable nature of luck rubbing up against opportunity.

From medical evacuation missions in Korea to a forced landing in the wilds of Venezuela; from a posh NATO assignment in Paris to Johnson's scandalous antics at the LBJ ranch; from being shot down in Vietnam to the prestigious Executive Flight Detachment for the White House; from being a Lockheed Director of Marketing in the Middle East to leading the "impossible" rescue and restoration of the Last Flight Helicopter – my life has been an exercise in defying the odds. And through it all, with thousands of flights all over the world, I never lost confidence in our country, in the importance of family and in people's basic desire to do the right thing.

That's how I was raised and what my parents expected of me, give or take a few shenanigans.

With Thanks

For their unwavering belief in us to accomplish the impossible, their willingness to contribute personal wisdom and for every helping hand they continue to extend, we thank our families: Guy and Robin (Boyer) LaFerrara, Curtis Boyer, CeCe Boyer, Dean Hupp, Dave and Stacey (Boor) Morgan, Jay Boor and Eric Boor. Additional bursts of inspiration continue to come from our grandchildren, Aryn and Ryan LaFerrara, and Elizabeth and Joseph Morgan. For their love and perpetual effervescence, we are forever grateful.

For her determination to start getting Exec Flight stories down on paper some twenty years ago, we send a special thank you to Gene's late sister-in-law, Barbara Mickens. She started the "blades spinning." Then, in the process of transforming a pile of notes into chapters, we received the invaluable benefit of keen-eyed viewpoints belonging to CW4 Carl Burhanan, Olivia Anastasiadis, COL William Golden, Suzanne Mattmiller, Marsha Lang, Colleen Truelson, COL and Mrs. Greg (Paige) Woodward, COL Frank Underwood, 2nd LT Chuck Bell, LTC Tom Lasser, CW4 Art Ransom, Rocky Lang, Vince Costello, Lois Eckart, LT Peter Anninos, Ron Walker, COL Vern Coffey, CPT Steve Curtain, MAJ Bill Shaw, MSGT Mike Hughes, CW4 Keith Borck, CW4 Benjamin Epps, LTC Bob Shain, MSGT Bill Robinson, MSGT John Summey, COL Steve Bosan, CPT Larry Wisneski and Marc Yablonka. Thank you all for helping us put together the pieces and for keeping us honest.

Finally, for her love of flight and the tales only pilots can tell, we acknowledge Nan Wisherd, our publisher. Her remarkable energy, thoughtful insights and seasoned expertise were a constant source of inspiration. To Nan and her talented Cable Publishing production crew of Debbie Zime, Norm Dodge, Larry Verkeyn and Flint Whitlock, we are extremely grateful for your attention to detail and team spirit.

To Gene from Jackie: it has been my honor to serve as your literary co-pilot.

To Jackie from Gene: thank you for your extraordinary efforts to commit my life's journey to paper.

And finally, to Amber, Gene's faithful dog and walking partner for her *always* happy-go-lucky attitude.

BIBLIOGRAPHY

Benson, Jackson L. *The True Adventures of John Steinbeck, Writer,* New York: Penguin, 1990.

Bowman, John S. *The Vietnam War: Day by Day.* New York: Bantam Books, 1989.

DeFrank, Thomas M. *Write It When I'm Gone: Remarkable Off-the-Record Conversations with Gerald R. Ford.* New York: G. P. Putnam's Sons, 2007.

Eisenhower, *Julie Nixon. Pat Nixon: The Untold Story.* New York: Simon & Schuster, 1986.

Gulley, Bill with Mary Ellen Reese. *Breaking Cover.* New York: Simon & Schuster, 1980.

Haldeman, H.R. *The Haldeman Diaries.* New York: G. P. Putnam's Sons, 1994.

Haley, J. Evetts. *A Texan Looks at Lyndon: A Study in Illegitimate Power.* Canyon, Texas: Palo Duro Press, 1964.

Johnson, Lyndon Baines, *The Vantage Point: Perspectives of the Presidency – 1963-1969.* New York, Chicago, San Francisco: Holt, Rinehart & Winston, 1971.

Kessler, Ron. *Inside the White House.* New York: Pocket Books, 1995.

Nixon, Richard M. *The Memoirs of Richard M. Nixon.* New York: Grosset & Dunlap, 1978.

Reston, James, Jr. *The Conviction of Richard Nixon: The Untold Story of the FROST/NIXON Interviews.* New York: Harmony, 2007.

Terhorst, Jerald F. and COL Ralph Albertazzie. *The Flying White House: The Story of Air Force One.* New York: Coward, McCann & Geoghegan, Inc., 1979.

White House Central Files: Presidential Daily Diary. Gerald Ford Presidential Library and Museum, Ann Arbor, MI. National Archives and Records Administration.

White House Central Files: Presidential Daily Diary. Richard Nixon Presidential Library and Museum, Yorba Linda, CA. National Archives and Records Administration.

ABOUT THE AUTHORS

LTC Gene T. Boyer (Ret.) was born in Akron Ohio, in 1929. Following graduation from Ohio University, he began a distinguished 22-year career in the U.S. Army and earned three Legion of Merit Awards for service to Presidents Johnson, Nixon and Ford as a White House pilot between 1964 and 1975. Currently residing in Huntington Beach, CA, Boyer led the restoration of the Last Flight Helicopter now on display at the Richard Nixon Presidential Library. The father of two and the grandfather of two, Boyer stays active walking his dog Amber, advocating for Veteran benefits and doing presentations on the history of Army One.

Jackie Boor began her freelance writing career in 1968 as a teen correspondent for two newspapers in Northern California. Currently an aspiring screenplay writer, she has worked as a reporter, ghostwriter, and forensic speech and debate coach. Long fascinated by the dynamics of human communication, she has also built a multilevel career as a dispute resolution expert specializing in large group facilitation, problem solving and civic engagement. A resident of Sacramento, CA, since 1975, Jackie is the mother of three and grandmother of two, and enjoys playing golf. *Inside the President's Helicopter* is her first full-length book.